P9-APF-751

Closing the Gender Gap

ACT NOW

OECD

BETTER POLICIES FOR BETTER LIVES

This work is published on the responsibility of the Secretary-General of the OECD. The opinions expressed and arguments employed herein do not necessarily reflect the official views of the Organisation or of the governments of its member countries or those of the European Union.

This document and any map included herein are without prejudice to the status of or sovereignty over any territory, to the delimitation of international frontiers and boundaries and to the name of any territory, city or area.

Please cite this publication as:
OECD (2012), *Closing the Gender Gap: Act Now*, OECD Publishing.
http://dx.doi.org/10.1787/9789264179370-en

ISBN 978-92-64-17936-3 (print)
ISBN 978-92-64-17937-0 (PDF)

European Union
Catalogue number: DS-30-12-887-EN-C (print)
Catalogue number: DS-30-12-887-EN-N (PDF)
ISBN 978-92-79-26795-6 (print)
ISBN 978-92-79-26793-2 (PDF)

The statistical data for Israel are supplied by and under the responsibility of the relevant Israeli authorities. The use of such data by the OECD is without prejudice to the status of the Golan Heights, East Jerusalem and Israeli settlements in the West Bank under the terms of international law.

Photo credits: Cover © Adeline Marshall.

Corrigenda to OECD publications may be found on line at: *www.oecd.org/publishing/corrigenda*.

© OECD 2012

You can copy, download or print OECD content for your own use, and you can include excerpts from OECD publications, databases and multimedia products in your own documents, presentations, blogs, websites and teaching materials, provided that suitable acknowledgement of OECD as source and copyright owner is given. All requests for public or commercial use and translation rights should be submitted to *rights@oecd.org*. Requests for permission to photocopy portions of this material for public or commercial use shall be addressed directly to the Copyright Clearance Center (CCC) at *info@copyright.com* or the Centre français d'exploitation du droit de copie (CFC) at *contact@cfcopies.com*.

Foreword

*I*n the aftermath of the Great Recession, there is an urgent need to focus on the economic case for gender equality and on how changes in the labour market might provide better economic opportunities for both men and women.

Building on its expertise, the OECD launched its OECD Gender Initiative in 2010 to examine existing barriers to gender equality in education, employment, and entrepreneurship (the "three Es"). The aim was to improve policies and promote gender equality in the economy in both OECD and non-OECD countries. The initiative was developed as an integral part of the wider policy imperative for new sources of economic growth, greater gender equality, and a more efficient use of everyone's skills. The OECD Gender Initiative presented its initial findings in its Gender Reports, published in May 2011 and May 2012 for the Meetings of the OECD Council at Ministerial Level in Paris. In addition, a special report on gender equality and the three Es in OECD countries in the Pacific Rim and other Asia-Pacific Economic Co-operation (APEC) countries was prepared for the APEC Women and the Economy Summit (WES) held in September 2011 in San Francisco.

This report is designed to inform, share policy experiences and good practices, and help governments promote gender equality in education, employment and entrepreneurship. It looks at the state of play from a gender perspective across all three issues, examines how and why inequalities have developed, and which obstacles must be overcome to move towards greater equality. It offers policy advice to governments on measures that can create a more level playing field.

Much of this advice is aimed at alleviating concerns over the experience of women and girls and removing obstacles to equal participation in the economy. Gender equality, however, is not just about the empowerment of women. This study also looks at why, in many countries, greater success at school for girls has gone hand in hand with less success for boys in some subjects, why fathers may find it difficult to take full advantage of family-friendly policies, and what can be done to bring about change.

Greater sharing of paid and unpaid work between women and men will involve changing norms, culture, mindsets, and attitudes. Such changes take time, but policy has a role to play in raising public awareness of gender biases in society and promoting change.

Mainstreaming the gender perspective at all levels of policy is one aspect of efficiently enhancing gender equality. Visible public gender agencies with sufficiently strong mandates, appropriate analytical tools, reliable evidence, and resources are needed to combat discrimination and enhance gender equality. Gender equality policies are most likely to be effective if both men and women are seen to actively promote such efforts: male and female role models are useful in breaking gender stereotypes. Effective mainstreaming, however, requires careful monitoring. To facilitate this process on a cross-national basis, the OECD has launched at the end of 2012 its one-stop gender data portal (www.oecd.org/gender). It shows the relative standing of countries in the various dimensions of gender equality in the three Es across the OECD and key partner countries.

Acknowledgements

The OECD *Gender Initiative* was carried out with the financial assistance of the European Union and the US Department of State, and the OECD would like to thank them for their support. Many colleagues in different directorates across the OECD have contributed to this report. The directorates include: the Centre for Entrepreneurship, SMEs and Local Development (CFE); the Development Centre (DEV); the Development Co-operation Directorate (DCD); the Directorate for Education (EDU); the Directorate for Employment, Labour and Social Affairs (ELS); the Directorate for Financial and Enterprise Affairs (DAF); the Directorate for Science, Technology and Industry (STI); the Public Affairs and Communications Directorate (PAC); the Public Governance and Territorial Development (GOV); and the Statistics Directorate (STD). We are very grateful to delegates to different OECD committees and networks, the Business Advisory Committee, and the Trade Union Advisory Committee who commented on earlier drafts. We would also like to thank various experts from across the world who helped shape our thinking about gender issues in OECD member and partner countries.

Table of contents

Executive summary   13

Part I

Gender equality: The economic case, social norms, and public policies

Chapter 1.   **The economic case for gender equality**   23
Chapter 2.   **Why social institutions matter for gender equality**   31
Chapter 3.   **Embedding gender equality in public policy**   37
Annex I.A1.   **Estimating the effects of human capital accumulation on growth**   45
Annex I.A2.   **Labour force projections for OECD countries not covered
in Figure 1.2.**   49
Annex I.A3.   **Gross domestic product projections for OECD countries not covered
in Figure 1.2**   54
References   59

Part II

Gender equality in education

Chapter 4.   **Keeping girls and boys in school**   65
Chapter 5.   **Aid in support of gender equality in education**   75
Chapter 6.   **Who is good at what in school?**   83
Chapter 7.   **Secondary school graduates: What next?**   91
Chapter 8.   **Science *versus* the humanities**   99
Chapter 9.   **Getting the job you studied for**   109
Chapter 10.   **Financial education for financial empowerment**   117
Annex II.A1.   **Supplementary tables to Chapter 4**   123
Annex II.A2.   **Supplementary table to Chapter 5**   133
Annex II.A3.   **Supplementary table to Chapter 8**   137
Annex II.A4.   **General background data on education**   138
References   141

Part III

Gender equality in employment

Chapter 11. **Who is in paid work?** 149

Chapter 12. **Does motherhood mean part-time work?** 159

Chapter 13. **A woman's worth** 165

Chapter 14. **The business case for women and addressing the leaky pipeline** 175

Chapter 15. **Women on boards** 183

Chapter 16. **Gender divides in the public domain** 191

Chapter 17. **Who cares?** 199

Chapter 18. **Supporting parents in juggling work and family life** 205

Chapter 19. **Male and female employment in the aftermath of the crisis** 215

Chapter 20. **The hidden workers: Women in informal employment** 221

Chapter 21. **Women in retirement** 229

Annex III.A1. **Supplementary tables to Chapter 11** 235

Annex III.A2. **The determinants of female labour force participation
and part-time work** 246

Annex III.A3. **Data sources for the analysis in Chapter 13** 249

Annex III.A4. **Supplementary table to Chapter 15** 252

Annex III.A5. **Supplementary table to Chapter 18** 253

Annex III.A6. **Supplementary tables to Chapter 20** 255

Annex III.A7. **General background data on employment** 258

References 261

Part IV

Gender equality in entrepreneurship

Chapter 22. **Trends in women entrepreneurship** 273

Chapter 23. **Motivations and skills of women entrepreneurs** 279

Chapter 24. **Is there a gender gap in enterprise performance?** 285

Chapter 25. **Does entrepreneurship pay for women?** 291

Chapter 26. **Women's access to credit** 297

Chapter 27. **Financing female-owned enterprises in partner countries** 303

Chapter 28. **Do women innovate differently?** 309

Chapter 29. **Formalising female-owned businesses** 315

Annex IV.A1. **Methodological issues and additional findings
to Chapters 22 and 24** 321

Annex IV.A2. **Methodological issues and additional findings
to Chapters 23 and 25** 328

Annex IV.A3. **Methodological issues and additional findings to Chapter 26** 330

Annex IV.A4. **Methodological issues and additional findings
to Chapters 27 and 29** 332

Annex IV.A5. **Methodological issues and additional findings to Chapter 28** 337

References 340

General note on figures and tables 345

References 347

Tables

I.A1.1. A general growth model with total human capital 47

I.A1.2. Basic growth model statistics 48

I.A2.1. Projected increase and decrease in labour force size from 2011 to 2030
under three scenarios of labour force participation 53

I.A3.1. Projected average annual growth rate in GDP and GDP per capita
in USD 2005 PPP, percentage, 2011-30 57

I.A3.2. Projected GDP in USD 2005 PPP, millions, 2020 and 2030 58

II.A1.1. Adjusted primary school net enrolment rates, 2000 and 2010 123

II.A1.2. Gross secondary school enrolment ratios, 2000 and 2010 128

II.A2.1. Gender equality focused aid in primary and secondary education,
percentage of 2009-10 annual average DAC members' aid commitments,
2010 prices 133

II.A3.1. Percentage of female students in higher education, 1985-2025 137

II.A4.1. Educational attainment, PISA scores, and field of tertiary education, 2009 . . 139

11.1. Women are over-represented in the service sector 152

III.A1.1. Labour force participation rates by gender, 1990, 2000 and 2010 235

III.A1.2. Employment by broad economic activity and gender, 2010 240

III.A1.3. Female employment as a proportion of total employment in each industry
sector according to ISIC Revision 3 and ISIC Revision 4 classifications, 2010 . . . 244

III.A2.1. Econometric estimates of the determinants of female labour force
participation, women aged 25-54, OECD, 1980-2007 247

III.A4.1. Quotas on boardroom representation in Europe and sanctions
for non-compliance 252

III.A5.1. Tax and benefit systems and their "neutrality" 253

III.A6.1. Informal employment in non-agricultural activities by gender 255

III.A6.2. Distribution of male and female informal employment by work category . . . 257

III.A7.1. Labour force participation, employment, part-time and temporary work,
gender wage gaps, boardroom membership and unpaid work 259

IV.A1.1. Women owned-enterprises lag behind in average productivity,
profits and generation of new jobs 326

IV.A1.2. Blinder-Oaxaca decompositions of the gender performance gap 326

IV.A2.1. Determinants of the earnings of male and female business owners 329

IV.A3.1. Differences in credit use and access for enterprises owned by women
and men, 2009 (16 European countries) 331

IV.A4.1. Description of the dataset used in Chapters 27 and 29 333

IV.A4.2. Statistics on small and micro-enterprises and their owners from surveys
used in Chapter 27 335

IV.A4.3. Differences in sales and sales per employee across gender
and formality status 336

IV.A5.1. Enterprises founded by women with previous entrepreneurial experience
are more likely to innovate and invest in R&D 338

IV.A5.2. The innovation gap by gender in the United States disappears
when controlling for other characteristics of firms and founders 339

IV.A5.3. Differences in expenditure on different forms of innovation by new
enterprises founded by women and men in the United States 339

Figures

1.1. Richer countries have higher and more gender-equal educational attainments 25

1.2. Converging male and female participation rates, the size of the labour force and the economy 28

2.1. Discriminatory attitudes are related to women's employment rates 32

2.2. The incidence of early marriage varies across regions 34

2.3. Early marriage is related to girls' secondary school enrolment. 34

3.1. Barriers to effective pursuit of gender mainstreaming and equality policies . 39

I.A2.1. The effect of converging participation rates between men and women on the size of the labour force 49

I.A3.1. The effect of converging participation rates between men and women on the size of the economy in GDP 54

4.1. Gender gaps in primary education still persist in some geographic regions . . 66

4.2. In secondary education girls are disadvantaged in regions with low overall enrolment rates. 67

4.3. In most OECD countries, young women are more likely to have completed upper secondary education than young men. 69

5.1. The education sector receives the highest volume of gender equality focused aid. 78

5.2. The education sector has the highest proportion of gender equality focused aid. 78

5.3. The proportion of OECD DAC donor aid targeting gender equality in primary and secondary education varies across regions 79

6.1. Girls significantly outperform boys in reading, but boys perform better than girls in mathematics 84

6.2. Girls continue to outperform boys in reading 85

6.3. The gender gap in reading is widest among the lowest performing students 86

6.4. Girls are more likely than boys to enjoy reading 87

6.5. Fathers are less likely than mothers to read to their children or have positive attitudes towards reading. 88

7.1. In low and middle income countries, NEET rates for women can be relatively high 92

7.2. Married and less educated young women aged 20-24 are more likely to be NEETs in Africa and India 93

7.3. After secondary school boys are more likely than girls to work 94

8.1. Today women are more likely to obtain a tertiary degree than men 100

8.2. More women enter health related degrees but remain underrepresented in computer science degrees. 102

8.3. Gender differences persist in technical vocational programmes 103

8.4. Women and men perform equally well at the tertiary level. 104

9.1. Male and female graduates who start their career in a skilled occupation . . . 110

9.2. Men and women who graduated from the same field often make different occupational choices 111

10.1. Women have slightly lower levels of financial knowledge than men 120

10.2. Young women typically have lower levels of financial literacy than their elders 121

11.1. In the OECD, gender gaps in labour force participation vary widely across countries 150

11.2. Gender gaps in labour force participation have narrowed but remain significant in South Asia, the Middle East and North Africa 151

11.3. Economic sectors with the highest feminisation rates are health and community services followed by education 153

11.4. Female employment is concentrated in a limited number of occupations . . . 154

11.5. In the OECD less than one-third of managers are women 156

11.6. More women are in paid work during childbearing years than in the past . . . 157

11.7. Women are at a higher risk of poverty than men, especially in old age 158

12.1. There are large gender gaps in part-time work and full-time equivalent employment rates 161

12.2. Motherhood makes part-time work much more likely 163

12.3. Women are more likely to work part-time in countries with high childcare costs 163

13.1. The gender pay gap: Narrowing but more slowly and still wide at the top . . . 167

13.2. Gender pay gap increases with age 169

13.3. The price of motherhood is high across OECD countries 170

13.4. The difference in take-home pay is wider because women work fewer hours 170

13.5. Differences in hours worked and the type of job explain part of the gender pay gap 171

13.6. Childcare and leave policies are inversely related to the pay gap 172

13.7. The gender pay gap is related to wage compression factors 173

14.1. The leaky pipeline: Women are under-represented in senior management . . 177

14.2. Cultural and corporate practices are perceived as the main barriers to women's rise to leadership 178

15.1. Norway has the largest proportion of women on boards of listed companies 186

16.1. Women make up a significant share of public sector employment 192

16.2. The government leaky pipeline: Women's under-representation in senior management in the central civil service 193

17.1. Women do more unpaid work than men in all countries 200

17.2. Women's unpaid work decreases with increases in the national levels of women's employment, but they always do more unpaid work than men . 201

17.3. Regardless of a woman's employment status, men do less unpaid work than their spouses 202

17.4. Gender gaps in unpaid and paid work increase with the arrival of children . . 202

18.1. In most OECD countries, dual-earner families are the norm 206

19.1. In most countries the employment gender gap narrowed during the economic crisis 216

19.2. Most employment losses are in male-dominated sectors 217

19.3. In most countries, women increased their hours worked to compensate for the employment loss of their partners during the crisis 218

19.4. The difference in unemployment rates between males and females
is on the rise 219

20.1. In Africa, Asia and Latin America informal employment is high and often
in non-registered companies 223

20.2. Women in informal non-agricultural employment tend to be concentrated
among the most vulnerable work categories 224

20.3. Both women and men earn less in non-agricultural informal employment
than in formal wage employment, but women earn even less than men 226

20.4. A significant proportion of women in non-agricultural informal
employment have indirect pension coverage through their spouses 226

21.1. Women pensioners are more likely to be poor than their male
counterparts 230

21.2. Most countries have a large pension gap 231

21.3. Women receive their pension for longer 232

22.1. The proportion of female entrepreneurs has not significantly increased
in most countries over the past decade. 274

22.2. The proportion of individually-owned enterprises with a female owner
varies between 20 and 40% across OECD countries...................... 276

22.3. The birth rate of female-owned enterprises is higher than
that of male-owned enterprises 276

22.4. Births of female-owned enterprises declined less than male-owned ones
during the crisis 277

23.1. Work-life balance is a motive for starting their business for more women
than men 280

23.2. More women than men start a business out of necessity, particularly
in Egypt and Mexico 281

23.3. Female business owners have higher educational attainment than men 282

24.1. There are wide international differences in the survival rates
of women-owned enterprises.. 286

24.2. Female and male-owned enterprises perform similarly in terms
of job creation 287

24.3. The share of female-owned enterprises falls among largest firms.......... 288

25.1. Female business owners earn significantly less than men 292

25.2. Most women tend to realise low profits, men being better represented
among average and top earners 293

25.3. In most OECD countries self-employed women work fewer hours
than men 294

25.4. Highly educated women earn more as salaried workers than
as self-employed... 294

26.1. More men than women use credit from banks to finance their start-up..... 298

26.2. There are large international differences in the difficulties perceived
by women in financing their start-up 300

26.3. Women create their enterprises with considerably lower amounts
of initial funds.. 301

27.1. The financial inclusion of women does not depend only on income 304

27.2. Women entrepreneurs in Africa are less likely to ask for loans than men ... 305

27.3. Neither male nor female micro-enterprise owners tend to use external loans to start up 306

28.1. Female founders perceive their activity as less innovative, particularly in terms of process innovation 310

28.2. Venture-capital investors are predominantly male, particularly in Asia 313

29.1. Women frequently own small and micro-enterprises, though less so in MENA countries 316

29.2. The percentage of female-owned micro and small businesses has increased in Mexico both in the formal and informal sectors 317

IV.A1.1. Gender differences in self-employment are much more pronounced among the self-employed with employees 323

IV.A1.2. Unemployed women are much less likely than men to consider self-employment 324

IV.A1.3. Enterprises run by women are significantly smaller than those run by men 324

IV.A1.4. Women are much less likely than men to run enterprises in manufacturing 325

IV.A4.1. Business owners in Brazil and Mexico consider level of prices and sales the most important business constraint 334

This book has...

StatLinks
A service that delivers Excel® files from the printed page!

Look for the *StatLinks* at the bottom right-hand corner of the tables or graphs in this book. To download the matching Excel® spreadsheet, just type the link into your Internet browser, starting with the *http://dx.doi.org* prefix.

If you're reading the PDF e-book edition, and your PC is connected to the Internet, simply click on the link. You'll find *StatLinks* appearing in more OECD books.

Executive summary

Gender equality is not just about economic empowerment. It is a moral imperative. It is about fairness and equity and includes many political, social and cultural dimensions. It is also a key factor in self-reported well-being and happiness across the world.

Many countries worldwide have made significant progress towards gender equality in education in recent decades. Girls today outperform boys in some areas of education and are less likely to drop out of school. But the glass is still only half full: women continue to earn less than men, are less likely to make it to the top of the career ladder, and are more likely to spend their final years in poverty.

Gender inequality means not only foregoing the important contributions that women make to the economy, but also wasting years of investment in educating girls and young women. Making the most of the talent pool ensures that men and women have an equal chance to contribute both at home and in the workplace, thereby enhancing their well-being and that of society.

The economic case for gender equality

Greater educational attainment has accounted for about half of the economic growth in OECD countries in the past 50 years – and that owes a lot to bringing more girls to higher levels of education and achieving greater gender equality in the number of years spent in education.

Greater educational equality does not guarantee equality in the workplace, however. If high childcare costs mean that it is not economically worthwhile for women to work full-time; if workplace culture penalises women for interrupting their careers to have children; and if women continue to bear the burden of unpaid household chores, childcare and looking after ageing parents, it will be difficult for them to realise their full potential in paid work. In developing countries, if discriminatory social norms favour early marriage and limit women's access to credit, girls' significant gains in educational attainment may not lead to increased formal employment and entrepreneurship.

The issues are complex and tackling them successfully means changing the way our societies and economies function. Men and women have to be able to find a work-life balance that suits them, regardless of family status or household income. Sharing childcare responsibilities can be difficult in a culture where men are considered professionally uncommitted if they take advantage of parental leave and mothers are sidetracked from career paths. And if good quality, affordable childcare is unavailable, it may simply be impossible for many parents, especially those on low incomes, to work full-time and take care of their families.

Well thought-out policies can help, but further action needs to be carefully considered to be sure that future change is as positive for growth and social outcomes as increased educational attainment has proved to be. To that end, general economic, labour market and entrepreneurship policy reform may be required and the lack of comprehensive and reliable information in some key areas must be overcome.

Increased gender equality has at least as many, if not more, benefits to offer developing countries, where women's economic empowerment is a prerequisite for sustainable development, pro-poor growth, and the achievement of all the Millennium Development Goals (MDGs). Investment in gender equality yields the highest returns of all development investments.

Education

Although most countries around the world have won the battle to provide universal primary education, the picture is much more mixed in secondary and higher education. Furthermore, policy needs to keep a firm eye on ensuring continuous improvement in the quality of education.

Girls are still less likely than boys to even start secondary education in Western, Eastern and Middle Africa and in South Asia. Enrolment is less of a problem in OECD countries, where education is generally compulsory up to the age of 15 or 16 years old. Boys, however, are more likely to drop out of secondary education, particularly in high-income countries.

As a result, young women are increasingly better educated than young men in many OECD countries. In reading skills, for example, boys lag behind girls at the end of compulsory education by the equivalent of a year's schooling on average. They are also far less likely to spend time reading for pleasure. Boys do perform better in mathematics, but the gender gap is narrower than in reading.

Girls are still less likely to choose scientific and technological fields of study and, even when they do, they are less likely to take up careers in those fields – a cause for concern given the skills shortages in the workplace, the generally more promising career and earnings prospects in science and technology, and the likelihood of positive spillover into innovation and growth.

Educational aspirations are formed early in life in OECD countries, so one answer should be to focus more attention on changing gender stereotypes and attitudes at a young age. Gender stereotyping frequently takes place in subtle ways at home, in schools, and in society. If primary teachers are mainly women, and secondary teachers, particularly in the sciences, are predominantly men, what messages are boys and girls getting about adult life? And if text books give examples of female nurses and male engineers, if teachers themselves project their beliefs about girls' and boys' abilities in mathematics or reading, what attitude towards those subjects will children form? Changing gender stereotypes in school is, however, only part of the equation: attitudes are also crucially determined by what happens at home.

In developing countries, where poor families may not be able to afford to send all their children to school, boys may come first. When primary schooling is made free, girls' attendance indeed rises. But the cost of education is not just a question of school fees. There are items such as uniforms and school meals – support in those areas can help get girls into school and keep them there all the way through secondary education. And education is the gift that keeps on giving: girls who have had schooling become mothers who, in turn, place high value on education for their own daughters.

To reap the highest economic and social return on education investment, therefore, it is important to find out just why there are gender differences in attitudes towards reading and mathematics, then to discover ways to reverse the imbalance. In the developing world, however, the prime focus must still be on getting girls into school and keeping them there, while ensuring that the schools they attend and the transport there and back are safe and that suitable sanitary facilities are provided.

Employment

The transition from education to paid work is a crucial moment which lays the foundation for many of the inequalities encountered throughout women's working lives. More women have entered the workforce in recent years, but often experience more difficulty than men in finding a first job, earn less than them, and are more likely to work part-time. Furthermore, the fields of study that young women and men choose perpetuate gender segregation in the labour markets, with women under-represented in the business sector and concentrated in health, welfare, education, and administrative jobs.

Such gender differences exist to a large extent because women still bear the burden of the unpaid, but unavoidable, tasks of daily domestic life, such as childcare and housework. In less developed countries, young women are more likely than young men to be neither in employment nor in education or training. When they do enter the labour market, there is more chance they will be confined to the most vulnerable jobs, frequently in the informal sector.

But irrespective of family commitments, many women find it difficult to climb the career ladder. In fact, inequalities increase the higher up the pay scale they go. The result is that, while in OECD countries women earn on average 16% less than men, female top-earners are paid 21% less than their male counterparts. The so-called "glass ceiling" exists: women are disadvantaged when it comes to decision-making responsibilities and senior management positions; by the time they get to the boardroom, there is only one of them for every 10 men.

The Norwegian experience shows that quotas can be effective in improving the gender balance at board level. However, the overall economic consequences of mandatory quotas have yet to become clear. In the meantime, a range of tools can be used to work towards the goal of gender balance – target setting, compliance with corporate governance codes and, in all cases, the monitoring and publication of progress.

Tensions between work and family life are at the heart of the employment puzzle when it comes to gender. Families with young children need affordable childcare if parents are to work. If childcare eats up one wage so that there is little or no financial gain in going out to work, parents (most often mothers) are less likely to seek a job. But how people manage life at home also plays a big part in the equation. Many systems still implicitly regard childrearing as a mother's responsibility: everywhere women are doing more unpaid work than men, regardless of whether they have full-time jobs or not.

Governments have an important role to play in promoting gender equality, not just by monitoring the gender dimension when crafting and evaluating policies, but also by ensuring equality of opportunity in the public service – with the government acting as a role model for other employers. Governments have indeed made great efforts in many countries, introducing policies like paid parental leave and childcare support that help parents reconcile work and family life. But the fact remains that it is primarily women who take advantage of family-friendly policies like flexible working arrangements, so perpetuating the idea that family responsibilities are a woman's affair.

Business, too, needs to think about the effect of corporate culture and working practices. If women are good for business, why do so few make it to the top, and why do so many simply give up trying? Teleworking and part-time or temporary work may sound attractive in the short term as ways of juggling work and family commitments, but the choice can be costly in the long term – in terms not just of salary, but of pensions and job security. Family-friendly workplace practices can make it easier to combine work and home life, but only if both men and women take advantage of them. Yet do employers make it easier for men and women to share domestic and family responsibilities outside the workplace? Are men who take their parental leave in full, for example, seen as uncommitted to their careers and passed over for promotion?

Change is not always easy, and it takes time for fundamental attitudes to shift in response to changing realities. Yet today's economies need all available talent to ensure a sustainable and prosperous future, while the right balance must be struck between responsibilities at home and at work to deliver better lives for all.

Entrepreneurship

Despite women's constantly increasing participation in the labour market over the past half-century, they remain substantially under-represented as entrepreneurs. When asked, fewer women than men say they would prefer to be self-employed. When they do choose to become entrepreneurs, they cite better work-life balance and/or economic necessity more often than men as the main motivation for starting a business. Yet female-owned businesses make a key contribution to household incomes and economic growth.

Entrepreneurship plays as important a role in developing countries as in developed ones in creating jobs, innovation, and growth. Fostering entrepreneurship is a key policy goal for governments of all countries which share the expectation that high rates of entrepreneurial activity will bring sustained job creation. Moreover, thriving new enterprises can boost the development of new products, processes, and organisational innovation.

But while more women are undertaking salaried work, the number of woman entrepreneurs has changed little in OECD countries. And when women do start businesses, they do it on a smaller scale than men and in a limited range of sectors. Self-employed women frequently earn 30 to 40% less than their male counterparts. Two key differences between male and female entrepreneurs help explain these relatively low returns: women start their enterprises with limited management experience and devote much less time to their businesses than men.

The proportion of women-owned businesses is currently stuck at around 30% of the total in OECD countries, and seems to plateau at around the same level in developing countries which have started from low levels. There is a clear need to provide more and better information about entrepreneurship as an attractive career option, both for young women in school and for women outside the labour force who are considering starting or getting back into work. About a quarter of women starting businesses in Europe gave as their reason for returning to work that their children were old enough to allow them to do so.

Women are also less likely than men to borrow money to finance their business. There are several reasons. Women might be charged higher interest rates and asked for more guarantees, as they often have shorter credit histories, less operating capacity, and less collateral. It may also be that women do not apply because they are afraid of refusal or lack confidence in the growth potential of their business. In a number of developing countries, the gap is narrowed by an array of microcredit and other financing arrangements targeted specifically at women and often administered by international agencies or NGOs. They are not, however, substitutes for the equitable treatment of loan requests from male and female entrepreneurs by the regular financial institutions and banks.

One of the main challenges when considering how to boost female entrepreneurship is the lack of solid, reliable data. Hence the need to collect more gender-specific data in this area.

Key findings

Economics, social norms and embedding gender equality in public policy

- The spread of education accounts for about half the economic growth in OECD countries in the past 50 years.
- Greater gender equality in education boosts female labour force participation and economic growth.
- Improving female labour market outcomes is needed to ensure strong, sustainable, balanced economic growth in the future.
- Persistent discriminatory social institutions and cultural norms restrict the economic and social role of girls and women in most countries across the world.
- Public gender agencies often lack the visibility, the authority and the resources to effectively advance gender equality across the "whole of government".

Education

- Enrolment in primary education is near universal in many countries. But, and particularly in high-income countries, boys are more likely to drop out of secondary education than girls, while younger women are increasingly better educated than young men.
- Girls outperform boys in reading but lag behind in mathematics, albeit to a lesser extent than boys in reading. Differences in attitudes are a major explanatory factor in these gender disparities.
- Although girls have high academic aspirations and employment expectations, there are systematic gender differences in areas of study at both tertiary level and in vocational training.
- In many low-income countries, young women are more likely than young men to be engaged neither in paid work nor in education or training.

Employment

- Female employment participation has generally increased and gender gaps in labour force participation have narrowed. Yet occupational segregation has not improved, gender pay gaps persist, and women are still under-represented at more senior job levels, especially among managers and on company boards.
- Formal childcare support is particularly important for boosting female employment levels and for achieving greater gender equality throughout working life.
- Women do more unpaid work than men in all countries, while the gender gap increases with the arrival of children.
- Women often work part-time as it facilitates combining work and family responsibilities, but this frequently comes at a cost to their long-term career and earning prospects.

Entrepreneurship

- Women are less keen than men on starting their own business and female entrepreneurs continue to be a minority in all countries.
- Enterprises owned by women are significantly smaller and less well represented in capital-intensive sectors. These and other factors tend to penalise their sales, profits and labour productivity.
- Women entrepreneurs rely substantially less than men on loans, both for starting up and financing their activities.

Key policy messages

General public policy

- Increase both the quantity and quality of data by gender and improve the evaluation of public policy.

- Strengthen the capacity of governments to apply a gender-responsive approach throughout the public financial management cycle and enhance gender impact assessments.

- Reform legal frameworks and ensure their enforcement to remove any obstacles to gender equality; prohibit discrimination, combat all forms of pay discrimination; uphold the notion of equal pay for work of equal value; and, provide economic support and incentives for individuals, families and communities to change discriminatory attitudes.

- Countries should set realistic targets for women in senior management positions in the public service.

Education

- Get girls more interested in mathematics and science and boys more interested in reading in OECD countries, for example, by removing the gender bias in curricula and raising awareness of the likely consequences of male and female choices of fields of study in their careers and earnings.

- Use apprenticeships to encourage women who have completed their science technology and mathematics (STEM) studies to work in scientific fields.

- Make schools safer and more affordable for girls in developing countries.

Employment

- Provide affordable, good-quality childcare for all parents and paid maternity leave for mothers in employment. Encourage more equal sharing of parental leave by, for example, reserving part of paid leave entitlements for the exclusive use of fathers.

- Remove disincentives to paid work created by taxes and benefit systems and ensure that work pays for both parents.

- Address cultural barriers and the stereotyping of women's roles in society, business and the public sector.

- Countries should introduce targets and measures to monitor progress on female representation on the boards of listed companies.

Entrepreneurship

- Ensure that policies for female-owned enterprises target not only start-ups and small enterprises, but encourage and support the growth ambitions of all existing firms.

- Promote comprehensive support programmes that target female-owned enterprises in high-tech sectors.

- Ensure equal access to finance for male and female entrepreneurs.

Gender equality: The economic case, social norms, and public policies

Greater gender equality and a more efficient use of skills are essential to achieving strong and sustainable growth. This section examines the contribution of gender equality in education and the labour market to economic growth. It also looks at the discriminatory social norms that restrict the economic and social roles of girls and women, and how policy can address such norms and practices. Finally, it considers how public institutions pursue gender equality policies and the institutional mechanisms that support the development of effective policies.

PART I

Chapter 1

The economic case for gender equality

Key findings

- Increases in educational attainment have accounted for around half of economic growth in OECD countries in the past 50 years.

- Greater gender equality in educational attainment has a strong positive effect on economic growth.

- Improved female labour market outcomes are needed to ensure continued economic growth in the future.

Greater gender equality in economic opportunity contributes to stronger, more sustainable economic growth. Similarly, investing in formal education and training increases individuals' lifelong skills sets, so improving the employment and entrepreneurial opportunities of both men and women. Gender equality also increases labour productivity and the available talent pool, affording businesses greater opportunities to expand, innovate and compete, which in turn provides governments with additional, much needed tax revenue and social security contributions as the population ages.

Gender equality in education: A matter of time and income?

Investment in human capital improves the economic and social opportunities of young people, thereby helping to reduce poverty and foster technical progress. In addition to its direct effects on economic participation, education also impacts on other societal outcomes such as child mortality, fertility, personal health outcomes, and greater investment in the education and health of future generations. Against that background, investing in the human capital of women is key to economic growth and social cohesion, especially in developing countries where the gender gap in education is still wide and the potential economic gains from educating girls consequently substantial (Barro and Lee, 1994; Schultz, 2002).

In countries where poverty and gender inequality are particularly pronounced – in parts of Africa, for example – an even greater, more urgent effort is required to actively and effectively engage women in economic, social and political life (OECD, 2007a). Good practice in pro-poor growth is about addressing social justice and higher economic returns as mutually supportive goals (OECD, 2009 and 2011a). In that light, gender equality in investment in education gives both men and women the means to contribute to a better society.

Gender equality is also a key driver in self-reported well-being and happiness across the world. Indeed, life satisfaction increases over time as gender equality does (Veenhoven, 2011 and 2012). However, there is concern that the double burden of paid and unpaid work makes it more difficult for women to achieve a similar degree both of satisfaction in the home and at work (Stevenson and Wolfers, 2009).

In global comparisons there is a strong positive association between countries' levels of development and educational attainment – a proxy for the level of human capital – for both men and women. Figure 1.1 plots levels of educational attainment by gender. Countries in the top right-hand corner have the highest levels of education for both men and women; in countries located above the diagonal line women on average have higher educational attainment than men. Since high-income countries are concentrated in the top right-hand corner, it can be inferred that in such countries young women have higher levels of educational attainment than young men. By contrast, in poorer countries the attainment rate is much lower and women are strongly disadvantaged. A similar picture could be shown for an older cohort of men and women (between the ages of 45 and 54).

Figure 1.1. **Richer countries have higher and more gender-equal
educational attainments**

Average number of years that 25-34 year-olds spend in education by gender

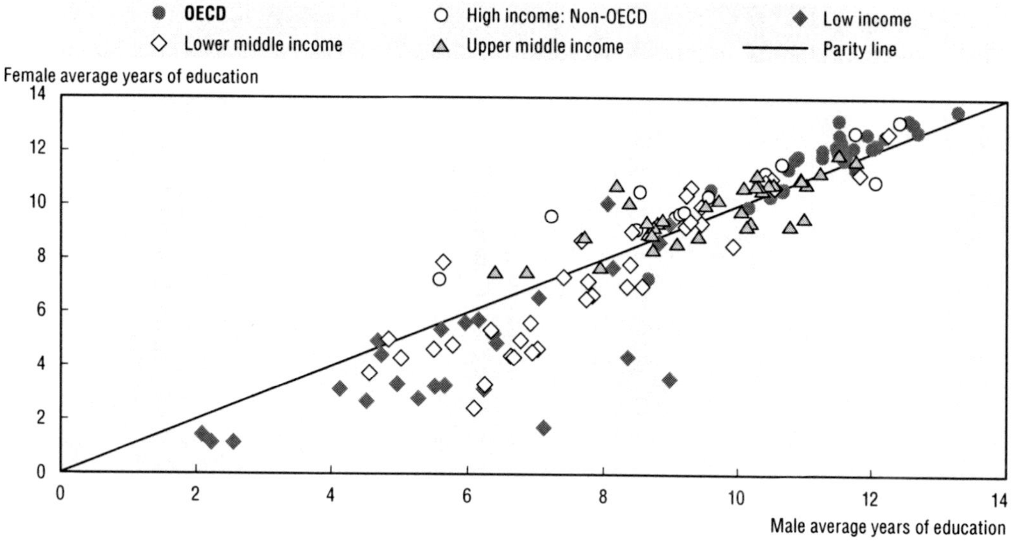

Note: Educational attainment is measured as the number of years spent in education. Countries are grouped by the World Bank Income Classification system.
Source: Barro, R.J. and J.W. Lee (2010), "A New Data Set of Educational Attainment in the World, 1950-2010", NBER *Working Paper*, No. 15902, Cambridge, United States.

StatLink ⟨⟩ http://dx.doi.org/10.1787/888932675253

However, compared with the previous generation, women have generally made gains in educational attainment, particularly in lower and middle-income countries; in terms of years of schooling developing countries are catching up.

The positive association between income and education may be interpreted in two ways. While it may reflect the positive effect of greater investment in education on countries' economic growth, it may also be related to the fact that richer countries invest more in human capital.

As regards gender equality, increased demand for human capital fosters incentives to invest more in women in whom hitherto investment was relatively small, and whose skills are on average identical to those of men. Growth and technological change can trigger further female education and empowerment, which in turn feeds back into economic development (Doepke *et al.*, 2011). This suggests that, as lower-income countries develop economically, female educational attainment will tend to expand as it did historically in developed countries. However, social institutions and norms like early marriage and assigned gender roles (addressed in Chapter 2) may have as much effect as education and labour market policies on the process of generating greater economic opportunities for women and for economies as a whole.

There is a large body of theoretical and empirical analysis of the link between investment in human capital and economic growth. Research conducted for this report suggests not only that building human capital has a strong positive effect on economic growth, but that a more equal gender distribution of education furthers that positive effect (Annex I.A1). A human-capital-augmented growth model was used to determine how much the growth of output per capita depends on the accumulation of human capital and on gender inequalities in educational attainment, while controlling for the effect of population growth, accumulation of physical capital and technological and economic efficiency (Annex I.A1).* The model was estimated using data that covered 30 OECD countries over the 1960-2008 period (Bassanini and Scarpetta, 2002; Arnold *et al.*, 2011). The main findings are as follows:

● Confirming recent studies, the empirical evidence suggests high returns on investment in education: one additional year of average education would raise output per capita by around 10% *per annum*.

● The increase in educational attainment accounted for around 50% of economic growth (2.1% *per annum* on average for the 30 countries from 1960 to 2008), of which over half was due to increased female educational attainment.

● Greater gender equality in the accumulation of human capital has an additional and significant positive effect on economic growth.

Labour market effects

While growth models used in the research conducted for this report allow an assessment of the overall effect of education and gender equality on long-term economic growth, they do not identify the mechanisms at work – i.e. the positive employment and productivity effects associated with higher levels of education and narrower gender gaps, and/or the effects of female education on fertility rates and the old-age dependency ratio. Moreover, in addition to increasing female participation in the labour force, better allocations of women workers across occupations and economic sectors can further contribute to growth. For example, Hsieh *et al.* (2012) suggest that between 17 and 20% of US economic growth between 1960 and 2008 might have been due to the changing allocation of under-represented groups in the workforce, which includes women.

The effect of growing (female) education on growth, in both the past and future, is perhaps nowhere more evident than in the Korean experience (Box 1.1). However, other countries, too, present a strong economic case for a more effective use of female labour supply.

Panel A of Figure 1.2 shows the effects that narrowing gender gaps in labour market participation may have on the potential size of the labour force. The figure's projections consider three different scenarios for men's and women's labour market participation over the next 20 years and their effect on the total labour force:

1. A no-change scenario: male and female participation rates remain at their 2010 levels over the whole period.

2. Convergence in participation rates: the male participation rate remains constant at its 2010 level, while the female participation rate increases over the period to converge with male participation in 2030.

3. Convergence in intensity of labour market participation: this scenario accounts for the difference in usual working hours between the genders and assumes that the male participation rate remains constant at its 2010 level, while the female full-time equivalent participation rate (see notes to Figure 1.2) increases to equal the full-time equivalent rate for men by 2030.

---

* The analysis requires a long time series on educational attainment as in Barro and Lee (2010). Educational attainment is expressed as years of schooling completed (Barro and Lee, 2010), which, however is a weak proxy of the progress in the quality of educational attainment as measured by the OECD *Education Database*. Nevertheless, even with this minimum-level indicator, the importance of greater gender balance in educational attainment is confirmed.

Box 1.1. **The Korean economic transformation: Can women continue the miracle?**

From a very poor country in 1950 with GDP per capita at less than USD 50, Korea has developed into a regional and global industrial powerhouse with per capita GDP exceeding USD 27 000 in 2011. This remarkable transformation is related, among other things, to the introduction in the 1960s of a sharp policy focus on investment in education and family-planning policies to curb birth rates, which fell from six children per woman in 1960 to 1.15 in 2009. The trend towards smaller families facilitates greater (public and parental) investment per child which, in Korea as in many other countries, is then spread equally among boys and girls (Behrman *et al.*, 1986; Kornich and Furstenberg, 2010; Shin *et al.*, 2008). At present, young Korean women are as well educated as their male peers (Chapter 4).

However, the Korean labour market has not kept pace with the rapid change in female educational attainment: female workforce participation rates are about the same now as they were 20 years ago. Men spend little time helping women with household chores (Chapter 17) and married women are still expected to leave their jobs upon giving birth (Kim, 2010). Women's position in the labour market is poor, as indicated by the wide gender pay gaps and limited number of female managers (Chapters 11 and 13). Korean policy is moving to further strengthen work-life balance policies, such as parental leave and childcare support, but as long as workplace culture involves long working hours, socialising after work, and a seniority-based pay system which punishes women for leaving their jobs to have children, social policy reform will have relatively little effect.

In the past, Korea's growing working population has contributed to strong economic growth. However, from 2018 the working-age population is projected to decline and Korea's demographic dividend will start to erode. The country, which has traditionally experienced little immigration, will need to use its human capital more effectively to face the challenge of a potentially dwindling pool of paid and unpaid workers. Korean men will have to do more at home, more Korean women will have to be part of the paid workforce, and Korean workplace practices will have to become more family-friendly.

Korea has used its demographic dividend for strong growth, but now needs to make better use of its female workers to avoid a shrinking labour force and economy

Korean population by broad age-group, 1950-2050

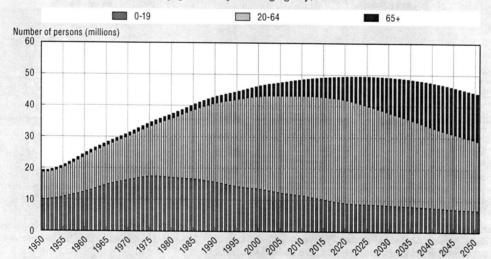

Source: OECD Demography and Population Database 2012.

StatLink ⏷ *http://dx.doi.org/10.1787/888932675272*

Figure 1.2. **Converging male and female participation rates, the size of the labour force and the economy**[a]

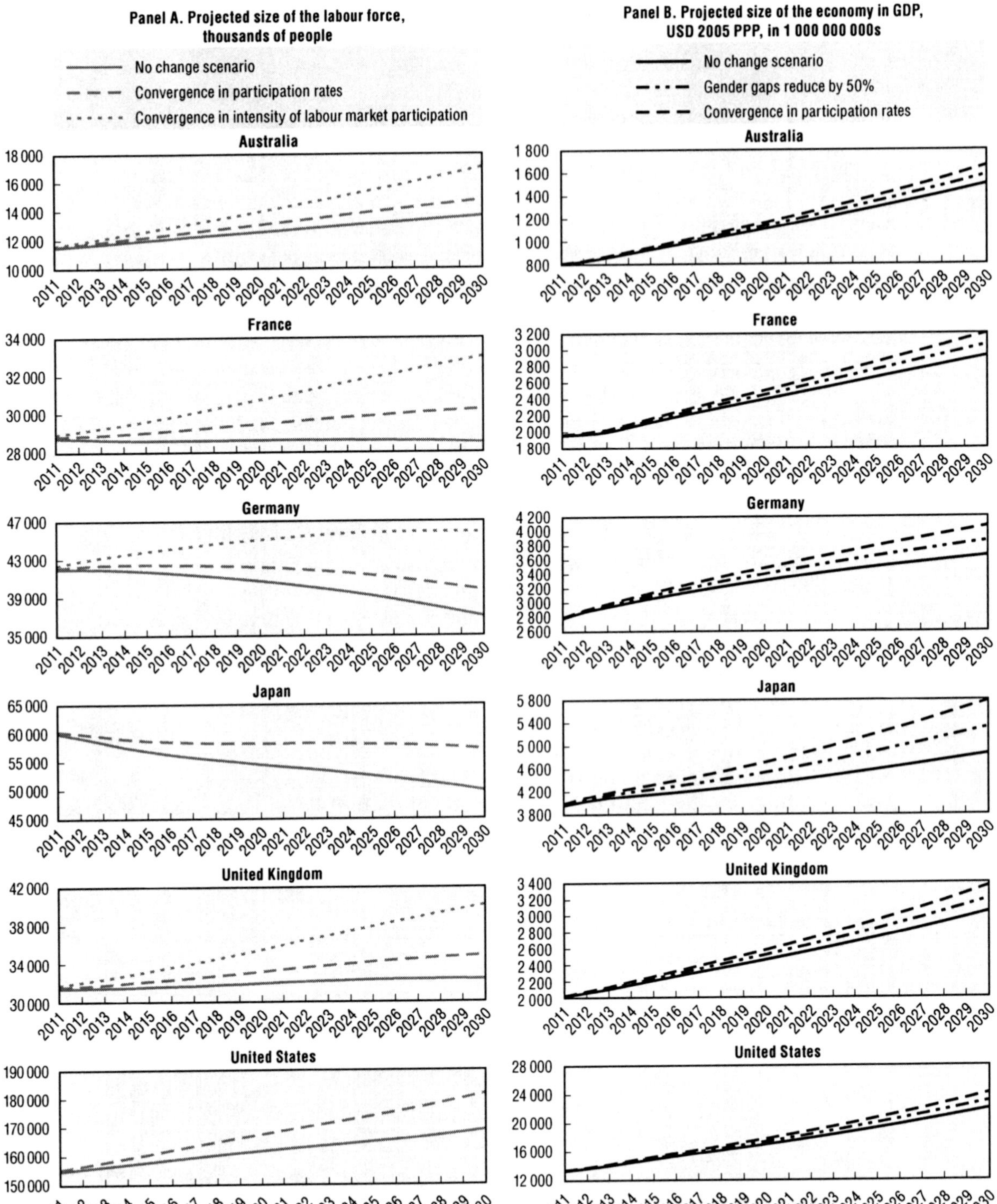

Panel A. Projected size of the labour force, thousands of people

- ——— No change scenario
- – – – Convergence in participation rates
- · · · · Convergence in intensity of labour market participation

Panel B. Projected size of the economy in GDP, USD 2005 PPP, in 1 000 000 000s

- ——— No change scenario
- – · – · Gender gaps reduce by 50%
- – – – Convergence in participation rates

a) The labour force projections are based on population projections for persons aged 15-64 years in the left-hand column and over 15 in the right-hand column, as reported by the *OECD Demography and Population Database*. For the remaining OECD countries not included in this chart and for definitions of the scenarios, see Annex I.A1 and I.A3.

Source: OECD Secretariat calculations based on OECD (2012), *OECD Economic Outlook*, No. 91, OECD Publishing, Paris; *OECD Demography and Population Database 2012*; *OECD Employment Database 2012*, available at *www.oecd.org/employment/database*.

StatLink ⟡⟡⟡ *http://dx.doi.org/10.1787/888932675291*

Ageing populations combined with dwindling fertility rates mean that many countries are expected to face a shrinking labour force over the next 20 years. Assuming constant male and female labour force participation rates, the projected decrease would be particularly severe (over 10%) in the Czech Republic, Germany, Japan, Poland, the Russian Federation, the Slovak Republic and Slovenia (Figure I.A2.1).

The convergence scenario for gender equality in labour force participation rates is projected to have the greatest effect in Brazil, Chile, the Czech Republic, Greece, Ireland, Italy, Japan, Korea, Luxembourg, Mexico, Poland, the Slovak Republic, and Spain. The projected increase in the size of the labour force will exceed 10% by 2030, as there are currently large gender gaps in participation in these countries (Figure I.A2.1).

Figure 1.2 also illustrates the further effect of convergence in the intensity of labour force participation. In line with this scenario, significant additional increases in the labour force are also projected in Australia, Austria, Belgium, Germany, Ireland, Luxembourg and the United Kingdom, where more than 30% of employed women work part-time. Labour force gains are potentially even higher in the Netherlands and Switzerland, where the incidence of part-time employment is highest among OECD countries (Figure I.A2.1).

Of course, these projections involve making certain assumptions regarding future population patterns that may not materialise. Nevertheless, they clearly illustrate the size of the potential female labour force and its effect in counteracting the decline in labour supply due to ageing populations. In this context, a key future challenge for both government and employers is to promote working conditions and pay that make being in work more attractive to women. At the same time, however, ageing populations will also increase the demand for long-term care (OECD, 2011b). In many emerging economies, the fulfilment of family obligations such as caring for aging relatives is a priority for women, regardless of their personal career ambitions. In China, this issue is of particular concern due to the prevailing one-child policy which, amongst other things, means that such care obligations cannot be shared between siblings (Hewlett and Rashid, 2011). There needs to be greater gender equality in both paid and unpaid work participation, while workplace practices will have to become more efficient to meet the demand for formal and informal labour.

Male and female labour force participation and economic growth

Research undertaken for this report gauges the potential effect on economic growth of women's increased participation in the labour force, drawing on the long-term growth scenario outlined in the *OECD Economic Outlook* (2012d). To illustrate effects, three scenarios for convergence between male and female labour force participation were considered (see Annex I.A1 for further detail):

1. A no-change scenario: the gap between male and female labour force participation rate remains at the levels observed in 2010.

2. Gender gaps reduced by 50%: the male participation rate remains constant at its 2010 level and the gap between male and female labour force participation rates is halved by 2030.

3. Convergence in participation rates: the male participation rate remains constant at its 2010 level, while the gender gap in labour force participation levels disappears by 2030.

Even in the absence of a reduction in the gender gap in labour force participation rates, the baseline projections estimate that the GDP per capita will grow at an average annual rate of between 0.8% (Luxembourg) and 3.4% (Estonia) among OECD economies over the next 20 years (Table IV.A3.1). This will be primarily due to an increase in multi-factorial productivity which will continue to be the main driver of growth over this period (OECD, 2012d).

A greater female labour supply will also add impetus to economic growth as measured by GDP (Figure 1.2, Panel B, Figure I.A2.1 and Figure I.A3.1). On average across the OECD, a 50% decrease in the gender gap in labour force participation rates will lead to an increase in the GDP per capita annual growth rate of 0.3 percentage points. If full convergence occurs by 2030, however, the increase will be 0.6 percentage points (equivalent to an overall increase of 12% in GDP over 20 years). The largest increases (more than 0.5 percentage points) from full convergence are projected in the Czech Republic, Greece, Hungary, Japan, Korea, Luxembourg, Poland, and the Slovak Republic. The rise is expected to be even higher in Italy – more than 1 percentage point (see Annex I.A3). To a large extent this trend reflects: i) persistently low birth rates which curtail growth of the working age population in the future; and ii) the wide existing gender gaps in participation and the consequently greater potential for growth through better utilisation of the female labour supply. At less than 5%, gains will be more limited in Finland, Iceland and Sweden where birth rates have held up better than in most OECD countries and gender employment gaps are narrow.

PART I

Chapter 2

Why social institutions matter for gender equality

Key findings

- Across the world, persisting gender gaps in education, employment and entrepreneurship are related to discriminatory social institutions, defined as laws, social norms and practices, which restrict the economic and social roles of girls and women.

- Across the OECD, countries with higher levels of discriminatory attitudes towards women's employment also have greater gender gaps in employment rates.

- For many developing countries, poorer education and subsequent labour market outcomes for women and girls are related to the prevalence of early marriage.

While recent decades have seen unprecedented numbers of girls succeeding in education, women entering the paid workforce and running successful businesses, patterns of gender inequality persist. Social institutions can help explain what is stopping women and girls from achieving equal outcomes in areas such as education, employment, business, health and political participation (IFC, 2011; Jones *et al.*, 2010; North, 1990; OECD, 2007b and 2010b; World Bank, 2011). They set the context for whether decisions, choices or behaviours are deemed acceptable or not in a society.

A key role in defining gender relations is played by social norms and attitudes – *e.g.* the division of paid and unpaid work and discriminatory practices such as early marriage – which influence social and economic outcomes for women and girls in developing countries. Too often, policy interventions that address gender inequalities are designed without regard for discriminatory social institutions. They consequently fail to tackle the underlying drivers of gender inequality.

Discriminatory social institutions worldwide

Figure 2.1 presents data on OECD countries' attitudes towards women and men's employment when jobs are scarce. These data give a rough indication of discriminatory social norms which reinforce the role of men as the primary breadwinners and female employment as secondary.

Figure 2.1. **Discriminatory attitudes are related to women's employment rates**

Gender gap in employment rates (male rate *minus* female rate) and discriminatory attitudes towards women's employment, OECD countries

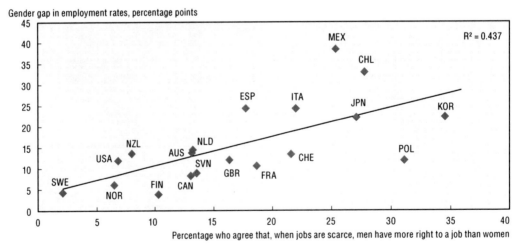

Source: World Values Survey Association (2009), "World Values Survey 2005", *www.worldvaluessurvey.org*; OECD *Employment Database 2012, www.oecd.org/employment/database.*

StatLink ᵐᵉˢᵖ *http://dx.doi.org/10.1787/888932675310*

Across OECD countries, an average of 10.3% of survey respondents agree that men are more entitled to a job than women when jobs are scarce. Swedes and Norwegians appear to have the least discriminatory attitudes, while about one-third of Poles and Koreans deem that men have more right to a job than women when labour demand is weak. Furthermore, Figure 2.1 suggests that the higher the percentage of respondents who find that men are more entitled to a job than women, the greater the gender gap in employment rates.

It seems that discriminatory attitudes towards women's employment are related to employment outcomes, and should therefore be taken into consideration when designing policy interventions aimed at achieving gender equality in economic participation. While countries may have anti-discrimination laws in place, there should also be a continued focus on changing underlying attitudes.

Although non-OECD countries have made great strides towards gender parity in primary school enrolment, gaps in secondary schooling persist, particularly in Sub-Saharan Africa and Southern Asia (Chapter 4). Discriminatory social institutions can help to explain why girls leave school prematurely, thereby contributing to persistent gender gaps in both educational and economic participation. The OECD Social Institutions and Gender Index (SIGI) is a composite measure of discriminatory social institutions across non-OECD countries capturing laws, social norms and practices which restrict women's economic and social role in five areas: 1) discriminatory family codes; 2) restricted physical integrity; 3) son bias; 4) restricted entitlements and resources; 5) restricted civil liberties.

One SIGI variable is "early marriage" as measured by the percentage of women aged 15-19 who are married. This variable often reflects practices such as forcing girls into marriage or their marrying before adulthood due to discriminatory social norms with respect to the status of women in the family and the reproductive role of women. Early marriage disproportionately affects young girls, who are much more likely to be married than young boys (UNICEF, 2005).

The prevalence of early marriage varies greatly across developing countries. Survey data nearest to 2012 indicate that the highest prevalence of early marriage is in the Niger (62%), Mali (50%) and Chad (49%). The practice varies across regions (Figure 2.2), with Sub-Saharan Africa exhibiting the highest regional average (26%), closely followed by Southern Asia (24%). Incidence is lowest in Eastern Europe (8%) and in Central and East Asia and the Pacific (9%).

Girls suffer negative consequences from early marriage on a number of counts. It limits their access to education, which has a knock-on effect on economic opportunities (UNICEF, 2005). It can also lead to high rates of adolescent fertility, infant mortality, poor maternal health, and increased vulnerability to HIV (Bruce and Clark, 2004; Jones et al., 2010). Early marriage can also have negative inter-generational effects as children are less likely to be educated or immunised if their mother has not received an education (World Bank, 2011).

Figure 2.3 shows the relationship between early marriage and gross female secondary school enrolment rates. Countries with a lower incidence of early marriage are more likely to have a higher gross female secondary school enrolment rate. In South Africa, for example, 3% of women aged 15-19 are married and the country has a gross female secondary school enrolment rate of 96%. By contrast, in Chad, 49% of women aged 15-19 are married and the gross female secondary school enrolment is 15%.

Figure 2.2. **The incidence of early marriage varies across regions**

Proportion of married women aged 15-19 worldwide by region

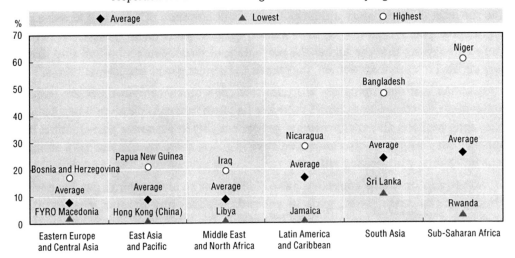

Source: OECD Gender, Institutions and Development Database 2012.

StatLink ᴍᴍ☐ http://dx.doi.org/10.1787/888932675329

Figure 2.3. **Early marriage is related to girls' secondary school enrolment**

Early marriage and girls' secondary school enrolment

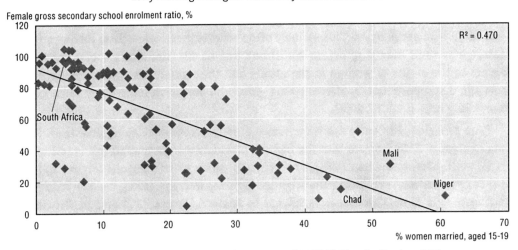

Source: OECD Gender, Institutions and Development Database 2012; and UNESCO Education Database 2012.

StatLink ᴍᴍ☐ http://dx.doi.org/10.1787/888932675348

The causal relationship between early marriage and girls' education is complex. Bates *et al.* (2007) and UNICEF (2005) found that access to formal education itself is a critical factor in delaying the age at which girls marry. Lloyd and Mensch (2008), however, found that almost 30% of young women who left secondary schooling before completion in Chad and Nigeria cited early marriage as the main reason. The persistence of gender gaps in secondary education in Sub-Saharan Africa and Southern Asia, where early marriage rates remain high, indicates that discriminatory social institutions need to be addressed to enable girls to reap the full benefits of education (Field and Ambrus, 2008).

> ### Box 2.1. **Missing women: A demographic crisis stemming from discrimination against daughters**
>
> The phenomenon of "missing women" due to sex-selective abortions and female infanticide has attracted growing attention in recent years. This phenomenon – a particular problem in Southern Asia, China and parts of the Caucasus and Western Balkans – is rooted in social norms that favour sons over daughters because they represent lifelong economic support while daughters are economic burdens (UNFPA, 2007).
>
> Klasen and Wink (2003) argue that increasing access to sex-selective abortions is one factor behind the missing women phenomenon, as well as restrictive family planning such as China's one-child policy. In the absence of gender discrimination and higher mortality rates among boys, the child-sex ratio should fall below 105. China's most recent census found that the sex-ratio for newborns was over 118 (Hudson, 2011). Using data from India's 2011 census, adjusted for excess mortality rates in girls, the estimates of the number of selective abortions of girls rose from 3 to 6 million in the 2000s. Jha *et al.* (2011) suggest the problem is becoming increasingly prevalent amongst the middle classes, the inference being that it cannot be attributed solely to poor socio-economic status.
>
> The rising number of missing women and girls in some countries presents a potential demographic crisis: skewed sex-ratios may have serious social consequences as men are unable to find female partners. The result could be social unrest, sexual violence, and increased trafficking of girls and young women.

Can policies change discriminatory social institutions?

Although rigorous evaluations of policy interventions to address discriminatory social institutions are limited, a three-pronged approach is emerging from the literature.

First, reforms (which include the harmonisation of laws) to ensure the equality of men and women before the law and prohibit discriminatory practices are a critical initial step in changing discriminatory social norms and practices. An enabling legal and policy environment has long been identified as critical to improving women's economic and social outcomes (OECD, 2010a; World Bank, 2011). For example, Tunisia introduced changes to its personal status law in 1993, establishing a minimum age of marriage and assigning men and women mutual obligations – the first country to introduce such reforms in the Middle East and North African region. The Tunisian reforms induced changes in norms regarding women's and men's roles in the family and society and have led to women marrying at a later age (OECD, 2010a).

Second, economic support and incentives for individuals and families can change behaviour and ultimately shift attitudes. The introduction of paid leave entitlements on a "use it or lose it" basis for fathers in a number of OECD countries has led to men taking longer parental leave (OECD, 2011c). One example of an economic incentive in a developing country context is the Indian programme called "*Apni Beti Apna Dhan*" (Our Daughter, Our Wealth). It provides cash incentives to girls and their families that are conditional on daughters remaining unmarried until the age of 18. Initial evaluation results suggest the programme has helped parents increase investment in their daughters' human capital (Sinha and Young, 2009).

Box 2.2. **Housing support for vulnerable women and children in Brazil**

"*Minha Casa Minha Vida*" (My House My Life) is a means-tested housing programme to support low-income families move into secure housing. The programme offers financing to support the purchase of homes and housing costs. It currently aims to extend the 1 million homes already provided to an additional 2 million houses and apartments by 2014. This is a federal programme delivered in partnership with states and municipalities, with eligibility criteria varying in rural and urban areas by income (*www.minhacasaminhavida.com.br*).

At the initiative of President Dilma Rousseff, the programme aims to address the issue of men leaving families and selling properties without providing for women and children. One of the conditions for providing support is that a property should "preferably" be registered in the woman's name, particularly because women are more likely to have custody of children. The programme, its application (to what extent the "preferable" condition is enforced) and its effect on women's behaviour (how they might behave in the event of domestic violence) is yet to be evaluated.

Last, a shift in public attitudes is required to bring about long-term change in discriminatory social institutions and address the gap between laws and practice. Interventions such as public awareness programmes or community mobilisation activities can be effective. The USAID "Safe Age of Marriage" programme in Yemen, for example, uses community education to tackle attitudes to early marriage. Initial results of the programme found an 18% increase in awareness of the benefits of delaying marriage, a 34% rise in the recognition that delaying marriage would increase educational opportunities, and a 19% increase among respondent who agreed that it would increase employment opportunities.

Key policy messages

Closing the gender gaps in education, employment and entrepreneurship requires governments to introduce policy interventions to shift discriminatory social institutions built on deep-seated social norms and gender stereotypes. A multifaceted approach is required. It should include:

- Reform of formal and informal legal frameworks and the harmonisation of laws to provide equality for women and men and the prohibition of discriminatory and harmful practices. Examples include reform of family codes to foster equality in marriage and inheritance and legislation that criminalises domestic violence.

- Economic support and incentives for individuals, families and communities to change behaviours and address discriminatory attitudes – *e.g.* support to encourage parents to invest in the education of their daughters as well as their sons.

- Community mobilisation, awareness, and empowerment initiatives to change discriminatory attitudes, social norms and practices through, for example, media campaigns reinforcing the value of daughters.

PART I

Chapter 3

Embedding gender equality in public policy

Key findings

- Limited government accountability and the public service's lack of awareness and capacity to assess the impacts of policy choices on men and women are among the barriers to more effective gender equality policies.

- Public agencies that support gender equality play an important role in mainstreaming gender considerations in policy development and service delivery. However, they often face challenges of visibility and authority in effectively pursuing coherent approaches to advancing gender equality across policy areas and tiers of government.

- The availability of gender-disaggregated data varies across policy areas and hampers government ability to undertake robust analysis of the gender effects of policy decisions and make informed policy choices.

The ability of governments to develop policies that are evidence-driven, responsive, and inclusive is fundamental to achieving genuine gender equality in OECD and non-member countries. The responsibility of government agencies for appropriately addressing issues of gender inequality and mainstreaming gender into policies and programmes was formalised in the 1995 Beijing Declaration and Platform for Action. The declaration was endorsed by 160 governments (United Nations, 1995) and incorporated into many national constitutions (*e.g.* Canada, Egypt, Germany, India, the Russian Federation, South Africa and Turkey) and other legal and policy provisions.

Box 3.1. Defining gender equality and gender mainstreaming

Gender equality describes the absence of obvious or hidden disparities among individuals based on gender. Disparities can include discrimination in terms of opportunities, resources, services, benefits, decision-making power and influence (Wikigender).

Gender mainstreaming is a process of assessing the implications for women and men of any planned action, so that the gender perspective becomes an integral dimension of the design, implementation, monitoring and evaluation of policies and programmes (United Nations, 1997). It encompasses the ability to anticipate the potentially differential impact of policy actions on women and men as well as the ability to design policy actions that are not "gender-blind" but "gender-sensitive". Policy actions are gender-sensitive if they recognise the potentially different interests and needs of women and men based on their potentially different social experiences, opportunities, roles and resources.

Despite governmental commitments, however, gender gaps persist. Figure 3.1 offers an overview of barriers to more effective pursuit of gender mainstreaming and equality policies. Countries that participated in the *2011 OECD Survey on National Gender Frameworks, Gender Public Policies and Leadership* (OECD, 2011d) report the chief obstacles as being:

● Limited accountability mechanisms across public agencies to advance gender equality and mainstreaming.

● A lack of awareness within the public service of how various policy options may have different effects on men and women.

● A lack of monitoring mechanisms to evaluate the effect of gender equality initiatives.

Furthermore, a co-ordinated approach for dealing with gender inequalities across policy areas and levels of government is often missing. Ireland, Norway, Spain, and Switzerland describe the limited nature of accountability mechanisms for gender equality commitments as their chief concern. The Czech Republic, Israel, Luxembourg, and Mexico note the lack of awareness of the need to mainstream gender considerations into the policy process as their key challenge (OECD, 2011d).

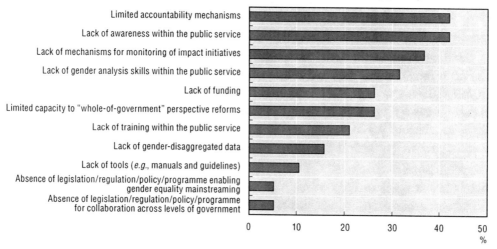

Figure 3.1. **Barriers to effective pursuit of gender mainstreaming and equality policies**

Percentage of country respondents who consider each barrier a top priority

Source: OECD (2011), "Survey on National Gender Frameworks, Gender Public Policies and Leadership", OECD Publishing, Paris.

StatLink ⊟ *http://dx.doi.org/10.1787/888932675367*

The barriers in Figure 3.1 may significantly impair the chances of reaching *de facto* gender equality. The evidence suggests that designing coherent, co-ordinated gender equality policies calls for a three-pronged approach (OECD, 2011d and 2011e):

1. Strong public institutions and mechanisms to ensure accountability for fulfilling gender equality and mainstreaming commitments.

2. Tools for evidence-based and inclusive policy making that account for potentially different effects on women and men.

3. Effective monitoring mechanisms and reliable gender-disaggregated evidence for making informed policy decisions.

Public institutions, incentives, and accountability

Many OECD and non-OECD countries have put in place institutional mechanisms – including central gender agencies and/or focal points – to support the development of policies that address gender inequalities and government accountability for closing gender gaps. Such mechanisms have a broad remit of government-wide policy-making responsibilities (OECD, 2011d):

● Report to Parliament on the state of gender equality (87%).

● Provide expert advice to other public bodies on gender equality (83%).

● Conduct policy research (65%).

● Make policy recommendations to other ministries (83%).

● Monitor the implementation of public gender initiatives (61%).

● Conduct analyses into the effects on men and women of different policy options as part of the policy-making process (48%).

These institutional mechanisms frequently act as catalysts to facilitate action by other government bodies and can influence legal reforms in ways that promote gender equality. For example, Mexico's National Women's Institute developed an institutional mechanism called "National System for Equality between Women and Men", which co-ordinates the gender-related work of 42 federal agencies.

Gender-related institutional frameworks differ widely across countries. There seems to be no common trend: data show that OECD countries are experimenting to test what institutional set-ups or models work best in their national contexts. Regardless of their structure, however, agencies in charge of gender equality portfolios may well face issues related to a lack of the authority, visibility and leverage required to effectively pursue a coherent government approach across various policy areas (Figure 3.1).

- *Single ministries or agencies:* 37% of OECD countries established stand-alone gender equality ministries or agencies. They ensure high visibility for gender issues and often have access to cabinet submissions, which facilitates the inclusion of gender considerations in policy decisions. (Belgium, Chile, Korea, Luxembourg, and New Zealand are among the countries with such set-ups.) However, if funding and authority are lacking, the single-agency framework may contribute to the marginalisation of gender issues while limited ownership by other public agencies may hamper their focus on gender issues.

- *Units in the centre of government:* 9% of OECD countries, such as Israel and the United States, have established gender institutions in the seat of government (*i.e.* in the office of the head of state or government) to facilitate co-ordination, monitoring, policy development and accountability at the highest level. If there is no designated minister for gender equality, however, this option may curtail the visibility of gender issues both in the seat of government and across government departments.

- *Combined portfolios:* in 54% of OECD countries, gender equality issues are paired with other portfolios in ministries. (Examples are the Czech Republic, Germany, Greece, Finland, Ireland, Norway, the Slovak Republic, Spain, Sweden, and Switzerland, as well as non-OECD countries like Morocco and Tunisia.) To be effective, this organisational framework requires strongly co-ordinated and coherent policy development and implementation. In addition, frameworks that combine gender equality with family and/or children's affairs may risk confining women narrowly to their roles as mothers and caregivers.

In addition to these focal points in government ministries, some countries (*e.g.* Belgium, Finland, Greece, Korea, Mexico and Spain) have established parliamentary committees with responsibility for gender matters. To oversee gender equality issues, others have independent commissions (Australia, Belgium, Israel, Luxembourg and New Zealand) and/or human rights commissions (Australia, Ireland, Mexico and New Zealand). A number of countries use "ombuds-offices" to oversee the implementation of gender initiatives and to keep gender concerns on the policy agenda (including the Czech Republic, Finland, France, Germany, Greece, Mexico, Norway, and Sweden).

Some of these bodies also consider complaints related to violations of the economic and social rights of both men and women. Such violations include issues of equal pay for equal work or equal access to education (OECD, 2008, describes measures against labour market discrimination in greater detail).

The use of institutional frameworks to oversee, report, and enforce the overall implementation of gender equality legislation and regulations varies between countries and can also differ between levels of government within a particular country. Less than half of

OECD countries systematically report to their parliaments or other high-level bodies either on the implementation of laws to reduce gender-related inequalities and discrimination or on the results of gender-impact assessments. Yet most gender-equality agencies are vested with this responsibility (OECD, 2011d). While audits or inspections also exist, they are very rare. Similarly, it is not common practice to incorporate the implementation of gender-relevant policies into managerial performance objectives and there are often little or no consequences for failing to meet gender equality targets (OECD, 2011d).

Tools for evidence-based policy making

Building awareness and understanding among policy makers of the potentially different effects of policy choices on men and women is key to effective, evidence-based policy making in various domains (Figure 3.1). Even seemingly gender-neutral policy decisions can have effects, whether intentional or not, on women's chances of become equal participants in society. They may make it more difficult for them to find employment, secure an education, start a business, meet the needs of their family, or ensure their human rights. For example, a workplace regulation that permits both parents to take leave to care for a sick child is more likely to affect women as primary caregivers (see Chapter 17).

Against that background, the Gender Impact Assessment (GIA) is a key policy-making tool that provides detailed, systematic information about the potentially differential effects of laws, policies and regulations on men and women. Israel, for example, reports that several GIAs showed how sports for men and boys enjoyed greater subsidies than sports for women and girls at national and local level (Swirski, 2011). GIAs can also help understand who will benefit from a particular set of policy options and can promote policy coherence by making the trade-offs inherent in public policies transparent.

The European Union defines a GIA as "a process to compare and assess, according to gender-relevant criteria, the current situation and trend with the expected development resulting from the introduction of the proposed policy" (European Commission, 1997). Such analysis can be conducted during the design stage of a law or regulation (*ex ante*) and/or during evaluations of the impacts of implemented laws, regulations and programmes (*ex post*). In Sweden, for example, a regulation stipulates that a "committee of enquiry" must carry out gender impact analysis of a policy proposal with a potential effect on gender equality. The committee extensively examines the proposal and drafts a report that is submitted to Parliament ahead of its decision. Spain has passed legislation, the Act for Effective Equality between Women and Men, that requires gender impact analyses for regulations and plans of specific "economic, social, cultural and artistic relevance" that are submitted to the Council of Ministers.

While many OECD countries (*e.g.* Finland, Korea, New Zealand, Switzerland, Sweden, Turkey and the United Kingdom) use gender impact assessments of policy choices, the extent and depth to which they actually conduct them varies. GIAs have yet to become a routine part of public policy making. For example, while they are well embedded in the law-making processes of most OECD countries (84%), fewer require them as part of the development of policies (68%) and programmes (74%) by the executive branch of government (OECD, 2011d). GIAs are also seldom used in evaluating the impacts of legislation, policies and regulations (*ex post* assessments). Whether a GIA is carried out *ex ante* or *ex post*, the availability of sex-disaggregated data is necessary for high quality analysis (OECD, 2011e and 2011f).

Overall, OECD countries report that the introduction of GIAs has improved awareness, agenda-setting practices, and dialogue on gender issues amongst policy makers. For instance, a gender analysis assessment of a draft Finnish bill on occupational health and safety revealed the need to redefine the concept of occupational safety and risks to include the aspects of violence and mental health (OECD, 2011e and 2011f).

Monitoring and gender-disaggregated evidence in policy making

OECD countries have identified limited mechanisms for monitoring the implementation of legal frameworks and government strategies as among the key barriers to addressing gender inequalities and advancing women's *de facto* equality. Indeed, less than half of the OECD countries that participated in the *2011 OECD Survey on National Gender Frameworks, Gender Public Policies and Leadership* report systematically measuring, evaluating and monitoring the performance of gender-relevant legislation and policies (OECD, 2011d).

Limited monitoring and measurement practices tend to be linked to the limited capacity of ministries either to define the need for data disaggregated by gender or to disaggregate the existing statistics – essential monitoring requirements (Box 3.2).

Box 3.2. **Gender-responsive budgeting**

Gender responsive budgeting (GRB) is arguably the best known form of Gender Impact Assessment. GRB inserts a gender perspective at all stages of the budgetary cycle: it aims to avoid "gender-blind spending" and improve the effectiveness of government programmes by identifying gender-disproportionate consequences (Council of Europe, 2005).

Several OECD and non-member countries (*e.g.* Egypt, Morocco, Nepal, Rwanda) have experimented with some form of gender budgeting over the past decade (OECD, 2010b and 2011g). In some countries – Austria, Belgium, Egypt, Korea, Spain and Mexico, for example – gender-responsive budgeting now has a legal basis. The Federal Government of Austria introduced a legal requirement to undertake gender-responsive budgeting through an amendment to the Federal Constitution in 2009. Other countries have opted for a more flexible legal approach. One is Norway, which issued guidelines to ministries for gender-sensitive analyses of their budgets.

OECD (2011d) shows that GRB is still in its early stages: about half of OECD countries "always" or in "some cases" require GRB at all levels of government – 47% of countries at central government level (*e.g.* Belgium, Finland, France, Israel, Korea, Mexico, Norway and Spain), 42% at regional level (*e.g.* France, Germany, Korea, Mexico, Spain and Switzerland), and 52% at local levels (*e.g.* the Czech Republic, Finland, Germany, Israel, Mexico, Korea, Spain and Switzerland).

A thorough gender analysis cannot be performed without gender breakdowns in data collection (Swirski, 2011). Some OECD countries, such as Israel since its 2008 Statistics Law, do require all data collected by government bodies to be disaggregated by gender (*ibid.*). However, over 40% of OECD countries participating in the *2011 OECD Survey on National Gender Frameworks, Gender Public Policies and Leadership* reported capacity issues as one of the chief barriers to developing a sufficient gender-disaggregated evidence base for designing inclusive policies and monitoring their impacts. Looking at data collection across sectors, results suggest that 74% of countries "always" collect gender-disaggregated data on

Box 3.3. **Gender statistics and the Busan partnership
for effective development co-operation**

Many countries are making concrete efforts to improve their gender statistics, recognising that better information is vital to progress towards gender equality. However, bringing gender issues into statistics is more complex than simply disaggregating data by sex. In fact, gender statistics should be able to "adequately reflect problems, issues and questions related to women and men in society" (United Nations, 1995). The development of gender statistics thus requires a comprehensive strategy that encompasses: a) a focus on subject areas where women and men do not enjoy the same opportunities; b) concepts, definitions, methods and tools that adequately reflect the diversities of women and men in society, taking into account stereotypes and cultural factors that might produce gender biases; and c) effective instruments to communicate findings to policy makers, civil society and other stakeholders. The mainstreaming of gender perspectives in statistics can improve the whole statistical system, pushing it to describe more accurately the activities and characteristics of the entire population (UNECE, 2010).

Despite progress, much remains to be done. In a number of areas of critical interest for policy makers, gender data and indicators are still insufficient or lack comparability across countries. Co-ordination among international agencies and strong ownership by statistical institutes (in both developing and high-income economies) are key to addressing these gaps. The dialogue between producers and users of gender statistics should also be strengthened. Doing so will ensure that high-priority policy issues are addressed first and that requests for new data are backed by sufficient funding, since many countries are facing serious fiscal constraints. The harmonisation and analysis of gender statistics in the three dimensions of education, employment and entrepreneurship ("the three Es") is a central element of the OECD Gender Initiative. In co-ordination with the InterAgency Expert Group on the Development of Gender Statistics (IAEG-GS), the OECD Gender Initiative has selected key indicators on gender differences in education and employment, drawing on existing compilations and data sets developed by international organisations, including the OECD.

At the 4th High Level Forum on Aid Effectiveness (HLF-4) in Busan (from 29 November to 1 December 2011), organised by the OECD and the Government of Korea, participants recognised that gender equality and women's empowerment were critical to achieving development results and a prerequisite for sustainable and inclusive growth. Participants also agreed to accelerate and deepen efforts to collect, disseminate, harmonise and make full use of gender-disaggregated data for informing policy decisions and guiding investments in order to ensure that public expenditures were targeted appropriately to benefit both women and men.

To support the implementation of the gender equality commitments it took in Busan, the HLF-4 launched the Evidence and Data for Gender Equality (EDGE) initiative. Led by UN Women and the UN Statistical Division, EDGE is a dynamic partnership of UN member countries, the World Bank, OECD and other stakeholders. It aims to improve the availability and use of statistics that capture gender gaps in economic activity. It capitalises on the May 2011 OECD Ministerial Council Meeting on development which called on international organisations to agree on a harmonised set of gender equality indicators in order to measure progress in education, employment and entrepreneurship for presentation at the Busan HLF-4. The resulting EDGE indicators are part of the broader "minimum set of gender indicators" as supported by the IAEG-GS under the aegis of the United Nations, which includes indicators on access to media, education, health, public life and decision making, and human rights.

The objective of EDGE is to build national capacity and strengthen national systems to collect data on critical areas of women's empowerment. The areas selected for initial focus are education, employment, entrepreneurship, and asset ownership. Activities will include the development of a database for international data compilation covering basic education and employment indicators, the drawing up of standards and guidelines for entrepreneurship and asset ownership indicators, and related pilot data collection in ten countries.

education, 58% on social protection, 63% on general public services, and only about 40% in the areas of health, public order and safety, economic affairs, recreation, culture and religion (OECD, 2011d). Yet the availability of these data is essential to understanding the effect of various policy decisions and to developing evidence-based solutions that are responsive to the needs of citizens, both men and women. For example, gender disaggregation of data and public policy analysis on participation in politics or community life, housing ownership, the use of public transport or income patterns can help inform and develop better, more responsive policies for better lives.

Many OECD countries have already taken steps to strengthen their information capacity (OECD, 2011d). Such steps include:

- Introducing formal requirements for gender disaggregation and incorporating a gender perspective within national statistical legislation (58% of respondents, including Germany, Israel, Korea, New Zealand, the Slovak Republic and Spain).

- Setting up gender units in national statistical agencies (53% of respondents including Belgium, Chile, the Czech Republic, Norway, the Slovak Republic and Sweden).

- Systematically identifying gaps in the availability of gender-disaggregated data (42% of respondents including Mexico, Finland, Spain, France and the United States).

- Establishing horizontal co-ordination mechanisms to determine gender-disaggregated data needs (42%, including Australia, Greece, Switzerland and the United States).

Yet further efforts are required to close the *de facto* gender gap and build a comprehensive evidence base for responsive policies that address remaining inequalities and foster inclusive growth.

Key policy messages

Although governments have made significant progress, they still need to do more to develop, monitor and evaluate public policies if they are to make gender policies more effective. In particular, they need to:

- Strengthen the capacity, skills and mechanisms for regular impact monitoring and evaluation of gender initiatives. Such capacity building should include the systematic collection of relevant gender-disaggregated data in all policy areas.

- Enhance the incorporation of gender impact assessments in the design, implementation and evaluation of laws, policies, regulations, programmes and budgets in a systematic and comprehensive manner.

- Strengthen incentives as well as compliance and accountability measures to make the implementation of gender equality and mainstreaming initiatives across government bodies more effective.

ANNEX I.A1

Estimating the effects of human capital accumulation on growth

To measure the effect of human capital accumulation on economic growth, a human capital augmented standard neoclassical growth model (for more detail, see Mankiw *et al.*, 1992; Bassanini and Scarpetta, 2002; Arnold *et al.*, 2011) has been estimated for this report. Given the straightforward assumptions on how the factors of production evolve over time, the steady-state level of output per capita can be expressed as a function of the propensity to accumulate physical and human capital, the population growth rate, the level and growth rates of technological and economic efficiency, and the (constant) rate of depreciation of capital. If countries were at their steady state – or if deviations from the steady state were random – growth equations could be based simply on the relationship linking steady-state output to its determinants. However, actual data may well include out-of-steady-state dynamics due, among other things, to slow convergence towards the steady state. Consequently, observed changes in output per capita at any point in time are likely to include, in addition to technological progress, both a convergence component and a level component, due to shifts in the steady-state output per capita arising from factors other than technology.

The baseline growth equation used for estimation is:

$$\Delta \ln Y_{(t)} = a_0 - \phi \ln Y_{(t-1)} + a_1 \ln k_{(t)} + a_2 \ln H_{(t)} - a_3 \ln N_{(t)} + a_4(t) + b_1 \Delta \ln k_{(t)} + b_2 \Delta \ln H_{(t)} + b_3 \Delta \ln Ni_{(t)} + \varepsilon(t)$$

where per capita income growth (ΔY) is related to the accumulation of physical capital (k), human capital (educational attainment H) and population (N), t is the time trend which accounts for the technological change that modifies the influence of education on output over time, while subscripts indicate country (i) and time (t). The b-regressors capture short-term dynamics and ε is the usual error term.

This basic growth equation can be further extended to include a variable which captures the growth rates in men's and women's human capital. The revised Barro and Lee dataset (Barro and Lee, 2010) provides information on educational attainment (as measured by years of schooling) from 1960 onwards. Although such a long timeframe is needed to obtain robust results, trends in male and female years in school over the period (Table I.A1.2) are strongly related. To avoid this multicollinearity issue the approach has been to include a direct measure of the gender gap in educational attainment in the growth equation – rather than separate indicators on male and female educational attainment (Klasen, 2002; Knowles *et al.*, 2002).

To estimate the growth equation in a cross-national set-up, annual data and pooled cross-country time series are used, which makes it more practical to control for country- and/or period-specific effects. This approach involves assuming common technological change, common population growth, and common growth convergence patterns. However, population growth differs considerably across countries, and the evidence on multifactor productivity growth patterns across countries does not fit with the assumption of common technological change (Lee *et al.*, 1997; Bassanini and Scarpetta, 2002). The Pooled Mean Group (PMG) approach is, therefore, used here. It allows short-run coefficients (speed of adjustment and error variances) to differ across countries, but constrains the long-run coefficients to be identical (which would be consistent with the diffusion of technological change and intense trade relations).

The long-run growth equations have been estimated for 30 OECD countries over the period 1960-2008 (see the notes to Table I.A1.1). The years 2009 and 2010 were deliberately excluded from the sample as their inclusion would introduce short-term disturbance in the estimation of a long-run relationships due to the recent economic recession. Five-year dummies are included to control for the effect of time, as the influence of education on growth might change over time with technological change. The results are presented in Table I.A1.1.

- The convergence parameters have a negative sign, which is consistent with the assumption that variables move towards a long-run equilibrium.
- Output per capita growth responds positively to investment in physical capital ($\log k$) and negatively to variation in population size ($\Delta \log N$).
- Increasing educational attainment has a clear positive effect on economic growth: one additional year of schooling in the population is estimated to raise output per capita by around 10% *per annum*.
- Greater gender equality has a clear positive effect on economic growth: a gender-balanced ratio of education ($R^{f/m} = 1$) might increase output per capita by around 0.8% in comparison to a scenario where women have no access to education.

Overall, one additional year of schooling in the population is estimated to raise output per capita by around 10% *per annum*. This is less than the 13% found by Topel (1999), but at the higher end of the range of results in Bassanini and Scarpetta (2002). The 10% rise in per capita output is not surprising since coverage encompasses a longer time period and a higher number of countries, including those where there was more pronounced growth in both educational attainment and output per capita.

The average number of years spent in education has increased, on average, by 1.2% *per annum* (from 6.13 years in 1960 to 11.1 in 2008). The second model specification points to a growth elasticity to the years of education of 0.94, suggesting human capital accumulation induced an increase in growth of 1.1% (= 0.94 * 1.2%) *per annum*. As GDP per capita actually grew by 2.2% *per annum* on average, the model specification suggests that the increase in years of education accounts for about 50% of economic growth, of which just over half was due to the increase in educational attainment among women.

The last column in Table I.A1.2 shows that output per capita growth is increased by a better gender composition of educational attainment. The elasticity of the output per capita growth to an increase in the average number of years in education is slightly lower than in the former specification: hence, the annual 1.2% increase in years of education is estimated here to have raised GDP per capita by 1.13% annually. But the higher ratio of female to male

Table I.A1.1. A general growth model with total human capital

	Pooled mean group, with non-linear period effects	
		Including the female-to-male ratio of educational attainment
Convergence coefficient		
Log Y_{t-1}	−0.28*** (0.04)	−0.33*** (0.062)
Long-run coefficients		
Log k	0.28*** (0.01)	0.30*** (0.01)
Log H	1.07*** (0.06)	0.94*** (0.07)
Log $R^{f/m}$	–	0.81*** (0.16)
Δ log N	−1.57*** (0.70)	
Δ log N^m	–	1.06 (1.05)
Δ log N^f	–	−4.80*** (1.33)
Time trend (5-years dummies)	Yes	Yes
Short-run coefficients		
Δ log k	0.20*** (0.02)	0.19*** (0.02)
Δ log H	−1.19** (0.57)	−1.83 (0.95)
Δ $R^{f/m}$	–	−1.75 (1.98)
Δ2 log N	−0.80 (1.44)	
Δ2 log N^m		0.81 (0.85)
Δ2 log N^f		−0.54 (0.46)
Number of countries	30	30
Number of observations	1 150	1 127
Log likelihood	3 184	3 184

Notes: Standard errors in brackets. ***, ** and *: significant at the 1%, 5% and 10%, respectively.
A Hausman test does not reject the homogeneity restrictions on long-run parameters imposed by PMG estimation; the stationarity of residuals is accepted by an Im-Pesaran-Shin test.
Dependent variable (Δ log Y): growth in real GDP per head of population aged 15-64 years expressed in (2005) purchasing power parities (PPP); convergence variable (ln Y_{t-1}): lagged real GDP per head of population aged 15-64 years, in PPP; physical capital accumulation (ln k): the propensity to accumulate physical capital is proxied by the ratio of real private non-residential fixed capital formation to real private GDP; population growth (Δ log N): growth in the working age population (15-64 years), also separately for men Δ log N^m and women Δ log N^f; stock of human capital (log H): average number of years of schooling of the population from 25 to 64 years of age; $R^{f/m}$: female-to-male ratio in education attainment (i.e. the ratio in the years of education for women aged 25 to 64 years to the male population of the same age).
Countries included are: Australia, Austria, Belgium, Canada, Chile, the Czech Republic, Denmark, Estonia, Finland, France, Germany, Greece, Hungary, Iceland, Ireland, Israel, Italy, Japan, Korea, Luxembourg, Mexico, the Netherlands, New Zealand, Norway, Poland, Portugal, the Slovak Republic, Slovenia, Spain, Sweden, Switzerland, Turkey, the United Kingdom and the United States.
Source: OECD Secretariat estimates based on OECD Economic Outlook, December 2011 for data on GDP and Capital accumulation. Information on educational attainment by gender is taken from the revised Barro-Lee dataset [Barro, R.J. and J.W. Lee (2010), "A New Data Set of Educational Attainment in the World, 1950-2010", NBER Working Paper, No. 15902, Cambridge, Mass.] which includes data on years in education, enrolment and completion rates for both men and women from 1960 onwards with a five-year interval (annual series were derived by means of linear interpolation).
StatLink ⏩ http://dx.doi.org/10.1787/888932677362

years in education has a positive and highly significant influence on output. As the gender ratio of education increased on average by around 0.09% each year, it suggests that it contributed to increasing annual economic growth by a further 0.07% *per annum* (i.e. 0.09% * 0.81).

Table I.A1.2. **Basic growth model statistics**

Variables	Year	Sample mean	Standard deviation
GDP per capita (in USD at 2005 PPP)	1960	16 295	5 711
	1990	35 503	10 622
	2008	46 745	18 963
Average years of education – men	1960	6.49	2.16
	1990	9.65	1.72
	2008	11.1	
Average years of education – women	1960	5.79	2.31
	1990	9.01	2.02
	2008	11.1	1.56
Capital per capita annual growth rate		2.13	8.51
% growth of male working age population		1.00	0.85
% growth of female working age population		0.91	0.94

Note: Countries included are: Australia, Austria, Belgium, Canada, Chile, the Czech Republic, Denmark, Estonia, Finland, France, Germany, Greece, Hungary, Iceland, Ireland, Israel, Italy, Japan, Korea, Luxembourg, Mexico, the Netherlands, New Zealand, Norway, Poland, Portugal, the Slovak Republic, Slovenia, Spain, Sweden, Switzerland, Turkey, the United Kingdom and the United States.

Source: OECD Secretariat estimates based on OECD Economic Outlook, December 2011 for data on GDP and Capital accumulation. Information on educational attainment by gender is taken from the revised Barro-Lee dataset [Barro, R.J. and J.W. Lee (2010), "A New Data Set of Educational Attainment in the World, 1950-2010", NBER Working Paper, No. 15902, Cambridge, Mass.] which includes data on years in education, enrolment and completion rates for both men and women from 1960 onwards with a five-year interval (annual series were derived by means of linear interpolation).

StatLink ⬛ᵫ᷉ http://dx.doi.org/10.1787/888932677381

ANNEX I.A2

Labour force projections for OECD countries not covered in Figure 1.2

Figure I.A2.1. **The effect of converging participation rates between men and women on the size of the labour force**

Projected number of persons aged 15-64 in the labour force, thousands, 2011-30[a]

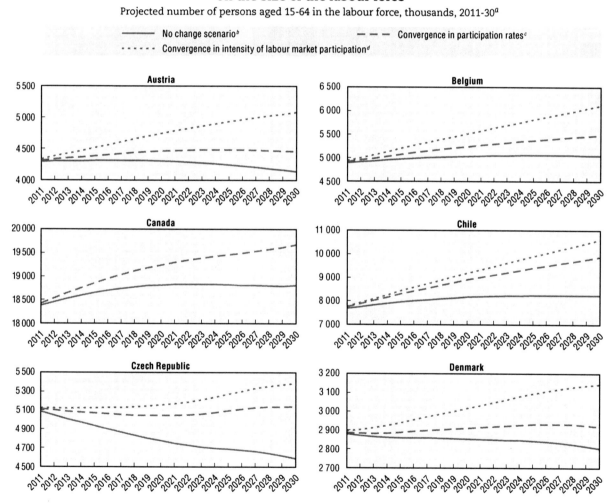

Figure I.A2.1. **The effect of converging participation rates between men and women on the size of the labour force** (*cont.*)

Projected number of persons aged 15-64 in the labour force, thousands, 2011-30[a]

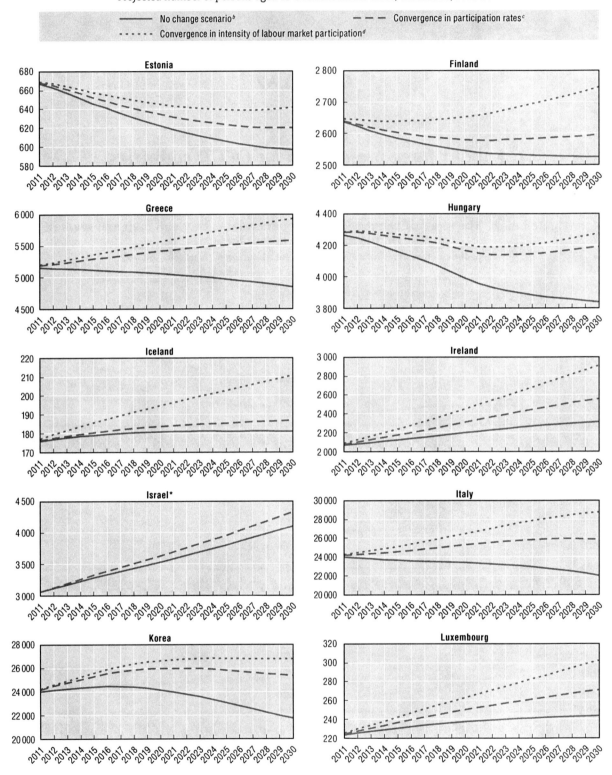

Figure I.A2.1. **The effect of converging participation rates between men and women on the size of the labour force** *(cont.)*

Projected number of persons aged 15-64 in the labour force, thousands, 2011-30[a]

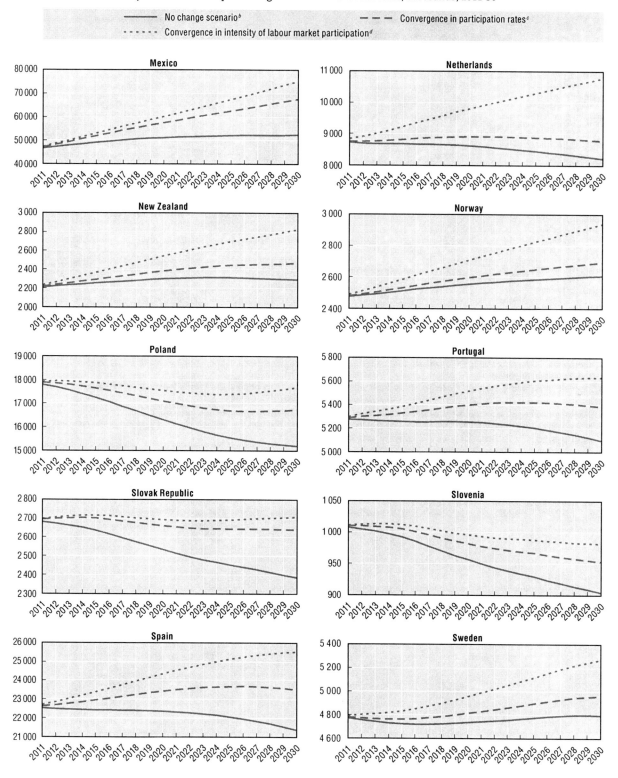

——— No change scenario[b]   – – – Convergence in participation rates[c]

·········· Convergence in intensity of labour market participation[d]

Figure I.A2.1. **The effect of converging participation rates between men and women on the size of the labour force** (*cont.*)

Projected number of persons aged 15-64 in the labour force, thousands, 2011-30[a]

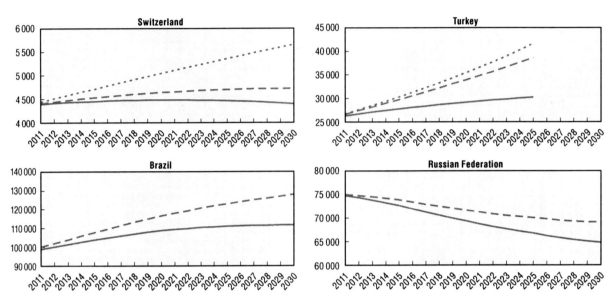

* Information on data for Israel: *http://dx.doi.org/10.1787/888932315602.*

a) The labour force projections are based on population projections for persons aged 15-64 years as reported by the *OECD Demography and Population Database.*

b) No-change scenario: the projected size of the total labour force aged 15-64 years if the labour force participation rates for men and women remain constant from 2011 to 2030 at the rates observed in 2010.

c) Convergence in participation rates: the projected size of the total labour force aged 15-64 years if the full-time equivalent rate for men remains constant from 2011 to 2030 at the rate observed in 2010, and the rate for women shows a gradual increase (steady growth rate) from 2011 to 2030 reaching the 2010 rate for men by 2030.

d) Convergence in intensity of labour market participation: the projected size of the total labour force aged 15-64 years if the full-time equivalent rate for men remains constant from 2011 to 2030 at the rate observed in 2010, and the full-time equivalent rate for women shows a gradual increase (steady growth rate) from 2011 to 2030 reaching the 2010 full-time equivalent rate for men by 2030. The full-time equivalent rate is calculated as the labour force participation rate, multiplied by the average usual hours worked per week by all employed men and women respectively, and divided by 40.

Source: OECD Secretariat estimates based on *OECD Population and Demography Database 2012* and *OECD Employment Database 2012.*

StatLink ⟶ *http://dx.doi.org/10.1787/888932677172*

Table I.A2.1. **Projected increase and decrease in labour force size from 2011 to 2030 under three scenarios of labour force participation**

	Total labour force size in 2011 (millions)	Projected increase/decrease in total labour force size in 2030 as a percentage of the levels observed in 2011[a]		
		No-change scenario[b]	Convergence in participation rates[c]	Convergence in intensity of labour force participation[d]
Australia	11.47	19.1	28.5	47.4
Austria	4.29	−3.6	3.5	17.4
Belgium	4.89	3.2	11.6	23.9
Canada	18.38	2.3	6.8	. .
Chile	7.68	7.2	27.6	36.8
Czech Republic	5.09	−9.9	0.5	5.1
Denmark	2.88	−2.7	1.2	8.6
Estonia	0.67	−10.5	−7.2	−4.1
Finland	2.64	−4.2	−1.7	3.8
France	28.72	−0.8	5.0	14.1
Germany	41.98	−11.9	−5.7	8.2
Greece	5.15	−6.0	7.7	14.1
Hungary	4.27	−10.1	−2.2	−0.3
Iceland	0.18	2.9	6.1	19.1
Ireland	2.06	12.0	23.4	39.7
Israel[e, *]	3.06	34.2	41.6	. .
Italy	24.00	−8.2	7.1	18.6
Japan	59.96	−16.8	−5.3	. .
Korea	24.01	−9.5	4.9	10.5
Luxembourg	0.22	8.9	20.8	34.2
Mexico	46.59	12.1	43.4	59.1
Netherlands	8.73	−6.0	0.3	22.2
New Zealand	2.21	3.7	11.2	26.6
Norway	2.47	5.3	8.6	18.2
Poland	17.80	−14.8	−6.5	−1.4
Portugal	5.27	−3.4	1.8	6.3
Slovak Republic	2.68	−11.0	−2.1	0.4
Slovenia	1.01	−10.3	−5.6	−2.9
Spain	22.51	−5.1	4.0	12.5
Sweden	4.77	0.5	3.8	9.9
Switzerland	4.39	0.2	7.2	27.6
Turkey[e]	26.25	15.0	45.2	56.2
United Kingdom	31.43	2.8	10.5	26.5
United States	154.74	9.2	17.0	. .
Brazil	98.81	13.0	28.0	. .
Russian Federation	74.80	−13.5	−7.9	. .

* Information on data for Israel: *http://dx.doi.org/10.1787/888932315602.*

a) The labour force projections are based on population projections for persons aged 15-64 years as reported by the OECD *Demography and Population Database.*

b) No-change scenario: the projected size of the total labour force aged 15-64 years if the labour force participation rates for men and women remain constant from 2011 to 2030 at the rates observed in 2010.

c) Convergence in participation rates: the projected size of the total labour force aged 15-64 years if the labour force participation rate for men remains constant from 2011 to 2030 at the rate observed in 2010, and the rate for women shows a gradual increase (steady growth rate) from 2011 to 2030 reaching the 2010 rate for men by 2030.

d) Convergence in intensity of labour market participation: the projected size of the total labour force aged 15-64 years if the full-time equivalent rate for men remains constant from 2011 to 2030 at the rate observed in 2010, and the full-time equivalent rate for women show a gradual increase (steady growth rate) from 2011 to 2030 reaching the 2010 full-time equivalent rate for men by 2030. The full-time equivalent rate is calculated as the labour force participation rate, multiplied by the average usual hours worked per week by all employed men and women respectively, and divided by 40.

e) For Israel, the figures reflect the percentage change from 2010 to 2030; for Turkey, the figures reflect the percentage change from 2011 to 2025.

Source: OECD Secretariat estimates based on *OECD Population and Demography Database 2012* and *OECD Employment Database 2012.*

StatLink ⬛⬛ *http://dx.doi.org/10.1787/888932677400*

ANNEX I.A3

Gross domestic product projections for OECD countries not covered in Figure 1.2

Figure I.A3.1. The effect of converging participation rates[a] between men and women on the size of the economy in GDP

Projected size of the economy in GDP, USD 2005 PPP, in 1 000 000 000s, 2011-30

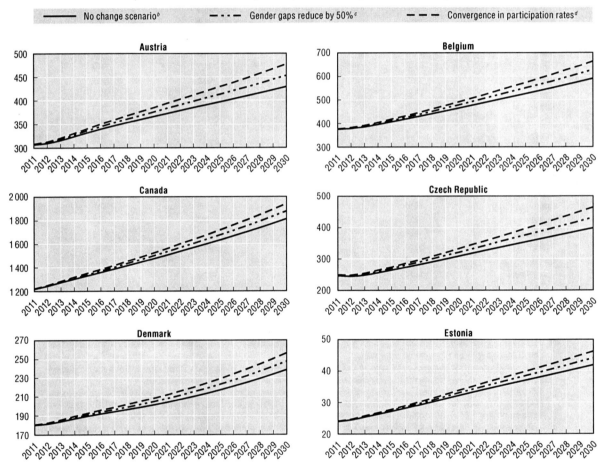

Figure I.A3.1. **The effect of converging participation rates[a] between men and women on the size of the economy in GDP** (*cont.*)

Projected size of the economy in GDP, USD 2005 PPP, in 1 000 000 000s, 2011-30

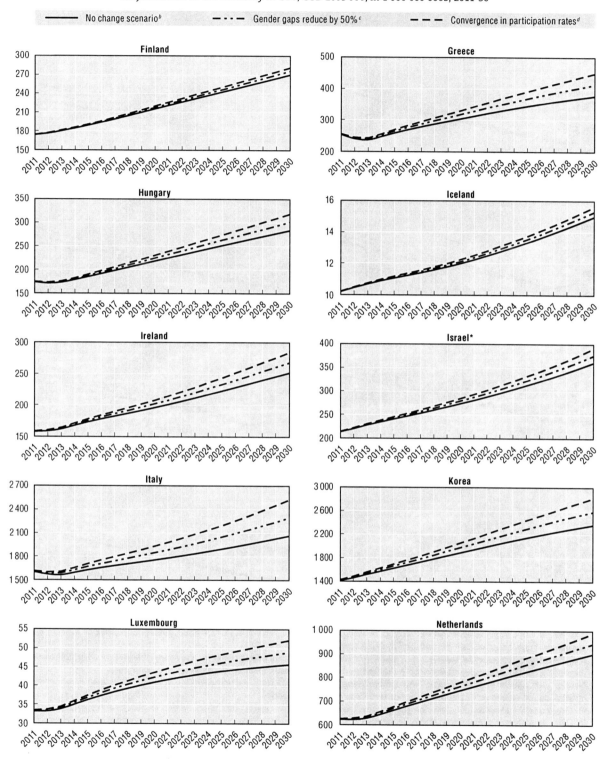

Figure I.A3.1. **The effect of converging participation rates[a] between men and women on the size of the economy in GDP** *(cont.)*

Projected size of the economy in GDP, USD 2005 PPP, in 1 000 000 000s, 2011-30

——— No change scenario[b]   — · — · Gender gaps reduce by 50%[c]   — — — Convergence in participation rates[d]

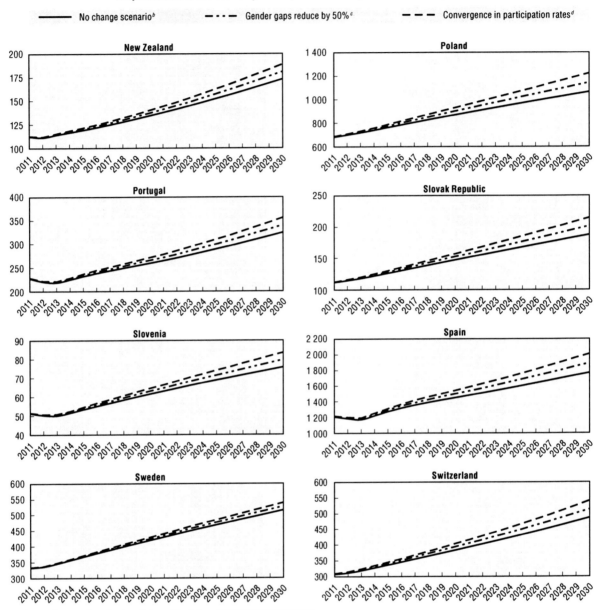

* Information on data for Israel: *http://dx.doi.org/10.1787/888932315602*.

a) The labour force projections are based on population projections for persons aged 15+ years, rather than persons aged 15-64, to be consistent with the growth model outlined in *OECD Economic Outlook*, No. 91.

b) No change: the gap between male and female labour force participation rate remains at the levels observed in 2010 (this scenario is identical to the baseline growth scenario presented in the *OECD Economic Outlook*, No. 91 long-term database).

c) Gender gaps narrow by 50%: the gap between male and female labour force participation levels observed in 2010 is reduced by 50% by 2030, based on a steady growth rate in female labour force participation.

d) Convergence in participation rates: the gap between male and female labour force participation levels observed in 2010 disappears by 2030, based on a steady growth rate in female labour force participation. Thus, in this scenario it is assumed that the female labour force participation rate will reach the levels observed for men by 2030 and the gender gap not longer exists.

Source: OECD Secretariat estimates based on the *OECD Economic Outlook*, No. 91 long-term database (Version 6, June 2012), *OECD Population and Demography Database* and the *OECD Employment Database*.

StatLink ⧉ http://dx.doi.org/10.1787/888932677191

Table I.A3.1. **Projected average annual growth rate in GDP and GDP per capita in USD 2005 PPP, percentage, 2011-30[a]**

	No change in labour force participation rate (LFPR)[b]		Male and female LFPR gap reduced by 50%, by 2030[c]			Male and female LFPR gap reduced by 75%, by 2030[d]			Male and female LFPR gap reduced by 100%, by 2030[e]		
	GDP	GDP per capita	GDP	GDP per capita	Increase in GDP per capita	GDP	GDP per capita	Increase in GDP per capita	GDP	GDP per capita	Increase in GDP per capita
	(1)	(2)	(3)	(4)	(4) – (2)	(5)	(6)	(6) – (2)	(7)	(8)	(8) – (2)
OECD	**2.2**	**1.8**	**2.5**	**2.1**	**0.3**	**2.6**	**2.3**	**0.5**	**2.7**	**2.4**	**0.6**
Australia	3.3	2.0	3.5	2.2	0.2	3.7	2.4	0.4	3.8	2.5	0.5
Austria	1.9	1.5	2.1	1.8	0.3	2.3	1.9	0.4	2.4	2.1	0.6
Belgium	2.5	1.8	2.8	2.1	0.3	2.9	2.3	0.5	3.1	2.4	0.6
Canada	2.1	1.4	2.2	1.6	0.2	2.3	1.7	0.3	2.4	1.8	0.4
Czech Republic	2.4	2.6	2.8	3.0	0.4	3.0	3.2	0.6	3.2	3.4	0.8
Denmark	1.5	1.2	1.6	1.4	0.2	1.7	1.5	0.3	1.8	1.5	0.3
Estonia	3.2	3.4	3.5	3.7	0.3	3.6	3.8	0.4	3.7	3.9	0.5
Finland	2.4	1.9	2.5	2.0	0.1	2.5	2.1	0.2	2.6	2.2	0.3
France	2.1	1.7	2.3	1.9	0.2	2.5	2.0	0.3	2.6	2.1	0.4
Germany	1.5	1.6	1.8	1.8	0.2	1.9	2.0	0.4	2.0	2.1	0.5
Greece	1.7	1.7	2.1	2.1	0.4	2.4	2.4	0.7	2.6	2.6	0.9
Hungary	2.6	2.8	2.9	3.1	0.3	3.1	3.3	0.5	3.2	3.4	0.6
Iceland	1.9	1.5	2.0	1.6	0.1	2.0	1.7	0.2	2.1	1.7	0.2
Ireland	2.3	1.6	2.6	1.9	0.3	2.7	2.1	0.5	2.9	2.2	0.6
Israel*	2.9	1.2	3.1	1.4	0.2	3.2	1.5	0.3	3.3	1.6	0.4
Italy	1.2	1.4	1.7	1.9	0.5	2.0	2.2	0.8	2.2	2.4	1.0
Japan	1.0	1.5	1.5	1.9	0.4	1.7	2.1	0.6	1.9	2.3	0.8
Korea	2.8	2.5	3.3	3.0	0.5	3.5	3.2	0.7	3.7	3.4	0.9
Luxembourg	1.4	0.8	1.7	1.1	0.3	1.9	1.3	0.5	2.0	1.4	0.6
Netherlands	1.9	1.6	2.2	1.9	0.3	2.3	2.0	0.4	2.4	2.1	0.5
New Zealand	2.3	1.8	2.5	2.0	0.2	2.6	2.1	0.3	2.7	2.2	0.4
Poland	2.4	2.7	2.8	3.0	0.3	3.0	3.2	0.5	3.1	3.4	0.7
Portugal	1.8	1.6	2.0	1.9	0.3	2.1	2.0	0.4	2.2	2.1	0.5
Slovak Republic	2.8	2.9	3.1	3.2	0.3	3.3	3.4	0.5	3.5	3.6	0.7
Slovenia	1.9	1.9	2.2	2.2	0.3	2.3	2.3	0.4	2.4	2.4	0.5
Spain	1.8	1.9	2.1	2.2	0.3	2.3	2.4	0.5	2.4	2.5	0.6
Sweden	2.4	1.9	2.6	2.1	0.2	2.6	2.1	0.2	2.7	2.2	0.3
Switzerland	2.5	1.9	2.7	2.2	0.3	2.9	2.3	0.4	3.0	2.4	0.5
United Kingdom	2.1	1.4	2.3	1.7	0.3	2.4	1.8	0.4	2.6	1.9	0.5
United States	2.6	1.7	2.9	1.9	0.2	3.0	2.0	0.3	3.1	2.2	0.5

* Information on data for Israel: *http://dx.doi.org/10.1787/888932315602*.

a) The labour force projections are based on population projections for persons aged 15+ years, rather than persons aged 15-64, to be consistent with the growth model outlined in *OECD Economic Outlook*, No. 91.

b) No change: the gap between male and female labour force participation rate remains at the levels observed in 2010 (this scenario is identical to the baseline growth scenario presented in the *OECD Economic Outlook*, No. 91 long-term database).

c) Gender gaps narrow by 50%: the gap between male and female labour force participation levels observed in 2010 is reduced by 50% by 2030, based on a steady growth rate in female labour force participation.

d) Gender gaps narrow by 75%: the gap between male and female labour force participation levels observed in 2010 is reduced by 75% by 2030, based on a steady growth rate in female labour force participation.

e) Convergence in participation rates: the gap between male and female labour force participation levels observed in 2010 disappears by 2030, based on a steady growth rate in female labour force participation. Thus, in this scenario it is assumed that the female labour force participation rate will reach the levels observed for men by 2030 and the gender gap not longer exists.

Source: OECD Secretariat's estimates based on the *OECD Economic Outlook*, No. 91 long-term database (Version 6, June 2012), *OECD Population and Demography Database* and *OECD Employment Database*.

StatLink ᵐˢᵖ *http://dx.doi.org/10.1787/888932677419*

Table I.A3.2. **Projected GDP in USD 2005 PPP, millions, 2020 and 2030**[a]

	Current	No change in labour force participation rate (LFPR)[b]		Male and female LFPR gap reduced by 50%, by 2030[c]			Male and female LFPR gap reduced by 75%, by 2030[d]			Male and female LFPR gap reduced by 100%, by 2030[e]		
	2010	2020	2030	2020	2030	% gain by 2030	2020	2030	% gain by 2030	2020	2030	% gain by 2030
		(1)	(2)	(3)	(4)	(4 – 2)/(2)	(5)	(6)	(6 – 2)/(2)	(7)	(8)	(8 – 2)/(2)
OECD	**1 146 968**	**1 426 392**	**1 764 281**	**1 468 055**	**1 870 133**	**6.0**	**1 487 863**	**1 923 060**	**9.0**	**1 507 081**	**1 975 986**	**12.0**
Australia	787 677	1 103 725	1 499 260	1 132 147	1 578 592	5.3	1 145 798	1 618 259	7.9	1 159 114	1 657 925	10.6
Austria	296 571	366 028	428 998	376 020	453 117	5.6	380 812	465 176	8.4	385 482	477 236	11.2
Belgium	363 807	464 547	590 432	478 477	626 957	6.2	485 126	645 220	9.3	491 588	663 483	12.4
Canada	1 205 278	1 475 420	1 813 020	1 500 800	1 876 699	3.5	1 513 162	1 908 538	5.3	1 525 321	1 940 378	7.0
Czech Republic	249 088	309 079	398 130	321 287	431 020	8.3	327 025	447 465	12.4	332 555	463 910	16.5
Denmark	178 731	201 428	238 668	205 109	247 565	3.7	206 899	252 013	5.6	208 657	256 462	7.5
Estonia	22 248	32 199	41 876	33 027	44 051	5.2	33 426	45 139	7.8	33 817	46 226	10.4
Finland	168 784	215 543	270 070	217 852	275 903	2.2	218 988	278 819	3.2	220 112	281 735	4.3
France	1 924 322	2 390 455	2 920 002	2 445 586	3 057 422	4.7	2 472 214	3 126 132	7.1	2 498 271	3 194 842	9.4
Germany	2 709 921	3 307 827	3 654 202	3 397 560	3 858 410	5.6	3 440 588	3 960 514	8.4	3 482 517	4 062 619	11.2
Greece	272 668	304 931	377 598	318 620	413 269	9.4	324 986	431 105	14.2	331 088	448 941	18.9
Hungary	170 098	218 119	284 050	224 622	301 391	6.1	227 733	310 062	9.2	230 760	318 732	12.2
Iceland	10 337	12 002	14 978	12 128	15 298	2.1	12 190	15 459	3.2	12 252	15 619	4.3
Ireland	161 219	195 733	251 754	201 898	268 185	6.5	204 831	276 400	9.8	207 677	284 615	13.1
Israel*	203 651	273 544	361 112	279 117	376 063	4.1	281 817	383 539	6.2	284 465	391 014	8.3
Italy	1 634 919	1 752 386	2 062 120	1 845 278	2 294 082	11.2	1 887 925	2 410 063	16.9	1 928 532	2 526 043	22.5
Japan	3 962 739	4 334 823	4 850 222	4 530 121	5 312 484	9.5	4 621 099	5 543 614	14.3	4 708 365	5 774 745	19.1
Korea	1 356 587	1 888 264	2 359 168	1 975 076	2 589 371	9.8	2 015 336	2 704 473	14.6	2 053 864	2 819 574	19.5
Luxembourg	34 817	40 861	45 625	42 251	48 849	7.1	42 909	50 461	10.6	43 547	52 073	14.1
Netherlands	614 886	745 198	900 762	762 827	944 508	4.9	771 325	966 381	7.3	779 631	988 253	9.7
New Zealand	110 672	134 014	173 101	137 041	181 098	4.6	138 503	185 096	6.9	139 933	189 095	9.2
Poland	659 719	869 235	1 065 297	900 243	1 144 181	7.4	914 924	1 183 622	11.1	929 130	1 223 064	14.8
Portugal	229 636	259 102	324 850	265 274	340 670	4.9	268 252	348 580	7.3	271 165	356 490	9.7
Slovak Republic	108 617	147 171	187 537	152 312	201 158	7.3	154 748	207 968	10.9	157 107	214 779	14.5
Slovenia	51 801	61 496	75 717	63 054	79 647	5.2	63 803	81 612	7.8	64 534	83 577	10.4
Spain	1 242 300	1 450 797	1 769 654	1 498 142	1 889 635	6.8	1 520 646	1 949 626	10.2	1 542 466	2 009 617	13.6
Sweden	318 671	419 650	515 569	424 468	527 489	2.3	426 836	533 449	3.5	429 176	539 409	4.6
Switzerland	300 186	383 625	487 121	393 912	513 984	5.5	398 847	527 415	8.3	403 657	540 847	11.0
United Kingdom	2 027 321	2 456 837	3 043 261	2 519 320	3 199 790	5.1	2 549 347	3 278 055	7.7	2 578 642	3 356 319	10.3
United States	13 031 760	16 977 717	21 924 279	17 388 073	23 013 113	5.0	17 585 799	23 557 531	7.4	17 779 013	24 101 948	9.9

* Information on data for Israel: http://dx.doi.org/10.1787/888932315602.

a) The labour force projections are based on population projections for persons aged 15+ years, rather than persons aged 15-64, to be consistent with the growth model outlined in *OECD Economic Outlook*, No. 91.

b) No change: the gap between male and female labour force participation rate remains at the levels observed in 2010 (this scenario is identical to the baseline growth scenario presented in the *OECD Economic Outlook*, No. 91 long-term database).

c) Gender gaps reduce by 50%: the gap between male and female labour force participation levels observed in 2010 is reduced by 50% by 2030, based on a steady growth rate in female labour force participation.

d) Gender gaps reduce by 75%: the gap between male and female labour force participation levels observed in 2010 is reduced by 75% by 2030, based on a steady growth rate in female labour force participation.

e) Convergence in participation rates: the gap between male and female labour force participation levels observed in 2010 disappears by 2030, based on a steady growth rate in female labour force participation. Thus, in this scenario it is assumed that the female labour force participation rate will reach the levels observed for men by 2030 and the gender gap not longer exists.

Source: OECD Secretariat's estimates based on the *OECD Economic Outlook*, No. 91 long-term database (Version 6, June 2012), *OECD Population and Demography Database* and *OECD Employment Database*.

StatLink ⬛≣► http://dx.doi.org/10.1787/888932677438

References

Arnold, J., A. Bassanini and S. Scarpetta (2011), "Solow or Lucas? Testing the Speed of Convergence on a Panel of OECD Countries", *Research in Economics*, Vol. 65, pp. 110-123.

Barro, R.J. and J.W. Lee (1994), "Sources of Economic Growth", *Carnegie-Rochester Conference Series on Public Policy*, Vol. 40, pp. 1-46.

Barro, R.J. and J.W. Lee (2010), "A New Data Set of Educational Attainment in the World, 1950-2010", *NBER Working Paper*, No. 15902, Cambridge, United States.

Bassanini, A. and S. Scarpetta (2002), "Does Human Capital Matter for Growth in OECD Countries? A Pooled Mean-group Approach", *Economic Letters*, Vol. 74, pp. 399-405.

Bates, L.M., J. Maselko and S.R. Schuler (2007), "Women's Education and the Timing of Marriage and Childbearing in the Next Generation: Evidence from Rural Bangladesh", *Studies in Family Planning*, Vol. 38, pp. 101-112.

Behrman, J.R., R. Pollak and P. Taubman (1986), "Do Parents Favor Boys?", *International Economic Review*, Vol. 27, pp. 31-52.

Bruce, J. and S. Clark (2004), *The Implications of Early Marriage for HIV/AIDS Policy*, Population Council and UNFPA, New York.

Council of Europe (2005), *Report on Gender Budgeting of the Committee for Equal Opportunities of Women and Men*, Parliamentary Assembly, Document, No. 10764, December, available at *http://assembly.coe.int/Documents/WorkingDocs/Doc05/EDOC10764.htm*.

Doepke, M., M. Tertilt and A. Voena (2011), "The Economics and Politics of Women's Rights", *NBER Working Paper*, No. 17672, Cambridge, United States.

European Commission (1997), "Employment, Social Affairs and Inclusion", *A Guide to Gender Impact Assessment*, available at: *http://ec.europa.eu/social/BlobServlet?docId=4376&langId=en*.

Field, E. and A. Ambrus (2008), "Early Marriage, Age of Menarche, and Female Schooling Attainment in Bangladesh", *Journal of Political Economy*, Vol. 116, No. 5, pp. 881-930.

Hewlett, S.A. and R. Rashid (2011), "Winning the War for Talent in Emerging Markets: Why Women are the Solution", Harvard Business School Publishing, Boston, United States.

Hsieh, C.T., E. Hurst, C.I. Jones and P.J. Klenow (2012), "The Allocation of Talent and US Economic Growth", unpublished manuscript.

Hudson, V. (2011), "China's Census: The One-Child Policy's Gender-Ratio Failure", *World Politics Review Briefing*, 4 May 2011, available at *www.worldpoliticsreview.com/articles/8731/chinas-census-the-one-child-policys-gender-ratio-failure*, accessed 15 February 2012.

IFC (2011), "Strengthening Access to Finance for Women-Owned SMEs in Developing Countries", Global Partnership for Financial Inclusion and International Finance Corporation, available at *www1.ifc.org/wps/wcm/connect/a4774a004a3f66539f0f9f8969adcc27/G20_Women_Report.pdf?MOD=AJPERES*.

Jha, P., M. Kesler and R. Kumar (2011), "Trends in Selective Abortions of Girls in India: Analysis of Nationally Representative Birth Histories from 1990 to 2005 and Census Data from 1991 to 2011", *The Lancet*, Vol. 377, No. 9781, pp. 1921-1928.

Jones, N., C. Harper and C. Watson (2010), "Stemming Girls' Chronic Poverty: Catalysing Development Change by Building Just Social Institutions", Chronic Poverty Research Centre, University of Manchester, United Kingdom.

Kim, J. (2010), "Women's Career Interruption and Labor Market Return", *Monthly Labour Review*, No. 65, Korea Labour Institute, Korea, pp. 36-50, August.

Klasen, S. (2002), "Low Schooling for Girls, Slower Growth for All? Cross-Country Evidence on the Effect of Gender Inequality in Education on Economic Development", *World Bank Economic Review*, Vol. 16, No. 3, pp. 345-373, Oxford University Press, United States, December.

Klasen, S. and C. Wink (2003), "Missing Women: Revisiting the Debate", *Feminist Economics*, Vol. 9, No. 2-3, pp. 263-299.

Knowles, S., P. Lorgelly and P.D. Owen (2002), "Are Educational Gender Gaps a Brake on Economic Development? Some Cross-Country Empirical Evidence", *Oxford Economic Papers*, Vol. 54, No. 1, pp. 118-149.

Kornich, S. and F. Furstenberg (2010), "Investing in Children: Changes in Parental Spending on Children, 1972 to 2007", *Working Paper*, United States Studies Center, University of Sydney.

Lee, K., M.H. Pesaran and R. Smith (1997), "Growth and Convergence in a Multi-country Empirical Stochastic Solow Model", *Journal of Applied Econometrics*, Vol. 12, pp. 357-392.

Lloyd, C. and B. Mensch (2008), "Marriage and Childbirth as Factors in Dropping Out from School: An Analysis of DHS Data from Sub-Saharan Africa", *Population Studies*, Vol. 62, No. 1, pp. 1-13.

Mankiw, G., D. Romer and D.Weil (1992), "A Contribution to the Empirics of Economic Growth", *Quarterly Journal of Economics*, Vol. 107, No. 2, pp. 407-437.

North, D. (1990), "Institutions", *Journal of Economic Perspectives*, Vol. 5, No. 1, pp. 97-112.

OECD (2007a), *Gender and Economic Empowerment of Women*, Africa Partnership Forum Support Unit, OECD Publishing, Paris.

OECD (2007b), *Informal Institutions: How Social Norms Help or Hinder Development*, Development Centre Studies, OECD Publishing, Paris, DOI: *http://dx.doi.org/10.1787/9789264039070-en*.

OECD (2008), *OECD Employment Outlook*, OECD Publishing, Paris, DOI: *http://dx.doi.org/10.1787/empl_outlook-2008-en*.

OECD (2009), "Promoting Pro-poor Growth: Employment", Document prepared by the DAC Network on Poverty Reduction (POVNET), OECD Publishing, Paris.

OECD (2010a), "Gender Inequality and the MDGs: What Are the Missing Dimensions?", *OECD Position Paper*, No. 2, OECD Development Center, OECD Publishing, Paris, September.

OECD (2010b), *Progress in Public Management in the Middle East and North Africa. Case Studies on Policy Reform*, OECD Publishing, Paris, DOI: *http://dx.doi.org/10.1787/9789264082076-en*.

OECD (2011a), "Women's Economic Empowerment", *Issue Paper*, DAC Network on Gender Equality (GENDERNET), OECD Publishing, Paris, April.

OECD (2011b), *Help Wanted: Providing and Paying for Long-Term Care*, OECD Publishing, Paris, DOI: *http://dx.doi.org/10.1787/9789264097759-en*.

OECD (2011c), *Report on the Gender Initiative: Gender Equality in Education, Employment and Entrepreneurship 2011*, Report prepared for the Meeting of the OECD Council at Ministerial Level, Paris, 25-26 May 2011, OECD Publishing, Paris.

OECD (2011d), "Survey on National Gender Frameworks, Gender Public Policies and Leadership", Developed by the MENA-OECD Governance Programme, OECD Publishing, Paris.

OECD (2011e), "Survey on Gender Analysis and Regulatory Impact Assessments", Survey conducted by the OECD on countries' regulatory management systems, OECD Publishing, Paris.

OECD (2011f), "Gender Analysis and Regulatory Impact Analysis", Document prepared by the DAC Network on Poverty Reduction (POVNET), OECD Publishing, Paris.

OECD (2011g), "Findings from the Gender Equality Module of the 2011 Paris Declaration Monitoring Survey", OECD Publishing, Paris, available at *www.oecd.org/dac/gender*.

OECD (2012a), *OECD Demography and Population Database*, OECD Publishing, Paris.

OECD (2012b), *OECD Employment Database*, OECD Publishing, Paris, available at *www.oecd.org/employment/database*.

OECD (2012c), *Gender, Institutions and Development Database*, OECD Development Center, OECD Publishing, Paris, available at *www.oecd.org/dev/gender*.

OECD (2012d), *OECD Economic Outlook*, No. 91, OECD Publishing, Paris, DOI: *http://dx.doi.org/10.1787/eco_outlook-v2012-1-en*.

Schultz, P. (2002), "Why Governments Should Invest More to Educate Girls", *World Development*, Vol. 30, No. 2, pp. 207-225.

Shin, Y.J., T. Sung T. and E. Choi (2008), "Study on the Burden of Childcare and Education Cost Affecting Fertility", *Policy Report*, No. 2008-17, Ministry of Health, Welfare and Family Affairs, Korea Institute for Health and Social Affairs.

Sinha, N. and J. Young (2009), "Long-Term Financial Incentives and Investment in Daughters: Evidence from Conditional Cash Transfers in North India", *Policy Research Working Paper*, No. 4860, World Bank, Washington, DC.

Stevenson, B. and J. Wolfers (2009), "The Paradox of Declining Female Happiness", *American Economic Journal: Economic Policy*, Vol. 1, No. 2, pp. 190-225.

Swirski, B. (2011), "Adva Center Information on Equality and Social Justice in Israel, Gender Mainstreaming Calls for Gender Breakdowns: Case Study", Israeli Ministry of Industry, Trade and Labour, available at *www.adva.org/default.asp?pageid=5*.

Topel, R. (1999), "Labor Markets and Economic Growth", in O. Ashenfelter and D. Card (eds.), *Handbook of Labor Economics*, Vol. 3C, North-Holland, Amsterdam.

UNECE (2010), *Developing Gender Statistics: A Practical Tool*, United Nations, Geneva.

UNESCO (2012), *Education Database*, UNESCO Institute for Statistics, available at *http://stats.uis.unesco.org/unesco/ReportFolders/ReportFolders.aspx*.

UNFPA (2007), "Sex-Ratio Imbalance in Asia: Trends, Consequences and Policy Responses", 4th Asia Pacific Conference on Sexual and Reproductive Health, UNFPA, New York.

UNICEF (2005), *Early Marriage: A Harmful Traditional Practice. A Statistical Exploration*, UNICEF, New York.

United Nations (1995), "Beijing Declaration and Platform for Action", United Nations Fourth World Conference on Women, Beijing, *www.un.org/womenwatch/daw/beijing/platform/*.

United Nations (1997), *Report of the Economic and Social Council for 1997*, United Nations, New York, 18 September, available at *www.un.org/documents/ga/docs/52/plenary/a52-3.htm*.

Veenhoven, R. (2011), "Social Development and Happiness in Nations 1990-2010", Presentation at Conference *Taking Stock: Measuring Social Development*, International Institute of Social Studies, 14-15 December.

Veenhoven, R. (2012), *World Database of Happiness*, Erasmus Universiteit Rotterdam, Netherlands.

World Bank (2011), *World Development Report 2012: Gender Equality and Development*, World Bank, Washington, DC.

Wikigender, "Gender Equality", *http://wikigender.org/index.php/Gender_Equality*.

PART II

Gender equality in education

In many developing countries girls are still less likely than boys to enter secondary education, while in many OECD countries educational attainment of women is now at least on par with that of men. Yet girls are still far less likely than boys to choose scientific and technological fields of study. This section looks at gender gaps in school enrolment rates, educational attainment and policies to address these gaps, including the role of aid in improving gender equality in education in developing countries. It examines gender differences in performance and attitudes in reading and maths, and the reasons why despite good performance women find it harder in many developing countries to find a job on leaving school. It considers how women still prefer to study humanities to sciences and asks what can be done to combat persistent stereotyping. Finally, it looks at the gender gap in financial literacy, and how to ensure women are as well-equipped as men to carry out long-term financial planning.

PART II

Chapter 4

Keeping girls and boys in school

Key findings

- Enrolment in primary education is near-universal in many countries and most countries worldwide have closed the gender gap. Exceptions are chiefly countries in South Asia and Sub-Saharan Africa.

- Enrolment in secondary education varies considerably across countries. In Eastern, Middle Central and Western Africa and in Southern Asia, teenage girls are less likely than boys to stay in school. By contrast, especially in high-income countries, boys are more likely to drop out of secondary education than girls.

- Attainment rates in upper secondary education among OECD countries reveal that young women in Iceland, Korea and Spain made the greatest gains in comparison with their male peers. Young Portuguese women enjoy the largest comparative advantage.

Who is in school?

Enrolment rates

With many countries mandating schooling from around the age of six onwards, primary school enrolment is near-universal in most regions of the world. In Western Africa, however, the primary enrolment rate is barely 70% and in Southern, Eastern, and Middle Africa it is only slightly above 80%. Moreover, regional averages mask inequality within regions. In Eastern and Middle Africa, for example, Eritrea and Djibouti have primary enrolment rates of 34% and 44%, respectively, compared with 98% in Burundi and Madagascar.

Out of the 154 countries for which net adjusted primary school enrolment data were available in 2010, some 112 countries have reached "gender parity" – as many girls as boys in primary schools.* Yet Figure 4.1 shows that, despite marked progress in Western, Eastern and Middle Africa and Southern Asia, gender gaps in primary school participation persist.

Figure 4.1. **Gender gaps in primary education still persist in some geographic regions**

Average net adjusted primary enrolment rates^a and gender parity index^b (GPI) by world region,^{c} 2000 and 2010

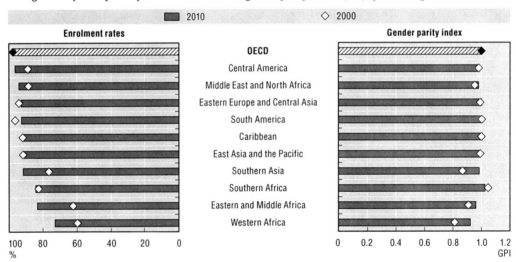

a) Adjusted primary net enrolment rate (ANER): total number of pupils in the official primary school age group who are enrolled at primary or secondary education levels, expressed as a percentage of the corresponding population.
b) Gender parity index (GPI): ratio of female to male values of a given indicator.
c) Country groupings are defined in the Annex II.A1. Regions are in order of decreasing 2010 enrolment rates.
Source: UNESCO *Education Database 2012*, UNESCO Institute for Statistics, *http://stats.uis.unesco.org/unesco/Report Folders/ReportFolders.aspx.*

StatLink ⫴ *http://dx.doi.org/10.1787/888932675386*

* According to the definition used by the UN Department of Economic and Social Affairs, countries are considered in gender parity when the gender parity index (GPI) is between 0.97 and 1.03.

The ten countries with the highest gender inequality in primary education are all found in these regions, with Benin, the Central African Republic, Niger, Pakistan and Yemen topping the list.

Both boys' and girls' enrolment rates in secondary school are lower than in primary education and vary significantly between the more and less economically developed regions. Compulsory schooling to the age of 15-16 means that almost all children of that age attend secondary education establishments in OECD countries. In Western, Eastern and Middle Africa, however, only four out of ten children are enrolled in secondary education.

Despite the gains made over the past decade in reducing gender disparities in secondary enrolment, girls are still less likely than boys to enrol in Western, Eastern and Middle Africa and Southern Asia (Figure 4.2). Girls are disadvantaged in regions with low overall enrolment rates, while in regions with higher rates – such as South America, Central America and Southern Africa – it is the other way round. As girls' educational expectations rise at a faster pace than boys", so does their academic performance. Once they have gained access to higher education, women outstrip men in grades, evaluations and degree completions (UNESCO, 2012a).

Figure 4.2. **In secondary education girls are disadvantaged in regions with low overall enrolment rates**

Average gross secondary enrolment ratios^a and gender parity index^b (2010 and 2000) by world region^c

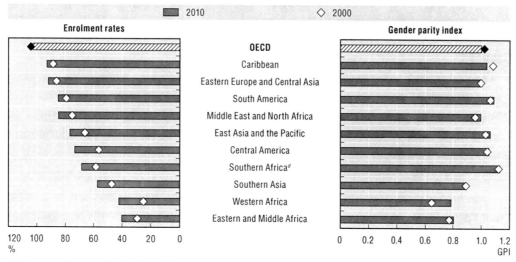

a) Gross enrolment ratio (GER): total enrolment in a specific level of education, regardless of age, expressed as a percentage of the eligible official school-age population in the same level of education in a given school year. GER can exceed 100% due to the inclusion of over-aged and under-aged pupils/students because of early or late entrants and grade repetition.
b) Gender parity index (GPI): ratio of female to male values of a given indicator.
c) Country groupings are defined in the Annex II.A1. Regions are in descending order of 2010 enrolment ratios.
d) The very high GPI value in Southern Africa is due to Lesotho (1.38) and Namibia (1.18), where the gross enrolment rate in secondary education in 2010 was low for both boys and girls. In Lesotho, the male and female secondary net enrolment rates were 39% and 54%, respectively.
Source: UNESCO Education Database 2012, UNESCO Institute for Statistics, http://stats.uis.unesco.org/unesco/ReportFolders/ReportFolders.aspx.

StatLink ⌨ http://dx.doi.org/10.1787/888932675405

Educational attainment and learning

Many developing countries have been successful in raising enrolment rates, but it is not clear to what extent learning has improved as a consequence. Evidence suggests that programmes which increased school participation, such as "deworming" (Miguel and Kremer, 2004) or the provision of school meals (Vermeersh and Kremer, 2005) and textbooks (Glewwe *et al.*, 2009) do not improve test scores. In fact, if greater participation is not accompanied by improvement in the quality of education and greater attention to children with weaker academic backgrounds, overcrowded schools or negative peer effects might actually lower test scores. Evidence from the Southern and Eastern African Consortium for Monitoring Education Quality (SACMEQ) for 15 Southern and Eastern African countries indicates that although many countries narrowed the gender gap in enrolment between 2000 and 2007, it remained stable in learning. Improvement was observed only in urban areas and among higher social economic status groups (Saito, 2011).

Sy (2011) found that in French-speaking African countries the quality factors that affect girls' achievement include female teachers, school location, class size, and teacher absenteeism. Language, ethnicity and family socio-economic background tend to compound gender inequality in learning, while speaking the language of instruction at home has a positive effect on student performance (Ouane and Glanz, 2010).

As for attainment rates in upper secondary education by gender, it appears that across OECD countries young women generally do at least as well as young men, except in Turkey. Three groups of countries emerge from comparison of the upper secondary educational attainments of younger (25-34 years old) and older (45-54 years old) men and women (see Figure 4.3):

● "Long-term male advantage countries": both younger and older women are less likely than men of the same age to have completed at least upper secondary education.

● "Recent female advantage countries": in contrast to older women, younger women are more likely than younger men to have completed at least upper secondary education.

● "Long-term female advantage countries": both younger and older women are more likely than their male counterparts to have completed at least upper secondary education.

Among the countries where lower proportions of women aged 45-54 than men of the same age have at least upper secondary education (the first two groups in Figure 4.3), progress in closing the gender gap was particularly pronounced in Australia, Iceland, Korea, Mexico and Spain (see Box 1.1 on Korea). In 2009, the proportion of women with at least upper secondary education was considerably higher than among men in Brazil, Greece, Iceland, Italy, Portugal and Spain.

Addressing gender gaps in education

Existing gender gaps in educational outcomes are related to a mixture of economic and socio-cultural factors, such as the costs and benefits of education, social norms and gender roles, discriminatory institutions, and personal safety. These factors are interrelated, which often makes it difficult to distinguish causes and effects and/or provide immediate, targeted policy responses.

The costs of schooling are both direct – school fees, books, uniforms, and transportation – and indirect – the opportunity cost of having children in education rather than engaged in economic activity. While the direct costs are the same for boys and girls, the indirect costs vary

Figure 4.3. **In most OECD countries, young women are more likely to have completed upper secondary education than young men**

Gender parity index[a] (GPI) for the percentage of population that has attained at least upper secondary education by age, 2009

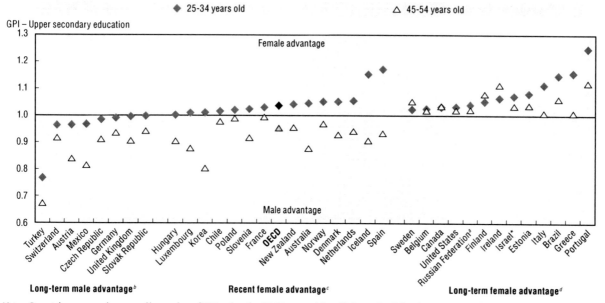

Note: Countries appear in ascending order of GPI value for 25-34 year-olds within each of the three groups – long-term male advantage; recent female advantage; and long term female advantage.

* Information on data for Israel: http://dx.doi.org/10.1787/888932315602.

a) Gender parity index (GPI): Ratio of female-to-male values of a given indicator.

b) Long-term male advantage: GPI smaller than 1 for both 25-34 and 45-54 year-olds.

c) Recent female advantage: GPI greater than 1 for 25-34 year-olds and smaller than 1 among 45-54 year-olds.

d) Long-term female advantage: GPI greater than 1 for both 25-34 and 45-54 year-olds.

Source: OECD (2011), Education at a Glance: OECD Indicators, OECD Publishing, Paris.

StatLink ⟡ http://dx.doi.org/10.1787/888932675424

with the prevailing gender roles. The opportunity costs of schooling include the foregone earnings of child work in the labour market or in the family business (*e.g.*, see the Understanding Children's Work [UCW] programme [*www.ucw-project.org*] on child labour and household chores). In addition to foregone earnings, the opportunity costs of schooling for girls include caring for younger siblings and unpaid domestic activities, which can take their toll on education. For example, it is frequently the duty of women and girls to fetch water – a chore which, depending on distances in rural areas and waiting times, may take up to four to five hours per day. Easier access to water, would therefore have a substantial beneficial effect on girls' enrolment in school.

In the past few decades, many countries have done away with tuition fees for primary education. But other education costs may still be barriers to participation. Kenyan parents, for example, have historically had to purchase school uniforms that cost about USD 6, accounting for a substantial proportion of the per capita income of USD 34 (Glewwe and Kremer, 2006). Interventions designed to reduce tuition fees and school uniform costs may encourage the enrolment of children from poor families. Other interventions in this direction are school meal programmes, flexible schooling models for working children, school-based malnutrition and health interventions, financial subsidies, scholarships and conditional cash transfers (Box 4.1).

Box 4.1. **Conditional and unconditional cash transfers**

In addition to general education policy, conditional cash transfers (CCTs) have also been introduced to build human capital through higher school participation rates. The success of cash transfers in Latin America in increasing educational participation is often attributed to their conditionality, whereby cash is received by households only if certain behavioural requirements are met (Behrman et al., 2011).

CCTs incentivise the demand side (students and parents) to overcome lack of motivation and encourage participation in schooling. At the same time, they are backed up with a provision of services to the target population. However, when low-school attendance is not principally related to parents' and students' low motivation, but is grounded in supply-side constraints (the lack of basic services in many developing countries), conditionality may not be an effective tool in boosting school attendance.

There are also differences across countries in the extent to which conditionality is applied. The Brazilian "Bolsa Familia" (Family Purse) programme provides benefits to low-income households – whose monthly per capita income is lower than half of the national minimum salary – and children of school age (6 to 15 years old). In the case of Bolsa Familia payments are conditional only on education and health services being delivered to children in the family. By 2010, the programme, launched in 2003, had reached 13 million beneficiary families (over 17 million children and adolescents of school age). The transfer amounts to a maximum of USD 112 per month to families on condition that their children attend school (on at least 85% of school days) and that family members use healthcare services. The application of eligibility criteria in Brazil is "soft": in the event of non-compliance the grant is not withdrawn. Instead, social services visit families to assess situations (Hanlon et al., 2010).

Before the introduction of Bolsa Familia, the net secondary enrolment rate in 2000 was 71% for girls and 66% for boys, compared with 86% and 78% in 2008 (UNESCO, 2011a). Soares et al. (2010) assert that Bolsa Familia increased the likelihood that a 15-year-old girl will remain in school by 19 percentage points. The largest gains occurred in the historically disadvantaged Northeast Region of Brazil, where enrolments have risen by 11.7 percentage points. Programme evaluations show that effects at primary school age are limited and mainly impact on the participation of older children.

Some CCTs are explicitly gender sensitive. The Mexican scheme "Oportunidades", for example, pays higher cash transfers for girls than boys, while the differential in support rates increases with grade levels in order to stem girls' relatively high drop-out rates after primary school in rural areas. Within two years of its implementation Oportunidades had contributed to a 9.3 percentage point increase in enrolment rates for girls in secondary school (from a base of 67%).

Another example is the Conditional Education Transfer (CET) programme for poor families implemented in Turkey since 2003. As for the majority of CCTs, the CET targets mothers and transfers cash into their bank accounts (www.unicef.org/turkey/sy11/ge45.html). The CET also channels higher amounts of assistance to girls than to boys in both primary and secondary school, with payments also varying according to age and the number of children in a household). The CET did not significantly affect primary school enrolment but had a noticeable effect on secondary school enrolment and attendance, subject to regional variations (Adato and Hoddinott, 2007; ADB, 2008).

> ## Box 4.1. **Conditional and unconditional cash transfers** (*cont.*)
>
> The South African Child Support Grant (CSG) is a means-tested benefit grant. Over the years, there has been a gradual age extension: as of 2012, children up to the age of 18 became eligible for the grant and about 60% of all children now receive it. The current amount is ZAR 240 (about USD 34) per month and in 2010, 9.4 million children benefitted from the CSG. Until recently it was an unconditional cash transfer. Since 2011, however, receipt of the CSG is conditional on furnishing proof of regular school attendance twice a year (Lund, 2011). The CSG can provide additional cash for children's uniforms or meals, which helps increase children's school participation. However, its impacts have been most visible on female labour force participation and children's nutrition.
>
> The effectiveness of the recently introduced conditionality in South Africa is debatable. Both girls' and boys' enrolment rates at primary and secondary school level are relatively high, while remaining problems with school attendance are largely related to gaps in education services in rural areas rather than the motivation of students or their parents. In this context, conditionality imposes an additional bureaucratic layer, and since the corresponding databases and infrastructure for monitoring and enforcing the conditionality are not in place, school attendance requirements remain "soft". It is not clear that introducing conditionality in these circumstances will be effective. Nevertheless, it serves as a policy signal that confirms the importance of education and may provide some reassurance to donors and tax payers.

Policies aimed at reducing the direct and indirect costs of education tend to benefit girls more than boys. This is because in poor families more girls than boys are on the margins of schooling and reduced education costs may tilt the balance towards school. Accordingly, countries which have introduced free primary education have seen the gender gap in enrolment narrow.

Most countries worldwide have school meal policies, although it is where the need is the greatest – in African countries and India – that coverage is lowest (WFP, 2009). Although school meal programmes do not specifically target girls, they nevertheless encourage more poor households to send their daughters to school. In India, for example, the introduction of school meals contributed to an increase in the number of years that girls, though not boys, attended primary school (Drèze and Kingdon, 2001), while in Ethiopia girls switched from agricultural to housework to reconcile their school participation with unpaid work commitments (Haile *et al.*, 2011).

A randomised school-based deworming programme has also been found to be cost-effective. As the programme reduces the incidence of the sickness and prompts parents to send their children to school, it is associated with significantly higher school participation rates, especially among girls and younger children (Edward and Kremer, 2000).

The benefits of education might also be different for boys and girls. Returns from education involve individual economic gains (better job, higher salary) and improved social outcomes (better health, higher social cohesion). Parents with limited financial resources might prefer to invest in boys' education rather than girls' to ensure they have the skills needed to get a decent job and marry. Although a growing body of literature suggests that mothers' education has strong social returns – lower child and maternal mortality, children more likely to attend school, and reduced gender inequality among siblings – parents usually do not consider the effect that their daughters' education might have on future generations. In poorer contexts, parents are more likely to think about the immediate benefits of marriage, such as greater family wealth or daughters-in-law who will care for them in old age. In determining how much to invest in their children's education, parents do not weigh up the wider social benefits which underlie the rationale for public investment in education.

Dropping out and staying on

Irregular attendance, poor school performance, and drop-out rates among adolescents – particularly boys – are a growing concern in many OECD countries. In OECD countries, an average of 73% of girls complete their upper secondary education on time compared to only 63% for boys, with the gender gap in this regard exceeding 15% in Israel and Norway (OECD, 2011a). Gender differences in completion rates are largely related to school performance and differences in socio-economic background: boys drop out because they do worse than girls throughout schooling, with those from low-income households especially affected (Falch et al., 2010). In OECD countries, boys and girls from lower socio-economic backgrounds or vulnerable social groups are twice as likely to be low performers and at a higher risk of dropping out (OECD, 2012a). In some countries in the MENA region, school drop-out among boys is due to the fact that they enjoy greater labour market opportunities than girls. In Abu Dhabi, for instance, boys lack the motivation to pursue education as they are practically assured of a career in the military, police, or family business (OECD, 2012b). Policies to prevent dropping out and support returns to education include a wide range of measures such as high-quality early education, tailored individual support to students when needed, and education and training opportunities that are attractive to boys (Council of the European Union, 2011; OECD, 2011a).

Policy makers need to continue to address the issue of unequal access to primary and secondary education and, where necessary, design tailored regional and local policies to address the needs of all students, including those who live in remote rural areas. Additional investment in schooling may well be most efficient if made in conjunction with investment in a range of other services that address health and care issues. Policies aimed at improving the quality of schooling, tackling poor school infrastructure, teacher shortages, and teacher absenteeism play an important role in increasing returns to education and boosting enrolment. Quality and equity in school is not a problem confined to developing countries: in OECD countries, almost one in five students fails to reach basic skill levels, while students from disadvantaged socio-economic backgrounds are twice as likely to be low performers (OECD, 2012a). Countries have to ensure that education, particularly vocational education, is relevant to labour market needs and that students do not have incentives to drop out of education too soon.

Increasing awareness among families and children of the benefits of education can be a successful, cost-effective policy for increasing school attendance and curbing drop-out rates with little cost to the public purse. A randomised evaluation of Madagascar found that providing information on returns to education for adolescents who finish primary school increased attendance by 3.5 percentage points (Nguyen, 2008). Similarly, Handa (2002) showed that adult literacy campaigns are nearly ten times more cost-effective than cash transfers in increasing primary school enrolment rates.

Getting girls into school and improving their educational outcomes requires policies to tackle such root causes of gender inequality in education as social norms, discriminatory institutions (see Chapter 2), violence against women (UNESCO, 2011a). A "girl-friendly" school environment can help get girls into school and lower barriers to their progress through the educational system (ibid.). Evidence from Africa, Asia, and the Middle East suggests that sexual harassment and other forms of gender-based violence may affect girls' school enrolment or lead to increased school drop-out rates (Morrison et al., 2007). Safe travel to and from school, female restroom facilities, and a balance between male and female teachers are all perceived as important in facilitating girls' enrolment.

To raise awareness of violence against women, NGOs around the world have used instruments like mass-media campaigns and community-based education. The most important lesson learned from experience is that programmes need to focus on changing the attitudes and behaviours of young men. A number of programmes that promote nonviolence among men and boys in developing countries – such as "Program H" in Brazil, "ReproSalud" in Peru, and "Men as Partners" in South Africa – have shown promising results (Guedes, 2004; Pulerwitz et al., 2004). Violence against women and sexuality-related gender norms put both girls and boys at increased risk of HIV infection. Appropriate measures in schools and communities to raise awareness of the risk of HIV infection are crucial.

Another practice that has also proven to have a positive impact on girls' attendance is hiring more female teachers. The evaluation of a randomised programme in India, for instance, has found that hiring additional female teachers increased girls' attendance by 50% (Glewwe and Kremer, 2006).

Key policy messages

Gender gaps in educational participation are related to a mixture of economic and socio-cultural factors. Narrowing them requires a comprehensive, multifaceted policy approach which, in developing countries, could include:

- Reducing the direct and indirect costs of schooling by reducing or abolishing school fees and providing free stationery, uniforms, and meals.

- Local infrastructure and institutional capacity need to be taken into account when deciding on CCT conditions as the quality and availability of education and ancillary services can be uneven across urban areas and remote rural ones.

- Reducing drop-out rates and encouraging returns to education through gender-sensitive awareness campaigns on the benefits of education, improving the quality of schools, hiring more female teachers, and making curricula more relevant to the labour market.

PART II

Chapter 5

Aid in support of gender equality in education

Key findings

- Aid from DAC members in support of gender equality amounted to around USD 25 billion in 2010 – 0.32% of DAC member countries' GNI. The figure is 31% of total bilateral sector-allocable aid.

- The education sector has the highest gender equality focus, reflecting donors' gender equality objectives and key international commitments like the Millennium Development Goals.

- The gender equality focus of aid to education is uneven across regions and is significantly lower in some regions with relatively high gender disparity in enrolment rates, notably in Sub-Saharan Africa.

Total aid flows from OECD Development Assistance Committee (DAC) donor countries reached a historic high of USD 129 billion in 2010, a 6.3% increase over 2009. The figure represented 0.32% of the combined gross national income (GNI) of DAC member countries. Of total DAC donor aid flow in 2009-10, USD 25.3 billion were reported as targeting gender equality and women's empowerment – 31% of bilateral sector-allocable aid screened against the DAC gender equality policy marker (Box 5.1).

Box 5.1. **The gender marker**

As part of annual reporting on their aid activities to the DAC Creditor Reporting System (CRS), DAC members are asked to indicate for each aid activity whether it targets gender equality as one of its policy objectives. To qualify as "gender equality focused", an activity must explicitly promote gender equality and women's empowerment. An activity can either target gender equality as its "principal" objective or as a "significant" objective. A "principal" score (2) is assigned if gender equality is an explicit objective of the activity and fundamental to its design – in other words, the activity would not be undertaken without that objective. A "significant" score (1) is attributed if gender equality is an important, but secondary, objective – i.e. not the principal reason for undertaking the activity. A "not targeted" score (0) is given if, after being screened against the gender equality policy marker, an activity is not found to target gender equality at all. Activities assigned a principal objective score should not necessarily be considered better than activities given a significant objective score, as donors that mainstream gender equality – and thus integrate it into their projects across a range of sectors – are more likely to score it as a "significant" objective.

All 24 DAC members now provide gender equality marker data to the DAC CRS, and 76% of all bilateral sector-allocable aid was screened against the marker in 2009-10. The remaining aid flows which were not screened against the marker were mainly attributable to the United States' reporting. The other 23 DAC members combined a total of 92% of their aid.

Almost all activities targeted gender equality as a significant – not principal – objective. USD 3.3 billion, or 5%, of total bilateral sector-allocable aid targeted gender equality as its principal objective. Canada stands out as the exception in this regard, with 42.4% of its aid targeting gender equality as a principal objective. One possible reason could be that Canada's development co-operation strategy includes measures to design programmes specifically aimed at reducing gender equality gaps.

A significant rise in Canada's spending on aid to gender equality has been supported by an emphasis on results-based management that incorporates descriptions of gender equality outputs into results frameworks. This approach helps planners to introduce these objectives into policy dialogue and to include them in the design phase of programmes.

Box 5.1. **The gender marker** (*cont.*)

**A high share of OECD DAC aid targets gender equality
as a significant objective**

Gender equality focus of donors' aid programmes, percentage of 2009-10 annual
average DAC members' aid commitments, 2010 prices

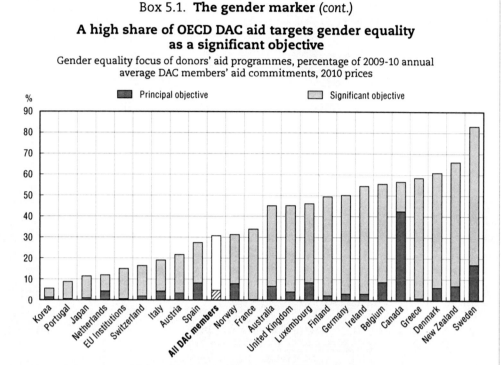

Notes: Countries are arranged left to right in ascending order of the percentage of gender equality focused aid (principal and significant objectives combined). The United States did not screen all its aid activities against the gender equality marker (21% coverage in 2009), so the share of aid that targets gender equality cannot be assessed.
Source: OECD Creditor Reporting System (CRS), *Aid Activity Database, www.oecd.org/dac/stats/idsonline.*

StatLink ᵐᵃᵖ http://dx.doi.org/10.1787/888932675481

The donor with the greatest overall proportion of gender equality focused aid is Sweden. Its prioritisation of gender equality is a whole-of-government effort, signalled through a tenfold increase in spending on gender equality across government between 2007 and 2010. As one of three thematic priorities within development co-operation, Sweden's main approach to gender equality has been to systematically mainstream it into all programmes. Policy directives require that context-specific analyses, including clear gender equality perspectives, guide the design of all programmes and operational measures.

International commitments drive DAC donor aid allocation for gender equality

Data on the distribution of aid that targets gender equality suggest that DAC donor allocation decisions are influenced by international commitments like the Millennium Development Goals (MDGs). The target for MDG3 – promote gender equality and women's empowerment – seeks to eliminate gender disparity in primary and secondary education, preferably by 2005 and, at all levels of education, by 2015. Gender equality marker data reveal that, in 2009-10, the education sector received one of the highest shares of gender equality focused aid –20%, or approximately USD 5.3 billion (Figure 5.1). This was equal to the government and civil society sector's allocation and just ahead of the health sector (19%).

Data show that education was the sector that targeted the highest share of its aid – 60% – at gender equality in 2009-10 (Figure 5.2). Next came the health sector with 51%, which reflects donor efforts to meet MDG5 (improve maternal health). Both sectors also

Figure 5.1. **The education sector receives the highest volume of gender equality focused aid**

Sectoral distribution of all aid targeting gender equality, 2009-10 annual average
DAC members' aid commitments, 2010 prices

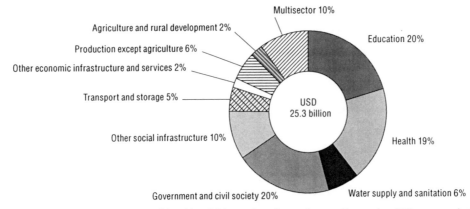

Note: The United States did not screen all its aid activities against the gender equality marker (21% coverage in 2009), so the share of aid that targets gender equality cannot be assessed.
Source: OECD Creditor Reporting System (CRS), *Aid Activity Database, www.oecd.org/dac/stats/idsonline.*

StatLink ⟨ms⟩ *http://dx.doi.org/10.1787/888932675443*

Figure 5.2. **The education sector has the highest proportion of gender equality focused aid**

Gender equality focused aid by sector, percentage of 2009-10 annual average
DAC members' aid commitments, 2010 prices

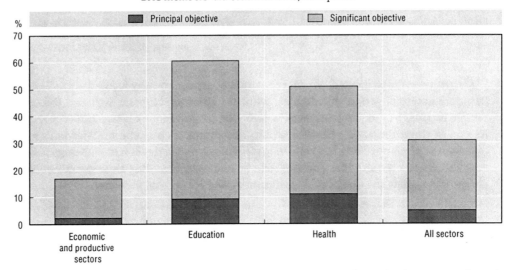

Note: The United States did not screen all its aid activities against the gender equality marker (21% coverage in 2009), so the share of aid that targets gender equality cannot be assessed.
Source: OECD Creditor Reporting System (CRS), *Aid Activity Database, www.oecd.org/dac/stats/idsonline.*

StatLink ⟨ms⟩ *http://dx.doi.org/10.1787/888932675462*

recorded relatively high shares of aid with gender equality as a principal objective: education with 9% and health with 11% (see definitions in Box 5.1). In contrast, Figure 5.1 reveals that the economic and productive sectors (banking, business, agriculture, transport) directed a significantly lower share of their aid (17%) at gender equality, despite their well documented gender inequalities (see Chapters 11, 22, 26, 27 and 29).

Setting international targets for gender equality in education has proven itself as an effective way to focus donor efforts on reducing gender enrolment gaps. More targeted international commitments could help increase donor efforts in other critical areas where the gender equality focus of aid is relatively low, such as the economic and productive sectors.

Does DAC aid to education target gender equality in regions with the greatest gender disparities?

Some regions are lagging behind in the effort to reach gender equality in education, with gender gaps persisting even in primary education enrolment (Chapter 4). Figure 5.3 illustrates the percentage of aid to primary and secondary education that was gender equality focused by region in 2009-10. The regions with wider gender gaps in primary enrolment are not necessarily the ones with the strongest gender focus in aid to education.

Figure 5.3. **The proportion of OECD DAC donor aid targeting gender equality in primary and secondary education varies across regions**

Gender equality focused aid in primary and secondary education, percentage of 2009-10 annual average DAC members' aid commitments, 2010 prices

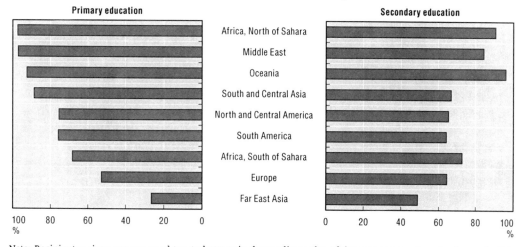

Note: Recipient regions are arranged top to bottom in descending order of the percentage of gender focused aid in primary education. Country groupings are defined in the Annex II.A2.

Source: OECD Creditor Reporting System (CRS), Aid Activity Database, www.oecd.org/dac/stats/idsonline.

StatLink ᔕᓬᐧ http://dx.doi.org/10.1787/888932675500

Donor aid to primary education was most heavily targeted on gender equality in North Africa and the Middle East at 97% (Figure 5.3, left-hand panel). Meanwhile, only 68% of the aid to primary education targeted gender equality in Sub-Saharan Africa where, except for some countries in Southern Africa, primary school enrolment had some of the highest levels of gender disparity (see Chapter 4). There is therefore scope for DAC members to increase the gender equality focus of their aid to primary education in Sub-Saharan Africa.

Data on aid to secondary education highlight an uneven spread in the shares of donors' aid focused on gender equality across regions. The focus is particularly low in the Sub-Saharan Africa region at 73% (Figure 5.3, right-hand panel), a percentage that is inadequate given that the region fares considerably worse than all others in terms of gender parity in secondary education enrolment (see Chapter 4). The South Asia region is also yet to reach gender parity in secondary education and enrolments, with the most significant gaps persisting in countries such as Afghanistan and India (Chapter 4). The gender equality focus of aid to secondary education to the South and Central Asia region was below average at 67%. Donors should increase efforts to ensure that their aid to secondary education in these regions includes objectives to increase the gender parity of enrolment as part of progress towards MDG2 (universal primary education) and MDG3 (promote gender equality and women's empowerment).

Policies and programmes that address the main barriers to gender parity in education

Regions face many daunting barriers to their efforts to increase girls' enrolment in primary and secondary schools (Chapter 4). A number of innovative examples from donors illustrate the role that well designed aid policies and programmes can play in helping developing countries to address challenges. AusAID, for example, has invested in facilities to train young women teachers in Papua New Guinea, while DFID has been working with state governments in Northern Nigeria to increase their capacity to deliver on increasing girls' school attendance (Boxes 5.2 and 5.3).

Box 5.2. **Educated women support Papua New Guinea's development**

About half of Papua New Guinea's (PNG) adult population cannot read or write. PNG, determined to change this, came up with an education wish list. It set an objective of at least 75% of children in primary school by 2015, with a focus on more girls not only in schools, but also in technical and vocational education. Aid provided by AusAID helped to eliminate school fees for the first few years of school, increasing primary school enrolments (many of them girls) from 53% in 2007 to 75% in 2010. The 2015 target was thus achieved five years ahead of schedule. An additional AUD 14 million in 2012 will further support the PNG government's own fee-free tuition programme, which will focus on lower secondary students in addition to primary school education.

As the number of girls enrolled increases, and as more girls complete primary school and go on to secondary school, the country needs more qualified teachers. Through AusAID support, work will soon start on improving facilities for women's colleges, such as building education rooms, health clinics, and extra female dormitories. This work will allow the colleges to accept more female students from across the country, enabling young women to receive an education and contribute to PNG's development. In doing so, it will also support PNG's own efforts to respond to a growing demand for education.

Box 5.3. **The Girls Education Project in Nigeria**

Over the past decade, Nigeria has made limited and uneven progress towards universal basic education, with its northern states suffering from particularly low enrolment rates and major gender disparities in primary school enrolment: 65% male to 35% female in 2010 (Nigeria Federal Ministry of Education, 2010). Unfortunately, the situation continues to worsen with 10.5 million children out of school in 2012, 3.6 million more than reported in 2000 and 42% of the primary school age population.

Box 5.3. **The Girls Education Project in Nigeria** *(cont.)*

Girls Education Project (GEP), a partnership bringing together Nigeria's Federal Ministry of Education, DFID and UNICEF, was launched in 2005. Since 2008, GEP has been implemented in four Northern Nigerian states. One of the project's objectives has been to build institutional capacity in state governments to address some of the biggest challenges facing the education system, such as overcrowded classrooms, poorly trained teachers, limited textbook availability, and outmoded teaching methods. Initial efforts helped a number of state governments to develop gender sensitive strategic plans for education. However, largely due to unaccountable government systems, these plans were rarely budgeted or implemented.

One way GEP addressed this was through the establishment of school-based management committees (SBMCs). State governments and donors co-financed grants awarded to SBMCs on the condition that local school plans made provisions for the improvement of the school environment; increased girls' enrolment and participation in the classroom; and improved the quality of educational inputs and services. Using the grants as incentives saw the SBMCs find innovative and practical ways to meet the conditions, *e.g.* by working with traditional and religious leaders, as well as conducting house-to-house campaigns to raise awareness of the importance of basic education for all children. Another positive intervention from the SBMCs was to help identify rural women candidates for co-financed scholarships to train as qualified teachers in their local communities. Ultimately, SBMCs proved a useful modality for channeling government resources towards raising the quality of schools and promoting female inclusion.

GEP has recently entered a third phase, and over the next eight years will be expanded into ten Northern Nigerian students. A measure of the programme's success has been the degree to which components of the project, such as the SBMC grants, have become increasingly co-financed and owned by state governments. Some states have performed better than others. For example, Bauchi State Government funded 86% of their female teacher scholarships, and the Niger State Government 78%. GEP is thus attempting to maximise the impact that aid resources can make on the achievement of MDG3 through efforts to mainstream reform into government systems and to strengthen government ability to deliver greater gender parity in education.

Key policy messages

- An increased gender equality focus is needed in aid to education in Sub-Saharan Africa and South and Central Asia to back countries' efforts to eliminate gender disparities and achieve the MDG3 targets in primary and secondary education.

- Partner countries need more support from donors to develop context-specific, innovative approaches to keeping girls in schools so that they complete a quality education.

- Setting international targets for gender equality in education has been an effective way to focus donor efforts on reducing gender gaps in school enrolment. More targeted international commitments could help increase donor efforts in other critical areas where the gender equality focus of aid is relatively low, such as the economic and productive sectors.

PART II

Chapter 6

Who is good at what in school?

Key findings

- At age 15, girls outperform boys in reading in every country and economy that participates in PISA. The reading performance gender gap is equivalent, across OECD countries, to one year's worth of schooling. In mathematics, boys outperform girls in most economies, though gaps are generally narrower than in reading. In science, gender differences are slight and there is no consistent pattern across countries.

- Students' attitudes play an important role in shaping the gender differences in academic performances observed in mathematics and reading. Gender-stereotypical attitudes towards these subjects arise early on.

- Gender gaps are much more pronounced among low- and high-achieving students. In reading, there are many more boys lacking basic skills than girls, while in mathematics it is boys who are more likely to be among the best performing students.

Concern over gender differences in education throughout much of the 20th century focused on the disadvantages and underachievement of girls. More recently, however, the underachievement of boys in reading and that of girls in mathematics have become the focus of policy attention (OECD, 2009a). Figure 6.1 illustrates the gender gaps in reading, mathematics and science in all PISA 2009 participant countries and economies. Evidence from other studies on African countries, such as the Southern and Eastern Africa Consortium for Monitoring Education Quality (SACMEQ) and the *Programme d'Analyse des Systèmes Éducatifs des Pays de la CONFEMEN** ("CONFEMEN Programme on the Analysis of Education Systems" – PASEC), also found that boys perform better in science-based subjects and girls are more successful in reading.

Figure 6.1. **Girls significantly outperform boys in reading, but boys perform better than girls in mathematics**

Difference in PISA score points (boys' scores *minus* girls' scores),[a] 2009

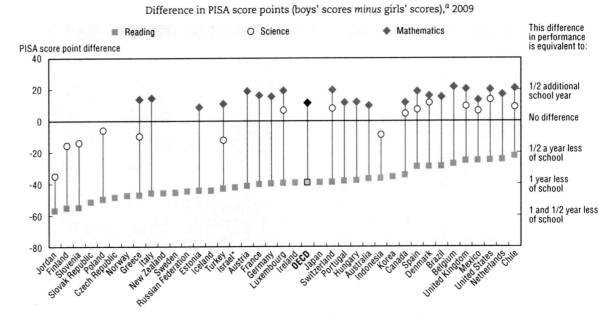

Note: Countries are arranged from left to right in order of decreasing gender gap in PISA reading scores.
* Information on data for Israel: *http://dx.doi.org/10.1787/888932315602.*
a) All PISA score point differences represented in the chart are statistically significant.
Source: OECD PISA Database 2009, *http://pisa2009.acer.edu.au.*

StatLink 🔗 *http://dx.doi.org/10.1787/888932675519*

In the PISA 2009 reading assessment, girls outperformed boys in every participant OECD country by an average of 39 PISA score points – equivalent to roughly one year of formal schooling (OECD, 2010a). The gap was much wider in some countries than in others.

* CONFEMEN is a French-language acronym for the *Conférence des ministres de l'Éducation des pays ayant le français en partage* (Conference of Ministers of Education of French-speaking Countries).

Figure 6.2. **Girls continue to outperform boys in reading**

Difference in PISA score points (boys' scores *minus* girls' scores),[a] 2009 and 2000

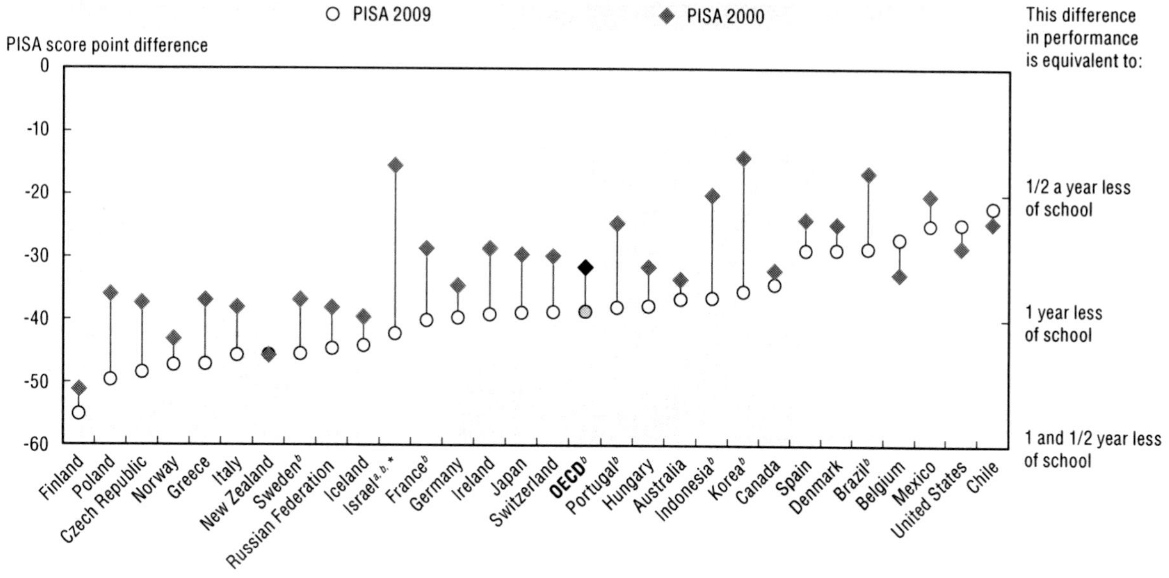

Note: Countries are arranged from left to right in ordered of decreasing gender gap in PISA reading scores.

* Information on data for Israel: *http://dx.doi.org/10.1787/888932315602.*

a) The Israel gender gap in reading in 2000 was non-statistically significant.

b) Gender gap in reading in 2009 was statistically significantly different from the reading gender gap in 2000.

Source: OECD PISA Database 2009, http://pisa2009.acer.edu.au.

StatLink ᵐˢᵖ *http://dx.doi.org/10.1787/888932675538*

With the exception of Denmark, Northern European countries have above-average gender gaps (Guiso *et al.*, 2008), while gender differences in East Asian countries tend to cluster just below the average, with Korea showing a gap of 35 points.

Gender performance in reading and mathematics

In 23 of the 34 OECD countries that participated in PISA 2009, boys performed better in mathematics than girls. Although gender differences varied widely across the countries, the average gender gap in mathematics tended to be much narrower than in reading. The widest disparities were observed in Belgium, Chile, the United Kingdom, and the United States, with an advantage of 20 score points or more for boys.

Gender differences in science performance tend to be small, both in absolute terms and relative to the wide gap in reading and the narrower one in mathematics. In 2006, when science was the main focus of the PISA assessment, gender differences were observed in two of the science processes assessed: identifying scientific issues and explaining scientific phenomena. Across OECD countries, girls scored higher when it came to identifying scientific issues, while boys outscored girls in explaining phenomena scientifically (OECD, 2007). The PISA 2000 and 2009 surveys both focused on reading, student attitudes, and engagement in reading activities. This provided the opportunity to analyse trends over that period for 38 countries, 26 of which were OECD members. The gender gap in reading performance did not narrow in any country between 2000 and 2009 and actually widened in seven.

Average differences in performance between boys and girls mask much greater gender differences between the lowest and the highest performing students. In reading, the gender gap is much larger among the lowest performing students: many boys lack basic reading skills, while only a few girls are not able to read texts and comprehend what they read (Figure 6.3).

Figure 6.3. **The gender gap in reading is widest among the lowest performing students**

Difference in PISA score points (boys' scores *minus* girls' scores) by performance level, 2009

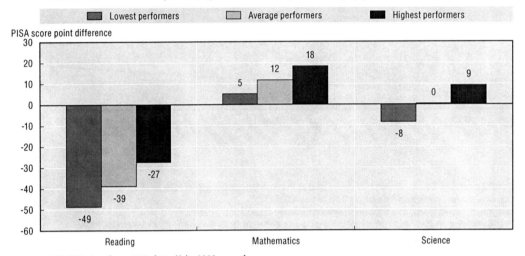

Source: OECD PISA Database 2009, http://pisa2009.acer.edu.au.

StatLink ⧉ http://dx.doi.org/10.1787/888932675557

In mathematics the gender gap is negligible among the lowest performing students, but increases to almost 20 score points – the equivalent of around half-a-year of formal schooling – among the best students. Thus, while the number of 15-year-old girls and boys struggling with mathematics is similar, boys outnumber girls among students with the highest proficiency levels in mathematics. Although gaps in science are generally smaller, girls outperform boys among the lowest performing students, while there are more boys than girls among 15-year-olds with the highest levels of proficiency.

Gender attitudes to reading and mathematics

Gender gaps in performance relate closely to gender differences in student attitudes and behaviours towards reading (OECD, 2004, 2007, 2010b). Girls are more likely to enjoy reading and to read for the sake of it (Figure 6.4). Differences in gender-based attitudes to reading and in reading habits widened between 2000 and 2009 – mostly because of a sharper decline in reading for enjoyment among boys than among girls (OECD, 2010c). Boys and girls not only differ in their propensity to read, but also in the types of reading material they favour: girls are significantly more likely than boys to read long, complex works of fiction and non-fiction, while boys are more likely than girls to read comic books (OECD, 2010b). Boys not only are less likely to read for enjoyment or to value reading as an activity, they are also less confident readers and see themselves as having lower skills than girls (Baker and Wigfield, 1999).

Figure 6.4. **Girls are more likely than boys to enjoy reading**

Percentage of boys and girls who read for enjoyment

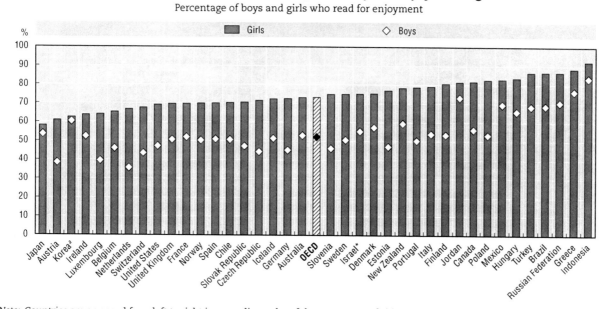

Note: Countries are arranged from left to right in ascending order of the percentage of girls who read for enjoyment.
* Information on data for Israel: *http://dx.doi.org/10.1787/888932315602.*
a) The difference between girls and boys in Korea is not statistically significant.
Source: OECD PISA Database 2009, http://pisa2009.acer.edu.au.

StatLink ⬛⬛ *http://dx.doi.org/10.1787/888932675576*

Boys show greater interest and ability in digital reading than in print reading (OECD, 2011b). Even though girls still outperform boys, the gender gap is narrower than in print reading. Among boys and girls with similar levels of proficiency in print reading, boys tend to have stronger digital navigation skills and therefore score higher in digital reading. This could be exploited to start a "virtuous cycle" where boys would read digital texts more frequently, so improving their digital reading proficiency which could, in turn, lead them to derive greater enjoyment from reading and to read printed matter more proficiently. Parents, educators, and policy makers should also take note of girls' weaker skills in digital navigation. Without them, students will find it more difficult to make their way in the digital age.

In mathematics, girls rate their own ability as lower than that of boys as early as the first year of primary school, even when their actual performance does not differ from that of boys (Fredericks and Eccles, 2002; Herbert and Stipek, 2005). Both boys and girls exhibit gender-stereotypical attitudes towards mathematics (Cvenecek *et al.*, 2011). Unlike mathematics and reading, gender differences in science performance cannot be traced back to differences in attitudes, motivation, or confidence (OECD, 2009a). Even in the absence of performance differences in mathematics and science, 15 year-old girls and boys are unlikely to expect to enter similar occupations: girls who anticipate working in fields such as engineering and computing are few and far between (Sikora and Pokropek, 2011).

PISA reveals that teenagers whose parents were reading to them when they started primary school tend to read better than their peers whose parents did not read to them (OECD, 2010d). It is especially important for fathers to read to their sons, as doing so helps change their perceptions and attitudes to reading. Yet fathers in all countries are less likely than mothers to read to their children or to harbour positive attitudes towards reading (Figure 6.5). Whether at

Figure 6.5. **Fathers are less likely than mothers to read to their children or have positive attitudes towards reading**

Proportion of mothers and fathers[a] who...

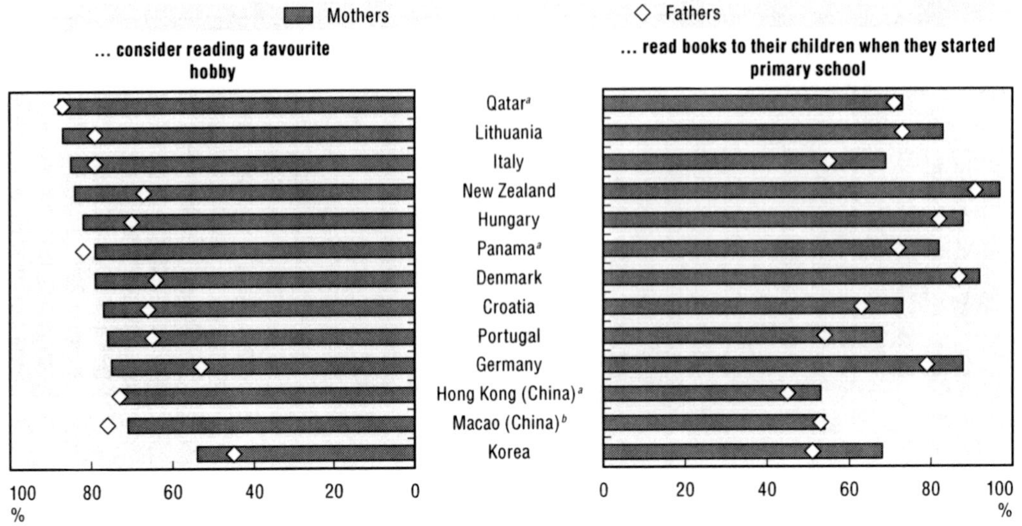

■ Mothers   ◇ Fathers

... consider reading a favourite hobby | ... read books to their children when they started primary school

Qatar[a]
Lithuania
Italy
New Zealand
Hungary
Panama[a]
Denmark
Croatia
Portugal
Germany
Hong Kong (China)[a]
Macao (China)[b]
Korea

Note: This chart is based on data collected through the Parental Questionnaire which was administered in 14 countries. (Poland is excluded from the chart, since Poland's survey did not include the question on parental engagement.) Countries are arranged from top to bottom in descending order of the proportion of mothers who consider reading a favourite hobby.

a) The difference between the proportion of mothers and fathers who consider reading a favourite hobby (left panel) is not statistically significant.

b) The difference between the proportion of mothers and fathers who read books to their child (right panel) is not statistically significant.

Source: OECD PISA Database 2009, http://pisa2009.acer.edu.au.

StatLink ᡵᡅᡦ http://dx.doi.org/10.1787/888932675595

home or school, providing boys with the kinds of books that appeal to them is an essential strategy for motivating them to read (OECD, 2010b). Finding the right books for children and parents to read together can significantly influence boys' perception of reading. Similarly, teachers can diversify their class reading lists and schools their libraries in order to appeal to the reading tastes of boys as well as girls. Parents and teachers can instil the pleasure of reading in boys by providing them with reading materials (such as comic books) they find interesting. Once the reading habit has gradually been built, longer and more complex texts such as novels and non-fiction books can be introduced. That said, simply engaging boys in discussions about what they like reading can also arouse their interest.

Turkey improved its mathematics performance between 2003 and 2009: boys by 21 score points and girls by 25. In reading, boys improved by 17 points and girls by 27. All this was achieved at a time when the enrolment of girls in education increased markedly (OECD, 2010c). In fact, Turkey implemented several projects that addressed equity issues. The aim of the campaign "Girls to Schools Now", launched in 2003, was that 100% of 6-14 year-old girls should attend primary school. Since 2003, the Ministry of National Education has supplied all primary school textbooks free of charge. More recently – in 2008 – the country initiated its Complementary Training Programme to provide all 10-14 year-olds who had never been to school or had dropped out with a basic education.

The gender gap in reading increased by 20 score points in Korea, mainly because of a marked improvement in girls' performance that was not matched by a similar trend among boys. The percentage of top performers increased among girls by more than nine percentage points, while among boys it rose by slightly less than five percentage points (OECD, 2010c). Overall, the average reading performance improved only among girls, while it remained at similar levels among boys. The improvement in girls' performance was recorded not only in reading, but also in other assessment areas covered by PISA and other international or national studies.

Since 2000, Korea has gradually introduced a more female-friendly science and mathematics curriculum. The effort has involved promoting female scientists or engineers as role models for girls, using more gender-neutral language in textbooks, and introducing learning materials considered more interesting to girls. At the same time, national assessments such as the NAEA were redeveloped to better monitor the different ways in which girls and boys acquire skills and to use formats that girls prefer, including, for example, the constructed response-item format.

Changes in Korean society may also be a factor in the drive to make science teaching more conducive to girls. Over the past few years, the family structure has changed as the number of children per household has fallen rapidly and the number of single-child families increased. While girls from larger families were once unlikely to get a good education, sociologists note that Korean parents today tend to set great store by their children's education, regardless of gender. New opportunities and incentives for learning may be additional reasons for the emphasis placed on teaching science to girls.

Key policy messages

- The teaching of STEM subjects (science, technology, engineering, mathematics) should be made more interesting for girls – by phasing out gender stereotypes from textbooks, promoting female role models, and using learning materials that appeal to girls.

- Boys' interest and abilities in digital reading could be exploited to start a "virtuous cycle": boys would read digital texts more frequently, so improving their digital reading proficiency which could, in turn, lead them to get more enjoyment from reading and read printed matter more proficiently.

- Parents and teachers can instil the pleasure of reading in boys by providing them with reading materials (such as comic books) they find interesting. Once the reading habit has gradually been built, longer and more complex texts such as novels and non-fiction books can be introduced.

PART II

Chapter 7

Secondary school graduates: What next?

Key findings

- In many low-income countries young women are more likely than their male peers to be neither employed nor in education or training (NEET).

- For young women the likelihood of being NEETs increases with age. In OECD countries being a NEET is often related to the end of compulsory education, while in developing countries it is associated with early marriage and child bearing.

- In general, NEET rates fall with higher levels of education. However, in some countries, especially in rural areas, informal employment and bad quality jobs may account for low NEET rates.

Across the world there has been marked progress in school participation and gender equality in education (Chapter 4). However, the school-to-work transition continues to pose numerous challenges. Young women are far more likely than young men to be neither employed nor in education or training (NEET), particularly in low- and middle-income countries. Failure to overcome other barriers which prevent women from making the transition from school to work as easily as men (Chapters 2, 4 and 18) can have effects that last a lifetime.

Being barred from the job market exacts a personal, social, and economic toll on young people. But being young and female, particularly in developing countries, is a double burden. While the recession further exacerbates youth unemployment, young women face even greater difficulty than young men in finding work (ILO, 2010). And in countries where women and girls are even more vulnerable to the effects of the global economic and food crises, there is a high risk that progress in gender equality and women's empowerment will be reversed (World Bank, 2009).

Employment eludes young women

In many OECD countries, NEET rates for boys and girls aged 15-24 are below 15% and do not show significant gender differences (Figure 7.1). Nor is there any clear gender

Figure 7.1. In low and middle income countries, NEET rates for women can be relatively high

Proportion of young people (aged 15-24) not in employment, education, or training (NEETs)

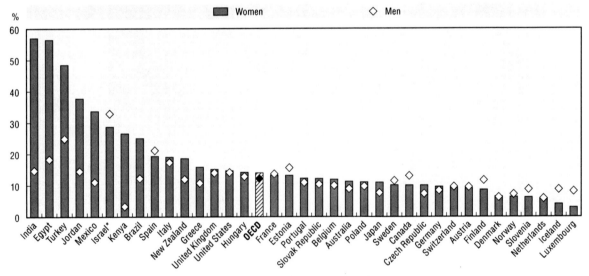

Note: Countries are arranged from left to right in descending order of young women who are NEETs.

* Information on data for Israel: *http://dx.doi.org/10.1787/888932315602.*

Source: OECD estimates based on OECD (2011), *Education at a Glance: OECD Indicators*, OECD Publishing, Paris; Kenyan estimations based on *Demographic and Health Survey 2008* and Indian estimations based on *Demographic and Health Survey 2005-06*; both references available at *www.measuredhs.com.*

StatLink ━━━ *http://dx.doi.org/10.1787/888932675614*

pattern in youth unemployment rates (ILO, 2012a). However, in some OECD countries, such as Mexico and Turkey, girls' NEET rates are much higher than young men's and comparable with those of non-OECD countries like Brazil, Kenya, Jordan, Egypt, and India.

Figure 7.2 shows that gender differences in NEET rates can be substantial in non-OECD countries. In India, for example the NEET rate among young men aged 15-24 is 15%, but at 57% India has an extremely high proportion of young women who are neither in education nor employment. In African countries the NEET rate for young men is about 20%, but 35% for young women.

Figure 7.2. **Married and less educated young women aged 20-24 are more likely to be NEETs in Africa and India**

Proportion of NEETs by age, educational levels, and marital status

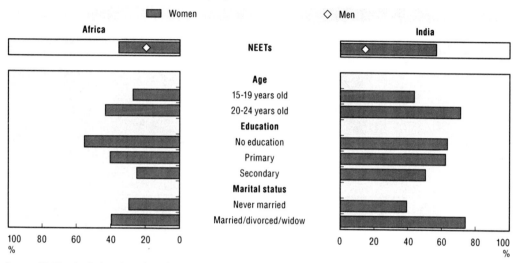

Source: OECD calculations based on the Gallup World Poll (2009-10) for African countries and *Demographic and Health Survey 2005-06* for India, *www.measuredhs.com*. (African analysis includes 27 countries.)

StatLink ᴍᴙ✎ *http://dx.doi.org/10.1787/888932675633*

Girls' NEET rates are likely to worsen as they enter their 20s. In OECD countries, it is because they may have just completed compulsory education, while in developing countries it is frequently because they have married early and/or have caring duties. Indeed, Figure 7.3 shows that in India young women who are married are more likely to be NEET than unmarried women of the same age. Figure 7.2 indicates a lower variation in the NEET rate by marital status for Africa, although this masks wide regional variations. In North Africa, the NEET rate was around 64% for married women and 40% for unmarried women.

A lack of qualifications also proves a significant barrier to female labour force participation. Figure 7.2 shows that the higher the level of educational attainment among women in Africa, the lower their NEET rates are. In India there does not seem to be such a pattern at national level. In urban areas, where there are more job opportunities, female NEET rates fall as education levels rise. In rural areas, however, where much of the population have very low levels of educational attainment, young women often work out of necessity and NEET rates tend to be lower. The Indian example illustrates how important both education and decent job opportunities are in providing "empowerment opportunities" to young women (Francavilla *et al.*, 2012; and Chapter 20).

Figure 7.3. **After secondary school boys are more likely than girls to work**

Proportion of students, workers and NEETs by age and gender in selected countries (age 15-29)

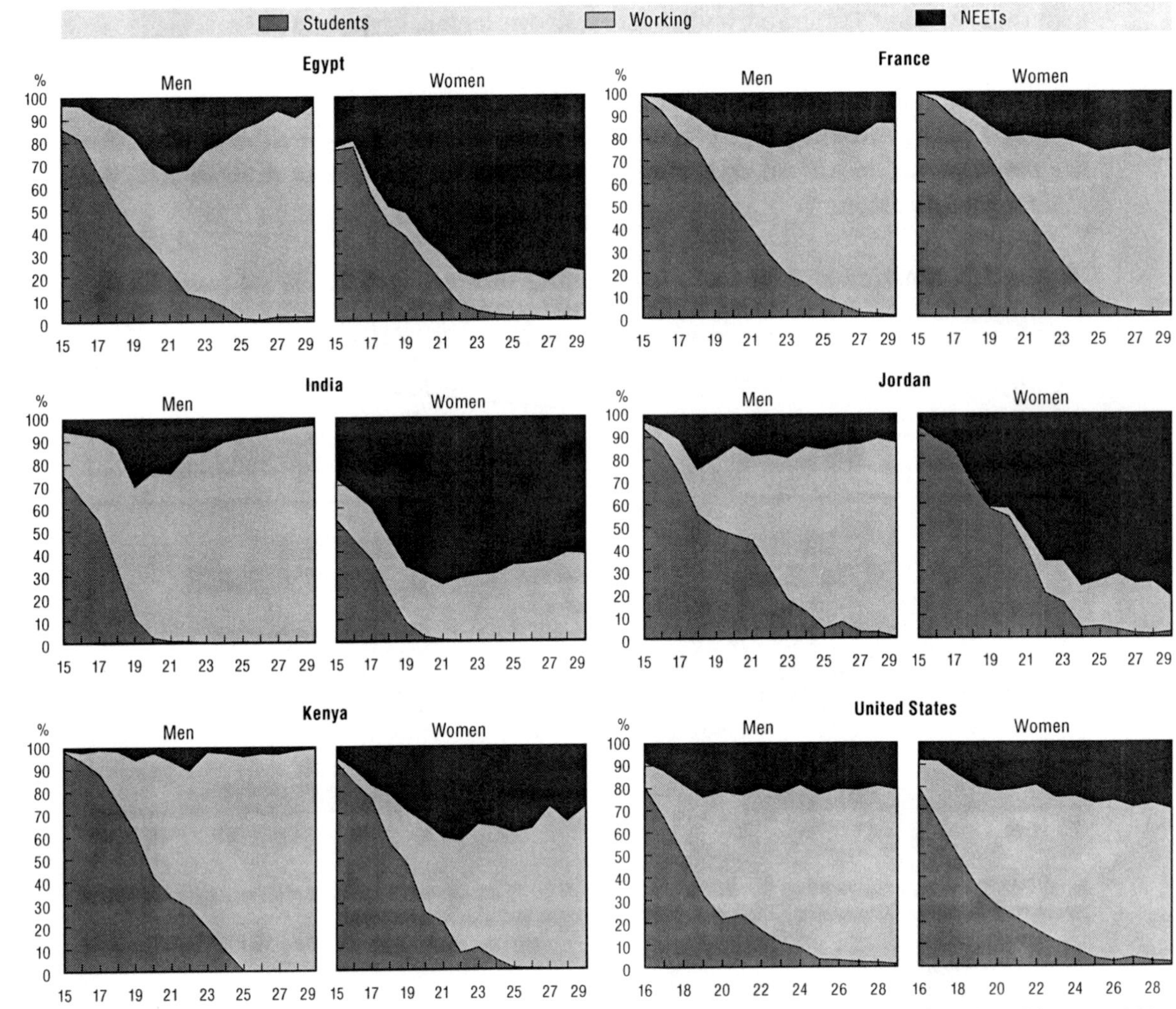

Students   Working   NEETs

Source: OECD estimates based on the *Kenya Demographic and Health Survey 2008*; the *Demographic and Health Survey 2005*, *www.measuredhs.com*; *France Labour Force Survey 2009*, Institut national de la statistique et des études économiques (INSEE); US Census (2009), "Results from the 2007 Survey of Business Owners", *www.census.gov/econ/sbo*.

StatLink ᵐˢᵖ *http://dx.doi.org/10.1787/888932675652*

School-to-work transition: Young women's missed opportunity

Figure 7.3 shows the shares of young people up to the age of 30 who are students, employed, or NEETs in selected countries. It reveals young women's NEET rates are similar of those of their male peers in France and the United States. In Egypt, India, Jordan and Kenya, however, they are much more likely to be NEETs from a very early age.

Adolescence is a decisive time for young people everywhere. In developing countries it is at that age that young men tend to drop out of school to enter the labour market. Young women, instead, usually leave school and take up the burden of unpaid household work, thus missing their chance to enter the labour market. In OECD countries, boys are likely to leave school earlier than girls. For example, in France and in the United States young women at age 24 are at least as likely to participate in formal education as young men of the same age. However, as women near the time when they typically form families, they are increasingly more likely to become NEETs than their male counterparts.

The role of policy

Fostering youth employment opportunities is vital for economic development across the globe, and investment in schooling is key (Chapter 4). However, the quality of schooling in developing countries often leaves much to be desired (Box 7.1). Too many children graduate from school without acquiring the basic skills in literacy and numeracy which are essential for labour market participation and progression. Youth literacy rates remain extremely low, especially for girls, in countries such as Benin, the Central African Republic, Chad, Guinea or Sierra Leone (UNESCO, 2009). MENA countries also still lag behind many other regions in adult literacy rates (72% for the period 2005-08), especially as regards women who account for about 65% of the region's illiterate population. Nevertheless, there has been considerable progress in recent years, as evidenced by literacy rates among young people that far exceed those of adults (UNESCO, 2010).

Box 7.1. Improving schools for better education for children:
Tailored country reviews to promote reform

The OECD has increased its efforts to promote effective education reforms across OECD member and partner countries (*www.oecd.org/edu/improvingschools*). As part of these efforts, the OECD has developed education policy country reviews tailored to address the specific challenges of a country's education system.

In 2008, the OECD produced a review tailored to help **Mexico** improve the quality of its education system. Challenges faced by the Mexican education system include a lack of capacity; unclear assignment of responsibilities across a decentralised system; and how to distribute resources across schools effectively along more institutionalised ways of consensus-building. The key recommendations, presented in two reports, can be summarised as follows:

- Develop and consolidate teacher career paths: define effective teaching, and attract, recruit, prepare, evaluate and develop a higher-quality teaching force.

- Improve school effectiveness: define effective school leadership, professionalise the training and appointment of directors, build instructional leadership capacity in and across schools, enhance school autonomy, ensure funding for all schools, and strengthen social participation.

In **Norway** in 2010-11, the OECD undertook a review to find ways of strengthening lower secondary education, where Norway faces a number of challenges. They include low student engagement and motivation, insufficiently prepared teachers, and a governance arrangement that does not necessarily fit with a decentralised education system. The key recommendations from the review were:

- Align policy design and implementation across different levels of governance.

- Raise the status of teaching and improve teacher performance: improve initial teacher education, raise salaries to attract high quality candidates, ensure teachers' continued skills and professional development.

- Improve school capacity: develop a national strategy to strengthen schools' capacities, enhance instructional leadership, and support the transition from primary to lower secondary school by creating a culture of student self-assessment and feedback for improvement.

> **Box 7.1. Improving schools for better education for children:
> Tailored country reviews to promote reform** *(cont.)*
>
> Further work with Norwegian policy makers and stakeholders (OECD Seminar for Leaders in Education Improvement) resulted in the design of an action plan specifically to improve lower secondary education in Norway.
>
> In **Iceland**, upper secondary educational attainment amongst young people has fallen as a result of the high dropout rate. Dropout rates seem to be related to the education system failing to address students' needs, whereas there ought to be more career and professional development opportunities. Recommendations include:
>
> - Support transition into upper secondary education: ensure that curricula across education levels do not overlap, strengthen the guidance and counselling of students in lower secondary education, and improve the capacity of schools to adapt to students' specific learning needs.
>
> - Strengthen the link between vocational education and the labour market: encourage social partners (employers and unions) to send the message to students that education is important, raise the status of vocational training programmes, and incentivise schools to recapture drop-out students.
>
> - Support teaching quality: increase the attractiveness of the teaching profession by, for example, providing career and professional development opportunities.
>
> - Promote a governance system that focuses on support and capacity building for schools: foster collaboration between stakeholders such as teachers' unions and ministries.

Some training schemes offer school-leavers valuable grounding in fields such as life skills (leadership, managing income and budgets, understanding employees' rights); employability (interpersonal and basic job skills, particularly those that young women may lack); and basic business skills training (developing business plans, financial management, and marketing). Other initiatives to help school leavers negotiate the transition to work include job placement support, providing access to micro-credit and/or savings accounts, and learning in small groups.

The World Bank Youth Employment Inventory shows that of 291 programmes in 84 countries, only 15% actively promote the inclusion of young women (Betcherman *et al.*, 2007). The Adolescent Girls Initiative (AGI) promoted by the World Bank is currently implemented in seven countries: Afghanistan, Jordan, Laos, Liberia, Nepal, Rwanda and South Sudan. It is a public-private partnership whose programmes are tailored to local contexts (World Bank, 2010). The AGI focuses not on low-paid, gender-stereotypical jobs like flower arranger or seamstress (Levine *et al.*, 2009), but on making non-stereotypical trades like electrician, mason and mobile phone technician attractive to young women. In some countries, AGI support programmes include: improving child care and transport services; placement and counselling services; financial incentives to recruit young women; job vouchers to incentivise firms to hire new graduates with no experience; and/or awareness campaigns to reach poorer, less educated and more vulnerable girls. All AGI programmes are first run as pilot schemes, then scaled up only if they have been found to be effective upon evaluation (World Bank, 2011).

Learning opportunities for young people also depend on the structure and development of the labour market. A study of seven cities in Western Africa shows that for those employed in the informal sector the returns from vocational schools are marginal. The main forms of vocational training are traditional apprenticeships and on-the-job training, the latter dominated by women (Nordman and Pasquier-Doumer, 2012). In South Africa, government training programmes have had limited success in helping youth with no job experience. To help reduce youth unemployment, the government is proposing a youth employment incentive that takes the form of a wage subsidy to help young workers into the unionised formal sector where entry wages are relatively high.

In many countries, supply-side policies alone are not sufficient to guarantee decent jobs for young men and women. For example, adequate industrial policies (such as investment in labour-intensive industry), technology and infrastructure are required, especially in rural areas. Policy approaches need to foster youth job opportunities through the creation of a good investment climate and the removal of barriers to competition like land and credit market imperfections.

Key policy messages

Successful school-to-work transitions require integrated, multi-sector policy approaches that address such critical areas as education, labour market, migration, family programmes, and social and cultural norms. Key policy interventions include:

- Facilitating the transition from school to work by ensuring a solid educational base, offering high quality education, establishing better links between the education sector and employers, and providing extensive labour market information.

- Promoting gender-sensitive vocational training programmes that are tailored to local contexts, focus on making non-stereotypical trades attractive to women, and include placement and counselling services. Before they can be scaled up, such programmes need first to be run as pilot projects and then evaluated.

PART II

Chapter 8

Science *versus* the humanities

Key findings

- There are no significant gender differences in performance amongst university graduates.
- In post-secondary education, boys tend to choose vocational training programs and girls higher education, which exacerbates gender differences in fields of study.
- Improving the quality of schooling for children from disadvantaged socio-economic backgrounds can in itself prompt more girls to go into science-related fields of study.

Women's greater gains in post-secondary education

Arguably, one of the greatest transformations in education to have occurred in OECD countries over the past few decades is the increased participation of women in tertiary education. Figure 8.1 shows that the graduation rates of both sexes at upper secondary (which includes programmes in post-secondary, non-tertiary education) and tertiary levels have risen across OECD countries. However, the share of women completing tertiary education has grown particularly rapidly. Although the numbers of men and women attaining upper secondary education have increased at similar rates, the proportion of men remains slightly higher (by 4 percentage points) simply because there are more men in post-secondary non-tertiary education programmes. If these were excluded, young women (25-34 age cohort) are actually more likely to complete both secondary and tertiary education than their male counterparts (OECD, 2011c).

Figure 8.1. **Today women are more likely to obtain a tertiary degree than men**

Proportion of men and women aged 25-64 with upper secondary or tertiary degrees across 27 OECD countries, 1998-2009

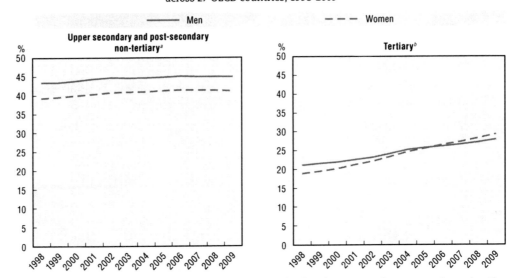

a) Includes graduates from upper secondary (ISCED 3A, 3B and 3C) and post-secondary non-tertiary education (ISCED 4). For a description of the ISCED classification see http://stats.oecd.org/glossary/detail.asp?ID=1436.

b) Include tertiary type A and advanced degrees.

Source: OECD (2011), Education at a Glance: OECD Indicators, OECD Publishing, Paris.

StatLink 🔗 http://dx.doi.org/10.1787/888932675671

Participation trends in higher education reveal a reversal in the gender gap: in 1985, the average share of female students was 46% in the OECD area; by 2005 it was 54%. If the trend continues, there will be an average of 1.4 female students for every male by 2025, and almost twice as many women in tertiary education in Austria, Canada, Iceland, Norway, and the United Kingdom (Table II.A2.1).

Gender differences in subject choices persist

Even if the gender gap in overall educational attainment is narrowing, it remains wide when it comes to the field of study. Women are still much under-represented in science, technology, engineering and mathematics (STEM). And even though more women are completing STEM degrees (particularly in biology and agriculture), they still account for a very small share of students in computing and engineering – subjects in great demand on the labour market in OECD countries and other regions (Box 8.1). Figure 8.2 clearly shows that women are a minority amongst computer science graduates and a majority in health and welfare degrees. Indeed, the proportion of female graduates in computer science degree courses in most OECD countries fell in the first decade of the 21st century due to the steeper rise in shares of male students. The largest drops in the proportion of female computer science graduates came in Korea, Ireland, and Sweden. On the other hand, more women entered health-related degrees in 2009 than in 2000 across all OECD countries, with the increase particularly pronounced in Denmark and the Slovak Republic.

Box 8.1. **Gender differences in subject choices at tertiary level in MENA countries and China**

Despite existing gender disparities in some Middle East and North African (MENA) countries in enrolment rates at the secondary (and sometimes primary) level of education, tertiary enrolment of young women has been growing and often exceeding that of young men (UNESCO, 2011b). Their rates rose from 42% in 1999 to 51% in 2009 in the region (UNESCO, 2012b), exceeding male rates in Algeria, Jordan, Kuwait, Lebanon, Qatar, Saudi Arabia, Tunisia and the United Arab Emirates (WEF, 2011).

Tertiary education: Female share in total enrolment by field of study in selected MENA countries, school year ending in 2007

Percentages

	Education	Humanities and arts	Social sciences, business and law	Science	Engineering, manufacturing and construction	Agriculture	Health and welfare	Services
Algeria	69	75	59	61	31	47	60	29
Bahrain	51	83	70	75	21	n.a.	85	69
Jordan	84	63	39	51	29	54	48	53
Lebanon	94	67	52	53	24	54	68	53
Morocco	38	52	50	41	29	38	67	48
Oman	63	69	43	56	23	74	66	n.a.
Palestinian Authority	70	65	40	46	30	18	57	31
Qatar	85	85	65	68	25	n.a.	76	n.a.
Saudi Arabia	73	73	53	59	2	23	44	n.a.
United Arab Emirates	92	76	55	55	29	74	80	30

Source: UNESCO (2010), Education for All Global Monitoring Report 2010, Paris, http://unesdoc.unesco.org/images/0018/001865/186558E.pdf.

StatLink ᴍ̶ᴏ̶ *http://dx.doi.org/10.1787/888932677305*

> Box 8.1. **Gender differences in subject choices at tertiary level in MENA countries and China** (*cont.*)
>
> However, as in OECD countries, distinct gender differences persist in fields of study at the tertiary level. The table below shows the female share of total enrolment. In nearly all the countries in the table (save Morocco), women are notably over-represented in the humanities, arts subjects, and education. With the exception of Jordan and Saudi Arabia, they also form the majority of university students in health and welfare and science in most countries. They are, however, significantly under-represented (less than one-third of students) in engineering, manufacturing and construction. The low female proportions in these subjects are, as in most OECD countries, related to attitudes rather than ability: for example, OECD (2010a) shows that 15 year-old girls in Jordan score better than boys in mathematics.
>
> In China, too, a highly disproportionate number of females choose the humanities over the science track in high school, which irreversibly affects their subject choices at tertiary level. The preference for the humanities is unlikely to be driven by girls' abilities in science and mathematics, since they score as well as boys, save at the upper end of the score distribution and in some, mostly rural, areas. Yet, the evidence suggests that the science track increases female students' chances of pursuing studies at university or in elite higher education institutes (Loyalka and Maani, 2012).

Figure 8.2. **More women enter health related degrees but remain underrepresented in computer science degrees**

Proportion of tertiary degrees awarded to women in 2000 and in 2009

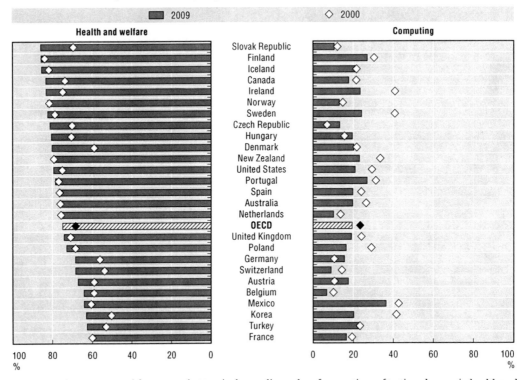

Note: Countries are arranged from top to bottom in descending order of proportions of tertiary degrees in health and welfare awarded to women in 2009.

Source: OECD (2011), *Education at a Glance: OECD Indicators*, OECD Publishing, Paris.

StatLink ᕳᕲᐧ *http://dx.doi.org/10.1787/888932675690*

The gender differences observed in higher education level are even more marked in vocational training programmes. More than one male student in two but less than one in ten females graduate from such programmes in the fields of engineering, manufacturing and construction in OECD countries (Figure 8.3). The exceptions are Korea and Indonesia, where the female graduation rates from vocational engineering programmes were 28.6% and 29.1%, respectively. Indonesia shows hardly any difference in male and female graduation rates or in subject choices at the tertiary level (OECD, 2011c).

Figure 8.3. **Gender differences persist in technical vocational programmes**

Proportions of women and men in upper secondary vocational education who completed their programmes in engineering, manufacturing and construction in 2009

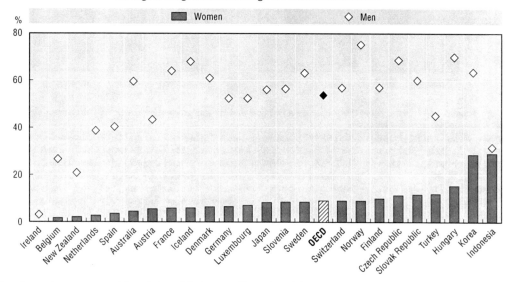

Note: Countries are arranged from left to right in ascending order of the proportion of female graduates.
Source: OECD (2011), *Education at a Glance: OECD Indicators*, OECD Publishing, Paris.

StatLink 🔗 *http://dx.doi.org/10.1787/888932675709*

Negligible gender performance disparities at tertiary level

Despite systematic gender differences in subject choices at tertiary level, male and female students graduate with very similar standards of performance. Panel A in Figure 8.4 shows that it is hard to discern gender-related performance disparities across subject areas, except that there are slightly more men than women amongst graduates with the lowest grades. Panel B reveals that the proportion of women among top performing students is very similar across fields of study, while men show a little more variation in this regard. Men and women graduate with very similar grades in science and in the social sciences, while women do slightly better in the humanities and men have the edge in the health area.

These broad trends, however, mask differences in individual countries. In Japan and the United Kingdom, for example, the proportion of female graduates with top grades is around 10 to 15% lower than for males, while in Estonia, Italy, and the Netherlands it is the other way around (Flabbi, 2011).

Figure 8.4. **Women and men perform equally well at the tertiary level**

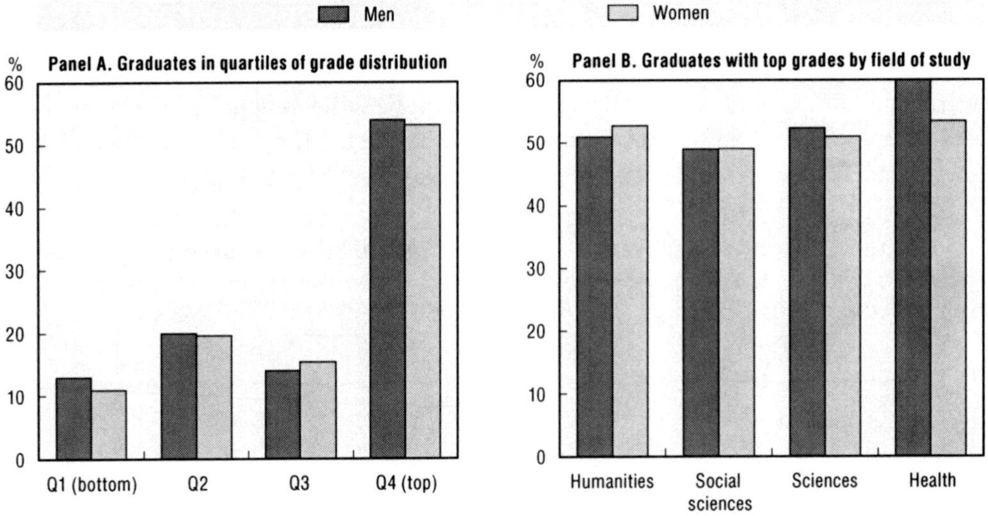

Note: Panel A and Panel B show the proportions of male and female graduates in a pooled sample of all tertiary graduates in the surveyed countries.
Source: Flabbi, L. (2011), "Gender Differentials in Education, Career Choices and Labour Market Outcomes on a Sample of OECD Countries", Background paper for the OECD Gender Initiative, using the REFLEX dataset which surveys 1999-2000 graduates from higher education (ISCED 5A, equivalent to bachelor or master degrees) who have about five years of work experience after leaving higher education in 14 OECD countries (Austria, the Czech Republic, Estonia, Finland, France, Germany, Italy, Japan, the Netherlands, Norway, Portugal, Spain, Switzerland and the United Kingdom).
StatLink ⧉ http://dx.doi.org/10.1787/888932675728

Cultural factors in subject choices at post-secondary level

Girls and boys might choose different fields of education because their personal preferences and expectations about labour-market outcomes are not the same (OECD, 2011a). For example, young women are more likely to plan intermittent participation in the labour force, so avoiding fields like the sciences that require high levels of on-the-job training, long working hours and where time taken out of work can be very costly (OECD, 2011c). They might also choose fields that allow more flexible work arrangements enabling them to combine work and caring for children and elderly relatives more easily. Such choices partly explain the trend towards the "feminisation" of the health and education sectors.

Different subject choices in higher education might also be driven by performance differences in reading, mathematics and science at secondary school. However, gender disparities in subjects chosen appear to be related more to student attitudes (such as motivation and interest) towards a particular subject rather than to ability and performance at school (Chapter 6). Attitudes are formed early in life and are undoubtedly influenced by traditional perceptions of gender roles and wide acceptance of the cultural values associated with particular fields of study (Kane and Mertz, 2011; OECD, 2009a). Moreover, traditional subject choices can be reinforced by early tracking in the education system. Further insights into the possible factors influencing choices made by students as they advance through their education can be obtained from the PISA longitudinal surveys (Box 8.2).

Box 8.2. **What drives gender differences in subject choices?**

New PISA longitudinal studies in a number of countries shed light on factors that determine gender differences in fields of study in post-secondary education. The studies considered male and female choices of subjects in different national education systems at tertiary level and in vocational training (VT) programmes. They show that a number of factors, such as individual attributes, family characteristics, and socio-economic background, play a role in determining whether boys and girls pursue science or arts subjects.

Typically, students who have high grades in mathematics in the last year of secondary school tend to choose science-related subjects when they go on to post-secondary education. The relationship is particularly pronounced for girls in most countries. Findings show that confidence in performing specific tasks in mathematics is a strong determinant among boys in choosing science and computing-related fields, whereas girls' perception of their own ability is essential to forming an idea of their future study and career paths.

The longitudinal studies do not generally find that mothers' or fathers' education has any significant effect on students' choices. In some countries, however, they may be associated with parental occupation. In Switzerland, parents' high occupational status seems to be an important predictor of whether students take science-based as opposed to arts-based degree courses, although the result is only significant for vocational training (Bergman et al., 2012). In the case of Uruguay, for example, if mothers work as teachers their daughters are significantly less likely to choose a humanities career and their sons less likely to choose medicine or social work. Fathers in engineering professions do not seem to influence their daughters' or sons' choices, whereas those who work as teachers, lawyers or administrators discourage boys from humanities and encourage them to enter law, the behavioural sciences and economics (Fernandez et al., 2012). In Australia, parents' occupations appear to have a greater effect on sons' choice of field of study than on their daughters.

The migration status of parents also influences the field of study their children choose. In Australia, for example, girls with both parents from overseas are more likely than those whose parents are born locally to choose traditional subjects, such as the humanities. In contrast, there is no such effect on boys, which might suggest that overseas perceptions of suitable careers for women differ from local ones. Families' socio-economic background might also play a role in the area of study chosen. In Uruguay, for example, lower economic status prompts girls to choose humanities subjects like teaching and the arts at the tertiary level. Indeed, girls from the middle and lower classes seem to favour occupations in such fields as a rung on the ladder of upward social mobility (Fernandez et al., 2012).

Young women are more likely to aspire to careers as professionals (OECD, 2009a) than young men and tend, therefore, to exhibit a preference for university study over vocational training. In Australia, young men associate science courses less with university entry than with vocational training schemes like apprenticeships. Since access to vocational training is not generally based on academic merit, performance in mathematics at the age of 15 has no significant effect on their choice of science course. Evidence for the Czech Republic shows a similar pattern: girls with high grades at secondary level choose to go to university while boys are more likely to pursue vocational training in a technical or science-related field. As in Australia and the Czech Republic, the segregation of subjects taught by different institutions influences gender differences in subject choices, so reinforcing typical male and female roles (Matějů et al., 2012; Polidano and Ryan, 2012).

To varying degrees from country to country, education systems may reinforce individual characteristics and cultural expectations. Thus, in addition to raising girls' interest and confidence in mathematics and science at school and at home, a wider provision of diverse, flexible educational pathways to the same career can help females pursue science-related occupations.

Policy interventions to address gender differences

The issue of gender disparities in subject choices is of concern because it affects women's career opportunities (Chapter 9), reduces their earnings potential, and underutilises available human capital (OECD, 2011c). As the global economy becomes increasingly knowledge-driven and there is ever fiercer competition in speed of innovation, the full use of a population's available stock of skills should be any government's priority.

Gender differences in subject choices are deeply rooted in cultural norms across all different socio-economic levels. Changing students' attitudes and behaviours is therefore particularly challenging, requiring considerable efforts from parents and teachers to change the stereotyped notions of what boys and girls excel in doing and what they enjoy. Interventions should start early in life before stereotypical perceptions and attitudes towards certain subjects are formed. A Canadian study, for example, shows that students aged 12-13 show the greatest interest in science and that their interest declines dramatically as they grow older (Ipsos Reid, 2010). A study of 4 000 children in the United Kingdom confirms the decline in interest in science as children progress through school. It reveals that science lessons are inspiring to 42% of 9 year-olds compared with 38% and 35% of 12 and 14 year-olds (Parvin and Porter, 2008). OECD (2008) found that interest in science and technology appears in primary school and remains stable until the age of 15 after which it declines. It is crucial that teachers embed mathematics and science activities in contexts that are interesting to both boys and girls and connect them to careers in ways that do not reinforce existing gender stereotypes (IES, 2007).

A positive attitude towards a subject (be it reading or mathematics) is also related to positive teacher-student relations since interaction with teachers helps shape the cognitive development and intellectual engagement of boys and girls (OECD, 2010b). Moreover, students tend to learn more when they feel that their teachers are taking them seriously because they gain confidence and perform better. Students who are better informed about what will help them learn also tend to perform better (OECD, 2009a). It therefore pays to have highly qualified teachers who address gender-specific attitudes within the classroom. Teacher-training programmes for graduates have proven to be effective in raising the quality of teaching in Turkey (OECD, 2011a). Valuable additions to existing teacher-training frameworks could be gender awareness courses, while gender mainstreaming concepts could be introduced in teacher training and teaching material. Examples include the "*Jungenarbeit und Schule*" (Working with Boys and School) project in Germany (*www.jungenarbeit-und-schule.de*), which focuses on how teachers can help boys succeed in school, or the gender mainstreaming approach in Austria (*www.bmukk.gv.at/ medienpool/9718/PDFzuPubID455.pdf*). The policy effectiveness of introducing single-sex schools – which are generally considered to increase girls' confidence and benefit their ability to learn mathematics – is not supported by data (Kane and Mertz, 2011).

With an eye on girls' future entry into the labour market, co-operation between educational establishments and the private sector can provide added support for increasing their interest in mathematics and science-related subjects. Introducing work-related learning to high-school students and explaining what subjects are required for different career options can also enhance students' interest in particular subjects (Crowley and Niesr, 2008).

Key policy messages

- Attracting girls to typically male-dominated fields of study and *vice versa* needs to start early both in schools and at home.

- Teacher-training programmes need to include courses that raise awareness of potential gender stereotypes.

- Governments, schools, and the private sector need to explore co-operation strategies such as job information days or career fairs in schools for both parents and students in order to increase girls' interest in science-related subjects and boys' interest in the humanities and arts-related subjects. Improving the quality of teaching staff and materials can further enhance pupils' academic motivation and learning outcomes for boys and girls.

PART II

Chapter 9

Getting the job you studied for

Key findings

- Even when women pursue STEM studies they are less likely than men to end up working in physics, mathematics and engineering.
- Gender differences in fields of study appear only marginally to respond to expectations of labour market outcomes and are likely to be related to a complex set of factors such as preferences, norms, and labour market characteristics.
- There is no clear indication of systematic gender differences in mismatches of skills with jobs.

In most OECD countries, young women are now at least as likely as men to complete their university education and perform just as well, regardless of the field of study. However, as Chapter 8 describes, gender differences still condition students' chosen fields of study and may well go on to affect men's and women's jobs, the sectors in which they work, and other labour market outcomes (see Chapters 11 and 13).

Gender imbalances in university-work transition

Although gender differences systematically shape the choice of study, over 50% of tertiary graduates find work as professionals or technicians, regardless of what they studied. Figure 9.1 depicts the distribution of university graduates from different fields of study across three occupational categories: managers, professionals and technicians.

Figure 9.1. **Male and female graduates[a] who start their career in a skilled occupation[b]**

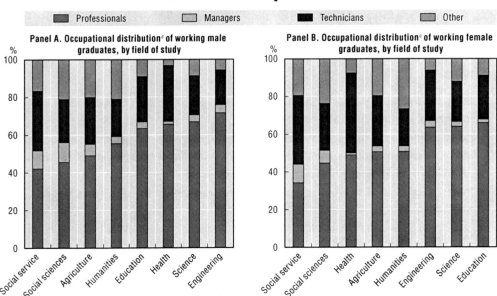

a) Fields of study are grouped into eight categories in ascending order of the proportion of graduates working as professionals.

b) The depicted occupations (i.e. managers, professionals and technicians) correspond to the main ISCO-88 categories (one-digit) (see www.ilo.org/public/english/bureau/stat/isco).

c) First job chosen after graduation.

Source: Flabbi, L. (2011), "Gender Differentials in Education, Career Choices and Labour Market Outcomes on a Sample of OECD Countries", Background paper for the OECD Gender Initiative. For more details see Figure 8.4.

StatLink ⬛⬛⬛ http://dx.doi.org/10.1787/888932675747

There are some gender differences. For both men and women the lowest proportion of professionals is observed amongst graduates from social services studies, while the highest proportion is amongst male engineering graduates and female education graduates. Furthermore, more men work in professional positions and more women are technicians. Among graduates who take up managerial positions on completing their studies the proportion of men (9.7%) is almost twice that of women (5.7%).

Even though differences in occupational choices can be traced back to differences in educational choices, occupational segregation is further reinforced in the transition from post-secondary education to employment. Figure 9.2 links the field of study to the choice of a career in teaching or in physics, mathematics and engineering. Among university graduates who work as professionals or technicians, about 66% of the female graduates who studied humanities work as teachers, compared with about 53% of male graduates. Conversely, 71% of male graduates from the science field work as professionals in physics, mathematics and engineering, as opposed to 43% of female graduates. In other words, even if women choose STEM subjects they are less likely to pursue a science career than men, although there is no gender difference in performance.

Figure 9.2. **Men and women who graduated from the same field often make different occupational choices**[a]

Distribution of graduates working as professionals and technicians by field of study and occupation

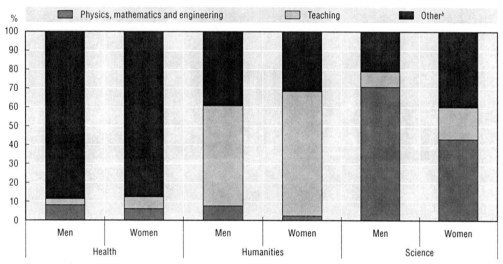

a) First job chosen after graduation.
b) "Other" includes all other professional and technical occupation fields.
Source: Flabbi, L. and M. Tejada (2012), "Fields of Study Choices, Occupational Choices and Gender Differentials", Background paper for the OECD Gender Initiative. For more details see Figure 8.4.

StatLink 🔗 http://dx.doi.org/10.1787/888932675766

Gender differences in the choice of field of study appear to be related to a complex set of factors. Flabbi and Tejada (2012) find that gender differences in the choice of field of study only marginally respond to expectations about labour market outcomes, as measured by wages and occupational segregation in a given occupation. The reasons that girls and boys make different choices in their educational career are thus presumed to be related to a range of factors, such as the historical predominance of men in manual occupations, innate preferences, considerations of future family obligations, as well as gender perceptions at home and amongst peers and teachers. The importance of socio-cultural factors is substantiated by the fact that employment expectations among 15 year-olds already attest gender segregation, regardless of differences in economic context and education system (OECD, 2012c). Although girls expect higher status

Box 9.1. **Adult learning in OECD countries**

Lifelong skills development enhances both individuals' human capital through greater personal and professional development and countries' economic growth through greater labour force employability and productivity. Across OECD countries in 2007, 41% of adults participated in learning activities (OECD, 2012d). The figure below shows no clear cross-national gender pattern in participation rates in adult education. The greatest gender difference in participation rates is recorded in Finland (12%, to the advantage of women), while no significant gender differences can be observed for Greece and Spain. In OECD countries, participation in adult learning declines with age and increases with educational attainment for both men and women (OECD, 2012d).

Participation of women and men in adult education*a* varies across countries

Percentage of 25-64 years old participating in adult education,*a* 2007*b*

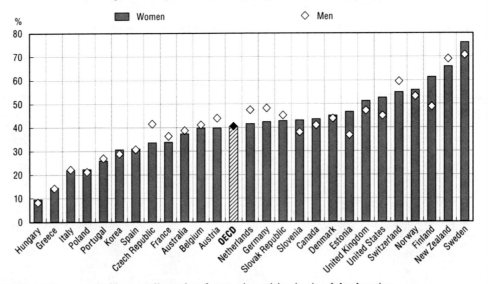

Note: Countries are ranked in ascending order of women's participation in adult education.
a) Adult learning includes formal and/or non-formal learning.
b) 2008 for Belgium, Canada, the Czech Republic, and the Netherlands; 2006 for Denmark, France, Finland, New Zealand, Hungary, Italy, Poland, and the United Kingdom; and 2005 for Sweden and the United States.
Source: OECD (2012), *Education at a Glance: OECD Indicators*, OECD Publishing, Paris.

StatLink ⫛ http://dx.doi.org/10.1787/888932675785

There are, however, significant gender differences in the number of hours spent in job-related education (*OECD Education at a Glance*, online data). In the majority of OECD countries, men spend on average four hours more than women in job-related education over their working lives. The widest disparities are observed in the Netherlands (19 hours) and in Norway (16 hours). The most striking exceptions are Finland and France where adult women receive on average 15 and 10 hours respectively more training than men. In Finland, women's active participation in work-related training can be traced back to 1990s. Between 1990 and 2006, participation in job-related education increased from 48% to 57% among women and only from 41% to 45% among men (see Panel A in the figure below). If schooling and training for the entire adult population (18-64 years) is considered, the participation rate of women has been at least 10 percentage points higher than that of men since 1980 (see Panel B in the figure below).

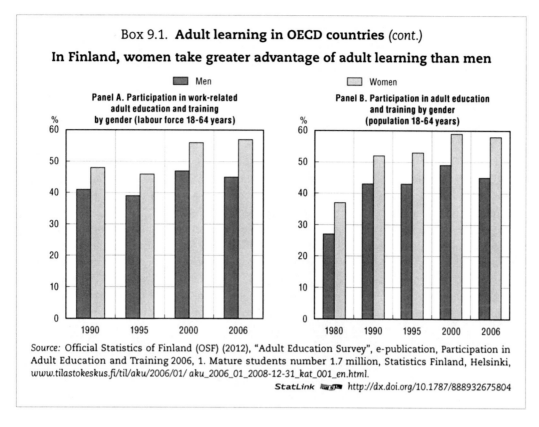

Box 9.1. **Adult learning in OECD countries** *(cont.)*

In Finland, women take greater advantage of adult learning than men

◼ Men   ◻ Women

Panel A. Participation in work-related adult education and training by gender (labour force 18-64 years)

Panel B. Participation in adult education and training by gender (population 18-64 years)

Source: Official Statistics of Finland (OSF) (2012), "Adult Education Survey", e-publication, Participation in Adult Education and Training 2006, 1. Mature students number 1.7 million, Statistics Finland, Helsinki, *www.tilastokeskus.fi/til/aku/2006/01/ aku_2006_01_2008-12-31_kat_001_en.html.*

StatLink http://dx.doi.org/10.1787/888932675804

employment than boys and more of them look forward to a career in health and medicine (*ibid.*), only 5% on average anticipate a career in engineering and computing compared with 18% of boys in OECD countries.

In OECD countries, women dominate teaching (especially at the lower levels of education). The 2008 OECD Teaching and Learning International Survey (TALIS) found that, on average, almost 70% of lower secondary school teachers were women. On the other hand, education management is, to a large extent, the province of men. Women were also more likely to teach languages, the arts (79%) and human sciences (57%), rather than mathematics and science (49%) (OECD, 2012c). This segregation within the teaching profession is a concern since it further reinforces existing gender stereotypes amongst students.

Gender skills mismatch real or perceived?

The mismatch between girls' aspirations and their actual career achievements is a cause for concern since well-educated women often end up in jobs where they do not use their full potential and skills. In addition to loss of talent, OECD findings show that being over-qualified and over-skilled reduces job satisfaction and increases the likelihood of women conducting on-the-job searches for fresh employment, which is likely to reduce productivity (OECD, 2011d).

Certain fields of study are associated with higher incidences of over-qualification. For instance, just over 10% of workers with qualifications in personal care services and teaching are over-qualified, compared with almost 30% of those with a background in social studies (Quintini, 2011). Women usually dominate such occupations, which may suggest that women are more likely to be over-qualified because of their educational background rather than their gender *per se*. Conversely, Quintini (2011) finds that women are more likely to be under-qualified than men, which could partly be driven by women's perceptions of their own abilities, which is borne out by Flabbi and Tejada (2012) who show that women more frequently declare they are under-qualified for their jobs. The mixed and, in some instances, counter-intuitive evidence of gender differences in skills assessment points to the need for further research in this area (Box 9.2).

Box 9.2. **A survey of adult skills**

The mismatch between workers' skills on one hand and job requirements on the other has been an ongoing concern of policy makers in the fields of education and employment. Since government investment in education and training is usually large, unused and misused human capital are a considerable waste of investment. Indeed, there is an increasing polarisation of skills in modern economies, whereby highly skilled workers are needed for technology-related jobs and low-skilled workers are hired for services that cannot be automated (e.g. personal care). The consequences for female labour market outcomes are significant because women are over-represented in low-skilled sectors and are consequently being pushed into low paying jobs. There is general agreement that the long-term trend in skills needs is towards jobs that require more education and cognitive skills (OECD, 2012e). To avoid further marginalisation of women in the labour market, therefore, a better understanding of how women's and men's skills are acquired and matched or mismatched throughout their working lives is essential.

A promising avenue is the new data being collected through an OECD survey of adult skills (the Programme for the International Assessment of Adult Competencies [PIAAC]) since it will measure skills (across age groups) along with indicators of the extent to which skills are used at work (OECD, 2012e). This approach will afford new insights into consequences for gender-related occupational differences and may suggest new ways of encouraging boys and girls to move away from traditional career choices.

How can governments change career stereotypes?

As suggested above, education performance or expectations about labour market outcomes do not shape gender differences in post-secondary fields of study, that are instead influenced by culture, students' attitudes and self-perception formed around or before the age of 15. Particular focus should therefore be placed on pupils still in school in addition to programmes that encourage non-traditional occupational choices among young people.

Supporting pupils with careful guidance on further study and university students with career advice that challenges stereotyped assumptions (e.g. "Carrefour des métiers" in France) can assist in encouraging "atypical" educational and occupational choices among young men and women. Other initiatives that seek to address early roots of segregation are motivational events and educational programmes. One example is the nationwide campaign in the United Kingdom, Women Into Science and Engineering (WISE), which aims to encourage young women to study mathematics and physics and consider careers in the areas of science, engineering and construction. First launched in 1984, WISE may have contributed to the doubling of the percentage of female engineering graduates from 7% in 1984 to 15% in 2009 (European Commission, 2009a).

It has been found that female mentors play an important role in attracting students into STEM careers and keeping them there. Accordingly, the US Department of Energy (DoE) created a mentoring programme that matches female college students with successful employees in the DoE (White House Council, 2012).

While many similar initiatives primarily encourage girls to enter male-dominated areas of work, there are also efforts to draw boys into predominantly female occupations such as teaching or caring. Examples include information drives such as the parallel campaigns "Girls' Day" and "New Pathways for Boys" in Germany and educational events like "National Future Day" in Switzerland. Some of these initiatives involve the participation of private firms (European Commission, 2009b), which helps smooth students' transition from education into the labour market (European Commission, 2010; IET, 2007; Lord and Jones, 2006; Mann, 2012).

Key policy messages

- Promoting early work experience through education programmes and apprenticeships could encourage women, particularly those who successfully completed STEM-related studies, to work in scientific fields.

- Careful career guidance and counselling at schools and universities can help young men and women to better match their acquired skills with the career path they choose.

- The OECD Programme for the International Assessment of Adult Competencies can help to build a data system that enables the assessment of available skills at the national level, informs skills policies, and minimises skills mismatches in the economy.

PART II

Chapter 10

Financial education for financial empowerment

Key findings

- Current evidence suggests that women typically have lower levels of financial literacy than men, exhibiting lower levels of financial knowledge and a lack of confidence in their financial skills.

- Women need to be financially literate in order to plan even more thoroughly than men for their retirement and health care expenditures, notably due to longer life expectancy.

- Both men and women need better tailored information, knowledge and skills development in order to efficiently address financial issues, make effective and confident financial decisions, and take advantage of income generation opportunities.

In the aftermath of the global financial crisis policy makers have recognised financial literacy as an essential life skill (OECD, 2009b). The growing policy attention stems from a number of factors:

- The transfer of a broad range of financial risks from governments and corporations to individuals.

- The mounting complexity of financial markets.

- The growing number of newly active consumers and investors in the financial sphere who need support and protection beyond that provided through regulation.

Financial education has become an important complement to market conduct and prudential regulation. Indeed, improving individuals' financial literacy is now a long-term policy priority in many developed and developing countries. The potential gains from financial education are substantial. Academic research shows that higher levels of financial knowledge are associated with a range of beneficial behaviour and positive outcomes, such as careful budgeting, controlled spending, planning for retirement, the accumulation of wealth, and the ability to understand the benefits of participating in financial markets (Hilgert et al., 2003; Lusardi and Mitchell, 2007; Perry and Morris, 2005; van Rooij et al., 2011; Stango and Zinman, 2009).

Box 10.1. **Defining financial education**

Financial education is the process by which individuals improve their understanding of financial products and concepts; and through information, instruction and/or objective advice develop the skills and confidence to become more aware of financial risks and opportunities, to make informed choices, to know where to go for help, and to take other effective actions to improve their financial well-being and protection (OECD, 2005).

Women must be sufficiently financially literate if they are to participate more effectively in economic activities and financial decision making in their households and communities. They should, for example, be able to access and choose the appropriate financial services to protect themselves and their families and to develop entrepreneurial activities (see Chapter 26). Such an ability is of special concern with the increasing prevalence of single-parent families, typically headed by women. Governments and development organisations have attempted to empower women by improving their financial literacy so that they can successfully start and manage small-scale or micro-enterprises (Hung et al., 2012). Examples of such programmes include: Australia, as a development activity for low-income countries (Australian Government, 2009); Cambodia (ILO, 2012b); Canada, for aboriginal women entrepreneurs (AANDC, 2010); Lebanon (Hung et al., 2012); and Uganda (Nordic Consulting Group, 2011).

Box 10.2 outlines some additional examples of how countries address gender-related differences in financial literacy.

Box 10.2. **Addressing gender differences in financial literacy**

Various countries, both developed and developing, have acknowledged the need to address the financial literacy of women and girls by studying their specific needs and implementing financial education programmes targeted at various subgroups.

In 2008, in a first step to help women build their financial security, Australia conducted the "Women Understanding Money" research campaign in order to identify the needs of women and girls. Analogously, the New Zealand Commission for Financial Literacy and Retirement Income is undertaking research into women's future retirement prospects in the country as part of an approach to address women's lower retirement outcomes.

Several other countries are engaged in developing programmes that exclusively or mainly target vulnerable women and girls. For example, Canada's "National Initiative for the Care of the Elderly" (NICE) holds money management workshops for low-income older women in Vancouver, Montreal and Toronto. Similarly, the Capital Markets Board (CMB) of Turkey launched a financial literacy programme in 2010 for unemployed, unbanked, and low-income women consisting of short seminars delivered by CMB experts. From Colombia, the project "Mujeres Ahorradorras en Acción" (Active Women Savers), launched in 2007 by the Presidential Agency for Social Action and International Co-operation, offers an example of a financial education programme dedicated to encouraging the use of formal saving products by women.

Several OECD countries also fund financial literacy programmes for women in developing countries. The UK Department for International Development (DFID) funded financial literacy training for girls and young women in rural areas of Zambia. It also contributed to funding a Population Council programme delivering financial education training and access to savings products for adolescent girls in Kenya and Uganda. Similarly, the Canadian International Development Agency (CIDA) is supporting financial education initiatives with a focus on female micro-entrepreneurs both in Pakistan and the Philippines.

Women are also more likely to take primary responsibility for child-rearing, make important decisions about allocation of household resources, and take a lead role in the education of their children on financial matters. This is an important issue given that the financial literacy of students is closely correlated with their mothers' education (Lusardi *et al.*, 2010).

Policy makers have not yet widely recognised the potential benefits of knowing the current levels of financial literacy amongst women and addressing any shortfalls. A recent stocktaking exercise across members of the OECD International Network on Financial Education (OECD/INFE) found that just eight of the 27 respondent countries recognised that the financial literacy of women and girls was an important issue (Hung *et al.*, 2012). And, because academics have not paid much attention to the question either, there is little research evidence. Nevertheless, it is possible to draw on existing survey data to identify differences in levels of financial literacy by gender and the associated policy issues.

Women have less financial knowledge and confidence

Short tests of financial knowledge around the world have shown that women have lower levels of financial knowledge than men. Lusardi and Mitchell (2011) report evidence from studies on eight countries – Germany, Italy, Japan, the Netherlands, New Zealand, the Russian Federation, Sweden, and the United States. These findings are largely confirmed by the responses to a set of eight knowledge questions used in the OECD/INFE financial literacy measurement survey (Atkinson and Messy, 2012). The survey includes a test of basic financial numeracy, as well as understanding of terms and concepts such as inflation, the time value of money, and the effect of compound interest rates. Figure 10.1 shows that the test scores of women are somewhat below those of men.

Figure 10.1. **Women have slightly lower levels of financial knowledge than men**

Mean number of correct responses (from minimum = 0 to maximum = 8)[a]

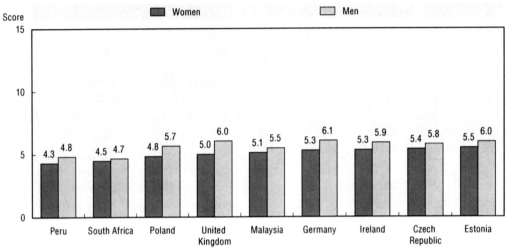

Note: Sample size ranges from 993 in Estonia to 3 112 in South Africa. Countries are arranged from left to right in ascending order of women's financial knowledge.

a) Differences are significant at the 5% level for each country.

Source: Atkinson, A. and F. Messy (2012), "Measuring Financial Literacy: Results of the OECD/International Network on Financial Education (INFE) Pilot Study", *OECD Working Papers on Finance, Insurance and Private Pensions*, No. 15, OECD Publishing, Paris.

StatLink ⌷⌷⌷ *http://dx.doi.org/10.1787/888932675823*

Women are also more likely than men to say they do not know the answer to a financial knowledge question rather than attempt to answer it (Lusardi and Mitchell, 2011). Moreover, they have been shown to have lower levels of confidence in both their knowledge and their ability with complex financial issues (Australian Government, 2008). Evidence suggests that gender differences in levels of confidence in financial knowledge start in school (the Capital One survey [2009] reports evidence from the United States). The combination of lower levels of knowledge and a lack of confidence means that women are less likely to feel capable when dealing with financial issues, services, and providers. They therefore fail to grasp potential opportunities for income generation through entrepreneurship or investment or apply for credit to develop their business potential (Morcos and Sebstad, 2011).

A wide range of factors influence women's generally lower levels of financial knowledge. Two particularly prominent ones are the socio-cultural context and access to financial services. For example, women's understanding and experience is partly shaped by the extent of their involvement in long-term financial investment strategies and related choices of financial products at the household level. Against that background, financial dependency on husbands or other male family members may be expected to impair the ability to learn from experience and the associated opportunities for improving self-confidence.

Financial education could start at school

Financial education is a complex, long-term process which involves changing individuals' attitudes, knowledge and behaviour in order to support more "savvy" financial decision making (OECD, 2005). Data also show that young people have lower levels of financial literacy than their elders, as Figure 10.2 illustrates with regard to women. What is more, adults with lower levels of education and those on low incomes are typically less financially literate than the general population (Atkinson and Messy, 2012). The 2012 PISA exercise and its new financial literacy option is a first international attempt to provide more detailed evidence on 15 year-olds' financial knowledge and their ability to apply it (OECD, 2010e and 2012f).

Figure 10.2. **Young women typically have lower levels of financial literacy than their elders**

Women's mean score for financial literacy^a (from minimum = 0 to maximum = 22)^b

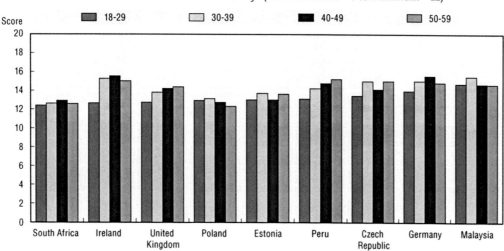

Note: See notes to Figure 10.1. Countries are arranged from left to right in ascending order of female financial literacy for 18-29 years old.

a) This score combines knowledge, behaviour and attitudes.

b) Differences are significant at the 5% level for the Czech Republic, Germany, Ireland, Peru and the United Kingdom.

Source: Atkinson, A. and F. Messy (2012), "Measuring Financial Literacy: Results of the OECD/International Network on Financial Education (INFE) Pilot Study", OECD *Working Paper on Finance, Insurance and Private Pensions*, No. 15, OECD Publishing, Paris.

StatLink ᵐˢ⁼ *http://dx.doi.org/10.1787/888932675842*

Against this backdrop, quality financial education in schools has the potential to bridge the income, gender and age gaps and influence students' financial attitudes and present behaviours (Elliot *et al.*, 2010). This explains why 23 out of 38 countries surveyed by the OECD/INFE had some form of financial education in schools in 2011 (Australia, the Czech Republic, Germany, Japan, New Zealand, South Africa, Spain and the United States were just some of those countries). The OECD/INFE is about to complete a three-year project which will provide specific guidance to policy makers to help them efficiently address challenges involved in introducing and developing financial literacy in schools. The project will also include the development of a learning framework for financial education (OECD, 2012g).

Women's money management and long-term planning

A number of national studies in OECD countries and the OECD/INFE survey suggest that women may be better than men in such short-term money management abilities as keeping an eye on their everyday expenditure (Atkinson et al., 2006; Atkinson and Messy, 2012; Irish Financial Regulator, 2009; McKay, 2011). At the same time, country evidence also suggests that women may be less likely than men to make long-term financial plans. In the United States, for example, over 50% of men, but only 45% of women, have set aside an emergency fund covering expenses for three months. Similarly, 45% of men and 39% of women have tried to assess how much they need to save for retirement (FINRA Investor Education Foundation, 2009). In the United Kingdom, a composite measure of attitudes and behaviour relating to long term planning suggests that women appear to be slightly worse at planning ahead than men – even after taking into account such explanatory factors as income or working status (Atkinson et al., 2006).

As women have to manage greater financial risks – they typically live longer than men but have lower life-time earnings – it is important that they are well equipped to carry out long-term financial planning, such as for retirement. The OECD will explore these issues in greater detail in 2012-13.

An interesting point to emerge from the OECD/INFE survey is that women appear at least as likely as men, if not more so, to have a positive attitude towards long-term financial planning. They should therefore be receptive to well-designed policies that strengthen their knowledge and encourage behavioural changes which could further improve their overall financial well-being and that of their households.

Key policy messages

Differences in financial literacy and behaviour by gender should be explored further: i) to gain a deeper understanding of the specific aspects of financial literacy that might negatively affect the financial well-being of women; and ii) design better targeted policy interventions. Given that financial literacy is a relatively new area of research, work in this area should focus primarily on:

- Gaining further insight into the gender differences in financial literacy and behaviours through internationally comparable surveys using the OECD/INFE Financial Literacy Core Questionnaire for adults and the PISA financial literacy international option introduced in 2012 for 15 year-olds.

- Developing financial education programmes tailored to girls' and women's needs and preferences. Such programmes should build on the current state of knowledge and good practice identified by the OECD/INFE and include – but are not limited to – financial education in schools in order to reach girls before they lose confidence in their abilities.

- Financial education programmes should incorporate regular monitoring to identify any divergence in expectations, confidence, or outcomes between male and female participants and to evaluate effectiveness.

ANNEX II.A1

Supplementary tables to Chapter 4

Table II.A1.1. **Adjusted primary school net enrolment rates, 2000 and 2010**

Total number of pupils of the official primary school age who are enrolled at primary or secondary education levels,
expressed as a percentage of the eligible official primary school age population

Region, country or economy[b]	2000				2010			
	All	Male	Female	GPI[a]	All	Male	Female	GPI[a]
OECD	**97.6**	**97.6**	**97.6**	**1.00**	**98.2**	**98.0**	**98.3**	**1.00**
Australia	94.6	94.2	95.0	1.01	97.2[m]	96.9[m]	97.5[m]	1.01[m]
Austria	90.1[d]	89.6[d]	90.6[d]	1.01[d]	..	..	..	..
Belgium	99.2	99.0	99.4	1.00	99.0[m]	98.9[m]	99.2[m]	1.00[m]
Canada	99.8[d]	99.6[d]	99.9[d]	1.00[d]	..	..	..	..
Chile	..	..	..	..	93.8[m]	94.0[m]	93.6[m]	1.00[m]
Czech Republic	95.9[d]	95.8[d]	96.0[d]	1.00[d]	..	..	..	..
Denmark	98.1	97.7	98.5	1.01	96.0[m]	94.9[m]	97.1[m]	1.02[m]
Estonia	99.3	99.4	99.2	1.00	96.3[m]	96.5[m]	96.0[m]	1.00[m]
Finland	99.7[e]	99.7[e]	99.8[e]	1.00[e]	97.6[m]	97.5[m]	97.7[m]	1.00[m]
France	99.7	99.5	99.8	1.00	99.2[i]	99.1[i]	99.3[i]	1.00[i]
Germany	84.5[c]	83.7[c]	85.2[c]	1.02[c]	..	..	..	..
Greece	97.7	97.6	97.9	1.00	98.5[k]	98.3[k]	98.7[k]	1.00[k]
Hungary	97.5	97.3	97.7	1.00	98.0[m]	97.8[m]	98.1[m]	1.00[m]
Iceland	99.2	100.0	98.3	0.98	99.4[m]	99.3[m]	99.6[m]	1.00[m]
Ireland	93.8	93.6	94.1	1.01	98.2[m]	97.5[m]	98.9[m]	1.01[m]
Israel*	97.9	98.1	97.6	1.00	97.0[m]	96.7[m]	97.3[m]	1.01[m]
Italy	99.7	99.8	99.7	1.00	99.4[m]	99.6[m]	99.2[m]	1.00[m]
Japan	..	..	..	..	..	..	..	..
Korea	99.8	99.5	100.0	1.00	99.6[m]	100.0[m]	99.1[m]	0.99[m]
Luxembourg	97.0	96.0	98.1	1.02	96.8[l]	96.1[l]	97.6[l]	1.02[l]
Mexico	99.5	99.1	99.9	1.01	99.6[m]	99.4[m]	99.8[m]	1.00[m]
Netherlands	99.4	100.0	98.8	0.99	99.4[k]	99.9[k]	98.9[k]	0.99[k]
New Zealand	99.0	98.8	99.1	1.00	99.5[m]	99.4[m]	99.6[m]	1.00[m]
Norway	99.7	99.6	99.8	1.00	99.0[m]	98.8[m]	99.1[m]	1.00[m]
Poland	97.5	97.7	97.2	0.99	96.0[m]	96.1[m]	95.9[m]	1.00[m]
Portugal	99.4[f]	99.3[f]	99.4[f]	1.00[f]	99.4[m]	99.2[m]	99.5[m]	1.00[m]
Slovak Republic	..	..	..	..	..	..	..	..
Slovenia	95.3	94.2	96.4	1.02	97.2[m]	97.3[m]	97.1[m]	1.00[m]
Spain	99.9	100.0	99.9	1.00	99.9[m]	99.9[m]	99.9[m]	1.00[m]
Sweden	99.4	99.7	99.1	0.99	99.3[m]	99.6[m]	99.0[m]	0.99[m]
Switzerland	99.3	98.9	99.7	1.01	98.9[m]	98.6[m]	99.1[m]	1.01[m]
Turkey	96.0	99.9	91.9	0.92	97.5[m]	98.2[m]	96.7[m]	0.98[m]
United Kingdom	100.0	100.0	100.0	1.00	99.8[m]	99.9[m]	99.7[m]	1.00[m]
United States	97.0	97.1	97.0	1.00	96.9[m]	95.9[m]	97.9[m]	1.02[m]

Table II.A1.1. **Adjusted primary school net enrolment rates, 2000 and 2010** (cont.)

Total number of pupils of the official primary school age who are enrolled at primary or secondary education levels, expressed as a percentage of the eligible official primary school age population

Region, country or economy[b]	2000				2010			
	All	Male	Female	GPI[a]	All	Male	Female	GPI[a]
Caribbean	**91.9**	**91.9**	**91.9**	**1.00**	**91.8**	**91.6**	**92.1**	**1.01**
Anguilla	99.3[e]	99.0[e]	99.6[e]	1.01[e]	92.9[l]	92.7[l]	93.0[l]	1.00[l]
Antigua and Barbuda	..	..	..	..	87.8	91.1	84.5	0.93
Aruba	98.7	99.0	98.4	0.99	99.7	99.5	99.9	1.00
Bahamas	87.7	88.7	86.7	0.98	95.1[l]	94.0[l]	96.2[l]	1.02[l]
Barbados	94.7	91.7	98.0	1.07	93.4[k]	89.8[k]	97.5[k]	1.09[k]
Bermuda	..	..	..	..	..	..	..	..
British Virgin Islands	95.5[h]	95.4[h]	95.5[h]	1.00[h]	95.0[m]	95.2[m]	94.7[m]	0.99[m]
Cayman Islands	93.8[f]	92.3[f]	95.3[f]	1.03[f]	83.9[l]	83.4[l]	84.4[l]	1.01[l]
Cuba	98.1	98.4	97.8	0.99	99.8	100.0	99.7	1.00
Dominica	..	..	..	..	95.5[l]	94.6[l]	96.4[l]	1.02[l]
Dominican Republic	84.8	84.3	85.3	1.01	93.0	95.5	90.4	0.95
Grenada	83.2	86.6	79.8	0.92	97.5[m]	95.7[m]	99.3[m]	1.04[m]
Haiti	..	..	..	..	..	..	..	..
Jamaica	93.8	94.0	93.7	1.00	82.8[m]	83.8[m]	81.9[m]	0.98[m]
Montserrat	..	..	..	..	..	..	..	..
Puerto Rico	..	..	..	..	85.9	83.5	88.4	1.06
Saint Kitts and Nevis	..	..	..	..	86.0	85.8	86.2	1.0
Saint Lucia	96.8	97.4	96.2	0.99	89.7	90.2	89.2	0.99
Saint Vincent and the Grenadines	..	..	..	..	98.3[l]	99.5[l]	97.0[l]	1.0[l]
Trinidad and Tobago	93.5	93.2	93.8	1.01	95.9[m]	97.5[m]	94.4[m]	0.97[m]
Turks and Caicos Islands	75.2[g]	75.3[g]	75.0[g]	1.0[g]	80.7[l]	77.5[l]	83.9[l]	1.1[l]
Central America	**88.9**	**89.8**	**88.0**	**0.98**	**96.3**	**97.0**	**95.7**	**0.99**
Belize	90.0	93.7	86.4	0.92	95.1[l]	99.7[l]	90.7[l]	0.91[l]
Costa Rica	..	..	..	..	..	..	..	..
El Salvador	86.0[e]	85.4[e]	86.5[e]	1.01[e]	94.6[m]	94.1[m]	95.0[m]	1.01[m]
Guatemala	86.7	90.0	83.4	0.93	98.6	99.6	97.6	0.98
Honduras	88.8	88.4	89.2	1.01	97.2	95.9	98.4	1.03
Nicaragua	83.2	82.4	84.1	1.02	93.9	93.2	94.5	1.01
Panama	98.6	98.7	98.6	1.00	98.7	99.1	98.2	0.99
South America	**96.3**	**96.2**	**96.4**	**1.00**	**92.7**	**92.6**	**92.9**	**1.00**
Argentina	99.4[d]	99.8[d]	98.9[d]	0.99[d]	..	..	..	..
Bolivia (Plurinational State of)	96.2	96.1	96.3	1.00	95.5[k]	95.2[k]	95.8[k]	1.01[k]
Brazil	94.5[h]	96.8[h]	92.1[h]	0.95[h]	95.1[l]	95.9[l]	94.2[l]	0.98[l]
Colombia	96.8	96.9	96.8	1.00	91.5	91.7	91.3	1.00
Ecuador	99.2[d]	98.5[d]	99.9[d]	1.01[d]	..	..	..	..
Guyana	98.3[g]	98.1[g]	98.4[g]	1.00[g]	84.1	82.4	85.9	1.04
Paraguay	97.9	97.5	98.2	1.01	85.7[m]	85.7[m]	85.7[m]	1.00[m]
Peru	99.5[c]	99.7[c]	99.4[c]	1.00[c]	97.2[m]	97.0[m]	97.5[m]	1.01[m]
Suriname	92.4[e]	90.4[e]	94.4[e]	1.04[e]	90.9[m]	90.9[m]	91.0[m]	1.00[m]
Uruguay	..	..	..	..	99.5[m]	99.8[m]	99.2[m]	0.99[m]
Venezuela (Bolivarian Republic of)	89.3	88.6	90.0	1.02	94.9	94.7	95.1	1.00
East Asia and the Pacific	**91.7**	**92.0**	**91.3**	**0.99**	**91.8**	**92.1**	**91.5**	**0.99**
Brunei Darussalam	..	..	..	..	..	..	..	..
Cambodia	90.5	94.4	86.6	0.92	95.9	96.4	95.4	0.99
China	..	..	..	..	..	..	..	..
China, Hong Kong Special Administrative Region	93.0[e]	93.4[e]	92.6[e]	0.99[e]	96.8[m]	96.2[m]	97.5[m]	1.01[m]
China, Macao Special Administrative Region	86.0	84.5	87.7	1.04	82.6	81.0	84.3	1.04
Cook Islands	94.3	93.0	95.9	1.03	98.7[k]	99.3[k]	97.9[k]	0.99[k]

Table II.A1.1. **Adjusted primary school net enrolment rates, 2000 and 2010** (cont.)

Total number of pupils of the official primary school age who are enrolled at primary or secondary education levels, expressed as a percentage of the eligible official primary school age population

Region, country or economy[b]	2000				2010			
	All	Male	Female	GPI[a]	All	Male	Female	GPI[a]
Fiji	94.7	94.7	94.7	1.00	99.1[m]	98.8[m]	99.3[m]	1.00[m]
Indonesia	94.0	95.6	92.3	0.97	95.1[i]	96.7[i]	93.5[i]	0.97[i]
Kiribati	..	..	..	..	..	..	..	..
Korea, Democratic People's Republic of	..	..	..	..	..	..	..	..
Lao People's Democratic Republic	78.1	81.3	74.7	0.92	89.0[l]	90.8[l]	87.0[l]	0.96[l]
Malaysia	97.8	97.8	97.8	1.00	..	..	..	..
Marshall Islands	85.0[e]	85.0[e]	85.1[e]	1.00[e]	..	..	..	..
Micronesia (Federated States of)	..	..	..	..	..	..	..	..
Mongolia	91.8	90.9	92.8	1.02	98.1[m]	98.3[m]	97.8[m]	0.99[m]
Myanmar	..	..	..	..	..	..	..	..
Nauru	..	..	..	..	..	..	..	..
Niue	98.5[d]	98.6[d]	98.4[d]	1.00[d]	..	..	..	..
Palau	..	..	..	..	..	..	..	..
Papua New Guinea	..	..	..	..	..	..	..	..
Philippines	89.8[d]	89.5[d]	90.1[d]	1.01[d]	88.7[m]	87.9[m]	89.5[m]	1.02[m]
Samoa	92.2	91.5	93.0	1.02	..	..	..	..
Singapore	..	..	..	..	..	..	..	..
Solomon Islands	..	..	..	..	82.0[k]	82.9[k]	81.1[k]	0.98[k]
Thailand	..	..	..	..	89.7[m]	90.0[m]	89.4[m]	0.99[m]
Timor-Leste	..	..	..	..	85.9	86.2	85.6	0.99
Tonga	..	..	..	..	..	..	..	..
Vanuatu	97.7[d]	98.3[d]	97.0[d]	0.99[d]	..	..	..	..
Viet Nam	..	..	..	..	..	..	..	..
Southern Asia	**76.5**	**81.4**	**71.3**	**0.87**	**91.7**	**92.3**	**91.0**	**0.98**
Afghanistan	..	..	..	..	..	..	..	..
Bangladesh	..	..	..	..	95.5[m]	91.2[m]	100.0[m]	1.10[m]
Bhutan	58.5	61.5	55.5	0.90	88.9[m]	87.6[m]	90.2[m]	1.03[m]
India	84.8	92.1	76.8	0.83	96.1[k]	97.8[k]	94.2[k]	0.96[k]
Iran (Islamic Republic of)	85.7	87.1	84.2	0.97	96.7[i]	97.6[i]	95.7[i]	0.98[i]
Maldives	98.6	98.0	99.2	1.01	96.8[n]	96.7[n]	96.8[n]	1.00[n]
Nepal	73.5	80.6	66.0	0.82	..	..	..	..
Pakistan	57.9[e]	68.9[e]	46.3[e]	0.67[e]	74.1	81.3	66.5	0.82
Sri Lanka	..	..	..	..	93.7[m]	93.5[m]	93.9[m]	1.00[m]
Eastern Europe and Central Asia	**94.1**	**94.6**	**93.7**	**0.99**	**92.8**	**92.7**	**92.9**	**1.00**
Albania	96.5[g]	97.5[g]	95.4[g]	0.98[g]	78.8	78.5	79.1	1.01
Armenia	93.2[e]	92.7[e]	93.6[e]	1.01[e]	79.5	78.2	81.1	1.04
Azerbaijan	88.2	88.5	88.0	0.99	84.7	85.3	84.1	0.99
Belarus	92.4[f]	92.6[f]	92.2[f]	1.00[f]	96.1[l]	95.0[l]	97.4[l]	1.02[l]
Bosnia and Herzegovina	..	..	..	..	87.4	86.5	88.4	1.02
Bulgaria	98.1	98.9	97.3	0.98	99.3[m]	98.9[m]	99.7[m]	1.01[m]
Croatia	92.4	92.8	92.0	0.99	93.2[m]	92.9[m]	93.5[m]	1.01[m]
Cyprus[o, p]	98.1	97.8	98.4	1.01	99.1[m]	99.4[m]	98.8[m]	0.99[m]
Former Yugoslav Republic of Macedonia (FYROM)	97.8	98.1	97.4	0.99	93.9[m]	93.0[m]	94.8[m]	1.02[m]
Georgia	90.2[h]	92.1[h]	88.3[h]	0.96[h]	95.3[k]	96.3[k]	94.2[k]	0.98[k]
Kazakhstan	94.0	92.8	95.3	1.03	99.5[n]	99.4[n]	99.7[n]	1.00[n]
Kyrgyzstan	92.3	92.5	92.2	1.00	95.3	95.5	95.1	1.00
Latvia	93.9[d]	94.3[d]	93.4[d]	0.99[d]	94.6[m]	94.1[m]	95.1[m]	1.01[m]
Lithuania	98.0	97.8	98.2	1.00	96.7[m]	96.5[m]	96.9[m]	1.00[m]
Moldova, Republic of	92.6	93.0	92.1	0.99	90.1	90.1	90.1	1.00
Montenegro	..	..	..	..	..	..	..	..

Table II.A1.1. **Adjusted primary school net enrolment rates, 2000 and 2010** *(cont.)*

Total number of pupils of the official primary school age who are enrolled at primary or secondary education levels, expressed as a percentage of the eligible official primary school age population

Region, country or economy[b]	2000				2010			
	All	Male	Female	GPI[a]	All	Male	Female	GPI[a]
Romania	92.7	92.9	92.6	1.00	92.4[m]	92.4[m]	92.5[m]	1.00[m]
Russian Federation	..	..	..	..	95.7[m]	95.1[m]	96.3[m]	1.01[m]
Serbia	..	..	..	..	94.5	94.7	94.4	1.00
Tajikistan	96.1	99.3	92.8	0.93	97.8	99.5	96.0	0.96
Turkmenistan	..	..	..	..	..	..	..	..
Ukraine	93.8[f]	93.9[f]	93.7[f]	1.00[f]	91.1	90.8	91.5	1.01
Uzbekistan	..	..	..	..	92.8[n]	94.1[n]	91.5[n]	0.97[n]
Middle East and North Africa	**88.5**	**90.3**	**86.6**	**0.95**	**94.1**	**94.9**	**93.3**	**0.98**
Algeria	93.0	94.5	91.5	0.97	97.3	98.2	96.4	0.98
Bahrain	98.4	97.1	99.8	1.03	99.3[j]	99.1[j]	99.6[j]	1.01[j]
Egypt	93.7	96.6	90.6	0.94	98.0[m]	99.7[m]	96.2[m]	0.96[m]
Iraq	87.4	93.4	81.0	0.87	89.2[k]	94.5[k]	83.7[k]	0.89[k]
Jordan	94.8	94.2	95.5	1.01	94.0[l]	93.1[l]	95.0[l]	1.02[l]
Kuwait	95.7	94.9	96.5	1.02	98.2[l]	96.6[l]	100.0[l]	1.03[l]
Lebanon	94.1[d]	95.4[d]	92.8[d]	0.97[d]	93.2	93.5	92.9	0.99
Morocco	76.3	80.7	71.6	0.89	96.2[n]	96.8[n]	95.6[n]	0.99[n]
Oman	82.4	81.3	83.5	1.03	98.1	97.9	98.4	1.01
Palestinian Authority	92.8	93.0	92.6	1.00	89.2	89.8	88.5	0.99
Qatar	96.2	93.0	99.8	1.07	96.2	95.7	96.6	1.01
Saudi Arabia	..	..	..	..	89.9[m]	90.4[m]	89.4[m]	0.99[m]
Syrian Arab Republic	..	..	..	..	99.1[m]	99.8[m]	98.4[m]	0.99[m]
Tunisia	96.5	98.1	94.8	0.97	..	..	..	..
United Arab Emirates	81.0	80.6	81.5	1.01	95.6[j]	93.6[j]	97.7[j]	1.04[j]
Yemen	56.7[d]	71.2[d]	41.6[d]	0.58[d]	78.2	85.5	70.5	0.82
Western Africa	**59.8**	**65.5**	**54.0**	**0.81**	**73.0**	**75.9**	**70.0**	**0.92**
Benin	85.6[g]	99.9[g]	71.5[g]	0.72[g]	88.0[i]	99.8[i]	76.3[i]	0.76[i]
Burkina Faso	34.5	40.3	28.6	0.71	61.5[m]	65.1[m]	57.7[m]	0.89[m]
Cape Verde	98.8[f]	99.4[f]	98.1[f]	0.99[f]	93.5	94.6	92.4	0.98
Côte d'Ivoire	56.8	65.5	48.2	0.74	61.5[m]	67.1[m]	55.8[m]	0.83[m]
Gambia	68.0	71.6	64.4	0.90	69.4	68.3	70.6	1.03
Ghana	65.0	65.7	64.2	0.98	84.2[n]	83.8[n]	84.6[n]	1.01[n]
Guinea	46.9	53.8	39.8	0.74	77.0	83.2	70.5	0.85
Guinea-Bissau	51.2	59.8	42.6	0.71	75.0	76.7	73.3	0.96
Liberia	46.5[d]	52.3[d]	40.5[d]	0.78[d]	..	..	..	..
Mali	42.2[d]	48.7[d]	35.5[d]	0.73[d]	65.8	70.6	60.8	0.86
Mauritania	61.1	62.0	60.2	0.97	74.4	72.8	76.0	1.04
Niger	27.1	31.6	22.3	0.71	58.3	64.2	52.0	0.81
Nigeria	64.5	70.0	58.9	0.84	62.1[k]	64.8[k]	59.3[k]	0.92[k]
Senegal	60.0	63.8	56.1	0.88	78.0	75.9	80.2	1.06
Sierra Leone	..	..	..	..	..	..	..	..
Togo	88.8	98.5	79.1	0.80	..	..	..	..
Eastern and Middle Africa	**62.4**	**64.9**	**59.9**	**0.91**	**83.3**	**84.7**	**81.9**	**0.96**
Angola	53.5[c]	57.6[c]	49.4[c]	0.86[c]	85.7	93.1	78.2	0.84
Burundi	44.9	49.0	40.8	0.83	99.1[m]	98.3[m]	99.8[m]	1.02[m]
Cameroon	..	..	..	..	93.8[m]	99.6[m]	88.0[m]	0.88[m]
Central African Republic	..	..	..	..	70.9	81.3	60.6	0.75
Chad	54.6	66.0	43.1	0.65	..	..	..	..
Comoros	73.4	79.4	67.4	0.85	77.8[k]	80.7[k]	74.8[k]	0.93[k]
Congo	..	..	..	..	90.8	92.3	89.3	0.97

Table II.A1.1. Adjusted primary school net enrolment rates, 2000 and 2010 (cont.)

Total number of pupils of the official primary school age who are enrolled at primary or secondary education levels, expressed as a percentage of the eligible official primary school age population

Region, country or economy[b]	2000				2010			
	All	Male	Female	GPI[a]	All	Male	Female	GPI[a]
Congo, Democratic Republic of	33.3[d]	34.2[d]	32.3[d]	0.95[d]	..	..	..	..
Djibouti	26.8	30.5	23.1	0.76	52.0[n]	54.9[n]	49.1[n]	0.89[n]
Equatorial Guinea	76.0[e]	81.2[e]	70.7[e]	0.87[e]	56.3	56.5	56.0	0.99
Eritrea	38.0	40.7	35.2	0.87	34.9	37.2	32.5	0.87
Ethiopia	40.4	46.6	34.2	0.73	82.2	84.8	79.5	0.94
Gabon	81.4[e]	81.6[e]	81.2[e]	1.00[e]	..	..	..	..
Kenya	65.7	64.7	66.7	1.03	84.0[m]	83.5[m]	84.5[m]	1.01[m]
Madagascar	67.2	66.8	67.6	1.01	..	..	..	..
Malawi	..	..	..	..	94.3[k]	91.0[k]	97.6[k]	1.07[k]
Mauritius	92.5	92.3	92.8	1.01	93.4	92.4	94.4	1.02
Mozambique	56.0	61.8	50.2	0.81	92.0	94.6	89.4	0.94
Rwanda	75.9[e]	74.9[e]	76.9[e]	1.03[e]	90.6[l]	89.0[l]	92.2[l]	1.04[l]
Sao Tome and Principe	89.5[d]	89.8[d]	89.2[d]	0.99[d]	97.3[l]	96.6[l]	97.9[l]	1.01[l]
Seychelles	91.8[e]	91.3[e]	92.4[e]	1.01[e]	95.1[i]	96.3[i]	94.0[i]	0.98[i]
Somalia	..	..	..	..	..	..	..	..
Sudan	..	..	..	..	..	..	..	..
Uganda	..	..	..	..	91.0	89.7	92.3	1.03
Tanzania, United Republic of	53.1	52.4	53.8	1.03	92.1	91.3	92.9	1.02
Zambia	71.0	71.7	70.2	0.98	92.7	91.4	93.9	1.03
Zimbabwe	..	..	..	..	..	..	..	..
Southern Africa	**82.6**	**80.7**	**84.4**	**1.05**	**84.3**	**83.3**	**85.3**	**1.02**
Botswana	81.0	79.3	82.8	1.04	85.8[k]	84.9[k]	86.7[k]	1.02[k]
Lesotho	76.2	73.3	79.2	1.08	73.7	72.2	75.3	1.04
Namibia	89.6	86.5	92.7	1.07	86.4[m]	83.9[m]	88.9[m]	1.06[m]
South Africa	93.9	93.2	94.7	1.02	90.0[m]	89.4[m]	90.7[m]	1.01[m]
Swaziland	72.1	71.3	72.9	1.02	85.6	86.1	85.1	0.99

* Information on data for Israel: http://dx.doi.org/10.1787/888932315602.
a) Gender parity index: ratio of female to male values of the adjusted net enrolment rate into primary education.
b) Country classification by world region is based on UN and World Bank classifications.
c) Data refer to 1998.
d) Data refer to 1999.
e) Data refer to 2001.
f) Data refer to 2002.
g) Data refer to 2003.
h) Data refer to 2004.
i) Data refer to 2005.
j) Data refer to 2006.
k) Data refer to 2007.
l) Data refer to 2008.
m) Data refer to 2009.
n) Data refer to 2011.
o) Footnote by Turkey: The information in this document with reference to "Cyprus" relates to the southern part of the Island. There is no single authority representing both Turkish and Greek Cypriot people on the Island. Turkey recognises the Turkish Republic of Northern Cyprus (TRNC). Until a lasting and equitable solution is found within the context of United Nations, Turkey shall preserve its position concerning the "Cyprus issue".
p) Footnote by all the European Union member states of the OECD and the European Commission: The Republic of Cyprus is recognised by all members of the United Nations with the exception of Turkey. The information in this document relates to the area under the effective control of the Government of the Republic of Cyprus.
Source: UNESCO Education Database 2012.

StatLink 🔗 http://dx.doi.org/10.1787/888932677457

Table II.A1.2. **Gross secondary school enrolment ratios, 2000 and 2010**

Total enrolment in secondary school, regardless of age, expressed as a percentage
of the eligible official secondary school-age population

Region, country or economy[b]	2000				2010			
	All	Male	Female	GPI[a]	All	Male	Female	GPI[a]
OECD	**104.4**	**103.0**	**105.8**	**1.02**	**102.8**	**102.8**	**102.9**	**1.00**
Australia	161.7	161.5	162.0	1.00	129.2[m]	131.8[m]	126.5[m]	0.96[m]
Austria	97.7	99.8	95.4	0.96	99.6[m]	101.8[m]	97.4[m]	0.96[m]
Belgium	145.1	138.4	152.2	1.10	110.5[m]	112.2[m]	108.8[m]	0.97[m]
Canada	102.5	101.6	103.4	1.02	101.3[l]	102.4[l]	100.2[l]	0.98[l]
Chile	82.7	81.8	83.6	1.02	87.9[m]	86.7[m]	89.2[m]	1.03[m]
Czech Republic	87.3	86.6	88.1	1.02	90.4[m]	89.9[m]	90.9[m]	1.01[m]
Denmark	126.7	124.0	129.6	1.04	117.4[m]	116.3[m]	118.5[m]	1.02[m]
Estonia	93.8	91.9	95.7	1.04	103.6[m]	102.7[m]	104.7[m]	1.02[m]
Finland	124.8	119.4	130.5	1.09	107.5[m]	105.0[m]	110.1[m]	1.05[m]
France	108.2	108.1	108.3	1.00	112.6[m]	112.4[m]	112.8[m]	1.00[m]
Germany	98.1	98.7	97.4	0.99	102.6[m]	105.3[m]	99.7[m]	0.95[m]
Greece	89.5	86.8	92.4	1.06	100.9[k]	103.5[k]	98.1[k]	0.95[k]
Hungary	95.1	94.8	95.5	1.01	98.3[m]	99.0[m]	97.6[m]	0.99[m]
Iceland	107.4	104.0	110.9	1.07	107.2[m]	105.7[m]	108.8[m]	1.03[m]
Ireland	106.7	102.6	111.1	1.08	117.5[m]	114.0[m]	121.1[m]	1.06[m]
Israel*	93.2	93.1	93.3	1.00	91.0[m]	90.3[m]	91.8[m]	1.02[m]
Italy	92.2[d]	92.6[d]	91.9[d]	0.99[d]	99.1[m]	99.8[m]	98.3[m]	0.98[m]
Japan	101.8	101.2	102.4	1.01	101.5[m]	101.4[m]	101.6[m]	1.00[m]
Korea	98.9	99.0	98.7	1.00	97.1[m]	97.6[m]	96.4[m]	0.99[m]
Luxembourg	97.0	94.2	99.9	1.06	97.6[l]	96.4[l]	98.8[l]	1.02[l]
Mexico	72.7	71.9	73.4	1.02	86.9[m]	83.7[m]	90.1[m]	1.08[m]
Netherlands	123.4	125.7	121.0	0.96	120.2[m]	121.1[m]	119.3[m]	0.99[m]
New Zealand	110.6	107.6	113.9	1.06	124.6[m]	122.9[m]	126.4[m]	1.03[m]
Norway	116.1	114.7	117.5	1.02	110.2[m]	111.5[m]	108.8[m]	0.98[m]
Poland	100.6	101.6	99.5	0.98	97.0[m]	97.5[m]	96.5[m]	0.99[m]
Portugal	104.7	101.4	108.1	1.07	106.7[m]	104.8[m]	108.7[m]	1.04[m]
Slovak Republic	84.6	83.8	85.4	1.02	89.4[m]	88.9[m]	90.0[m]	1.01[m]
Slovenia	100.8	99.1	102.6	1.04	97.1[m]	97.3[m]	96.8[m]	1.00[m]
Spain	111.4	108.3	114.7	1.06	119.0[m]	116.5[m]	121.6[m]	1.04[m]
Sweden	151.8	134.3	170.2	1.27	100.3[m]	100.6[m]	99.9[m]	0.99[m]
Switzerland	95.4	98.4	92.3	0.94	95.2[m]	97.1[m]	93.3[m]	0.96[m]
Turkey	71.4	82.5	60.1	0.73	77.6[m]	80.9[m]	74.1[m]	0.91[m]
United Kingdom	101.6	101.1	102.1	1.01	101.8[m]	100.8[m]	102.9[m]	1.02[m]
United States	93.0	92.4	93.7	1.01	96.5[m]	95.8[m]	97.1[m]	1.01[m]
Caribbean	**88.8**	**85.6**	**92.0**	**1.08**	**93.0**	**91.4**	**94.7**	**1.04**
Anguilla	107.0	108.2	105.9	0.98	79.7[l]	81.8[l]	77.6[l]	0.95[l]
Antigua and Barbuda	78.9	82.5	75.5	0.92	105.4	104.8	106.0	1.01
Aruba	97.0	95.4	98.5	1.03	89.6	89.3	90.0	1.01
Bahamas	81.9	85.8	77.9	0.91	94.0[m]	92.9[m]	95.0[m]	1.02[m]
Barbados	104.8	99.5	110.5	1.11	100.6	96.4	105.1	1.09
Bermuda	79.2[e]	76.5[e]	81.9[e]	1.07[e]	78.7	72.3	85.4	1.18
British Virgin Islands	95.7[h]	92.9[h]	98.5[h]	1.06[h]	98.4[m]	96.9[m]	99.8[m]	1.03[m]
Cayman Islands	102.5	102.6	102.5	1.00	83.2[l]	78.2[l]	88.4[l]	1.13[l]
Cuba	82.5	80.8	84.3	1.04	89.4	90.0	88.8	0.99
Dominica	105.5	99.1	112.0	1.13	98.2	94.0	102.8	1.09
Dominican Republic	59.5	53.5	65.5	1.23	76.4	72.0	81.0	1.12
Grenada	108.1[f]	100.7[f]	115.6[f]	1.15[f]	107.9	106.3	109.4	1.03
Haiti	..	..	..	..	..	..	..	..
Jamaica	86.7	85.8	87.6	1.02	95.6[m]	94.9[m]	96.3[m]	1.01[m]

Table II.A1.2. **Gross secondary school enrolment ratios, 2000 and 2010** (cont.)

Total enrolment in secondary school, regardless of age, expressed as a percentage
of the eligible official secondary school-age population

Region, country or economy[b]	2000				2010			
	All	Male	Female	GPI[a]	All	Male	Female	GPI[a]
Montserrat	102.0[f]	96.3[f]	109.0[f]	1.13[f]	102.1[k]	101.1[k]	103.2[k]	1.02[k]
Puerto Rico	..	..	..	..	82.2	79.9	84.5	1.06
Saint Kitts and Nevis	75.4	72.8	78.0	1.07	97.5	97.8	97.2	0.99
Saint Lucia	73.4	63.8	82.7	1.30	96.1	96.7	95.6	0.99
Saint Vincent and the Grenadines	82.5	70.5	94.6	1.34	109.4[m]	107.4[m]	111.5[m]	1.04[m]
Trinidad and Tobago	75.7	72.1	79.4	1.10	89.9[l]	87.0[l]	93.0[l]	1.07[l]
Turks and Caicos Islands	88.2[g]	88.4[g]	88.1[g]	1.00[g]	86.0[i]	88.7[i]	83.2[i]	0.94[i]
Central America	**56.3**	**55.0**	**57.7**	**1.04**	**73.3**	**71.4**	**75.3**	**1.06**
Belize	65.1	63.4	66.8	1.05	74.8	75.7	74.0	0.98
Costa Rica	60.7	58.2	63.5	1.09	99.7	97.0	102.5	1.06
El Salvador	54.0	54.2	53.9	0.99	63.1[m]	62.4[m]	63.7[m]	1.02[m]
Guatemala	38.0	40.3	35.6	0.88	58.5	60.5	56.6	0.93
Honduras	..	..	..	..	73.5	66.0	81.2	1.23
Nicaragua	53.1	49.0	57.4	1.17	69.4	66.2	72.7	1.10
Panama	67.0	65.0	69.1	1.06	74.1	71.7	76.7	1.07
South America	**79.4**	**77.1**	**81.7**	**1.06**	**85.2**	**81.8**	**88.7**	**1.09**
Argentina	86.6	84.6	88.6	1.05	85.8[l]	80.5[l]	91.4[l]	1.14[l]
Bolivia (Plurinational State of)	79.8	81.5	78.1	0.96	81.0[l]	81.9[l]	80.1[l]	0.98[l]
Brazil	104.4	99.5	109.5	1.10	101.3[l]	96.4[l]	106.5[l]	1.11[l]
Colombia	71.8	68.4	75.3	1.10	96.4	92.0	100.9	1.10
Ecuador	57.1	56.7	57.6	1.02	80.4[m]	78.6[m]	82.4[m]	1.05[m]
Guyana	94.6	94.5	94.8	1.00	91.0	86.6	95.7	1.11
Paraguay	61.3	60.3	62.3	1.03	66.9[m]	65.5[m]	68.5[m]	1.05[m]
Peru	85.8	88.8	82.6	0.93	91.6[m]	92.6[m]	90.6[m]	0.98[m]
Suriname	73.4[e]	67.3[e]	79.8[e]	1.19[e]	74.8[m]	67.3[m]	82.6[m]	1.23[m]
Uruguay	98.3	92.1	104.8	1.14	85.0[m]	79.4[m]	90.8[m]	1.14[m]
Venezuela (Bolivarian Republic of)	59.8	54.6	65.3	1.20	82.5	78.8	86.4	1.10
East Asia and the Pacific	**66.1**	**64.1**	**68.2**	**1.03**	**76.9**	**74.6**	**80.1**	**1.06**
Brunei Darussalam	89.2	86.9	91.7	1.06	107.3[m]	105.9[m]	108.7[m]	1.03[m]
Cambodia	16.6	21.4	11.7	0.55	46.2	48.5	43.7	0.90
China	63.3[e]	64.8[e]	61.6[e]	0.95[e]	80.1[m]	77.6[m]	82.9[m]	1.07[m]
China, Hong Kong Special Administrative Region	77.1[e]	77.6[e]	76.5[e]	0.98[e]	83.0	82.4	83.7	1.02
China, Macao Special Administrative Region	83.0	81.6	84.4	1.03	92.4	95.9	88.9	0.93
Cook Islands	76.7	72.0	82.0	1.14	83.4[m]	78.7[m]	88.6[m]	1.13[m]
Fiji	78.5	75.1	82.0	1.09	86.5[m]	82.7[m]	90.5[m]	1.09[m]
Indonesia	52.8	54.1	51.5	0.95	75.1[m]	75.4[m]	74.7[m]	0.99[m]
Kiribati	100.2	76.3	125.0	1.64	85.6[l]	81.3[l]	90.0[l]	1.11[l]
Korea, Democratic People's Republic of	..	..	..	..	..	..	..	..
Lao People's Democratic Republic	34.9	40.9	28.7	0.70	44.7[l]	49.4[l]	39.8[l]	0.81[l]
Malaysia	66.2	63.4	69.1	1.09	69.1[l]	66.6[l]	71.6[l]	1.08[l]
Marshall Islands	67.8[d]	65.7[d]	69.9[d]	1.06[d]	98.8[m]	97.5[m]	100.3[m]	1.03[m]
Micronesia (Federated States of)	82.2[h]	79.9[h]	84.8[h]	1.06[h]	83.2[i]	80.2[i]	86.6[i]	1.08[i]
Mongolia	65.0	58.5	71.6	1.22	92.9[m]	89.5[m]	96.3[m]	1.08[m]
Myanmar	39.9	38.6	41.1	1.07	54.3	52.6	56.0	1.06
Nauru	47.1	43.3	50.8	1.17	62.9[l]	57.6[l]	68.9[l]	1.20[l]
Niue	97.0	89.9	104.7	1.16	105.1[l]	82.9[l]	147.8[l]	1.78[l]
Palau	91.6[e]	91.3[e]	91.9[e]	1.01[e]	..	..	..	..
Papua New Guinea	19.3[c]	22.6[c]	15.9[c]	0.70[c]	..	..	..	..
Philippines	74.3[d]	70.8[d]	77.9[d]	1.10[d]	84.8[m]	81.5[m]	88.3[m]	1.08[m]

Table II.A1.2. **Gross secondary school enrolment ratios, 2000 and 2010** *(cont.)*
Total enrolment in secondary school, regardless of age, expressed as a percentage
of the eligible official secondary school-age population

Region, country or economy[b]	2000				2010			
	All	Male	Female	GPI[a]	All	Male	Female	GPI[a]
Samoa	77.9	73.1	83.3	1.14	84.7	79.3	90.7	1.14
Singapore	..	..	..	..	..	..	..	..
Solomon Islands	20.7	23.0	18.2	0.79	35.5[k]	38.4[k]	32.4[k]	0.84[k]
Thailand	62.2[e]	62.9[e]	61.5[e]	0.98[e]	77.2	74.2	80.4	1.08
Timor-Leste	56.6[h]	57.3[h]	55.9[h]	0.98[h]	56.3	56.1	56.4	1.01
Tokelau	92.3	91.9	92.7	1.01	..	..	..	..
Tonga	106.5	101.0	112.7	1.12	101.3[j]	101.2[j]	101.5[j]	1.00[j]
Tuvalu	79.5[e]	76.2[e]	83.7[e]	1.10[e]	..	..	..	..
Vanuatu	34.7	32.4	37.0	1.14	54.7	54.3	55.1	1.02
Viet Nam	64.0	66.9	61.0	0.91	77.2[l]	75.4[l]	79.1[l]	1.05[l]
Southern Asia	**47.4**	**50.5**	**49.5**	**0.89**	**57.4**	**60.2**	**54.4**	**0.89**
Afghanistan	11.5[e]	22.1[e]	..	..	45.5	59.8	30.2	0.51
Bangladesh	48.2	47.4	49.0	1.03	49.3[m]	47.1[m]	51.5[m]	1.09[m]
Bhutan	40.7	44.7	36.7	0.82	60.8[m]	61.0[m]	60.7[m]	1.00[m]
India	45.3	52.6	37.4	0.71	60.2[l]	63.8[l]	56.2[l]	0.88[l]
Iran (Islamic Republic of)	79.7	82.2	77.1	0.94	83.5[m]	85.9[m]	81.1[m]	0.94[m]
Maldives	52.8	50.8	54.9	1.08	82.1[j]	79.4[j]	85.1[j]	1.07[j]
Nepal	35.0	40.6	29.0	0.71	43.5[j]	46.1[j]	40.8[j]	0.89[j]
Pakistan	27.7[g]	31.1[g]	24.1[g]	0.77[g]	34.2	38.9	29.4	0.76
Sri Lanka	85.5[f]	82.9[f]	88.1[f]	1.06[f]	..	..	..	..
Eastern Europe and Central Asia	**86.4**	**86.5**	**86.3**	**1.00**	**92.0**	**92.5**	**91.5**	**0.99**
Albania	71.5	73.0	70.1	0.96	78.2	79.0	77.3	0.98
Armenia	87.7[e]	85.2[e]	90.2[e]	1.06[e]	92.0	91.0	93.1	1.02
Azerbaijan	74.8	76.7	73.0	0.95	84.5[k]	86.2[k]	82.7[k]	0.96[k]
Belarus	87.2	85.7	88.8	1.04	95.9[k]	94.9[k]	97.0[k]	1.02[k]
Bosnia and Herzegovina	..	..	..	..	89.6	88.5	90.7	1.03
Bulgaria	93.0	94.0	92.0	0.98	88.0[m]	89.6[m]	86.3[m]	0.96[m]
Croatia	85.2	84.3	86.1	1.02	95.3[m]	93.7[m]	97.0[m]	1.04[m]
Cyprus[o, p]	93.4	92.4	94.4	1.02	98.4[m]	97.8[m]	99.0[m]	1.01[m]
Former Yugoslav Republic of Macedonia (FYROM)	83.9	85.2	82.6	0.97	82.8[m]	83.6[m]	81.9[m]	0.98[m]
Georgia	78.8	79.4	78.2	0.99	89.0[l]	91.4[l]	86.6[l]	0.95[l]
Kazakhstan	93.7	92.8	94.6	1.02	99.6[n]	101.0[n]	98.3[n]	0.97[n]
Kyrgyzstan	84.3	83.1	85.5	1.03	84.0	84.5	83.5	0.99
Latvia	90.6	89.4	91.9	1.03	94.1[m]	93.8[m]	94.4[m]	1.01[m]
Lithuania	97.9	98.3	97.6	0.99	98.0[m]	98.1[m]	97.9[m]	1.00[m]
Moldova, Republic of	81.6	80.7	82.5	1.02	88.0	87.0	89.0	1.02
Montenegro	..	..	..	..	104.0	103.5	104.6	1.01
Romania	81.9	81.3	82.5	1.02	95.1[m]	95.4[m]	94.8[m]	0.99[m]
Russian Federation	91.6[g]	91.7[g]	91.5[g]	1.00[g]	88.6[m]	89.6[m]	87.5[m]	0.98[m]
Serbia	90.0	89.1	91.0	1.02	91.4	90.5	92.4	1.02
Tajikistan	74.2	79.8	68.5	0.86	87.2	93.4	80.9	0.87
Turkmenistan	..	..	..	..	..	..	..	..
Ukraine	98.9	98.6	99.2	1.01	95.6	96.7	94.4	0.98
Uzbekistan	87.5	88.9	86.2	0.97	105.7[n]	106.8[n]	104.5[n]	0.98[n]
Middle East and North Africa	**75.2**	**75.7**	**74.7**	**0.96**	**84.9**	**84.5**	**85.4**	**1.00**
Algeria	74.9[f]	73.2[f]	76.7[f]	1.05[f]	94.9[m]	94.1[m]	95.8[m]	1.02[m]
Bahrain	98.7	94.7	103.0	1.09	103.1[j]	100.9[j]	105.3[j]	1.04[j]
Egypt	82.6	85.9	79.1	0.92	..	..	..	..
Iraq	37.5	46.0	28.5	0.62	52.9[k]	60.3[k]	45.1[k]	0.75[k]

Table II.A1.2. **Gross secondary school enrolment ratios, 2000 and 2010** (cont.)

Total enrolment in secondary school, regardless of age, expressed as a percentage
of the eligible official secondary school-age population

Region, country or economy[b]	2000				2010			
	All	Male	Female	GPI[a]	All	Male	Female	GPI[a]
Jordan	84.2	82.4	86.2	1.05	91.1[l]	89.3[l]	93.0[l]	1.04[l]
Kuwait	107.9	105.9	109.9	1.04	101.0[l]	97.9[l]	104.3[l]	1.07[l]
Lebanon	76.7[d]	73.4[d]	80.1[d]	1.09[d]	81.4	76.8	86.2	1.12
Libya	110.3[f]	107.0[f]	113.7[f]	1.06[f]	93.4[j]	86.1[j]	101.2[j]	1.18[j]
Morocco	38.1	42.5	33.7	0.79	56.1[k]	60.3[k]	51.8[k]	0.86[k]
Oman	75.5	75.8	75.2	0.99	101.3	101.8	100.7	0.99
Palestinian Authority	80.6	78.9	82.4	1.04	86.0	82.7	89.4	1.08
Qatar	87.5	81.9	94.2	1.15	93.7	85.8	103.7	1.21
Saudi Arabia	..	..	..	..	104.3	110.6	97.9	0.89
Syrian Arab Republic	44.8	46.7	42.9	0.92	72.4	72.2	72.6	1.01
Tunisia	76.1	74.8	77.4	1.03	90.5[m]	88.0[m]	93.1[m]	1.06[m]
United Arab Emirates	85.2	82.9	87.7	1.06	92.3[j]	91.7[j]	93.0[j]	1.01[j]
Yemen	42.5	59.9	24.5	0.41	44.1	54.1	33.7	0.62
Western Africa	**25.2**	**29.9**	**20.4**	**0.65**	**42.3**	**46.6**	**38.0**	**0.79**
Benin	23.1	32.3	14.2	0.44	37.1[i]	48.4[i]	26.0[i]	0.54[i]
Burkina Faso	9.7	11.7	7.7	0.66	20.7	23.4	17.9	0.76
Cape Verde	67.9[e]	66.5[e]	69.2[e]	1.04[e]	87.5	79.7	95.4	1.20
Côte d'Ivoire	23.6	30.6	16.6	0.54	..	..	..	..
Gambia	..	..	..	..	54.1	55.6	52.6	0.95
Ghana	40.5	44.4	36.5	0.82	67.3[n]	70.6[n]	63.9[n]	0.91[n]
Guinea	16.0	23.1	8.6	0.37	38.1[m]	47.7[m]	28.1[m]	0.59[m]
Guinea-Bissau	18.5	23.9	13.1	0.55	..	..	..	..
Liberia	34.8	40.3	29.2	0.73	..	..	..	..
Mali	16.5	21.1	11.9	0.56	37.7	44.3	30.9	0.70
Mauritania	18.2	20.9	15.5	0.74	24.4	26.4	22.4	0.85
Niger	7.0	8.8	5.2	0.60	13.4	16.1	10.6	0.66
Nigeria	24.3	26.3	22.2	0.85	44.0	46.8	41.2	0.88
Senegal	16.5	19.9	13.0	0.65	37.4	39.9	34.9	0.88
Sierra Leone	27.6[e]	33.0[e]	22.5[e]	0.68[e]	..	..	..	..
Togo	33.7	46.7	20.8	0.44	45.5[k]	59.8[k]	31.4[k]	0.53[k]
Eastern and Middle Africa	**29.5**	**32.2**	**26.7**	**0.77**	**40.2**	**43.2**	**37.3**	**0.80**
Angola	14.9	16.4	13.4	0.82	31.3	37.2	25.5	0.69
Burundi	11.1[g]	12.6[g]	9.7[g]	0.77[g]	24.8	28.9	20.7	0.72
Cameroon	26.1[d]	28.4[d]	23.8[d]	0.84[d]	42.2[m]	46.0[m]	38.4[m]	0.83[m]
Central African Republic	..	..	..	..	12.6	16.0	9.3	0.58
Chad	10.8	16.9	4.8	0.28	25.7	36.3	15.0	0.41
Comoros	28.9	31.8	26.0	0.82	46.3[i]	52.7[i]	39.9[i]	0.76[i]
Congo	35.6	41.8	29.4	0.70	..	..	..	..
Congo, Democratic Republic of	19.0[d]	24.9[d]	13.1[d]	0.53[d]	37.9[m]	48.5[m]	27.2[m]	0.56[m]
Djibouti	13.6	16.4	10.8	0.66	36.1[n]	40.1[n]	31.9[n]	0.80[n]
Equatorial Guinea	31.4	43.5	19.2	0.44	..	..	..	..
Eritrea	25.0	29.7	20.4	0.69	31.9	36.3	27.6	0.76
Ethiopia	14.5	17.4	11.6	0.66	35.7	39.3	32.1	0.82
Gabon	48.0	51.6	44.4	0.86	..	..	..	..
Kenya	39.2	40.2	38.2	0.95	60.2[m]	63.2[m]	57.1[m]	0.90[m]
Madagascar	16.6[c]	17.1[c]	16.2[c]	0.95[c]	31.1[m]	32.0[m]	30.2[m]	0.94[m]
Malawi	32.2	36.7	27.6	0.75	32.1	33.6	30.6	0.91
Mauritius	75.3	76.6	73.9	0.96	89.4	89.5	89.3	1.00
Mozambique	6.1	7.5	4.7	0.63	25.5	28.0	22.9	0.82
Rwanda	11.1	11.4	10.8	0.95	32.2	31.9	32.4	1.02

Table II.A1.2. **Gross secondary school enrolment ratios, 2000 and 2010** (cont.)

Total enrolment in secondary school, regardless of age, expressed as a percentage
of the eligible official secondary school-age population

Region, country or economy[b]	2000				2010			
	All	Male	Female	GPI[a]	All	Male	Female	GPI[a]
Sao Tome and Principe	38.4[g]	35.3[g]	41.5[g]	1.18[g]	59.2[n]	55.2[n]	63.4[n]	1.15[n]
Seychelles	104.5	101.8	107.4	1.06	114.7[m]	108.2[m]	122.0[m]	1.13[m]
Somalia	..	..	..	..	7.8[k]	10.7[k]	4.9[k]	0.46[k]
Sudan	..	..	..	..	..	..	..	..
Uganda	16.3	18.5	14.1	0.76	28.1	30.4	25.8	0.85
Tanzania, United Republic of	..	..	..	..	..	..	..	..
Zambia	..	..	..	..	..	..	..	..
Zimbabwe	..	..	..	..	..	..	..	..
Southern Africa	**58.4**	**55.6**	**61.2**	**1.12**	**68.5**	**65.1**	**71.9**	**1.13**
Botswana	74.6	72.7	76.5	1.05	80.0[k]	77.9[k]	82.1[k]	1.05[k]
Lesotho	30.1	26.0	34.3	1.32	46.4	39.0	53.9	1.38
Namibia	60.1	56.6	63.7	1.13	64.0[k]	58.9[k]	69.3[k]	1.18[k]
South Africa	85.3	81.0	89.5	1.10	93.8[m]	91.6[m]	96.0[m]	1.05[m]
Swaziland	41.9	41.7	42.1	1.01	58.1	58.1	58.1	1.00

* Information on data for Israel: *http://dx.doi.org/10.1787/888932315602*.
a) Gender parity index: ratio of female to male values of the gross enrolment ratio into secondary education.
b) Country classification into world regions is based on UN and World Bank classifications.
c) Data refer to 1998.
d) Data refer to 1999.
e) Data refer to 2001.
f) Data refer to 2002.
g) Data refer to 2003.
h) Data refer to 2004.
i) Data refer to 2005.
j) Data refer to 2006.
k) Data refer to 2007.
l) Data refer to 2008.
m) Data refer to 2009.
n) Data refer to 2011.
o) *Footnote by Turkey:* The information in this document with reference to "Cyprus" relates to the southern part of the Island. There is no single authority representing both Turkish and Greek Cypriot people on the Island. Turkey recognises the Turkish Republic of Northern Cyprus (TRNC). Until a lasting and equitable solution is found within the context of United Nations, Turkey shall preserve its position concerning the "Cyprus issue".
p) *Footnote by all the European Union member states of the OECD and the European Commission:* The Republic of Cyprus is recognised by all members of the United Nations with the exception of Turkey. The information in this document relates to the area under the effective control of the Government of the Republic of Cyprus.

Source: UNESCO Education Database 2012.

StatLink *http://dx.doi.org/10.1787/888932677476*

ANNEX II.A2

Supplementary table to Chapter 5

Table II.A2.1. **Gender equality focused aid in primary and secondary education, percentage of 2009-10 annual average DAC members' aid commitments, 2010 prices**

Recipient region, country or economy	Primary education	Secondary education
North and Central America, all[a]	**75.6**	**65.6**
North and Central America, regional	98.2	99.2
West Indies, regional	..	100.0
Anguilla	..	..
Antigua and Barbuda	..	..
Barbados	..	..
Belize	100.0	..
Costa Rica	98.5	99.9
Cuba	15.8	57.0
Dominica	..	..
Dominican Republic	57.1	72.6
El Salvador	48.5	95.5
Grenada	0.0	..
Guatemala	39.2	46.2
Haiti	91.0	77.2
Honduras	89.7	34.6
Jamaica	100.0	100.0
Montserrat	..	0.0
Nicaragua	63.0	24.7
Panama	100.0	37.0
Saint Kitts and Nevis	..	..
Saint Lucia	..	..
Saint Vincent and the Grenadines	..	..
Trinidad and Tobago	..	..
South America, all[a]	**76.1**	**64.4**
South America, regional	99.8	91.2
Argentina	67.1	96.8
Bolivia (Plurinational State of)	64.2	61.7
Brazil	59.5	52.1
Colombia	90.5	65.2
Ecuador	41.0	68.0
Guyana	0.0	..
Paraguay	63.0	23.7
Peru	81.7	62.5
Suriname	..	..
Uruguay	86.5	57.8
Venezuela (Bolivarian Republic of)	96.1	46.3

Table II.A2.1. **Gender equality focused aid in primary and secondary education, percentage of 2009-10 annual average DAC members' aid commitments, 2010 prices** (cont.)

Recipient region, country or economy	Primary education	Secondary education
Far East Asia, all[a]	**26.7**	**48.8**
Far East Asia, regional	100.0	100.0
Cambodia	16.7	31.5
China	38.5	47.1
Indonesia	10.5	79.2
Korea, Democratic People's Republic of	100.0	100.0
Lao People's Democratic Republic	87.5	76.2
Malaysia	51.1	5.8
Mongolia	49.9	8.9
Philippines	72.4	58.9
Thailand	55.4	38.2
Timor-Leste	67.2	93.4
Viet Nam	88.3	25.9
Oceania, all[a]	**91.4**	**88.5**
Oceania, regional	100.0	91.3
Cook Islands	100.0	100.0
Fiji	10.4	12.6
Kiribati	97.3	..
Marshall Islands	..	..
Micronesia (Federated States of)	0.0	..
Nauru	..	..
Niue	100.0	..
Palau	..	..
Papua New Guinea	86.8	97.8
Samoa	70.6	53.0
Solomon Islands	91.0	0.0
Tokelau	100.0	..
Tonga	100.0	96.3
Tuvalu	76.1	17.3
Vanuatu	100.0	91.9
South and Central Asia, all[a]	**88.7**	**67.1**
Central Asia, regional	85.0	100.0
South Asia, regional	100.0	100.0
Afghanistan	84.0	90.3
Armenia	97.4	0.3
Azerbaijan	67.3	100.0
Bangladesh	87.2	49.5
Bhutan	0.0	93.2
Georgia	8.2	1.5
India	97.4	69.4
Kazakhstan	52.2	86.5
Kyrgyzstan	100.0	98.9
Maldives	0.0	100.0
Myanmar	80.3	3.5
Nepal	94.2	97.4
Pakistan	79.5	99.3
Sri Lanka	56.9	66.7
Tajikistan	99.9	75.9
Turkmenistan	..	7.4
Uzbekistan	0.7	44.9

Table II.A2.1. **Gender equality focused aid in primary and secondary education, percentage of 2009-10 annual average DAC members' aid commitments, 2010 prices** (cont.)

Recipient region, country or economy	Primary education	Secondary education
Europe, all[a]	**53.0**	**64.7**
Europe, regional	98.2	99.7
Albania	39.8	36.2
Belarus	0.0	78.1
Bosnia and Herzegovina	9.6	77.7
Croatia	100.0	94.9
Former Yugoslav Republic of Macedonia (FYROM)	50.6	37.7
Kosovo	26.7	58.8
Moldova, Republic of	74.2	68.5
Montenegro	100.0	6.5
Serbia	33.1	84.4
Ukraine	92.2	65.9
Africa, South of Sahara, all[a]	**68.5**	**72.9**
South of Sahara, regional	98.0	88.2
Angola	87.3	20.5
Benin	52.2	98.0
Botswana	91.0	8.6
Burkina Faso	96.6	78.6
Burundi	56.3	94.3
Cameroon	88.2	94.9
Cape Verde	100.0	0.1
Central African Republic	89.2	88.7
Chad	47.2	84.3
Comoros	100.0	1.8
Congo	87.0	94.3
Congo, Democratic Republic of	60.1	92.9
Côte d'Ivoire	89.0	78.3
Djibouti	100.0	100.0
Equatorial Guinea	17.6	24.9
Eritrea	0.0	39.6
Ethiopia	62.1	88.8
Gabon	0.0	18.6
Gambia	84.4	7.4
Ghana	58.1	24.2
Guinea	99.2	87.5
Guinea-Bissau	27.3	24.8
Kenya	52.6	54.2
Lesotho	99.8	..
Liberia	100.0	100.0
Madagascar	49.9	97.2
Malawi	99.1	7.1
Mali	90.4	36.5
Mauritania	78.8	75.8
Mauritius	100.0	100.0
Mayotte	100.0	100.0
Mozambique	66.3	41.3
Namibia	50.6	15.0
Niger	97.8	56.7
Nigeria	46.5	82.0
Rwanda	95.5	34.7
Saint Helena	..	0.0
Sao Tome and Principe	0.0	0.0

Table II.A2.1. **Gender equality focused aid in primary and secondary education, percentage of 2009-10 annual average DAC members' aid commitments, 2010 prices** (cont.)

Recipient region, country or economy	Primary education	Secondary education
Senegal	64.6	87.9
Seychelles	100.0	. .
Sierra Leone	94.1	69.9
Somalia	58.4	37.1
South Africa	3.0	62.7
Sudan	81.3	94.3
Swaziland	49.5	67.4
Tanzania, United Republic of	98.6	93.5
Togo	96.3	81.8
Uganda	25.3	24.2
Zambia	41.0	54.2
Zimbabwe	34.8	69.6
Middle East, all[a]	**97.2**	**84.4**
Middle East, regional	100.0	96.1
Iran (Islamic Republic of)	100.0	24.8
Iraq	93.8	90.1
Jordan	95.0	89.5
Lebanon	95.6	99.7
Oman	100.0	0.0
Palestinian Authority[b]	98.8	54.9
Syrian Arab Republic	97.0	71.2
Yemen	99.3	99.8
Africa, North of Sahara, all[a]	**97.5**	**90.5**
North of Sahara, regional	71.4	90.8
Algeria	100.0	98.6
Egypt	97.1	89.9
Libya	100.0	100.0
Morocco	97.7	89.4
Tunisia	98.5	93.8

. .: There were no commitments made to primary or secondary education for this country in 2009-10 or this aid was not screened against the gender equality policy marker.

a) Regional weigthed average.

b) Referred to as "West Bank and Gaza Strip" in the DAC List of ODA Recipients.

Source: Creditor Reporting System (CRS), *Aid Activity Database, www.oecd.org/dac/stats/idsonline.*

StatLink *http://dx.doi.org/10.1787/888932677495*

ANNEX II.A3

Supplementary table to Chapter 8

Table II.A3.1. **Percentage of female students in higher education, 1985-2025**

	1985	1995	2005	2015	2025
OECD	**46**	**50**	**54**	**56**	**58**
Australia	. .	50	54	55	56
Austria	44	48	54	61	72
Belgium	47	49	54	58	60
Canada	49	53	58	60	64
Czech Republic	. .	48	53	53	54
Denmark	48	52	57	59	60
Finland	49	53	54	54	53
France	52	55	55	56	57
Germany	. .	43	50	54	58
Greece	. .	49	51	53	53
Hungary	. .	52	58	59	60
Iceland	. .	58	65	67	68
Ireland	43	49	55	58	59
Italy	45	52	57	57	57
Japan	. .	44	46	47	48
Korea	. .	35	37	38	40
Luxembourg	. .	. .	. .	. .	. .
Mexico	. .	47	50	52	52
Netherlands	41	47	51	53	54
New Zealand	46	55	59	59	60
Norway	50	55	60	63	65
Poland	. .	. .	58	58	58
Portugal	53	57	56	56	56
Slovak Republic	. .	. .	55	58	59
Spain	48	53	54	55	55
Sweden	52	55	60	62	63
Switzerland	32	37	46	49	52
Turkey	31	38	42	43	43
United Kingdom	45	51	57	65	71
United States	52	55	57	60	62

Source: OECD (2008), *Higher Education to 2030*, OECD Publishing, Paris.

StatLink ⬛🔗 http://dx.doi.org/10.1787/888932677514

ANNEX II.A4

General background data on education

Table II.A4.1. Educational attainment, PISA scores, and field of tertiary education, 2009

	Proportion of the population with at least upper secondary education				Proportion of the population with tertiary education[a]				PISA scores						Proportion of degrees[b] awarded to women			
	25-34 years old		55-64 years old		25-34 years old		55-64 years old		Reading[c]		Mathematics[d]		Science[e]		Computing	Engineering, manufacturing and construction	Education	Health and welfare
	Men	Women	Men	Women	Men	Women	Men	Women	Boys	Girls	Boys	Girls	Boys	Girls	Women	Women	Women	Women
OECD	**80.1**	**82.9**	**65.6**	**57.0**	**32.7**	**41.5**	**24.2**	**20.6**	**474**	**513**	**501**	**490**	**501**	**501**	**18.9**	**26.3**	**76.8**	**74.8**
Australia	81.0	84.8	65.9	50.2	38.1	51.5	29.7	28.9	496	533	519	509	527	528	19.6[g]	24.8[g]	74.0[g]	75.6[g]
Austria	90.0	86.8	81.5	62.5	19.6	22.5	21.2	11.0	449	490	506	486	498	490	17.5	25.5	80.3	67.1
Belgium	82.1	84.2	56.7	50.7	36.3	48.7	25.9	20.8	493	520	526	504	510	503	6.8	27.2	75.8	64.1
Canada	90.5	93.4	80.4	80.4	49.0	63.2	39.2	42.1	507	542	533	521	531	526	17.8[g]	23.5[g]	76.8[g]	83.2[g]
Chile	84.9	86.3	46.2	39.4	35.6	34.3	17.2	16.1	439	461	431	410	452	443	22.1	27.5	74.3	70.4
Czech Republic	94.9	93.5	92.4	79.9	18.1	22.5	13.6	8.3	456	504	495	490	498	503	13.3	25.6	78.5	81.1
Denmark	83.5	87.9	74.3	61.7	37.1	52.5	25.6	26.1	480	509	511	495	505	494	20.2	31.8	72.5	80.1
Estonia	82.9	89.7	80.0	85.8	27.5	45.7	26.4	37.6	480	524	516	508	527	528	28.8	37.6	92.1	84.0
Finland	88.1	92.8	65.5	69.4	30.3	49.0	27.4	30.5	508	563	542	539	546	562	27.0	22.8	83.6	85.6
France	82.6	85.1	59.3	50.5	38.7	47.5	18.3	17.7	475	515	505	489	500	497	16.5	28.8	74.6	59.3
Germany	86.4	85.7	88.8	76.8	24.4	26.9	32.4	18.4	478	518	520	505	523	518	15.6	22.3	72.5	68.4
Greece	69.6	80.6	42.1	37.1	25.0	34.1	19.4	10.8	459	506	473	459	465	475	..	..	..	..
Hungary	85.9	86.1	80.8	65.7	20.4	29.8	17.6	15.2	475	513	496	484	503	503	19.5	24.2	78.7	80.4
Iceland	65.1	75.2	67.9	45.0	30.2	41.9	25.6	19.8	478	522	508	505	496	495	21.1	35.3	84.5	85.4
Ireland	83.1	88.5	45.1	50.2	41.2	53.8	20.5	19.9	476	515	491	483	507	509	23.4	21.2	74.2	83.1
Israel*	84.3	90.4	73.8	74.7	35.1	50.6	44.1	45.8	452	495	451	443	453	456	24.6	24.2	83.3	77.8
Italy	66.5	74.1	40.7	32.9	15.8	24.6	11.1	9.5	464	510	490	475	488	490	..	..	..	56.6
Japan	..	..	..	..	52.3	59.2	31.9	23.1	501	540	534	524	534	545	8.0	10.8	59.3	63.0
Korea	97.0	98.1	55.3	30.1	62.8	63.4	19.1	7.5	523	558	548	544	537	539	20.1	22.5	71.6	64.1
Luxembourg	83.4	84.2	77.5	62.9	42.7	47.4	30.7	19.0	453	492	499	479	487	480	..	..	..	..
Mexico	42.6	41.3	24.7	18.2	21.5	19.0	14.5	5.5	413	438	425	412	419	413	36.4	28.3	72.0	75.2
Netherlands	80.1	84.6	71.1	53.9	37.1	43.2	33.0	21.8	496	521	534	517	524	520	10.2	18.7	81.1	79.5
New Zealand	77.6	80.9	67.7	55.4	41.4	51.8	32.1	35.3	499	544	523	515	529	535	23.0	29.8	81.2	82.4
Norway	81.5	85.8	81.3	76.0	37.6	56.4	28.1	26.3	480	527	500	495	498	502	13.1	24.5	74.5	72.8
Poland	92.5	94.5	79.9	75.4	28.2	42.7	12.4	12.8	476	525	497	493	505	511	16.3	33.6	77.8	72.8

Table II.A4.1. Educational attainment, PISA scores, and field of tertiary education, 2009 (cont.)

| | Proportion of the population with at least upper secondary education | | | | Proportion of the population with tertiary education[a] | | | | PISA scores | | | | | | Proportion of degrees[b] awarded to women | | | |
| | 25-34 years old | | 55-64 years old | | 25-34 years old | | 55-64 years old | | Reading[c] | | Mathematics[d] | | Science[e] | | Computing | Engineering, manufacturing and construction | Education | Health and welfare |
	Men	Women	Men	Women	Men	Women	Men	Women	Boys	Girls	Boys	Girls	Boys	Girls	Women	Women	Women	Women
Portugal	43.0	53.6	14.9	13.3	17.8	29.0	7.8	7.1	470	508	493	481	491	495	26.9	29.4	85.3	78.5
Slovak Republic	94.8	94.7	89.9	76.5	17.5	23.8	14.1	10.4	452	503	498	495	490	491	10.6	31.1	78.2	85.9
Slovenia	92.4	94.6	81.1	66.4	21.9	39.5	15.9	17.5	456	511	502	501	505	519	10.4	31.0	84.2	72.9
Spain	59.1	69.4	34.6	26.2	33.3	43.5	20.4	12.9	467	496	493	474	492	485	19.7	33.9	78.7	75.9
Sweden	90.1	92.3	72.8	78.5	36.5	48.4	23.5	30.4	475	521	493	495	493	497	24.1	28.4	79.3	82.3
Switzerland	91.7	88.4	89.1	76.0	42.5	37.4	38.6	18.1	481	520	544	524	520	512	8.9	19.1	74.3	68.3
Turkey	46.9	36.0	22.6	14.8	17.4	15.9	12.2	6.7	443	486	451	440	448	460	23.3	26.7	54.6	62.6
United Kingdom	81.7	81.5	73.1	55.2	42.9	46.8	30.4	27.0	481	507	503	482	519	509	19.0	22.5	76.3	74.1
United States	86.9	89.7	88.5	89.2	36.1	46.1	42.6	39.2	488	513	497	477	509	495	20.8	21.4	77.7	79.3
Brazil	48.8	56.1	24.9	24.2	9.6	13.5	9.3	8.6	397	425	394	379	407	404	17.9	28.8	79.7	75.2
China	..	..	..	..	..	..	..	..	..	..	..	..	..	..	..	..	..	..
India	..	..	..	..	..	..	..	..	..	..	..	..	..	..	..	..	..	..
Indonesia	..	..	..	..	..	..	..	..	383	420	371	372	378	387	..	..	..	..
Russian Federation	89.2[f]	92.8[f]	73.1[f]	69.8[f]	49.1[f]	61.6[f]	44.3[f]	45.2[f]	437	482	469	467	477	480	..	..	..	..
South Africa	..	..	..	..	..	..	..	..	..	..	..	..	..	..	..	..	..	..

Note: The OECD average is calculated as the unweighted average for OECD countries for which data is available.

* Information on data for Israel: http://dx.doi.org/10.1787/888932315602.

a) Refers to ISCED levels 5 and 6.
b) Degrees awarded at the tertiary level.
c) PISA reading literacy is scored based on a weighted OECD average of 500 and standard deviation of 100: the unweighted OECD average for all countries for girls is 513, and for boys is 474.
d) PISA mathematics ability is scored based on a weighted OECD average of 500 and standard deviation of 100: the unweighted OECD average for all countries for girls is 490, and for boys is 501.
e) PISA science ability is scored based on a weighted OECD average of 500 and standard deviation of 100: the unweighted OECD average for all countries both girls and boys is 501.
f) Data refer to 2002.
g) Data refer to 2008.

Source: OECD (2010), *PISA 2009 Results: What Students Know and Can Do*, OECD Publishing, Paris; OECD (2011), *Education at a Glance*, OECD Publishing, Paris.

StatLink http://dx.doi.org/10.1787/888932677533

References

AANDC (2010), "Backgrounder – Aboriginal Women's Entrepreneurship: Key Issues", Aboriginal Affairs and Northern Development Canada, *www.aadnc-aandc.gc.ca/eng/1292345911615*, accessed on 2 March 2012.

Adato, M. and J. Hoddinott (2007), "Conditional Cash Transfer Programs: A 'Magic Bullet for Reducing Poverty'?", *2020 Focus Brief on the World's Poor and Hungry People*, October.

ADB (2008), "Conditional Cash Transfer Programs", *ERD Policy Brief Series*, No. 51, Economics and Research Department, Asian Development Bank, Manila.

Atkinson, A. and F. Messy (2012), "Measuring Financial Literacy: Results of the OECD/International Network on Financial Education (INFE) Pilot Study", *OECD Working Papers on Finance, Insurance and Private Pensions*, No. 15, OECD Publishing, Paris.

Atkinson, A., S. McKay, E. Kempson and S. Collard (2006), "Levels of Financial Capability in the UK: Results of a Baseline Survey", *Consumer Research*, Vol. 47, Prepared for the Financial Services Authority by Personal Finance Research Centre University of Bristol, Financial Services Authority.

Australian Government (2008), *Financial Literacy – Women Understanding Money*, Australian Government, Financial Literacy Foundation.

Australian Government (2009), *Financial Services for the Poor: A Strategy for the Australian Aid Program 2010-15*, AusAID.

Baker, L. and A. Wigfield (1999), "Dimensions of Children's Motivation for Reading and their Relations to Reading Activity and Reading Achievement", *Reading Research Quarterly*, Vol. 34, pp. 452-477.

Behrman, J.R., S.W. Parker and P.E. Todd (2011), "Incentives for Students and Parents", Paper presented at Conference on "Educational Policies in Developing Countries", University of Minnesota.

Bergman, M., S. Hupka-Brunner and S. Kanji (2012), "Gender Differences in the Transition from Secondary to Post-secondary Education: The Case of Switzerland", Background paper for the OECD Gender Initiative.

Betcherman, G., M. Godfrey, S. Puerto, F. Rother and A. Stavreska (2007), *Global Inventory of Interventions to Support Young Workers: Synthesis Report*, World Bank, Washington, DC.

Capital One (2009), "Capital One Survey of High School Seniors Reveals Gender Gaps in Financial Literacy", Capital One Financial Corporation, available at *http://phx.corporateir.net/phoenix.zhtml?c= 70667&p=irolnewsArticle&ID=1301899&highlight*, accessed 6 February 2012.

Council of the European Union (2011), "Legislative Acts and Other Instruments", Brussels, June, available at *http://ec.europa.eu/education/school-education/leaving_en.htm*.

Crowley, T. and H.R. Niesr (2008), "Work-related Learning for an Innovation Nation: Engaging with Employers to Improve Work-related Learning Opportunities for Young People Aged 14-19", National Endowment for Science, Technology and Arts (work commissioned by NESTA), United Kingdom.

Cvenecek, D., A.N. Meltzoff and A.G. Greenwald (2011), "Math-gender Stereotypes in Elementary School Children", *Child Development*, Vol. 82, No. 3, pp. 766-779.

Drèze, J. and G. Kingdon (2001), "School Participation in Rural India", *Review of Development Economics*, Vol. 5, No. 1, pp. 1-24.

Edward, M. and M. Kremer (2000), "Child Health and Education: The Primary School Deworming Project in Kenya", available at *http://are.berkeley.edu/courses/DEVELWORK/papers/miguel_oct00.pdf*.

Elliott, W., M. Sherraden, L. Johnson and B. Guo (2011), "Financial Capability in Children: Effects of Participation in a School-Based Financial Education and Savings Program", *Journal of Family and Economic Issues*, Vol. 32, No. 3, pp. 385-399.

European Commission (2009a), "EU Programme of Exchange of Good Practices on Gender Equality: Gender Stereotyping in Germany", Seminar on Gender Stereotypes, 13-14 May 2009, Köln.

European Commission (2009b), "Gender Segregation in the Labour Market: Root Causes, Implications, and Policy Responses in the EU", European Commission's Expert Group on Gender and Employment, Directorate-General for Employment, Social Affairs and Equal Opportunities, European Commission, Luxembourg.

European Commission (2010), *New Skills for New Jobs: Action Now*, Report prepared by the Expert Group on New Skills for New Jobs prepared for the European Commission, European Union.

Falch, T. *et al.* (2010), "Completion and Dropout in Upper Secondary Education in Norway: Causes and Consequences", Centre for Economic Research at Norges Teknisk-Naturvitenskapelige Universitet, Trondheim.

Fernandez, T., M. Bucheli and S. Cardozo (2012), "Gender Differences in the Transition from Secondary to Post-secondary Education: The Case of Uruguay: A PISA Longitudinal Study", Background paper for the OECD *Gender Initiative*.

FINRA Investor Education Foundation (2009), *Financial Capability in the United States – Initial Report of Research Findings From the 2009 National Survey – A Component of the National Financial Capability Study*, FINRA Investor Education Foundation, Washington, DC.

Flabbi, L. (2011), "Gender Differences in Education, Career Choices and Labour Market Outcomes on a Sample of OECD Countries", Background paper for the OECD *Gender Initiative*.

Flabbi, L. and M. Tejada (2012), "Fields of Study Choices, Occupational Choices and Gender Differentials", Background paper for the OECD *Gender Initiative*.

Francavilla, F., G.C. Giannelli and L. Grilli (2012), "Mothers' Employment and their Children's Schooling: A Joint Multilevel Analysis for India", World Development, Elsevier, in press.

Fredericks, J.A. and J.S. Eccles (2002), "Children's Competence and Value Beliefs from Childhood through Adolescence: Growth Trajectories in Two Male-sex-typed Domains", *Developmental Psychology*, Vol. 38, No. 4, pp. 519-533.

Gallup (2009/10), "Gallup World Poll", *www.gallup.com/consulting/worldpoll/24046/About.aspx*.

Glewwe, P. and M. Kremer (2006), "Schools, Teachers, and Education Outcomes'", in E.A. Hanushek and F. Welch (eds.), *Handbook of the Economics of Education*, Vol. 2, Edition 1, Elsevier, September.

Glewwe, P., S. Moulin and M. Kremer (2009), "Many Children Left Behind? Textbooks and Test Scores in Kenya", *American Economic Journal: Applied Economics,* Vol. 1, No. 1, pp. 112-135.

Guedes, A. (2004), "Addressing Gender-based Violence from the PHN Sector: A Literature Review and Analysis", USAID, Bureau for Global Health, Washington, DC.

Guiso, L., F. Monte, P. Sapienza and L. Zingales (2008), "Culture, Gender and Math", *Science*, Vol. 320, No. 5880, pp. 1164-1165.

Haile, G., R. Poppe and M. Frölic (2011), "School Meals Programme in Ethiopia: A Mixed-methods Based Impact Study'", University of Mannheim, and the UN-World Food Programme Country Office Ethiopia, March.

Handa, S. (2002), "Raising Primary School Enrolment in Developing Countries. The Relative Importance of Supply and Demand", *Journal of Development Economics*, Vol. 69, No. 1, pp. 103-128.

Hanlon, J., A. Barrientos and D. Hulme (2010), *Just Give Money to the Poor*, Kumarian Press, United States.

Herbert, J. and D.T. Stipek (2005), "The Emergence of Gender Differences in Children's Perceptions of their Academic Competence", *Journal of Applied Developmental Psychology*, Vol. 26, No. 3, pp. 276-295.

Hilgert, M., J. Hogarth and S. Beverly (2003), "Household Financial Management: The Connection Between Knowledge and Behaviour", *Federal Reserve Bulletin*, Vol. 89, pp. 309-322.

Hung, A., J. Yoong and E. Brown (2012), "Empowering Women Through Financial Awareness and Education", OECD *Working Papers on Finance, Insurance and Private Pensions*, No. 14, OECD Publishing, Paris, available at *http://dx.doi.org/10.1787/5k9d5v6kh56g-en*.

IES (2007), "Encouraging Girls in Math and Science", Institute of Education Sciences, National Center for Education Research, US Department of Education.

IET (2007), "STEM Engagement: The Perspectives of Educationalists, Teachers and Pupils", Stevenage: Institution of Engineering and Technology, United Kingdom.

ILO (2010), "Global Employment Trends for Youth", *Special Issue on the Impact of the Global Economic Crisis on Youth*, International Labour Office, Geneva, August.

ILO (2012a), "Key Indicators of the Labour Market (KILM)", 7th Edition, ILO Department of Economic and Labour Market Analysis, Geneva, available at *http://kilm.ilo.org*.

ILO (2012b), "ILO's Women's Entrepreneurship Development Programme (ILO-WED)", International Labour Organization, *www.ilo.org/wed*.

Ipsos Reid (2010), "Canadian Youth Science Monitor", Canada Foundation for Innovation, May.

Irish Financial Regulator (2009), *Financial Capability in Ireland: An Overview*, available at *www.financialregulator.ie/publications/Documents/Financial%20Capability%20An%20Overview.pdf*.

Kane, J.M. and J.E. Mertz (2011), "Debunking Myths about Gender and Mathematics Performance", *Notices of the American Mathematical Society*, Vol. 59, No. 1, pp. 10-21.

Levine, R., C. Lloyd, M. Greene and C. Grown (2009), *Girls Count a Global Investment and Action Agenda: A Girls Count Report on Adolescent Girls*, Center for Global Development, Washington, DC.

Lord, P. and M. Jones (2006), *Pupils' Experiences and Perspectives of the National Curriculum and Assessment: Final Report for the Research Review*, National Foundation for Educational Research (NFER), Slough, United Kingdom.

Loyalka, P. and M. Maani (2012), "Does Choosing the Science Track Matter for Females Aspiring to go to College? Evidence from the STEM Education Pipeline in China", *Working Paper*, China Institute for Educational Finance Research (CIEFR), Peking University.

Lund, F. (2011), "A Step in the Wrong Direction: Linking the South Africa Child Support Grant to School Attendance", *Journal of Poverty and Social Justice*, Vol. 19, No. 1, pp. 5-14.

Lusardi, A. and O.S. Mitchell (2007), "Baby Boomer Retirement Security: The Roles of Planning, Financial Literacy, and Housing Wealth", *Journal of Monetary Economics*, Vol. 54, No. 1, pp. 205-224.

Lusardi, A. and O.S. Mitchell (2011), "Financial Literacy Around the World: An Overview", *Journal of Pension Economics and Finance*, Cambridge University Press, Vol. 10, No. 4, pp. 497-508.

Lusardi, A, O.S. Mitchell and V. Curto (2010), "Financial Literacy Among the Young", *Journal of Consumer Affairs*, Vol. 44, No. 2, pp. 358-380.

Mann, A. (2012), "It's Who You Meet: Why Employer Contacts at School Make a Difference to the Employment Prospects of Young Adults", Education and Employers Taskforce, London, United Kingdom.

Matějů, P., P. Soukup, J. Straková and M. Smith (2012), "Gender Differences in the Transition from Secondary to Post-secondary Education: The Case of the Czech Republic", Background paper for the OECD *Gender Initiative*.

McKay, S. (2011), "Understanding Financial Capability in Canada Analysis of the Canadian Financial Capability Survey", Research Paper prepared for the Task Force on Financial Literacy, University of Birmingham, available at *http://publications.gc.ca/collections/collection_2011/fin/F2-213-2011-eng.pdf*.

Miguel, E. and M. Kremer (2004), "Worms: Indentifying Impacts on Education and Health in the Presence of Treatment Externalities", *Econometrica*, Vol. 72, No. 1, pp. 159-217.

Morcos, C. and J. Sebstad (2011), *Financial Education for Adolescent Girls*, Youth-Inclusive Financial Services (YFS), available at *www.yfslink.org/resources/general-resources/Financial_education_for_adolescent_girls*, accessed 7 February 2012.

Morrison, A., M. Ellsberg and S. Bott (2007), "Addressing Gender-Based Violence: A Critical Review of Interventions", *World Bank Research Observer*, Vol. 22, No. 1, pp. 25-51.

Nigeria Federal Ministry of Education (2010), *The Nigeria Digest of Education Statistics 2006-2010*, Federal Ministry of Education, Nigeria.

Nguyen, T. (2008), "Information, Role Models, and Perceived Returns to Education: Experimental Evidence from Madagascar", *Working Paper*, Department of Economics, Massachusetts Institute of Technology, Cambridge, United States.

Nordic Consulting Group (2011), "End Review of the Project – Strengthening Women Entrepreneurs in Uganda 'Enterprise Uganda'", available at *www.oecd.org/aidfortrade/47399575.pdf*.

Nordman, C.J. and L. Pasquier (2012), "Vocational Education, On-the-Job Training and Labour Market Integration of Young Workers in Urban West Africa", Background paper for *2012 EFA Global Monitoring Report: Youth, Skills and Work*, UNESCO, Paris.

OECD (2004), Learning for Tomorrow's World. First Results from PISA 2003, OECD Publishing, Paris, DOI: http://dx.doi.org/10.1787/9789264006416-en.

OECD (2005), Improving Financial Literacy: Analysis of Issues and Policies, OECD Publishing, Paris, DOI: http://dx.doi.org/10.1787/fmt-v2005-art11-en.

OECD (2007), PISA 2006 Science Competencies for Tomorrow's World, OECD Publishing, Paris, DOI: http://dx.doi.org/10.1787/9789264040014-en.

OECD (2008), Encouraging Student Interest in Science and Technology Studies, Global Science Forum, OECD Publishing, Paris, DOI: http://dx.doi.org/10.1787/9789264040892-en.

OECD (2009a), Equally Prepared for Life? How 15 Year old Boys and Girls Perform in School, OECD Publishing, Paris, DOI: http://dx.doi.org/10.1787/9789264064072-en.

OECD (2009b), "Financial Crisis and Financial Education: Analytical Note and Recommendations", OECD/INFE Working Paper, OECD Publishing, Paris.

OECD (2010a), PISA 2009 Results: What Students Know and Can Do – Student Performance in Reading, Mathematics and Science, OECD Publishing, Paris, DOI: http://dx.doi.org/10.1787/9789264091450-en.

OECD (2010b), PISA 2009 Results: Learning to Learn – Student Engagement, Strategies and Practices, OECD Publishing, Paris, DOI: http://dx.doi.org/10.1787/9789264083943-en.

OECD (2010c), PISA 2009 Results: Learning Trends – Changes in Student Performance since 2000, OECD Publishing, Paris, DOI: http://dx.doi.org/10.1787/9789264091580-en.

OECD (2010d), PISA 2009 Results: Overcoming Social Background – Equity in Learning Opportunities and Outcomes, OECD Publishing, Paris, DOI: http://dx.doi.org/10.1787/9789264091504-en.

OECD (2010e), PISA Framework on Financial Literacy, OECD Publishing, Paris, available at www.pisa.oecd.org/dataoecd/8/43/46962580.pdf.

OECD (2011a), Education at a Glance: OECD Indicators, OECD Publishing, Paris, DOI: http://dx.doi.org/10.1787/eag-2011-en.

OECD (2011b), PISA 2009 Results: Students on line – Digital Technologies and Performance, OECD Publishing, Paris, DOI: http://dx.doi.org/10.1787/9789264112995-en.

OECD (2011c), Report on the Gender Initiative: Gender Equality in Education, Employment and Entrepreneurship 2011, Report prepared for the Meeting of the OECD Council at Ministerial Level, Paris, 25-26 May 2011, OECD Publishing, Paris.

OECD (2011d), "Survey on National Gender Frameworks, Gender Public Policies, Leadership and Employment in the Middle East and North Africa", Developed by the MENA-OECD Governance Programme, OECD Publishing, Paris.

OECD (2012a), Reviews of National Policies for Education: Abu Dhabi, United Arab Emirates, OECD Publishing, Paris, forthcoming.

OECD (2012b), Equity and Quality in Education – Supporting Disadvantaged Students and Schools, OECD Publishing, Paris, DOI: http://dx.doi.org/10.1787/9789264130852-en.

OECD (2012c), "What Kinds of Careers Do Boys and Girls Expect for Themselves?", OECD PISA in Focus 14, OECD Publishing, Paris.

OECD (2012d), Education at a Glance: OECD Indicators, OECD Publishing, Paris, DOI: http://dx.doi.org/10.1787/eag-2012-en.

OECD (2012e), OECD Skills Strategy: Better Skills, Better Jobs, Better Lives: A Strategic Approach to Kills Policies, Report prepared for the Ministerial Council Meeting, OECD, Paris, May.

OECD (2012f), Financial Education in Schools: Policy Guidance, Challenges and Case Studies, OECD Publishing, Paris, forthcoming, DOI: http://dx.doi.org/10.1787/9789264174825-en.

OECD (2012g), "Recommendation on Guidelines for Financial Education in Schools and Guidance on Learning Framework on Financial Education", OECD Publishing, Paris, forthcoming.

Ouane, A. and C. Glanz (2010), "Why and How Africa Should Invest in African Languages and Multilingual Education. An Evidence and Practice-based Policy Advocacy Brief", in collaboration with the Association for the Development of Education in Africa, UNESCO Institute for Lifelong Learning, Germany.

Parvin, J. and C. Porter (2008), Learning to Love Science: Harnessing Children's Scientific Imagination, Report from the Chemical Industry Education Centre, University of York, United Kingdom.

Perry, V.G. and M.D. Morris (2005), "Who Is in Control? The Role of Self Perception, Knowledge, and Income in Explaining Consumer Financial Behavior", *Journal of Consumer Affairs*, Vol. 39, No. 2, pp. 299-213.

Polidano, C. and C. Ryan (2012), "Gender Differences in the Transition from Secondary to Post-secondary Education: The Case of Australia", Background paper for the OECD *Gender Initiative*.

Pulerwitz, J., G. Barker and M. Segundo (2004), "Promoting Healthy Relationships and HIV/STI Prevention for Young Men: Positive Findings from an Intervention Study in Brazil", Horizons Research Update, Population Council, Washington, DC.

Quintini, G. (2011), "Over-Qualified or Under-Skilled: A Review of Existing Literature", *OECD Social, Employment and Migration Working Papers*, No. 121, OECD Publishing, Paris, DOI: *http://dx.doi.org/10.1787/5kg58j9d7b6d-en*.

Saito, M. (2011), "Trends in the Magnitude and Direction of Gender Differences in Learning Outcomes", *Southern and Easter Africa Consortium for Monitoring Educational Quality (SAQMEC) Working Paper*, September.

Sikora, J. and A. Pokropek (2011), "Gendered Career Expectations of Students: Perspectives from PISA 2006", *OECD Education Working Papers*, No. 57, OECD Publishing, Paris, DOI: *http://dx.doi.org/10.1787/5kghw6891gms-en*.

Soares, F., R. Ribas and R. Osorio (2010), "Evaluating the Impact of Brazil's Bolsa Familia: Cash Transfer Programs in Comparative Perspective", *Latin American Research Review*, Vol. 45, No. 2, pp. 173-190.

Stango, V. and J. Zinman (2009), "Exponential Growth Bias and Household Finance", *Journal of Finance*, Vol. 64, No. 6, pp. 2807-2849.

Sy, V. (2011), *Gender Equality in Education: Looking Beyond Parity. Summary of the Report on Gender and Educational Achievement in French-Speaking Africa: Study of Performances by primary-School Pupils*, UNESCO, Paris.

UNESCO (2009), *World Atlas of Gender Equality in Education*, UNESCO, Paris.

UNESCO (2010), *Education for All Global Monitoring Report 2010*, UNESCO, Paris.

UNESCO (2011a), *The Hidden Crisis: Armed Conflict and Education*, UNESCO, Paris.

UNESCO (2011b), *Education for All Global Monitoring Report 2011*, UNESCO, Paris.

UNESCO (2012a), *World Atlas of Gender Equality on Education*, UNESCO, Paris.

UNESCO (2012b), *Education Database*, UNESCO Institute for Statistics, available at *http://stats.uis.unesco.org/unesco/ReportFolders/ReportFolders.aspx*.

van Rooij, M., A. Lusardi and R. Alessie (2011), "Financial Literacy and Stock Market Participation", *Journal of Financial Economics*, Vol. 101, No. 2, pp. 449-472, August.

Vermeersch, C. and M. Kremer (2005), "School Meals, Educational Achievement, and School Competition: Evidence from Randomized Evaluation", *World Bank Policy Research Working Paper*, No. 3523, Washington, DC.

WEF (2011), *Global Gender Gap Report 2011*, World Economic Forum, Geneva, available at *http://reports.weforum.org/global-gender-gap-2011/#=*.

WFP (2009), *Feed Minds, Change Lives School Feeding: Highlights and New Directions*, World Food Programme, Rome.

White House Council (2012), "Keeping America's Women moving forward: The Key to an Economy Built to Last", White House Council on Women and Girls, April.

World Bank (2009), "Women in 33 Countries Highly Vulnerable to Financial Crisis Effects", *Press Release*, No. 2009/245/PREM, Washington, DC, 6 March.

World Bank (2010), *The Adolescent Girls Initiative: An Alliance for Economic Empowerment*, World Bank, Washington, DC, October.

World Bank (2011), *World Development Report 2012: Gender Equality and Development*, World Bank, Washington, DC.

PART III

Gender equality in employment

Compared to men, women are less likely to work full-time, more likely to be employed in lower-paid occupations, and less likely to progress in their careers. As a result gender pay gaps persist and women are more likely to end their lives in poverty. This section looks at how many men and women are in paid work, who works full-time, and how having children and growing older affect women's work patterns and earnings differently to men's. It looks at how women bear the brunt of domestic and family responsibilities, even when working full-time. It also considers the benefits for businesses of keeping skilled women in the workplace, and encouraging them to sit on company boards. It looks at women's representation in parliaments, judicial systems, and the senior civil service. It examines male and female employment in the wake of the crisis, and how women tend to be confined to the most vulnerable categories within the informal sector in developing countries.

PART III

Chapter 11

Who is in paid work?

Key findings

- Female employment participation has generally increased and gender gaps in labour force participation have narrowed, although they remain considerable in South Asia, the Middle East and North Africa.

- Mothers and women with low levels of educational attainment are least likely to be in paid work.

- Occupational segregation has not improved since the turn of the century.

- Women are still under-represented at more senior job levels.

Gains in female educational attainment have contributed to a worldwide increase in women's participation in the labour force in recent decades (Chapter 4), so helping narrow the employment gender gap in most countries. Nevertheless, considerable gaps do remain – in working hours (Chapter 12); in conditions of employment, occupations and sectors; and in earnings (Chapter 13). Women continue to undertake a much higher load of unpaid work than men (Chapter 17), which restricts their opportunities to take on paid work.

Across OECD countries the gender gap in labour force participation narrowed by an average of 9 percentage points between 1990 and 2010 (Figure 11.1). Outside the OECD, the gap shrank in an even more pronounced manner in Central and South America – more than 12 percentage points. By contrast, East Asia and the Pacific (with 4 percentage points), together with Eastern Europe and Central Asia (less than 2), saw much more limited progress (Figure 11.2).

In 2010, an average of 65% of women were in the labour force in OECD countries, compared with 58% in 1990. However, there is considerable variation across countries. In 2010, female labour force participation ranged from over 75% in China, the Nordic countries and Switzerland to below 50% in India, Mexico, South Africa and Turkey (Annex III.A1).

Figure 11.1. In the OECD, gender gaps in labour force participation vary widely across countries

Gender gap in labour force participation (male rates *minus* female rates) in OECD, enhanced engagement countries, and selected developing countries,[a] 15-64 years old, 1980-2010

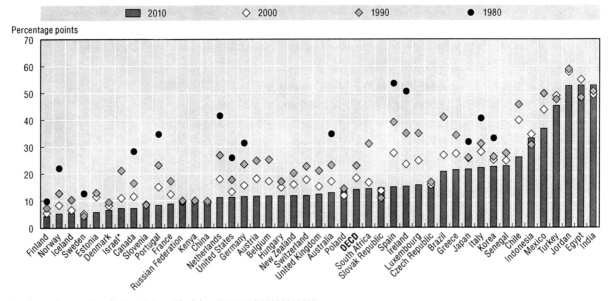

* Information on data for Israel: *http://dx.doi.org/10.1787/888932315602*.

a) Countries are arranged from left to right in ascending order of 2010 gender gap in labour force participation.

Source: *OECD Employment Database 2012* and ILO (2012), "Key Indicators of the Labour Market (KILM)", 7th Edition, *ILO Department of Economic and Labour Market Analysis*, Geneva, available at *www.kilm.ilo.org*.

StatLink ⟐ *http://dx.doi.org/10.1787/888932675861*

Figure 11.2. **Gender gaps in labour force participation have narrowed but remain significant in South Asia, the Middle East and North Africa**

Gender gaps in labour force participation (male rates *minus* female rates) by world region,[a] 15-64 years old, 1990-2010

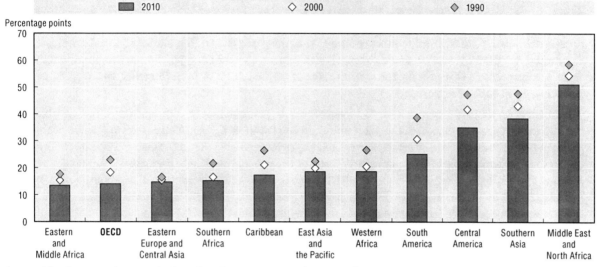

a) Unweighted averages for countries in each region. Country groupings are defined in the Annex III.A1. Regions are arranged from left to right in ascending order of 2010 gender gap in labour force participation.

Source: OECD Employment Database 2012 and ILO (2012), "Key Indicators of the Labour Market (KILM)", 7th Edition, ILO Department of Economic and Labour Market Analysis, Geneva, available at www.kilm.ilo.org.

StatLink ᵃᵢₛ▓ *http://dx.doi.org/10.1787/888932675880*

In non-OECD countries, despite progress, gender gaps are noticeably high in Central America, Southern Asia, and the Middle East and North Africa (MENA): they can be as high as 30 percentage points as female labour force participation is limited. Many governments are seeking to foster female employment. India and South Africa, for example, have introduced measures to attract more women into their public work programmes (Box 11.1).

Today, in most regions around the world, workers are employed predominantly in the service sector, where women are over-represented (Table 11.1). In the OECD, services account for more than 80% of women's employment compared to 60% of men's, with the agriculture sector employing the lowest numbers of both men and women.

In less developed regions, except for the Caribbean and South America, agriculture does continue to be an important source of employment, especially for women. In fact, recent decades have seen a "feminisation of agriculture" in many developing countries. In 2010, 58% of women against 52% of men in Eastern and Middle Africa worked in the agricultural sector, whilst in South Asia the proportions were 51% and 35% respectively (Table 11.1). Women often remain marginalised in low-status, unskilled, frequently unpaid agricultural work (Jütting and Morrisson, 2009; Jütting *et al.*, 2012). Discriminatory social institutions (Chapter 2) play a key role in explaining gender disparities in the agricultural sector.

Across the OECD there is a strong feminisation of most services sectors. An average of almost one in three women employed in the services sector works in sales, hotels and restaurants; the highest proportions of women are observed in health and community services (78%), followed by education (70%). Transport, storage, and communication are the exception, having low feminisation rates (i.e. low proportions of women among workers in each activity) (see Figure 11.3). There are, however, wide differences across countries both in the distribution of female employment by sector and in feminisation rates (Annex III.A3).

Box 11.1. **Public work programmes through a gender lens**

A number of developing and emerging economies use public works programmes as instruments for delivering social protection to the working-age poor as well as a response to slack labour demand. Although early programmes suffered from low levels of female participation, some have developed a range of approaches over time to involve more women. Examples are the Indian National Rural Employment Guarantee Act (NREGA) and, to some extent, South Africa's Expanded Public Works Programme (EPWP). Both are important safety nets for women: about 50% of NREGA beneficiaries and 63% of EPWP beneficiaries in 2010 were women.

Both NREGA and EPWP have sought to increase female participation in different ways, one of which is through explicit quotas: NREGA set a target of one-third and EMWP 40%. NREGA also seeks to promote women's participation in the workforce by establishing equal wages for men and women; allowing childcare facilities to be provided on worksites; and by requiring that places of work should be close to participants' homes (i.e. within a radius of eight kilometres). As a result of NREGA's equal wage policy, women are able to earn more – up to INR 60 (USD 1.2) more than in private rural employment (Holmes and Jones, 2011). A further requirement is that women should be included in monitoring and managing the scheme.

Yet, even though both public works schemes have high female participation rates, there is scope for improvement. Mainly for reasons of technical capacity and cost (employment costs exceed the hourly wage), the South African EPWP has a very limited outreach. It could be improved if it were to establish equal wages for men and women and provide better day-care facilities through closer links with the subsidised Early Childhood Development Centres programme. NREGA, too, has been criticised for high costs and low efficiency (Niehaus and Sukhtankar, 2009); the issue of corruption has also been widely debated since evidence came to light in some districts that the higher status households in the villages are more likely to participate in the programme (Liu and Deininger, 2010). NREGA has also been reproached for lacking day-care facilities at or near the work sites (Bhatty, 2006), even though they were designed into the scheme. Both the South African and Indian programmes could benefit from allowing flexible women working hours to support their dual work and caring responsibilities.

Table 11.1. **Women are over-represented in the service sector**

Distribution of employment by sector, region and sex, 2010[a, b]

	Women				Men			
	Agriculture	Industry	Services	All activities[c]	Agriculture	Industry	Services	All activities[c]
Caribbean	3	9	88	100	11	29	60	100
Central America	8	16	76	100	34	23	42	100
East Asia and the Pacific	31	12	56	100	33	20	46	100
Eastern and Middle Africa	58	8	34	100	52	14	34	100
Eastern Europe and Central Asia	23	14	63	100	23	30	47	100
Middle East and North Africa	21	7	72	100	12	29	58	100
OECD	**5**	**12**	**83**	**100**	**6**	**34**	**60**	**100**
South America	12	12	76	100	20	28	52	100
Southern Africa	12	11	77	100	21	26	53	100
Southern Asia	51	19	28	100	35	20	41	100
Western Africa	53	7	36	100	60	11	27	100

a) 2010 or most recent year, unweighted averages for countries in each region for which data was available after 2005.

b) See the Annex III.A1 for more detail on the countries and years used to calculate regional averages.

c) Data for all activities may also include "activity not adequately defined", here not reported. The sum of agriculture, industry and services may not therefore equal exactly 100.

Source: OECD Employment Database 2012; for OECD countries (excluding France, Luxembourg and the United States) and Brazil; ILO (2012), "Key Indicators of the Labour Market (KILM)", 7th Edition, ILO Department of Economic and Labour Market Analysis, Geneva, www.kilm.ilo.org for France, Luxembourg, the United States and non-OECD countries (excluding Brazil).

StatLink ⟶ http://dx.doi.org/10.1787/888932677324

Figure 11.3. **Economic sectors with the highest feminisation rates are health and community services followed by education**

Female employment in service activities in OECD countries, 2010

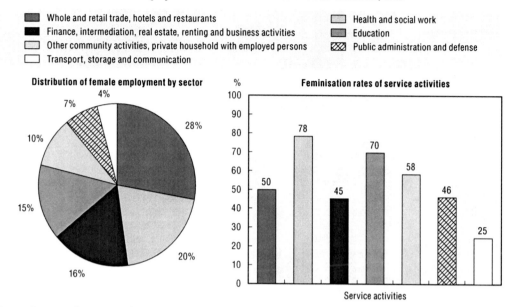

Source: OECD Employment Database 2012, www.oecd.org/employment/database, excluding France, Luxembourg and the United States.

StatLink 🔗 http://dx.doi.org/10.1787/888932675899

Women continue to choose different occupations from men (Chapter 9). In the 1990s, the development of new technologies and the change in the organisation of work were believed to be factors that could contribute to widening women's occupational choices (OECD, 1994). But Figure 11.4 shows that female employment in Europe is concentrated in fewer occupations than male employment, with gender differences varying across countries and little change over the last decade. Bettio and Verashchagina (2009) for Europe and Hegewisch et al. (2010) for the United States corroborate that since the mid-1990s there has been little change in "horizontal segregation" – i.e. where a workforce is made up chiefly of one gender, race, or other ascribed characteristic. In 2009, the greatest spread of female workers across occupations amongst European countries was in the Czech Republic, where ten occupations accounted for half of total employment. The comparably high diversification of female occupations in the Czech Republic is related to their past as communist regimes, while the subsequent move to a market economy has brought the shift back to a more traditional model of economic segregation (Box 11.2).

In addition to horizontal segregation, women across the world also face a "glass ceiling" or "vertical segregation issues" – i.e. where opportunities for career advancement for a particular gender, race, or other ascribed characteristics, are narrowed. On average, in OECD countries for which information is available, less than one-third of managers are women, with small variations across countries (Figure 11.5). The proportion of female managers is highest in France, Poland and the United States (35%). The proportion of women with managerial responsibilities is lowest in Luxembourg (21%). Overall, women face many more obstacles to promotion and reaching the top echelons of the corporate world than men do (Chapter 15).

Figure 11.4. **Female employment is concentrated in a limited number of occupations**

Minimum number of occupations[a] that account for half of employed men and women, 2002-09

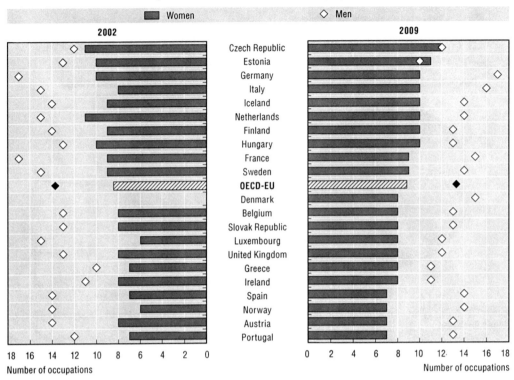

Note: Countries are arranged in descending order of the number of occupations in which women were employed in 2009.

a) The 3-digit ISCO88 classification of occupations has been used, with 111 occupations distinguished.

Source: Eurostat (2012), *European Union Labour Force Survey 1995-2009*, available at *http://circa.europa.eu/irc/dsis/ employment/info/ data/eu_lfs/index.htm.*

StatLink ᵐˢ⁹ᵐ *http://dx.doi.org/10.1787/888932675918*

Female employment has evolved differently not only across regions and countries, but also across age groups, education, and family status. In all OECD countries, except Iceland and Sweden, mothers' employment rates are lower than those of women aged 25 to 49 (OECD, 2012a). During the prime childbearing years, women often tend to reduce their work-participation while men maintain or increase the number of hours worked. However, as children grow up and enter compulsory schooling (around the age of 6) women frequently re-enter the labour market or switch from part-time to full-time work (Chapter 12). The number of children can also play an important role in female employment decisions: in many countries, mothers with three or more children are significantly less likely to be in employment than those with one or two (OECD, 2012a). Such patterns very across countries and are related to the availability of formal childcare support facilities and other family-friendly arrangements in the workplace (Box 11.3 and Chapter 18).

Box 11.2. Effects of the economic transition on occupational segregation in the Russian Federation

The equality of men and women was one of the avowed objectives of the communist system, where the policy of full employment applied to both men and women (including mothers). Due to the size of the industrial sector and prevailing labour demand, women were encouraged to a certain extent to take up physical, traditionally male jobs (Kamerman and Moss, 2009). As a result, and officially at least, horizontal gender segregation in the former Soviet Union was considerably lower than in Western economies.

However, during the transition period in the early 1990s, the industrial sector declined and both men and women moved out and into other jobs related to science, technology, engineering and mathematics (STEM). The change was more visible among women, who left the industrial sector more quickly than men (see figure below) and entered sectors with traditionally high levels of female concentration, such as healthcare, social services and education. Many men either quit or combined their former employment with economic activities in the private sector (which took over a number of state-owned industrial enterprises).

During transition from communism to capitalism, many women left the industrial sector and moved into traditionally female jobs

Change in the proportion of women and men employed in the industrial and education sectors

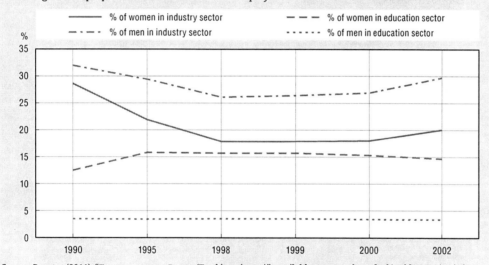

Source: Rosstat (2011), "Труд и занятость в России (Trud i sanjatost)", available at www.gks.ru/bgd/regl/b11_36/Main.htm.
StatLink ⬛⬛⬛ http://dx.doi.org/10.1787/888932675937

Women's movements in and out of employment have noticeably changed in recent decades (Figure 11.6). Before 1990, in the OECD area, women's age-employment profiles generally showed a marked trough during the childbearing years (between the ages of 25 and 34). This trough has gradually evened out as more women remain in the labour market after childbirth. Indeed, employment rates in OECD countries have increased for women of all ages, except for those in the youngest age group (20 to 24 years old).

Figure 11.5. **In the OECD less than one-third of managers are women**
Proportion of women among staff with managerial responsibilities, 2007[a]

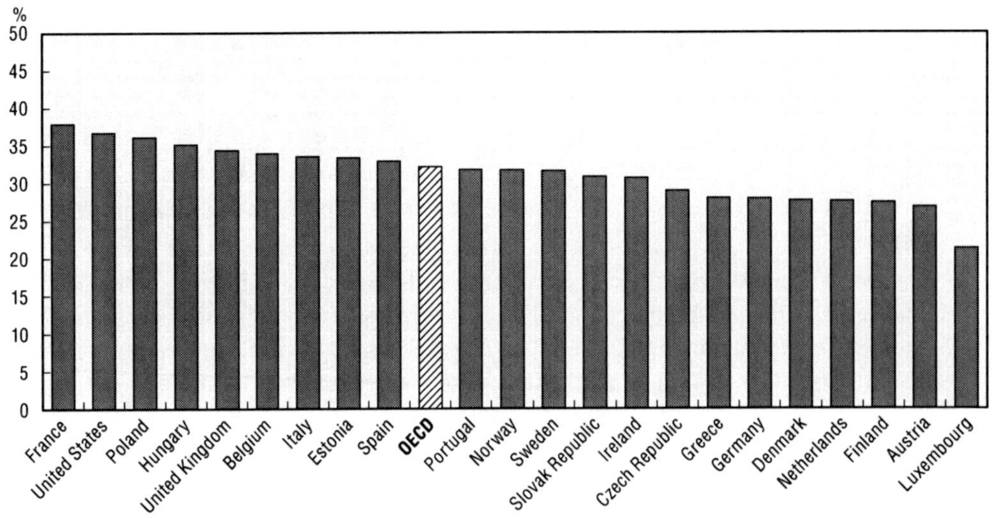

Note: Countries are arranged from left to right in descending order of the proportion of women among staff with managerial responsibilities.
a) March 2009 data for the United States.
Source: OECD Family Database 2012.

StatLink ⬛⬛⬛ http://dx.doi.org/10.1787/888932675956

Box 11.3. **Female labour force participation in MENA countries**

Many countries in the Middle East and North African (MENA) region have made significant progress towards reducing gender gaps in key dimensions of education and health. Improvements in employment outcomes are limited, however. The increase in female labour force participation over the past two decades has been slight: from 22% in 1990 to 30% in 2010, almost 40 percentage points below the male labour force participation rate in the region. There is, however, considerable cross-national variation: female labour force participation rates range from 15% in Iraq to 53% in Qatar.

In the MENA region, women are often employed in the public sector (WEF, 2011). In Egypt, for example, the public sector accounts for 56% of employed women compared with 30% of men (Hendy, 2012). Even within the public sector, women tend to work in traditionally feminised areas in many MENA countries, although degrees of gender segregation do vary across countries.

Lack of work-life balance policies (Chapter 18) is one of the main barriers to women's employment opportunities in the region. Family responsibilities are considered the domain of women and marriage plays a key role in their labour force participation, particularly among those employed in the private sector. In Morocco, only 12% of married women join the labour force (compared with 79% of married men). In Egypt and Jordan, the share of women in private jobs falls sharply when they first marry (Hendy, 2012), regardless of education level. Marriage has less of an effect on employment patterns among women in public sector employment: in Morocco, for example, 57% of married female employees work in the public sector (MMSP, 2011). As in OECD countries, women earn lower salaries than men in both private and public sector employment and do not have equal access to leadership training. They are less well represented in senior positions and leadership in both the private and public sectors.

Box 11.3. Female labour force participation in MENA countries *(cont.)*

Other institutional, legal, economic and social norms also account for the slow progress in the region's female labour force participation. They include norms that determine the type of work women should do, the hours they should work, and the need to obtain the permission of husbands or fathers to work. Some MENA countries (*e.g.* Egypt, Jordan and Yemen) also report that safe public transport and a more suitable working environment would improve the employment prospects of women, particularly those in remote areas (Hendy, 2012; OECD, 2011a).

Many MENA governments have nevertheless taken steps to improve women's employment prospects. One such measure is an increased commitment to conducting research into women's participation in economic activities. Morocco, for example, regularly reports on gender employment trends and women's access to leadership positions in the civil service (OECD, 2010a). Egypt, Jordan, Morocco and Tunisia have introduced measures to guarantee public sector pay equity. Policy initiatives to promote female employment through entrepreneurship in MENA countries are also outlined in Chapter 23.

Figure 11.6. **More women are in paid work during childbearing years than in the past**

Age-employment profiles of women, 1960-2010

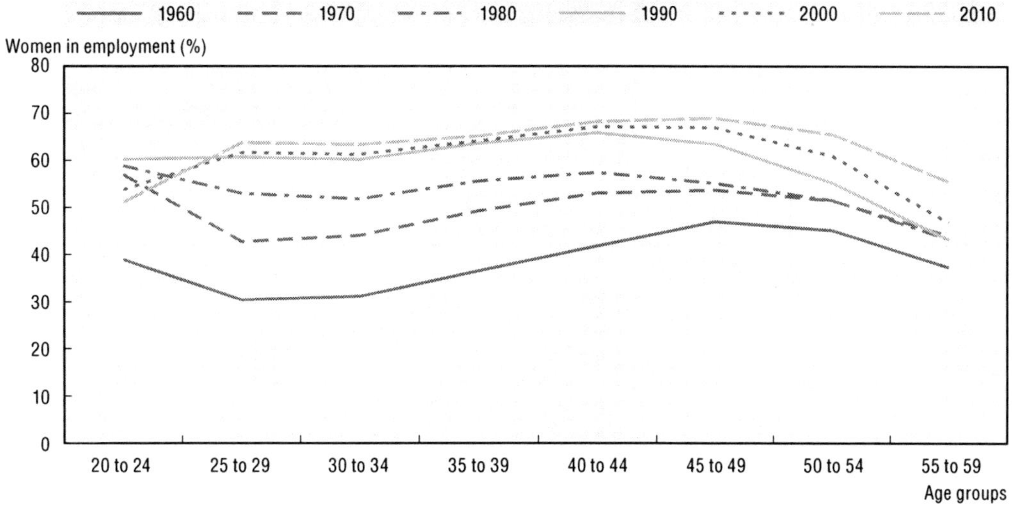

Source: OECD Employment Database 2012.

StatLink ⬛⬛ *http://dx.doi.org/10.1787/888932675975*

Figure 11.6 masks the differences in age-employment profiles that exist across countries. In Nordic countries, women's age-employment participation profiles often closely resemble those of men. In countries like the Czech Republic, Hungary, Japan, Korea and the Slovak Republic, a more traditional profile is observed, as mothers find it more difficult to combine work with family commitments. A fuller understanding of the factors influencing changes in female and male employment patterns across age groups and over time requires comparable and sufficiently detailed longitudinal datasets.

Because of their looser attachment to the labour market and lower earning outcomes, women are at a higher risk of poverty than men, particularly in old age (Figure 11.7). Greater female labour force participation mitigates that risk.

Figure 11.7. **Women are at a higher risk of poverty than men, especially in old age**

Relative poverty risk of men and women by age, OECD average, mid-2000s

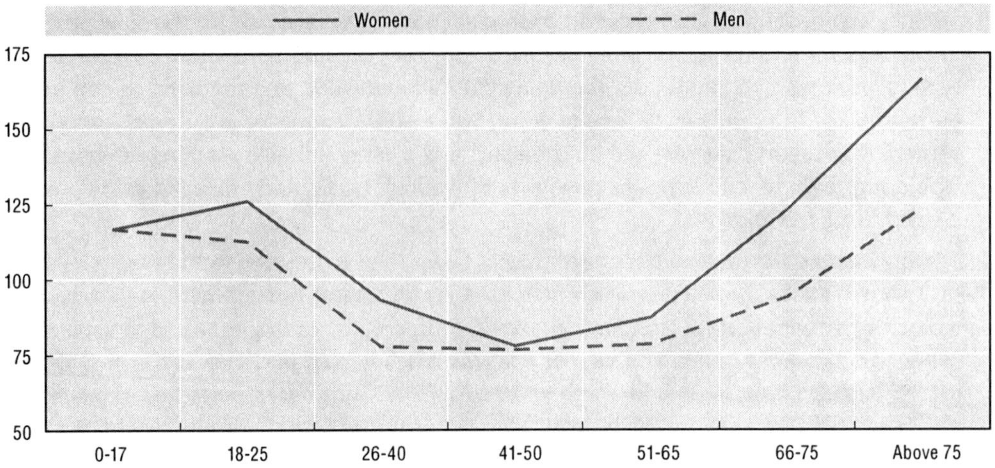

Note: The relative poverty risk is the age-specific poverty rate of men and women divided by the poverty rate for the entire population multiplied by 100. The poverty threshold is set at 50% of the median income of the entire population.
Source: OECD (2008), *Growing Unequal? Income Distribution and Poverty in OECD Countries*, OECD Publishing, Paris.
StatLink http://dx.doi.org/10.1787/888932675994

Educational attainment helps to explain differences in labour force participation for both men and women. In all OECD countries (except Japan, Korea and Turkey) employment rates increase and gender employment gaps decrease as educational attainment rises. In the OECD, while an average of 79% of women with tertiary education were in paid work, only 48% of women with less than upper-secondary education were (OECD, 2012a). Similarly, the employment rates of women with post-secondary education in Egypt and Jordan are three times as high as for the female population in general.

There remain substantial differences in employment outcomes between men and women. Women's employment decisions too often appear to be constrained by various factors which lead to them being more likely than men to end up in low-paid work with limited prospects of advancement.

Key policy messages

● Governments should promote further development of work-life balance policies and other public employment supports to facilitate female labour force participation.

● Future policy development should focus on remaining gender gaps in employment outcomes, such as the concentration of males or females in certain occupations and sectors.

PART III

Chapter 12

Does motherhood mean part-time work?

Key findings

- Across the OECD, gender differences in working hours and participation in part-time work remain wide.
- Childcare costs and time constraints often make part-time work an attractive option for mothers wishing to reconcile work and family commitments. But it is rarely a stepping stone to full-time employment and many mothers work part-time on a long-term basis.

The incidence of part-time work has increased in recent decades, particularly during the 1980s and the early 1990s (OECD, 2010b), while the past decade has seen it grow further still (Figure 12.1, Panel A). With the exception of Poland, male participation in part-time employment has also increased. But by and large, part-time work is a women's affair. The substantial gender imbalance in part-time employment leads to wide gender employment gaps when accounting for working hours (Figure 12.1, Panel B). As part-time employment among women is most widespread in the Netherlands (Box 12.1) and Switzerland, it is in those two countries that differences between female employment rates and their full-time equivalents are most pronounced.

Part-time employment often lasts for years, especially in countries where its incidence is high. Only a very small proportion of workers use part-time work as a stepping stone into full-time employment: 3% of European women and 1.5% of European men who have worked part-time for up to six years move into full-time employment. By contrast, in the United States, where women generally either work full-time or not at all, part-time workers are more likely to go full-time (Buddelmeyer et al., 2005; Macunovich, 2010; OECD, 2010b).

Econometric analysis conducted for this report illustrates the importance of the factors that determine female labour force participation on a full or part-time basis (Annex III.A2). It considers how labour market characteristics and government policies to help parents balance work and family commitments affected aggregate female labour participation in 30 OECD countries from 1980-2007. The results show that:

- The increase in female employment was driven by two separate factors: the increase in part-time work in some countries and the expansion of public employment in others.

- Educational attainment is an important driver of female labour force participation and has contributed to the rise in part-time employment.

- The growing enrolment of children in childcare has enhanced female employment on a full-time and part-time basis. However, higher public spending on childcare does not necessarily lead to more part-time employment, as it may facilitate moves into full-time work or improve the quality of childcare without affecting hours worked per week.

- Increasing public spending for paid maternal and/or parental leave tends to raise the incidence of full-time employment relative to part-time work, while the extending the duration of paid maternal and/or parental leave decreases the probability of working part-time.

- Finally, higher tax rates on the second earner in a family reduce female labour force participation; but women are more likely to work part-time when two-earner households are taxed less than one-earner households with the same earnings.

There is a part-time premium in that part-time workers have more control over their working time and suffer less from stress and health worries than their full-time counterparts (OECD, 2010b). But part-time work also penalises, despite the development of a regulatory framework to ensure equal treatment of part-time and full-time workers. The drawbacks of

Figure 12.1. **There are large gender gaps in part-time work and full-time equivalent employment rates**

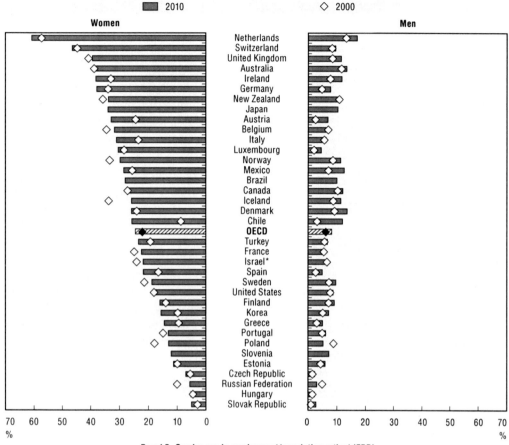

Panel A. Percentage of men and women in part-time employment,ᵃ 2000 and 2010

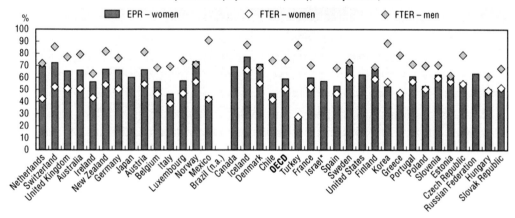

Note: Countries are arranged in descending order of the proportion of women working part-time.

* Information on data for Israel: *http://dx.doi.org/10.1787/888932315602*.

a) Part-time employment refers to persons who usually work less than 30 hours per week in their main job.

b) The employment/population ratio (EPR) is defined as the proportion of employed in the working age population.

c) The full-time equivalent rate (FTER) is calculated as the employment/population ratio, multiplied by the average usual hours worked per week per person in employment, then divided by 40.

Source: OECD Employment Database 2012.

StatLink ⟪ɪɪsɪ⟫ *http://dx.doi.org/10.1787/888932676013*

> ### Box 12.1. **Mothers' popularised part-time work in the Netherlands**
>
> From 1860 to 1960, there was hardly any change either in men's labour force participation rates, around 90%, or in women's, which stood the internationally low level of 30% (Visser *et al.*, 2004). However, between 1975 and 2010 female employment rates climbed from 30 to 70%. The bulk of gains went to part-time work, while the employment rate of women who work full-time has oscillated around 21% since the early 1990s (Dijkgraaf and Portegijs, 2008).
>
> Part-time employment started to expand in response to the recession in the early 1970s, which caused a steep rise in unemployment and in social spending (de Beer and Luttikhuizen, 1998; Visser and Hemerijck, 1998). To limit spending and fight youth unemployment, public policy during the 1970s and 1980s provided subsidies to employers who split existing full-time jobs into two part-time jobs. In turn, employers favoured part-time work to get around union demands for collective reductions in the standard working week to less than 38 hours.
>
> However, part-time work took off not because of a redistribution of work among younger or older workers, but because women, particularly mothers, wanted to be and stay in work. This was related to a sea-change in attitudes. In 2005, about three-quarters of women had no issue with mothers who had young children being in paid work and using care facilities, while the proportion was only a quarter in 1970. However, because of childcare and out-of-school-hours care constraints, women have often chosen to work part-time rather than full-time (Ribberink, 1998). In all, only one in ten mothers with a child not yet ten years of age was in paid work in the Netherlands in 1971: a quarter of a century later that proportion had increased to over 50%. The "normalisation" of part-time work in the Netherlands has been formalised in legislation, with laws such as the ones that stipulate equal pay per working hour regardless of weekly working hours; employees' right to request changes in weekly working hours; and/or the entitlement to request parental leave on a part-time basis (Visser *et al.*, 2004).

part-time employment are: lower hourly earnings (Chapter 13); fewer training and promotion opportunities; less job security; less access to unemployment insurance; and reduced pension entitlements (although pensions systems, as in Switzerland, can cover childcare responsibilities and ensure minimum payments).

Evidence on job satisfaction suggests that women who work part-time voluntarily often accept lower earnings potential and less job security in exchange for better working arrangements and less stress. The advantages must outweigh the disadvantages for a vast majority of part-timers, as more than eight out of ten choose to work part-time "voluntarily" and women are more likely to do so than men (OECD, 2010b).

Mothers are generally more likely than women without children to work part-time as it helps families reconcile work, care responsibilities and school hours (Chapter 17). Mothers in Austria, Germany, Ireland, Luxembourg, the Netherlands and the United Kingdom are particularly likely to be in part-time employment (Figure 12.2).

The lack of access to affordable, good quality childcare and short and/or irregular school hours also force many mothers to work part-time (OECD, 2011b). This explains why the share of part-time work in total female employment is greater in countries with significantly higher childcare costs (Figure 12.3).

Figure 12.2. **Motherhood makes part-time work much more likely**

Percentage in each category of women aged 25-54 (childless/with children under 15), 2009

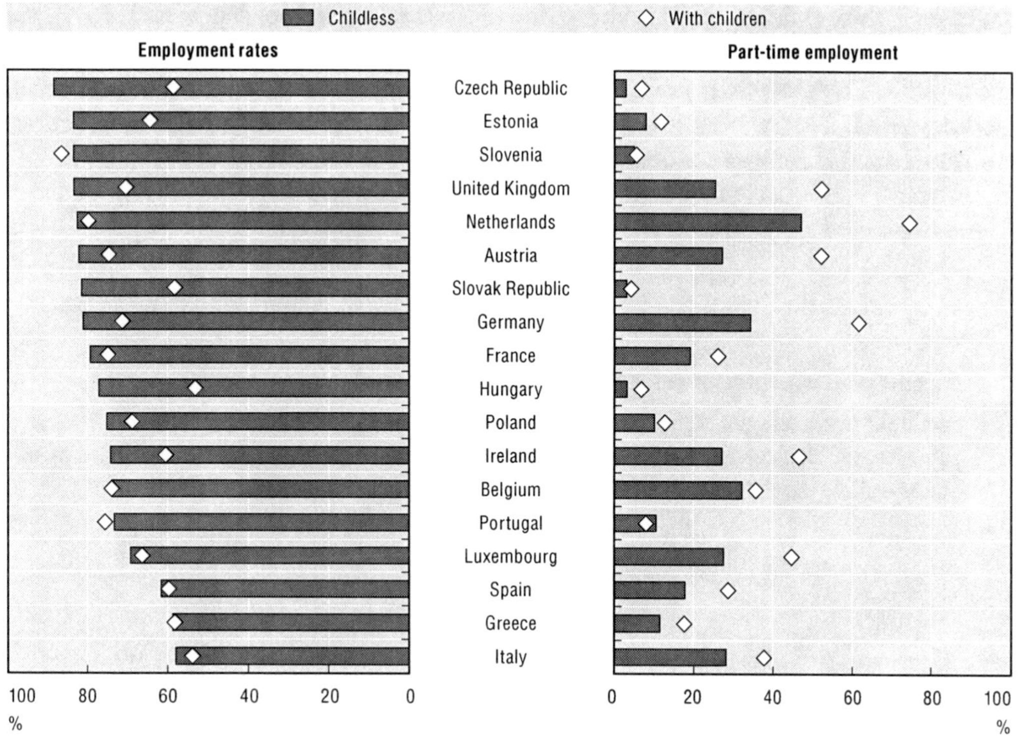

■ Childless   ◇ With children

Employment rates   Part-time employment

Czech Republic
Estonia
Slovenia
United Kingdom
Netherlands
Austria
Slovak Republic
Germany
France
Hungary
Poland
Ireland
Belgium
Portugal
Luxembourg
Spain
Greece
Italy

100 80 60 40 20 0   0 20 40 60 80 100
%   %

Note: Countries are arranged from top to bottom by decreasing employment rates of childless women.

Source: Eurostat (2012), *European Union Labour Force Survey 1995-2009, http://circa.europa.eu/irc/dsis/employment/info/data/eu_lfs/index.htm.*

StatLink ᵐⁱˢᵖ *http://dx.doi.org/10.1787/888932676032*

Figure 12.3. **Women are more likely to work part-time in countries with high childcare costs**[a]

Women's part-time employment and childcare costs

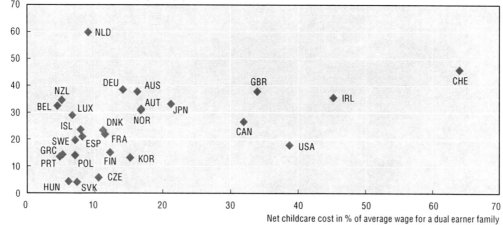

Share of part-time in total women employment (%)

Net childcare cost in % of average wage for a dual earner family

Note: Information on fees for the Netherlands concerns guidelines. Fees are often considerably higher.

a) Net childcare costs among couple families where one adult earns 100% of the average wage and the other earns 50% of the average wage.

Source: OECD (2011), *Doing Better for Families* and *Benefits and Wages: OECD Indicators*, OECD Publishing, Paris.

StatLink ᵐⁱˢᵖ *http://dx.doi.org/10.1787/888932676051*

The presence of young children in the family is one factor that limits transition from part-time to full-time employment. Mothers are more likely to increase their working hours once their children enter primary, or even secondary, school (Thévenon, 2009). The combination of more flexible working hours with provision of longer hours of care and out-of-school care services is likely to facilitate an increase of working hours among mothers (OECD, 2011c), thus strengthening their pension rights while helping to address the labour force shortages projected in some countries (Chapter 1).

Key policy messages

- Promote part-time work as a temporary rather than a permanent solution to work and care issues.
- Encourage a more gender-equitable use of part-time work.
- Facilitate the transition from part-time to full-time work by: i) making (full-time) work pay after childcare cost; and ii) expanding the provision of high quality childcare and out-of-school care services.

PART III

Chapter 13

A woman's worth

Key findings

- Women are paid less than men, discrepancies being largest among top earners. In many countries the pay gap has narrowed in the past decade. In recent years, however, it has closed at a slower pace and wide gaps persist in a number of countries.

- The wage gap is narrow for young women, but there is a wage penalty for motherhood.

- Much of the wage penalty is explained by women working shorter hours in lower-paid occupations than men. However, in many countries, unobserved factors account for a sizable component of the gender pay gap.

- Family policy (childcare costs and parental leave) and wage-bargaining institutions affect the gender pay gap.

Gender wage gaps have narrowed and vary with earnings levels

Almost all OECD countries have legislated to ensure equal pay for equal work, regardless of gender (OECD, 2008a). Yet gender pay gaps persist. In all OECD countries, men's median wages are higher than women's. Among full-time employees, women earned on average 16% less than men in 2010. This figure actually represented a four percentage point closing of the wage gap compared with 2000. However, the improvement had been largely achieved by 2005, and progress has been limited since. Cross-country variations are significant too. In Mexico, Hungary, and New Zealand, the gender wage gap at median earnings is relatively small – between 5 and 7% in 2010. At the other end of the spectrum, the gender wage gap in Japan in 2009 was 29% and even higher at 39% in Korea (Figure 13.1, Panel A).

In many OECD countries, the wage gap at the top of the earnings distribution is wider than at the median point. Top female earners make, on average, 21% less than their male counterparts (Figure 13.1, Panel B). The discrepancy suggests the presence of the so-called "glass ceiling", which prevents women from moving up the career ladder to top-level salaries. The glass-ceiling appears still to be there, even when controlling for differences in occupation and sector affiliation (Albrecht *et al.*, 2003; Arulampalam *et al.*, 2007; De la Rica *et al.*, 2008). Exceptions to the wider gap at the top include Belgium, Canada and Italy, where the gap is similar throughout the income distribution, and Mexico, Poland and Southern European countries, where it is relatively small among the highest 10% of wage earners. The relatively small pay gap at the top in Mexico and Southern Europe reflects a "selection effect", whereby only the most highly qualified women are able to remain in the labour force, so enjoying wage levels closer to men's (De la Rica *et al.*, 2008; Olivetti and Petrongolo, 2008).

In some countries – notably Germany, Austria, and to a lesser extent Spain and Italy – the gap is also wider between male and female low earners, as indicated by the wage gap measured in the first decile of the earnings distribution (the so-called "sticky floor" effect). In Germany, gender wage gaps have narrowed substantially among the top earners, but not among the lowest. Wider gaps in the lower portion of the wage distribution are often linked to the poor provision of affordable childcare – a barrier to employment for low-wage earners who cannot pay for private childcare.

The gender pay gap increases with age and during childbearing

Although younger women's earnings are drawing closer to those of their male counterparts in many OECD countries, women still face important wage penalties as they age and have children. In 2010, across the 16 OECD countries for which data were available, the gender wage gap for 25-29 year-olds was around 9%, compared with 24% for 55-59 year-olds (Figure 13.2, Panel A). Some countries with the highest overall pay gaps, such as Germany or Korea, have below-average or close-to-average pay gaps for young women. This pattern can, in part, be explained by a lessening from one generation to the next of gender differences in the

Figure 13.1. **The gender pay gap: Narrowing but more slowly
and still wide at the top**

Panel A. Slow-down in convergence for the gender pay gap
Gender pay gap in earnings[a] for full-time employees,[b, c] 2000,[d] 2005[e] and 2010[f]

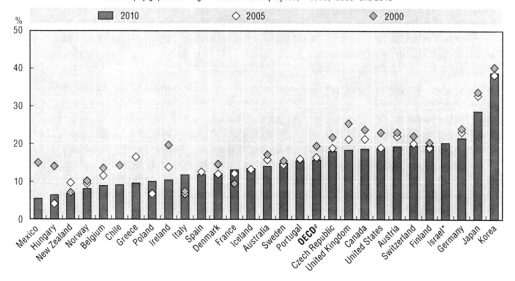

Panel B. The pay gap is higher for incomes at the top of the earnings distribution
Gender pay gap in earnings[a] for full-time employees,[b, c] across the earnings distribution, 2010[f]

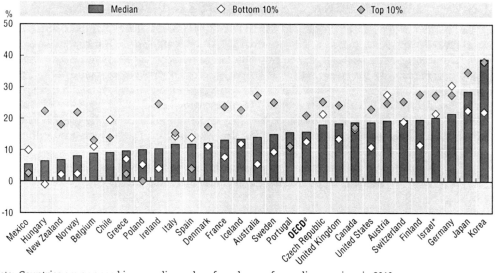

Note: Countries are arranged in ascending order of gender gap for median earnings in 2010.

* Information on data for Israel: *http://dx.doi.org/10.1787/888932315602.*

a) In Panel A, the wage gap is defined as the difference between male and female median wages divided by male median wages; in Panel B it is defined as the difference between male and female wages divided by male wages (at the first decile, median and ninth decile of the earnings distribution).

b) Estimates of earnings used in the calculations refer to gross earnings of full-time wage and salary workers. Self-employed women and unpaid family workers are not included in the calculations. However, this definition may slightly vary from one country to another. Further information on the national data sources and earnings concepts used in the calculations can be found at: *www.oecd.org/employment/outlook.*

c) Data is not adjusted for parity of time worked among full-time employees.

d) Data refer to 1999 (instead of 2000) for the Czech Republic.

e) Data refer to 2004 (instead of 2005) for Italy and Switzerland.

f) Data refer to 2009 (instead of 2010) for Austria, the Czech Republic, Denmark, Finland, Germany, Ireland, Israel, Korea, Sweden and Switzerland; to 2008 for Belgium, France, Greece, Iceland, Italy, Poland, Portugal and Spain.

g) OECD unweighted average excluding Mexico and Chile.

Source: OECD Database on Earnings Distribution; OECD Secretariat estimates based on CASEN (2009) and ENIGH (2010) (Annex III.A3).

StatLink ⬛⬛⬛ *http://dx.doi.org/10.1787/888932676070*

Box 13.1. **Gender pay gaps in emerging economies and MENA countries**

Emerging economies show great diversity in terms of the pay gap and its evolution over time. In China, Indonesia and South Africa, pay gaps are relatively high, while Jordan has a gender pay gap that is smaller than in any OECD country. As in OECD countries, differences in women's sectors of work, work experience, and educational attainment account for only a relatively small part of the pay gap. Much of the pay gaps remains unexplained, especially in Brazil (Marques Garcia *et al.*, 2009).

The narrow gender pay gap in MENA countries is related to the small group of women who are in wage employment – *e.g.* Egypt (23%) and Jordan (16%) – who tend to be more educated than men (Sweidan, 2012). Most women in the MENA region are neither in paid work nor participate in the family business and are therefore not captured in the calculations. Horizontal job segregation appears to be an important factor in Egypt, where a large percentage of women have public sector jobs, which typically pay less than private sector jobs (Ahmed, 2012). In Jordan, segregation across grades within occupations is greater, because women tend to work in low-skill occupations where the pay gap is relatively small, unlike professional occupations where it is larger.

In Indonesia, the average gender wage gap was 22% in 2011, a narrowing of 15% since 1996; women's increased educational attainment accounted for 50% of that improvement (Matsumoto, 2011). While the educational attainment of male and female employees has become broadly similar over time, a large proportion of women continue to work as unpaid family workers. The likelihood of engaging in such work for those who have only been in primary education has increased over time, suggesting that the overall pay gap might in fact be wider if unpaid family workers were to engage in paid work or receive a salary.

The gender wage gap in China and South Africa, in contrast, has widened since the mid-1990s (Muller, 2009). In China, it was around 16% in 1995, while by 2007 it had increased to 26% (Li and Song, 2011). However, due to difficulties in gathering comprehensive national data, the gap reflects only the mean wages of urban workers in five regions using the China Household Income Project. Much of the gender wage gap remains unaccounted for, possibly reflecting discrimination and other factors. This unexplained component has increased over time, particularly for low-wage workers. Possible explanations include the growth in the labour supply from female migrant workers and the privatisation of state-owned enterprises.

**Gender pay gap in emerging economies and MENA countries
are not necessarily higher than in the OECD**

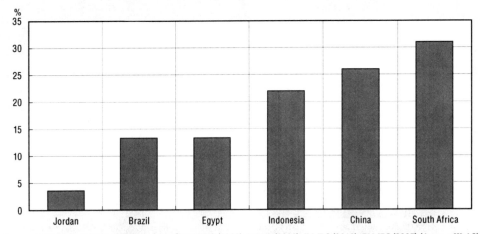

Source: OECD Secretariat estimates based on NIDS (2008), PNAD (2009), JLMPS (2010), ELMPS (2005) (Annex III.A3); Li, S. and J. Song (2011), "Changes in the Gender Wage Gap in Urban China, 1995-2007", *CIBC Working Paper Series*, No. 2011-20; Matsumoto, M. (2011), "Wage Inequality in Indonesia: 1996-2009", *mimeo*, Hitotsubashi University.

StatLink ⟨⟨⟨ http://dx.doi.org/10.1787/888932676089

Figure 13.2. **Gender pay gap increases with age**

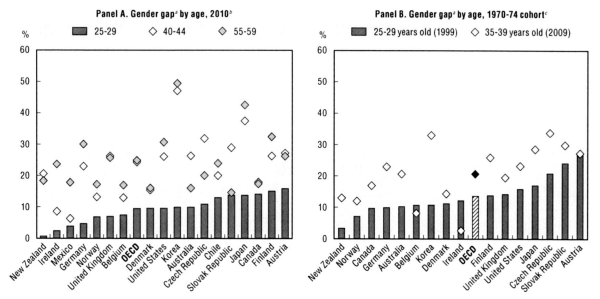

Note: Countries are arranged in ascending order of gender pay gap for 25-29 year-olds in each of the two panels.

a) Defined as the difference between male and female mean wages divided by male mean wages.

b) Data refer to 2008 for Australia, Austria, Denmark, Finland, Germany, Korea, Norway and the Slovak Republic; to 2007 for Belgium, the Czech Republic and Ireland. For Austria, 25-29 refers to 20-29, 40-44 refers to 40-49, and 55-59 refers to 50-59.

c) Data for 25-29 years old refers to 1998 (instead of 1999) for Denmark, Korea, Norway and the Slovak Republic; to 1997 for Ireland. Data for 35-39 years old refers to 2008 (instead of 2009) for Australia, Austria, Denmark, Finland, Germany, Norway, Korea, and the Slovak Republic; to 2007 for Belgium, the Czech Republic and Ireland. For Austria, 25-29 refers to 20-29, 35-39 refers to 30-39.

Source: OECD Database on Earnings Distribution; OECD Secretariat estimates based on CASEN (2009) and ENIGH (2010) (Annex III.A3).

StatLink ⟐⟐⟐ *http://dx.doi.org/10.1787/888932676108*

factors most closely linked with wage levels, such as human capital and occupation choices (Blau and Kahn, 2006). However, differences in the gender wage penalty across ages still persist, even after controlling for generational effects (Figure 13.2, Panel B).

The steep increase in the gender wage gap that women experience during their childbearing and childrearing years points to the presence of a so-called "motherhood penalty". Among women of child-bearing age who work full-time, those with children earn significantly less than men compared with childless women (Figure 13.3). The wage penalty for having children is on average 14%, with Korea showing the greatest wage gap between childless women and those with children, while Italy and Spain have almost none.

Women often work part-time in order to reconcile work and family life (Chapters 11, 12 and 18). If part-time work is taken into account, the gender pay gap in take-home pay doubles in many European countries and triples in Ireland and the Netherlands (Figure 13.4).

Working hours, job choices and family policies matter

Do pay gaps reflect discrimination, especially towards mothers? Personal characteristics and career choices in part explain earning differences between men and women. The fewer hours worked by women explain, on average, one-third of the gender earnings gap among employees in the OECD, which rises to over 50% in Germany and the Netherlands. Working in different occupations and sectors from men, which may be more compatible with family life, is another important explanatory factor. For example, lower geographical mobility might restrict job choice and impact on job earnings. Occupational segregation and reduced

Figure 13.3. **The price of motherhood is high across OECD countries**

Gender pay gap[a] by presence of children,[b] 25-44 years old[c]

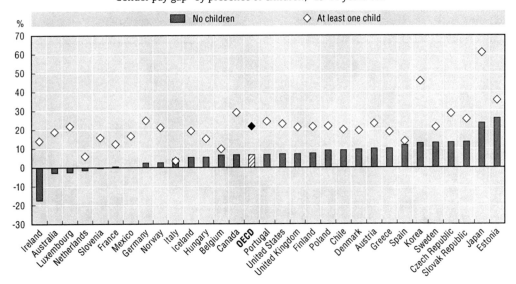

Note: Countries are arranged from left to right in ascending order of the gender pay gap for childless workers.

a) Defined as the difference between male and female median wages divided by male median wages.

b) Children defined as aged less than 16 years old.

c) Wage gap calculated for men and women aged 25-44 working full-time.

Source: OECD Secretariat estimates based on EUSILC (2008), HILDA (2009), CPS (2008), SLID (2008), KLIPS (2007), JHPS (2009), CASEN (2009) and ENIGH (2010) (Annex III.A3).

StatLink ᴹᴵˢᴸ *http://dx.doi.org/10.1787/888932676127*

Figure 13.4. **The difference in take-home pay is wider because women work fewer hours**

Gender pay gap[a] for full-time and all workers

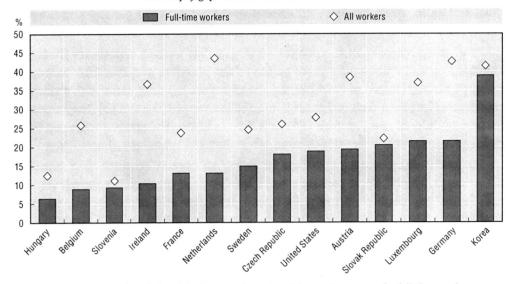

Note: Countries are arranged from left to right in ascending order of the gender pay gap for full-time workers.

a) Defined as the difference between male and female median wages divided by male median wages.

Source: OECD Database on Earnings Distribution; OECD Secretariat estimates based on EUSILC (2008), CPS (2008), KLIPS (2007) (Annex III.A3).

StatLink ᴹᴵˢᴸ *http://dx.doi.org/10.1787/888932676146*

working hours, together with education and work experience, explain slightly more than 30% of wage differences and more than 60% in Germany, the Netherlands, and the United Kingdom. When comparing hourly wages, sector and/or occupation are the most important factors driving the gender wage gap (Blau and Kahn, 1997; Flabbi and Tejada, 2012).

In general, gender differences in measured human capital, age (as a proxy for experience) and other demographic characteristics (such as marital status) do not account for much of the gender wage gap (Figure 13.5). Actual work experience appears to explain on average 5% of the wage gap, while education in general reduces the pay gap – except in Korea.

Figure 13.5. **Differences in hours worked and the type of job explain part of the gender pay gap**

Decomposing the gender pay gap

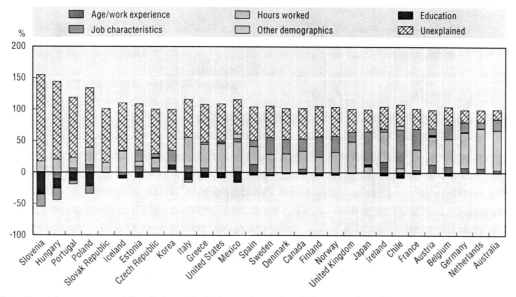

Note: Countries are arranged from left to right in descending order of the proportion of the unexplained gender pay gap. The countries selected differ from Figure 13.1 because survey data for the decomposition analysis are lacking for some countries.
Source: OECD Secretariat estimates, based on EUSILC (2008), HILDA (2009), CPS (2008), KLIPS (2007), SLID (2008), JHPS (2009), CASEN (2009) and ENIGH (2010) (Annex III.A3).

StatLink ᴧᴥ᷿ *http://dx.doi.org/10.1787/888932676165*

Lack of childcare options can lead to career interruptions and discontinuous employment, which in turn may explain women's lower wages when they enter motherhood. Countries with generous work-family policies tend to have a lower unexplained wage gap (Christofides *et al.*, 2010). Figure 13.6 shows that formal care enrolment for young children is associated with a lower gender wage gap. At the same time, the gender pay gap is higher at the extremes of the wage distribution in countries with more generous family policies (Arulampalam *et al.*, 2007; Christofides *et al.*, 2010). For women at the top of the distribution, this discrepancy may be explained the fact that they are penalised for interrupting their careers to have children. The results below indeed suggest that longer periods of maternity and parental leave are associated with a wider wage gap. Both types of policies tend to be inversely correlated: countries with longer parental leave often have lower formal childcare enrolment (*e.g.* Austria, the Czech Republic and the Slovak Republic).

Figure 13.6. **Childcare and leave policies are inversely related to the pay gap**

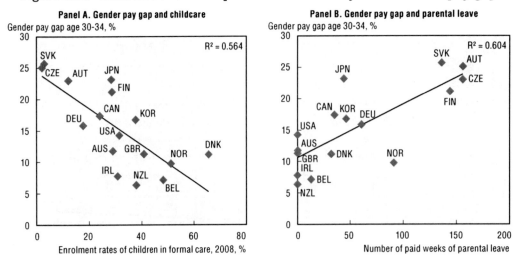

Source: OECD Family Database 2012; OECD Database on Earnings Distribution.

StatLink ⬛⬛ http://dx.doi.org/10.1787/888932676184

Workplace and institutional factors can play a role

Observed characteristics cannot account for a great part of the gender earnings gap in several countries, particularly in Eastern and Central Europe and Korea. What unobserved factors may be behind the gap? Flexible hours, distance to work, teleworking, working in the evenings or other unsociable hours can play a role. When focusing on a sample of women who do not adjust their working hours, who stay with their original employer, hold the position after maternity leave, and experience no changes in other non-pecuniary dimensions, such as working inconvenient hours, the gender pay gap becomes insignificant (Felfe, 2012). This would suggest that employers play a crucial role: workplace support and family-friendly practices can contribute to women earning equal pay.

Wage-setting policies, mechanisms, and institutional practices that affect overall wage distribution also influence the gender pay gap. Indeed, the gap tends to be somewhat higher in countries where overall wage inequality is higher (Figure 13.7, Panel A). The narrower gap among low earners in many countries reflects the influence of statutory minimum wages and workplace agreements to protect low-income workers. Higher union coverage and minimum wages (with respect to the median wage) are associated with narrower gender pay gaps (Figure 13.7, Panel B). The two factors may be linked, since countries with higher unionisation rates tend to have lower wage dispersion, while the drop in union coverage in the past two decades has been accompanied by rising wage inequality (OECD, 2011c). Wage policies which reduce overall pay inequality and those which target low-paid and/or female-dominated sectors can help promote equal pay for women.

It is likely that one aspect of the unexplained component of the gender pay gap is discrimination, against which most OECD countries have legislated. Empirical evidence of the impact of such anti-discrimination legislation is nonetheless scarce, although it does point to some positive effects. At the same time, it is costly and complex to enforce regulations because many women remain unaware of their rights, which points to the need

Figure 13.7. **The gender pay gap is related to wage compression factors**

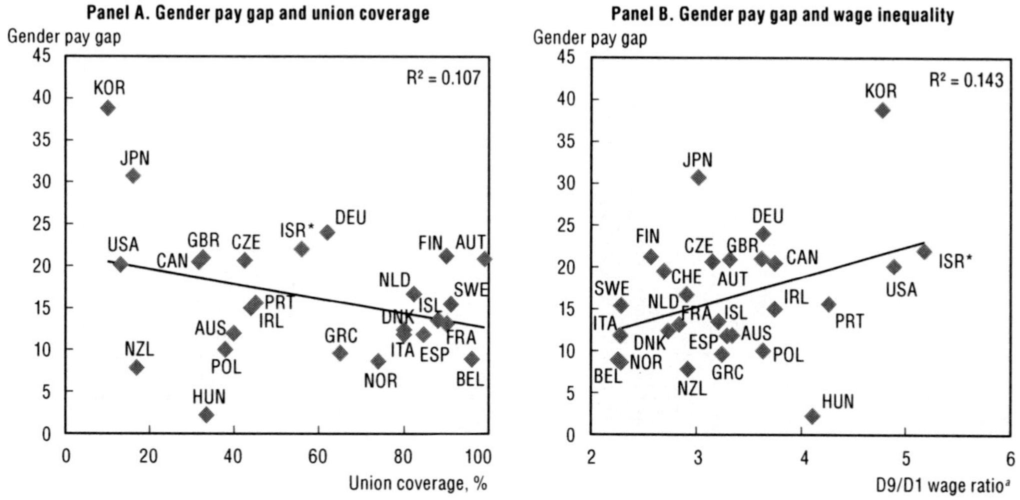

Panel A. Gender pay gap and union coverage

Panel B. Gender pay gap and wage inequality

* Information on data for Israel: http://dx.doi.org/10.1787/888932315602.

a) Ratio between the wages in the ninth and first deciles of the earnings distribution.

Source: OECD Employment Database and Visser, J. (2009), *The ICTWSS Database: Database on Institutional Characteristics of Trade Unions, Wage Setting, State Intervention and Social Pacts in 34 Countries between 1960 and 2007*, Amsterdam Institute for Advanced Labour Studies (AIAS).

StatLink ⬛ http://dx.doi.org/10.1787/888932676203

for public awareness campaigns (OECD, 2008a). Mediation could help but, more importantly, the law will have greater impact if specialised bodies are empowered to investigate companies, take legal action against discriminating employers, and impose sanctions (which, however, they do not appear equipped to do). Transparent pay systems are also an important factor in implementing equal pay.

Key policy messages

- Promote a more gender-equal use of flexible workplace practices that reconcile work and family life and which fit into career patterns. For example, promote a better transition to full-time, permanent, better paid jobs and extend affordable childcare opportunities so as to enhance continuous employment patterns.

- Strengthen public awareness of anti-discrimination laws, promote pay transparency and improve enforcement of equal pay provisions.

- Conduct further research into the contribution of social and informal factors to the persistence of the gender pay gap and produce policy responses to address the issue.

PART III

Chapter 14

The business case for women and addressing the leaky pipeline

Key findings

- There is increasing recognition of the business case for having more women in business and at more senior levels. However, there is a "leaky pipeline" in business with many women leaving or not advancing.

- Firms can do much themselves to empower women and a range of good practices are emerging. In practice, much will depend on the commitment of senior and middle management to driving the necessary change.

The business case for women

To focus the attention of CEOs and senior managers on improving gender balance it is essential that a clear and compelling business case be made, backed by the best possible evidence and analysis. There are several reasons why businesses should be – and increasingly are – interested in enhancing the role of women in their companies. Such reasons include: *a)* to attract and retain the best talent; *b)* to enhance diversity and improve overall performance in the workplace; *c)* to better serve consumer markets, including those in which women are the main customers.

With growing competitive pressures, firms are constantly looking for the best talent. Women account for a growing share of the talent emerging from the education system, and more and more graduate with science degrees (OECD, 2011d). Firms risk losing out if they do not leverage this talent pool. With rapid ageing in OECD countries and beyond, the search for talent is of growing importance to many businesses, and giving women a greater role is increasingly seen as part of the solution. Firms that are not able to address gender equality in the workplace also risk not being seen as attractive career prospects by the next generation of talent. Drawing on new, improved talent pools can also be good for economic growth: Hsieh *et al.* (2012) suggest that between 17 and 20% of economic growth between 1960 and 2008 in the United States can be attributed to the greater intake of under-represented groups in the workforce, notably women.

Tapping into the best talent is not the only reason why many firms are actively engaged in gender initiatives. Initiatives to strike a better balance between work and family life, for example, may reduce stress, sickness and absenteeism, and make a firm more attractive as a place of work, thus increasing staff retention. A recent review of the literature (Beauregard and Henry, 2009) finds that the introduction of work-life balance practices does not necessarily resolve potential conflicts between work and life. It does, though, point to the benefits of such practices for company performance, which include improved perceptions and recruitment. That being said, benefits also depend on context, *e.g.* national factors, job levels, and managerial support.

A greater role for women also enhances diversity, which can be valuable for a firm's performance in an increasingly complex world, enabling it to draw on diverse perspectives to solve problems, take decisions, and enhance leadership. This is important both at board level (Chapter 15) and other levels of decision making. More women in leadership positions can have a positive trickle-down effect, easing in more inclusive workplace cultures and providing younger women with role models and mentors.

Several studies have also argued that there is a positive relationship between a firm's financial performance and women's presence on boards or at senior management levels (McKinsey and Company, 2008). While most empirical analysis has yielded mixed results on this question to date (Terjesen *et al.*, 2009), a recent study by Dezso and Ross (2011), covering the enterprises included in Standard and Poor's 1 500 Composite Index for the period 1992-2006, found that female representation in top management does improve firm performance – but only insofar as its business strategy focuses on innovation. Another study of over 700 firms in France, Germany, the United Kingdom and the United States (Bloom *et al.*, 2009 and 2010) found that, while family-friendly policies yield no direct financial benefits, neither do they hurt financial performance and may deliver other positive results, such as making the firm a more attractive place to work.

Women also account for a large share of the global consumer market and purchasing decisions in households. Companies – in particular those serving consumer markets – may therefore seek out women to better understand buying patterns and help develop and market products aimed at them. Such an approach is important in developing countries, where several firms leverage women's networks to reach rural markets that would otherwise be difficult to reach. For example, the social enterprise Solar Sister uses women's rural networks to create access to solar energy applications, such as solar lamps or phone chargers. Firms may also look for other non-financial benefits, such as an improved image or strong female role models, that can indirectly contribute to company strategies.

Plugging the leaky pipeline

Despite the potential benefits that firms can derive from giving women a more prominent role (as described above), they remain under-represented in the business sector in most countries. Figure 14.1 illustrates the significant gap between the participation of women in the labour force and their presence in senior management functions in OECD countries and

Figure 14.1. **The leaky pipeline: Women are under-represented in senior management**

Women's shares in the labour force and senior management,[a] 2010[b]

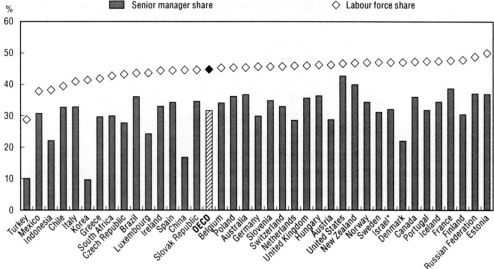

Note: Countries are arranged from left to right in order of the increasing share of women in the labour force.

* Information on data for Israel: *http://dx.doi.org/10.1787/888932315602*.

a) Senior managers cover Category 1 of the International Standard Classification of Occupations (ISCO), which includes legislators, senior officials and managers.

b) Senior managers data refer to 2008 for Australia, Canada, Indonesia, Israel, Korea, Mexico, New Zealand, the Russian Federation, South Africa and the United States; to 2005 for China; and to 2002 for Chile.

Source: Women as a percentage of the labour force from OECD *Employment Database 2012*; women as percentage of professionals and senior managers based on employment by occupation (ISCO-88) from ILO, KILM data.

StatLink 🖳 *http://dx.doi.org/10.1787/888932676222*

emerging economies. While they represent on average 45% of the labour force across OECD countries, they constitute only some 30% of legislators, senior officials and managers.

As of January 2012, only 6.6% of executive directors in the United Kingdom's FTSE 100 companies were female, whereas 15% of all directors were (Cranfield University, 2012; BIS, 2012). However, these numbers were an improvement on 2010, when only 5.5% of executive directors in the FTSE 100 companies and 12.5% of all directors were female (Cranfield University, 2010). The figures suggest that some good may have come of the recommendations in Lord Davies' independent review of women in the boardroom (BIS, 2011).

The Economist (2011) revealed that gender equality in business was reasonably well established for professionals in the United States in 2010. However, only between 15 and 20% of all executives were women, less than 10% of all top earners, and fewer than 5% of all CEOs. (Chapter 22 of this report shows that women are also under-represented as entrepreneurs.) There are several factors and policies that contribute to the leaky pipeline, highlighted in Figure 14.2. The biggest barriers are general norms and cultural practices within countries, corporate culture, and the lack of role models.

Figure 14.2. **Cultural and corporate practices are perceived as the main barriers to women's rise to leadership**

Barriers to women's rise to leadership, average ratings from 1 (least problematic) to 5 (most problematic)

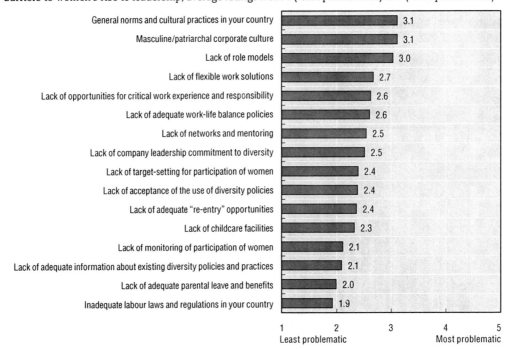

Source: WEF (2010), *The Corporate Gender Gap Report 2010*, World Economic Forum Geneva.

StatLink ⟐ *http://dx.doi.org/10.1787/888932676241*

Many firms are currently actively engaged in efforts to strengthen the role of women and fix the leaky pipeline, which suggests that they find that the benefits outweigh any costs (BIAC/OECD/AmCham, 2012; McKinsey and Company, 2011 and 2012). The business literature suggests that these objectives are more often pursued by firms which already have relatively high numbers of female managers and are often driven by strong commitment from the CEO and senior management.

Some companies, such as Deutsche Telekom and GDF Suez, have set voluntary quotas for increasing the number of women in top management positions, while mandated quotas are in place in some countries in Europe. However, as Chapter 15 shows, there is ongoing debate about the pros and cons of such measures (AIM, 2012). But by setting targets and measuring performance, whether on a voluntary or mandatory basis, companies make managers accountable. This helps focus the attention of middle and senior managers and enables gender initiatives to become an integral part of the firm's decision making. For example, the online bank ING links parts of its business unit's bonus pool specifically to diversity goals (McKinsey and Company, 2008).

An OECD workshop in February 2012 brought together the Business and Industry Advisory Committee to the OECD and the American Chamber of Commerce. Known as the "BIAC/OECD/AmCham workshop", it highlighted the fact that many companies have focused on changing human resources practices in recruitment, promotion, remuneration, flexible work, mobility, and re-entry in order to remove potential biases against women. Such action can involve training recruiters and managers in the importance of diversity, identifying potential prejudice, and improving the female focus of recruitment campaigns or quotas in lists of top management candidates.

Other corporate initiatives include coaching and mentoring for women from senior mentors. The latter point is important in the light of research from the United States: it suggests that mentors for men are often more senior than women's, which may help explain why more men make it to the top (Catalyst, 2011). In addition, it is particularly important to foster networking between women in order to improve access to resources and information. Lalanne and Seabright (2011) also stress the role of social networks and the job-related benefits they yield.

Policies to help plug the leaky pipeline

While individual firms may make it their own responsibility to enhance the role of women in business, governments may want to play an active role in supporting their efforts in light of the broader social and economic benefits that can flow from women's empowerment. Governments can strengthen the policy framework for supporting business by making changes in education, employment and social policies. Such moves help firms change corporate practices in their own contexts. For example, Denmark has pioneered a "flexicurity" employment policy which is designed to offer a balance of flexibility and security through workforce training as well as social and employment security measures (OECD, 2011e). Policies related to education, training and apprenticeship are also important, as they can further increase the pool of female talent. One example is the Goldman Sachs initiative, "10 000 Women", which seeks to provide underserved female entrepreneurs with business and management education in developing and emerging markets.

Influencing formal and, in particular, informal corporate practices is more difficult. However, governments can play a role in addressing cultural barriers and the stereotyping of women in society and business by collaborating with business, NGOs, academia and the media on awareness campaigns. Such efforts may include reports or indices with metrics about women in business which could, in turn, help both to raise awareness and measure progress within and between countries. Similar initiatives could be to disseminate profiles through the media, schools and communities of successful business women, so helping to change public perceptions and create role models for young women. In addition, and along

---

Box 14.1. **A toolkit for advancing women in business**

The Business and Industry Advisory Committee (BIAC) to the OECD and the American Chamber of Commerce in France co-hosted a workshop at the OECD on February 2012 to address the business case for advancing women's economic empowerment. The resulting report included a toolkit for advancing women in business that drew on the best practices collected from their member companies (BIAC/OECD/AmCham, 2012). The key elements of the toolkit include:

1. *Set the tone: top management leadership and commitment.* Evidence from practice shows that top corporate leadership commitment is critical but that action and support is also needed at all levels of management.

2. *Gender as core to the business strategy: measurement and accountability.* Diversity and inclusion should be integrated into business strategy with clear, measurable targets set. Monitoring key performance indicators help to enforce accountability and highlight progress.

3. *Provide the enabling framework: human resource and operational policies.* Recruitment and development processes should be continually evaluated and adjusted as needed to avoid subtle biases against women. This includes policies on pay and promotion.

4. *Provide a robust and relevant support system for women executives.* Education, leadership training, and skills development, in areas such as science, technology, engineering and math (STEM) are important for developing female executive talent.

5. *Change mindsets and organisation culture: change management and communication.* Perceptions and stereotypes of the roles of men and women can create barriers within the corporate culture. Effective communication programmes are needed to change cultural biases.

6. *Address the broader social context.* Cultural and societal traditions can create barriers for women's empowerment. Business can support policies, within and outside their companies, to help address issues.

---

the lines of Catalyst Awards in the United States, governments can support awards for women in business, in traditionally male-dominated fields such as science and technology, and/or for companies with policies to promote women.

In addition to business, government can lead by example through enhancing the role of women at senior levels within the public sector, semi-public agencies and enterprises that are fully or partially state-owned. Government schemes can be taken at the national, regional or local level, through the establishment of councils, centres and other initiatives (Chapter 16).

Many governments actively support female-owned businesses of all sizes. They should also support the development of women's business networks within local communities and tap more extensively into such female entrepreneur talent pools and help companies identify experienced women to hire for senior management or board positions. The European Commission recently set up a Mentor Network for Women Entrepreneurs, which it has launched in countries across Europe.

Finally, Bloom *et al.* (2009) find that better managed firms use more family-friendly workplace practices. Family-run firms are typically poorly managed compared with other businesses, including multinationals (Bloom *et al.*, 2011). Governments can thus take measures to remove distorsions that favour family ownership, such as inheritance tax provisions, and by fostering product market competition to help reduce the number of badly managed firms.

Key policy messages

● Address cultural barriers and stereotypes relevant to the role of women in society and business. Awareness campaigns and role models are important. Data and statistics can be useful tools for measuring progress.

● Foster a broader talent pool of women by identifying women entrepreneurs and female leaders outside of business who can be strong candidates for leadership roles in the corporate world.

● Foster good management practices, such as making managers accountable. Such practices support gender balance and enable gender initiatives to become an integral part of the firm's decision making.

PART III

Chapter 15

Women on boards

Key findings

- Women are still under-represented in top corporate jobs. In 2009, women on average occupied only 10% of board seats in listed companies of 35 countries.

- A greater proportion of women on boards may positively affect the governance of badly performing companies, although there is no conclusive evidence that it generally increases company performance.

- In order to take company and country-specific circumstances into account, many countries have updated voluntary measures to encourage women's participation on boards.

The issue of diversity on boards of listed companies has gained considerable attention in the gender debate in recent years. Improving the gender balance at the top of companies is seen as one way of fostering wider gender equality within firms (Box 15.1). However, there is considerable debate on whether the best way for policy to achieve its objectives is by promoting self-regulatory corporate governance codes or imposing board quotas by law. In parallel, there are also a plethora of voluntary or private sector-led initiatives, involving shareholders or investor groups, chief executives, universities, search firms, institutes of directors, and other stakeholders seeking to both widen the pool of qualified female candidates and create incentives as well as peer pressure on companies to have a more formal and transparent board nomination process that favours diversity.

Box 15.1. **The effect of gender-diverse boards on governance and performance**

The effects of gender diversity in boards can be considered in terms of how it impacts on companies' governance and performance. According to the OECD *Principles of Corporate Governance* (OECD, 2004a), corporate governance is a set of relationships between a company's management, its board, its shareholders and other stakeholders. The board of a company is entrusted by shareholders with key tasks, such as guiding corporate strategy, monitoring management performance, achieving an adequate return for shareholders, while preventing conflicts of interest and balancing competing demands on the corporation.

Governance. More gender-diverse boards can contribute to better corporate governance for a multitude of reasons. A heterogeneous board can be a stronger monitor of executive behaviour (Adams and Funk, 2009; Nielsen and Huse, 2010). Since women are generally under-represented in "old boys' networks", more female directors might bring more independent views into the boardroom and strengthen its monitoring function (Rhode and Packel, 2010). Moreover, gender-diverse boards tend to have a wider range of backgrounds, experiences, perspectives, and problem-solving skills. They can be passed on to top managers and potentially improve a firm's governance (Terjesen *et al.*, 2009). Carter *et al.* (2003) and Adams and Ferreira (2009) suggest that more diverse boards are more likely to hold CEOs accountable for poor stock prices and encourage better attendance at board meetings while Bianco *et al.* (2011) find that boards meet more frequently when independent, rather than family affiliated, board members are involved. McKinsey and Company (2010) find that women are more likely than men to use leadership skills such as employee development, rewards, role models, inspiration, and participative decision making. Brown *et al.* (2002) suggest that when there are more women on boards there is closer scrutiny of the handling of conflicts of interest.

Performance. The economic argument for bringing more women into the boardroom is based on the proposition that firms which fail to select the most competent candidates for their boards impair their financial performance. Catalyst (2008) and McKinsey and Company (2007, 2010) assert that better-performing firms tend to have more women on

---

> ### Box 15.1. **The effect of gender-diverse boards on governance and performance** (*cont.*)
>
> their boards. However, this does not prove causality: it cannot be said that more gender-diverse boards generate better firm performance (Terjesen *et al.*, 2009; Coles *et al.*, 2008; Linck *et al.*, 2008). It may well be that firms with better performance are more likely to seek women or, if women are scarce commodities, that they have the opportunity to work in better-performing firms (Farrell and Hersch, 2005). Moreover, the effects of more balanced boards may vary across companies: some benefit from more diversity, others may not (Adams and Ferreira, 2009).
>
> Taking a sample of Fortune 1 000 companies and controlling for various characteristics – including firm and board size, industry, share of inside board members and others – Carter *et al.* (2003) found a positive relationship between the presence of women on boards and Tobin's Q (*i.e.* the ratio between the market value of a firm divided by the replacement cost of its assets). The positive link between female board presence and return on equity is confirmed by Lückerath-Rovers (2011) in their studies of Dutch firms. Smith *et al.* (2006) also document the beneficial effects on various company performance measures. Other country-specific studies have found positive stock market reactions to the appointment of women (Campbell and Minguez-Vera, 2009; Ding and Charoenwong, 2004) and higher volatility in the stock returns of firms with lower proportions of women directors (Adams and Ferreira, 2004). However, there are probably at least as many studies that find no – or negative – relationships between women on the board and financial performance (Ahern and Dittmar, 2010; Böhren and Ström, 2005; Rose, 2007; Lee and James, 2007; Marinova *et al.*, 2010; Randøy *et al.*, 2006).
>
> The ambiguous empirical evidence may be partly explained by differences in study design and the type of data used – *e.g.* different country and institutional settings; samples (type of firms or periods of study); definitions of gender diversity (proportion or presence of female directors); accounting or market measures of performance; and methodologies. There is much room for improving analysis through greater sensitivity to the possible influences of the institutional context, of unobservable heterogeneity, of reverse causality, and of other factors that might influence a firm's performance and directors' characteristics (Ahern and Dittmar, 2010; Grosvold and Brammer, 2011).

Women on boards, the numbers today

Women today generally play a more important role in the boardroom than in the past. In 2010, "Catalyst Census: Fortune 500 Women Board Directors" (Catalyst, 2010) reported that women held 16.1% of seats on boards – up from 9.6% in 1995. Despite this increase, however, change is slow and women remain a minority. Some countries, though, are doing better than others. Study of the boards of publicly listed companies in 35 countries for which data from a single source is available reveals that, in 2009, the proportion of women was highest in Norway at close to 40% in listed companies, prompted by the introduction of quota legislation in 2006 (Figure 15.1). In Sweden, Finland, France and Indonesia, the proportion of women on boards in listed companies was between 15% and 20%, whereas in Germany, Japan and the Netherlands, it was less than 5%. According to European Commission data, the proportion of women on the boards of the largest listed companies was between 22 and 27% in Finland, France and Sweden, whereas in Germany it was 16% and in the Netherlands it was 19% (European Commission, 2012a).

Figure 15.1. **Norway has the largest proportion of women on boards of listed companies**

The share of women on the boards of listed companies by country, 2009

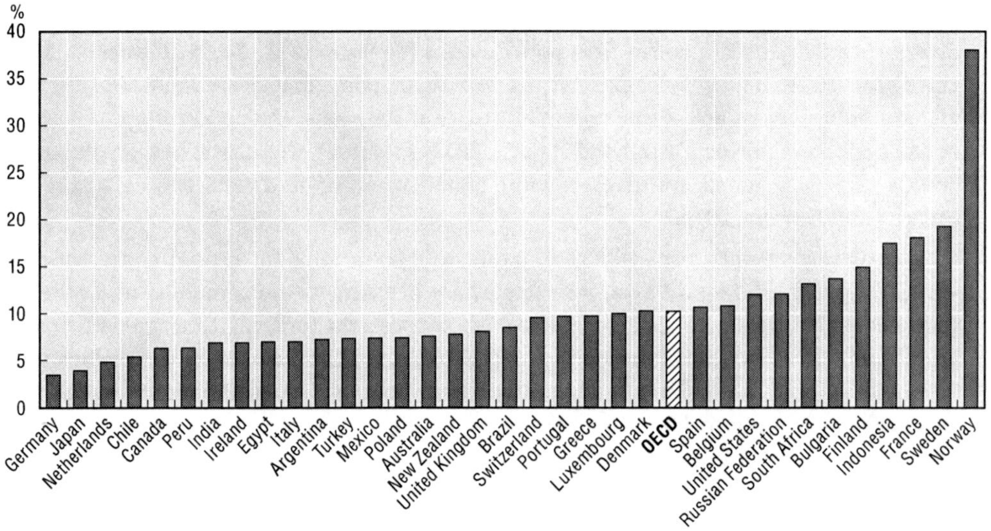

Note: Countries are arranged from left to right in order of the share of women on boards. The minimum sample size is 200 observations. Results for Austria, the Czech Republic, Estonia, Hungary, Iceland, the Slovak Republic and Slovenia were dropped due to small sample sizes.
Source: OECD Secretariat tabulations on the basis of ORBIS data.

StatLink ᵃᵗᵃˢᵖ *http://dx.doi.org/10.1787/888932676260*

Results from a 2012 OECD survey on gender-balanced boards in listed companies suggest that in a number of countries there is a significant percentage of companies with no women at all on their boards. In 2010, for example, 90% of the most liquid listed companies had no women on their boards in Chile, while the figure was 57 % for New Zealand in the same year and 41.9% for Canada in 2009.

Women are even more under-represented among executive directors who sit on boards of publicly-traded companies. Adams and Kirchmaier (2012) analyse the board composition of publicly traded companies in 21 OECD countries and India and find that in 2010 on average women accounted for 11% of non-executive directors but only 5% of executive directors in company boards.

Examples of policy initiatives: Why the push for gender-balanced boards

Corporate Governance Codes and other soft measures

Corporate Governance Codes (CGC) are self-regulatory measures increasingly used to promote gender-balanced company boards. CGCs typically apply to listed companies and rely on peer pressure to influence companies from within and pressure from stakeholders, including shareholders, and the media from outside (European Commission, 2010). Non-compliance does not usually result in a penalty but it does require an explanation. Reference to gender in CGCs – in countries like Austria, Denmark, Finland, France, Germany, the Netherlands, Poland, Spain, Sweden and the United Kingdom – is deemed to have some influence on the composition of boards in listed companies. However, the situation differs between countries. In Finland, for example, where there is an obligation to "comply or explain" compliance with the code, the percentage of listed companies with women on boards went up from 51% in 2008 to 74% in 2010 (Finland Central Chamber of Commerce, 2010).

The scope of CGC recommendations varies. In Finland, they require both men and women to be represented on the board. The Netherlands code states that "the supervisory board shall aim for a diverse composition in terms of such factors as gender and age"; in 2011, the CGC was supplemented with an amendement of the Civil Code to create an obligation for larger companies to strive for "a well-balanced composition of the board and supervisory board", by which 30% should be female (Corporate Governance Code Monitoring Committee, 2010). In Sweden, the CGC stipulates that "the company should strive for equal gender distribution on the board".

The Australian Stock Exchange CGC requires, since January 2011, that companies set measurable objectives for the increased representation of women on boards, amongst executives and throughout the organisation. They are also required to address pay equity, and to report publicly against their targets on a "comply or explain" basis. These changes brought about an immediate change at board level. The percentage of women on boards was 8.3% in July 2010, 10.9% in March 2011 and 13.8% in January 2012. As of February 2012, women have comprised 33% of all board appointments (BIAC/OECD/AmCham, 2012, p. 11).

Similar results were achieved in the UK after *The Davies Report*, a Government-commissioned report released in early 2011, required that the chairs of the top 350 UK companies (known as the FTSE 350) set out the percentage of women they aim to have on their boards in 2013 and 2015. FTSE 100 boards were asked to aim for a minimum of 25% female representation by 2015. CEOs are also required to review goals for the percentage of women on executive committees in 2013 and 2015. A progress report in March 2012 showed the largest-ever annual increase in the percentage of women on boards. Within the FTSE 100, women accounted for 15.6% of all directorships in March 2012, up from 12.5% a year before. It was also reported that should momentum be maintained, a record 26.7% female board representation in FTSE 100 companies would be achieved by 2015 (Lord Davies of Abersoch, 2012).

Regulatory alternatives similar to CGC are disclosure requirements, such as those recently adopted in the United States. The US Securities and Exchange Commission (SEC) now requires companies to disclose whether and how the nominating committee "considers diversity in identifying nominees" for directors (GMI, 2011). In Austria, firms must publish all measures undertaken to promote women to management boards and, in Canada, the province of Québec has made gender parity on the boards of its Crown corporations a statutory requirement (BIS, 2011).

Denmark announced in May 2012 a series of legislative amendments to strike a balance between the need for real progress in increasing the share of women on boards of directors and flexibility for companies. First, the 1 100 largest companies are required to set a target for the proportion of the under-represented gender on the board, which needs to be realistic and ambitious. Second, these companies must have a policy – which must be presented in the company's annual report – for increasing the proportion of the under-represented gender at the management level of the companies. Third, companies must report on the status of fulfilling the target set out in the annual report, and explain, if so, why the companies failed to achieve the target set. Fines can be applied to companies that fail to report (*http://miliki.dk/ fileadmin/ligestilling/PDF/PHplan/Facts_The_ Danish_model_on_women_in_management.doc.pdf*).

Mandatory legal quotas

Mandatory legal quotas have been introduced in some countries. Thus far, the issue has received most attention in Europe, where gender board quotas for publicly listed companies have been established in Belgium, France, Iceland, Italy, the Netherlands, Norway and Spain (Annex III.A4). The European Commission will examine progress in women's representation at board level and has launched a public consultation that will help assess the effects of possible EU measures (including legislation) and the commitment of countries to redressing gender imbalance on boards (Gómez Ansón, 2012).

After Norway introduced a law in 2006 stipulating that women had to make up 40% of the boards of publicly traded companies, the increase in the proportion of women on boards was steep: from 9% in 2003 to 40% five years later. However, the rapid rise was supported by a receptive national policy environment in a country that boasted the second highest female employment rate in the OECD (OECD, 2011f) and a comprehensive set of work-life balance policies.

There are strict penalties for non-compliance with the quota in Norway: companies that do not meet the target can be de-listed. In Spain, in contrast, the Law of Equality does not spell out a penalty in the event of non-compliance; and while the proportion of women sitting on the boards of Spain's largest listed companies rose from 5% in 2006 to almost 10% in 2009, progress has not been as pronounced as in Norway (European Commission, 2010).

The Norwegian experience shows that legal quotas can be effective in advancing gender balance at board level, though the economic consequences have yet to become clear. A few years might not be long enough to judge the effects of the law, particularly as it was introduced only two years before the financial crisis struck. Moreover, the Norwegian experience shows that introducing quota legislation may affect board membership, but does not immediately change the number of women in top management positions. The holes in the "leaky pipeline" are not plugged that easily (Chapter 14). The law also had some unintended consequences: some companies changed their legal status with the aim to either prevent or choose not to comply with the new legislation (*http://ec.europa.eu/justice/gender-equality/files/quota-working_paper_en.pdf*).

As mentioned in the BIAC report (BIAC/OECD/AmCham, 2012), a positive consequence of quotas is the dynamic public debate they have fostered around diversity, even beyond gender. The Italian move towards a quota supported by law, for example, created active debate throughout the business world. Even the expectation of quota enforcement can be a compelling incentive to motivate change. Figures in France testify to this. Prior to final enactment of the law in France, percentages of women on boards rose from 8.4% in March 2009 to 12.7% in March 2011 and to 16.0% by January 2012.

Gender-balanced boards in the future

The general arguments for more women on boards seem apparent – larger talent pool, better representation of diverse experiences and competencies, better understanding of consumer needs, etc. Nevertheless, gender-balanced boardrooms remain rare. Looking to the future, there are multiple tools for helping to redress the imbalance and fostering greater boardroom diversity.

Public target setting is one such tool, while another way forward is to work through new or existing CGCs that increasingly address board diversity. Compliance with codes is typically a listing requirement. Also, the "comply or explain" nature of voluntary codes makes it possible to accommodate both company-specific needs, including board size and composition, as well as national differences in terms of the available female director talent pool.

Until research is conclusive, proposals for mandating quotas of women on boards must be carefully assessed. Countries that have introduced mandatory quotas should also evaluate the effectiveness of legislation. Moreover, if a country does introduce quotas, it could do so as a temporary measure and be part of broader plans to enhance female participation in economic activity so that distorting consequences are avoided. To reduce recognised obstacles in a career path, complementary instruments could include: flexibility in working conditions, measures to favour work-life balance and, more specifically, board induction.

Key policy messages

- Consider how corporate governance codes can effectively improve gender balance on boards. If quotas are introduced, they should be complemented by other measures.

- Ensure that conditions are in place to support the effective role of women on boards and expand the pool of qualified candidates.

- If quotas are introduced, they should be preceded by a full regulatory economic impact assessment, carefully monitored and reviewed.

Closing the Gender Gap
Act Now
© OECD 2012

PART III

Chapter 16

Gender divides in the public domain

Key findings

- Governments are taking steps to ensure equal opportunity for their female and male employees. Early evidence suggests that countries that have implemented proactive measures to ensure equal opportunity and gender balance are making progress in closing gender-representation gaps in the public sector.

- Yet, gender imbalances remain in parliaments, judicial systems, the executive branch of government, and the senior civil service. Women are well represented in public-sector employment, but they are over-represented in contractual employment, lower job categories, and part-time work. As a consequence, they often earn less than their male counterparts.

In recent decades, governments in OECD countries have worked to establish public sector employment frameworks that guarantee efficiency, productivity and effectiveness as well as fundamental values, such as merit and transparency to maintain public confidence (OECD, 2008b). There is indeed increasing recognition among policy makers that diversity measures, which include gender representation, contribute to: i) creating a public sector which is fair and representative of the citizens it serves; ii) improving the quality of public policies and services through a better understanding of citizens' needs; iii) making the best use of the talent pool; and iv) enhancing social mobility (OECD, 2011g). At the same time, and in the context of tight fiscal constraints, governments seek to continue to deliver high quality services with fewer resources. At a time of knowledge-based societies, attracting talented women and men to the public sector has, as this report has argued thus far, become a question of competitiveness (WEF, 2011). However, it is also about social responsibility and public credibility.

In 2008, women accounted for about 58% of the total public sector workforce (Figure 16.1) and the public sector about 20% of overall employment (Chapter 11). Overall, the public sector provides such attractive employment conditions as diverse career options and paths, relatively stable jobs, flexible working hours, and good pay and benefit packages. A study commissioned by the *OECD Gender Initiative* (Anghel *et al.*, 2011) found that for jobs with similar characteristics, female wages in a number of OECD countries'

Figure 16.1. **Women make up a significant share of public sector employment**

Percentage of women in total employment and in public sector employment, 2008

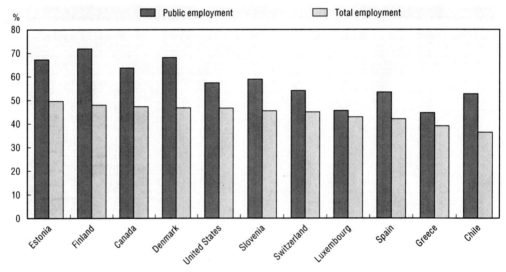

Note: Countries are arranged from left to right in descending order of the proportion of women in total employment. The total public sector workforce includes national, regional and local governments and government-controlled institutional units such as public corporations. Data for Canada include the federal/provincial/municipal levels of government.
Source: ILO (2012), *LABORSTA Database*, ILO Department of Statistics, available at *www.laborsta.ilo.org.*

StatLink http://dx.doi.org/10.1787/888932676279

public sectors (*e.g.* France and the United States) tended to be comparable to or higher than those in the private sector (Chapter 11) – at least at entry and middle management level, where women are well represented.

Horizontal occupational segregation and gender pay gaps also tend to be lower in the public sector (OECD, 2009a; and Anghel *et al.*, 2011). In Austria, for example, the estimated gender pay gap at median earnings was 16% in 2011 in the federal civil service as compared to 21% in the entire labour market (Government of Austria, 2011). Many OECD governments are also taking measures to create family-friendly workplaces, with childcare, leave, and working time support generally exceeding similar provisions in the private sector in countries like Austria, France and Switzerland (OECD, 2011h). Such arrangements help to attract women to public sector employment (Anghel *et al.*, 2011).

Women a minority in public sector upper tiers

As Figure 16.2 shows, women are significantly under-represented in public sector leadership positions. Barriers to top jobs in the public sector include limited opportunities for women to reconcile leadership responsibilities and working hours with family life (European Commission, 2012b; OECD, 2009a).

Figure 16.2. The government leaky pipeline: Women's under-representation in senior management in the central civil service

Percentage of women in senior management and among central government employees, 2010-11

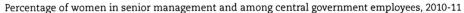

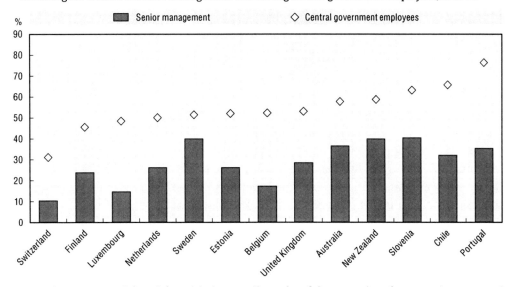

Note: Countries are arranged from left to right in ascending order of the proportion of women who are central government employees. Data for Estonia includes officials in special services (police, military, and judges). "Central civil service" is defined as those branches of the public sector that are not legislative, judicial, or military and where employment is usually based on competitive examination.
Source: OECD (2011), "Survey on Gender in Public Employment"; data for Belgium, Luxembourg, New Zealand and Sweden from 2011; all other data from 2010.

StatLink ⟡ *http://dx.doi.org/10.1787/888932676298*

There is also a tendency for women to occupy senior positions in ministries without key economic or strategic functions. Within the European Union, women occupy 33% of the highest positions in socio-cultural ministries, but only 22% in the ministries with economic and key strategic functions. In 2008, out of the 1 022 ministerial portfolios held by women, only six were defence portfolios (IPU, 2008). Evidence also suggests that women are under-represented in top public positions with wide-ranging responsibilities: for example, Guégot (2011) shows that in France, 17 out of 155 ambassadors and 19 out of 192 prefects were female in 2008.

Across federal ministries and agencies, women are more likely to head the human resources or communication department than the budget or information technology department. Women are over-represented in the lower civil service levels in many OECD countries (OECD, 2011h) and in "feminised" areas like care, education, and health (OECD, 2011i). By contrast, they are under-represented in others, such as the police, justice, interior, and economic affairs. Across 13 OECD countries the proportion of female police personnel ranged from 3 to 26% in 2009 (UNODC, 2010), while across the OECD 55% to 77% of teachers and academic staff were female (OECD, 2011j).

An additional pay-related finding emerges from some countries (e.g. France, Canada, the United Kingdom and the United States). It suggests that the increasing "feminisation" of certain public sector professions (e.g. physicians) or entire subsectors (health, education) may trigger reduced wage growth in these so-called "pink collar professions", as for example among physicians in post-Soviet countries (Connolly and Holdcroft, 2009; Guégot, 2011; Lo Sasso et al., 2011; Ross, 2003).

As in the private sector, women are also more likely to work part-time than men in the public sector (OECD, 2011h). However, working part-time on a long-term basis tends to have a negative effect on their career opportunities as it limits their abilities to develop leadership skills and take on jobs with high levels of responsibility. Women who work part-time tend to be less widely represented in management positions, as evidence from Austria, Germany and Switzerland suggests.

Furthermore, in the civil service of some countries (e.g. Australia, Austria and Germany), women tend to be over-represented in contractual employment, where job security, net wages and pension benefits are limited (Campbell and Minguez-Vera, 2009; Government of Germany, 2010). In Austria, for example, women represented 40.3% of the total federal civil service staff in 2010, but made up 60.3% of contractual employees and only 26.1% of civil servants (Government of Austria, 2011). To some extent, these discrepancies are related to the over-representation of women in the lower and middle job categories, where there are traditionally higher percentages of contractual employment.

Frequently, gender pay gaps persist within the public sector. The primary causes are occupational choices and career patterns (leading to horizontal and vertical segregation), and women's greater use of child-related leave and part-time work (Government of Austria, 2011; Government of Germany, 2010; Government of New Zealand, 2010; OECD, 2011h).

Job classification and pay schemes generally offer advantages compared to individual salary agreements in the private sector, yet seem inadequate for overcoming pay gaps (Government of Switzerland, 2009; Guégot, 2011; OECD, 2011g and 2012b). In New Zealand, for example, although the gender pay gap in the public sector shrank from 16.4% in 2005 to 14.4% in 2010, women overall still earned about NZD 10 000 less per year than men (Government of New Zealand, 2010). The evidence from some OECD countries also suggests that, within the public sector, gender pay gaps tend to be highest among occupational groups in the top tiers (Guégot, 2011).

Box 16.1. **Facts: Women in the public domain**

Women in the judiciary. Across the globe women's participation in law schools now equals that of men. Nevertheless, women are not yet equally represented in the highest tiers of legal systems. Courts function as a prime site of accountability for gender equality, yet women average only 27% of judges worldwide (UN Women, 2011). Shares of women fall even further for more senior positions. For example, in the European Union, 33% of Supreme Court judges and only two out of 18 Presidents of Administrative Courts are female (European Commission, 2011). Evidence confirms that the presence of women as jurists is vital to ensuring the implementation and safeguarding of equal rights (UN Women, 2011). Courts that operate free of gender bias and other forms of discriminatory practices can be powerful drivers of social change. Female judges can create fairer, more conducive environments for women and counter social and institutional barriers in the justice system that deny women access to legal redress. An American study, for example, demonstrates that female judges are 11% more likely to rule in favour of the plaintiff in employment discrimination cases (UN Women, 2011).

Women in parliament. More women in parliament co-operating across party lines in "women's caucuses" could be an important way of pushing ahead with gender equality legislation and the supervision of its implementation (IPU, 2008). The figure below shows that, overall, the proportion of female members of parliament (single chamber or lower house) has increased in most OECD countries. At 40% or above, the highest proportions of female members of parliament (MPs) in 2011 were in Iceland, Norway, Sweden, Finland, and South Africa. They were lowest, at below 10%, in Brazil and Hungary. Countries which saw large increases (of 20 percentage points and over) in the numbers of parliamentary seats occupied by women between 1995 and 2011 include Australia, Belgium, Denmark, Iceland, Portugal, South Africa and Spain. A benchmark widely recognised by political scientists, the media, and women's movements is the 30% legislative participation: they consider it a critical threshold for female political representation (Dahlerup, 1988; Childs and Krook, 2008). In December 2011, 28 countries – of which ten were OECD members – reached or passed the threshold (UN Statistics, 2012). Of those countries, 21 have electoral systems that use some form of proportional representation (*IPU Database*, 2011).

The proportion of women in parliament increased in most countries in the last decade but is still below the share of men

Percentage of parliamentary seats[a] occupied by women, 1995 and 2011

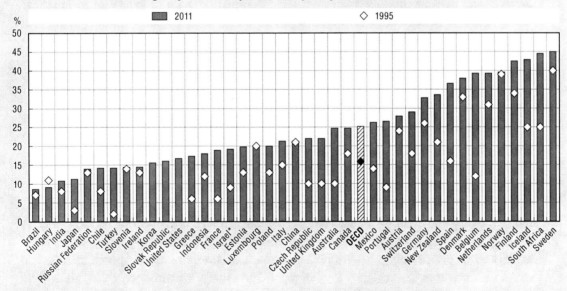

Note: Countries are arranged in ascending order of the percentage of parliamentary seats occupied by women in 2011.

* Information on data for Israel: *http://dx.doi.org/10.1787/888932315602*.

a) Seats in single or lower chambers of parliament. For South Africa, the data on the distribution of seats do not include the 36 special rotating delegates appointed on an *ad hoc* basis. For the United States, the data refers to all voting members of the House.

Source: IPU Database (2011), "Women in National Parliaments", Inter-Parliamentary Union, *www.ipu.org/wmn-e/classif.htm*.

StatLink ᴹᔕᐧ *http://dx.doi.org/10.1787/888932676317*

Policy responses

Most OECD countries have introduced specific measures that address any form of gender-based discrimination. They aim particularly to ensure equal employment opportunities for women and men and to close the representation gaps in the public sector at different levels of the career ladder and across policy sectors. Measures include: diversity targets or quotas; leadership development and mentoring programmes; the integration of gender considerations into strategic workforce management; external oversight mechanisms; work-life balance initiatives; and initiatives to ensure pay equality and equity in practice.

To close gender gaps in top management positions and across policy sectors on the demand side, half of OECD countries regularly assess the gender balance of the current central government workforce (OECD, 2011h). Some have made gender quotas in the civil service a statutory obligation (*e.g.* France introduced a progressive 40% quota for appointed senior civil servants by 2018). Other countries (*e.g.* Austria, Germany, Ireland, the Netherlands, Switzerland and the United Kingdom) use a range of mandatory or voluntary target-setting mechanisms for closing the representation gap, while continuing to emphasise merit-based employment by giving preference to female job candidates in the event of parity of qualification (OECD, 2011g). A number of countries, like Austria and Spain, have integrated diversity targets into performance agreements for senior managers (OECD, 2011h), while state-owned enterprises in Finland have been required to have at least 40% of both genders on boards since 2004 (Chapter 15).

On the supply side a number of OECD countries (*e.g.* Austria, Belgium, Germany, Sweden and the United Kingdom) use a range of leadership development and mentoring programmes to afford both women and men opportunities to develop the skills and competencies they need to lead in the public sector. These initiatives seek to support women and men in career networking, offer them the chance of exposure to practical learning methods, evaluation of key managerial skills, develop personal training plans, and prepare for job interviews. Early evaluations indicate the programmes' positive contributions to achieving gender balance in the top echelons: Belgium, for example, increased the share of female applicants for senior civil service positions from 20% in 2008 to 30% in 2009.

Most OECD countries have also established a range of safeguards – such as transparent, standardised, merit-based competency tests and gender-balanced interview panels – to ensure that job selection processes, appointments and promotions consider performance alone and do not create biases or barriers that limit female and male candidates' opportunities (OECD; 2007a and 2010c). As part of further efforts to support merit, transparency, and equal treatment, several countries (*e.g.* Belgium, Denmark, Estonia, Iceland, the Netherlands, Spain, Switzerland and the United States) have set up independent oversight, complaint, and disciplinary mechanisms (OECD, 2011h). They have proven their efficiency in promoting gender-equal treatment and employment opportunities. For example, data from the US Equal Employment Opportunity Commission (2009) show that the federal government's workforce has become more gender-balanced in the past 25 years and that a dwindling percentage of employees believe that they experience gender discrimination in recruitment, promotion or access to leadership.

Most survey respondents to the *OECD Survey on Gender in Public Employment* (OECD, 2011h) have, in addition, introduced measures to improve work-life balance in the public sector. Measures include flexible working hours, part-time work, and maternity, paternity, and parental leave arrangements that include time off to care for a sick family member. About 80% of respondents have taken steps to accommodate the special needs of pregnant or breastfeeding women; about 70% provide teleworking solutions and the possibility of working compressed weeks (OECD, 2011h); and 56% facilitate childcare solutions for public sector staff.

Work-life balance measures and flexible work arrangements are reported as important to all employees, including women who work in the top echelons of the public sector. In fact, the absence of work-life balance mechanisms was found to be one of the factors that discourage women from applying for leadership positions. Conversely, when work-life balance measures are in place they have been found to have a significant impact on job satisfaction, organisational productivity, and bottom-line results (Conference Board of Canada, 2003). At the same time, as discussed in Chapters 12 and 18, it is important to ensure that maternity leave provisions and part-time work arrangements do not harm long-term earnings and career prospects (OECD, 2011c and Box 18.2). Efforts are also needed to give men an incentive to take an active part in childcare and household duties and even make use of work-life balance measures.

Finally, to reduce and close persisting pay gaps, 95% of all respondents to the *2011 OECD Survey on Gender in Public Employment* (OECD, 2011h) have introduced legal provisions that seek to guarantee pay equality (equal pay for women and men for the same work) and 85% to guarantee pay equity (equal pay for work of equal value requiring similar qualifications, though not necessarily the same work). Moreover, 40% conduct regular assessments of jobs of equal value to ensure pay equity (*e.g.* Austria, Belgium, the Netherlands, Spain, Sweden, and Switzerland). Some countries (*e.g.* Germany and Switzerland) also use the equal pay self-test tool, called Logib, which allows managers to statistically review their pay policies, identify potential gender wage inequalities, assess enterprise wage gaps, and account for the qualification characteristics of male and female employees. In Switzerland, public procurement regulations stipulate that public contracts can only be awarded to firms with an unexplained wage gap of less than 5% (as evidenced by Logib). In Germany, employers analyse their pay structures on a voluntary basis (Beblo, 2011). In the United States the government has launched an open competition – "Equal Pay App Challenge" – to develop new tools to educate the public about the pay gap and promote equal pay for women (White House Council, 2012).

Broader, more cause-specific measures may, however, be needed to address the persisting gender pay gaps. Such measures may take the form of policy actions to address women's educational and career choices, parental leave, part-time work arrangements that include both partners, the expansion of childcare facilities, phased plans to promote women's access to executive leadership, and the systematic detection and analysis of wage gaps.

Key policy messages

Gaps remain in women's equal access to senior positions, pay and working conditions in the public domain. This calls for a comprehensive and systematic set of measures to:

- Develop specific mechanisms that improve the gender-balance in leadership positions and across different policy sectors, *e.g.* target-setting for managers.

- Strengthen the flexibility, transparency, and fairness of public sector employment systems and policies to ensure fair pay and equal opportunities for talented women and men with a mix of backgrounds and experience.

- Improve work-life balance options, particularly opportunities for flexible work arrangements and workload management.

- Develop broader, more cause-specific measures to address the persisting gender pay gap.

PART III

Chapter 17

Who cares?

Key findings

- Women do more unpaid work than men in all countries and the gender gap increases with the arrival of children.

- Domestic work has a negative effect on the female supply of hours in paid employment and on the gender wage gap.

- Encouraging fathers to make better use of parental leave arrangements, part-time employment and other flexible work arrangements could contribute to more equally shared working and caring.

Women, much more than men, devote a significant part of their time to unpaid household work, which includes caring for children, sick household members, and the elderly. Time-use surveys of 26 OECD countries and three OECD enhanced engagement countries (China, India and South Africa) show that women devote, on average, more than twice as much time to household work as men (Figure 17.1). By the same token, men spend on average about 50% more time in paid employment. As a result, the gender difference in total working time – the sum of paid and unpaid work, including travelling time – is close to zero in many countries. The allocation of time between paid and unpaid work is in part driven by preferences, but also by the availability and affordability of policies to reconcile work and family life, like childcare and part-time employment opportunities. Women are more likely to work part-time in countries with high childcare costs (OECD, 2011c), while in those where part-time work is uncommon, e.g. Portugal and Greece, the presence of children frequently leads to a mother's exit from the labour market (Lewis et al., 2008).

Figure 17.1. **Women do more unpaid work than men in all countries**
Female *minus* male total, paid and unpaid working time in minutes per day[a]

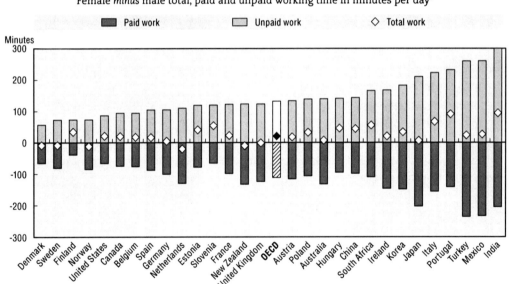

Note: Countries are arranged from left to right in ascending order of the gender gap in unpaid work.

a) The years covered are: Australia: 2006; Austria: 2008-09; Belgium: 2005; Canada: 2010; China: 2008; Denmark: 2001; Estonia: 1999-2000; Finland: 2009-10; France: 1998-99; Germany: 2001-02; Hungary: 1999-2000; India: 1999; Italy: 2002-03; Ireland: 2005; Japan: 2006; Korea: 2009; Mexico: 2009; the Netherlands: 2006; New Zealand: 2009-10; Norway: 2000-01; Poland: 2003-04; Portugal: 1999; Slovenia: 2000-01; South Africa: 2000; Spain: 2002-03; Sweden: 2000-01; Turkey: 2006; the United Kingdom: 2000-01; and the United States: 2010.

Source: OECD Secretariat estimates based on national time-use surveys. For further detail, see Miranda, V. (2011), "Cooking, Caring and Volunteering: Unpaid Work Around the World", OECD *Social, Employment and Migration Working Papers*, No. 116, OECD Publishing, Paris.

StatLink ▧▧▦ http://dx.doi.org/10.1787/888932676336

The gender gap in unpaid work decreases with the increase in the female employment rate. From a cross-country perspective, there is a strong negative correlation between a country's female employment rate and women's average unpaid working time (Figure 17.2). At the same time, there is some substitution between female paid work and male unpaid work: the higher the female employment rate, the more men are engaged in unpaid work.

Figure 17.2. **Women's unpaid work decreases with increases in the national levels of women's employment, but they always do more unpaid work than men**

Unpaid work and women employment rate

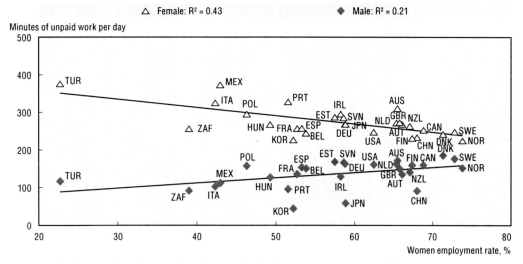

Source: OECD Secretariat estimates based on national time-use surveys and OECD *Labour Force Surveys* for employment rates. For further detail on national time-use surveys, see Miranda, V. (2011), "Cooking, Caring and Volunteering: Unpaid Work Around the World", OECD *Social, Employment and Migration Working Papers*, No. 116, OECD Publishing, Paris.

StatLink ⬛⬛⬛ http://dx.doi.org/10.1787/888932676355

Women undertake a disproportionally high amount of unpaid work no matter what type of household they live in. Regardless of a woman's employment status, men in couple families do less unpaid work than their partners (Figure 17.3). In couples where both partners work, women spend more than two hours per day extra in unpaid work. Although this gender gap is related to the fact that many women work part-time (Chapter 12), it hardly narrows when both partners work full-time. Even in female-earner couples men only do as much housework as women. Gender gaps in childcare provision are even wider: working mothers devote about 50% more time to childcare than non-working fathers (Miranda, 2011).

The greatest change in the time individuals devote to domestic work is when children are born. It is also typically a point at which traditional gender divisions of work in the home assert themselves, even if there was more equality up to then (Lewis, 2009). Having to take care for children tends to negatively affect both women's decisions to participate in the labour market and the number of hours they can put in (Del Boca *et al.*, 2009), as they tend to devote more time to unpaid work. As for men, the time they spend in both paid and unpaid work slightly increases when children arrive in the household (Figure 17.4).

Figure 17.3. **Regardless of a woman's employment status,
men do less unpaid work than their spouses**

Minutes devoted to unpaid work per day by gender, for single- *versus* dual-earner couples (OECD average)

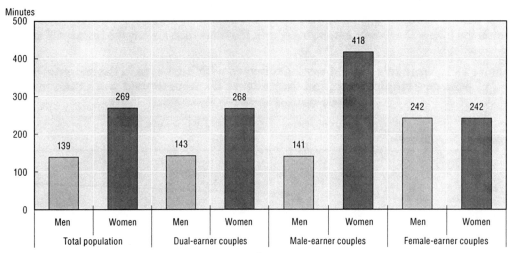

Source: OECD Secretariat estimates based on national time-use surveys. For further detail, see Miranda, V. (2011), "Cooking, Caring and Volunteering: Unpaid Work Around the World", *OECD Social, Employment and Migration Working Papers*, No. 116, OECD Publishing, Paris.

StatLink ᵐˢᵖ *http://dx.doi.org/10.1787/888932676374*

Figure 17.4. **Gender gaps in unpaid and paid work increase
with the arrival of children**

Minutes devoted to paid and unpaid work per day by gender, for people with and without children (OECD average)

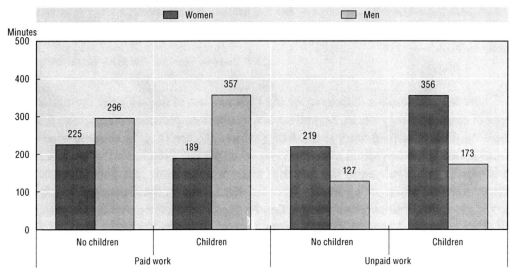

Source: OECD Secretariat estimates based on national time-use surveys. For further detail, see Miranda, V. (2011), "Cooking, Caring and Volunteering: Unpaid Work Around the World", *OECD Social, Employment and Migration Working Papers*, No. 116, OECD Publishing, Paris.

StatLink ᵐˢᵖ *http://dx.doi.org/10.1787/888932676393*

Across the OECD countries, more than one in ten adults aged over 50 provide informal (usually unpaid) help with personal care to the elderly, sick and disabled (OECD, 2011k). Close to two-thirds of such carers are women, typically caring for close relatives such as their parents or spouse. High-intensity care giving is associated with a lower labour supply for paid work, a higher risk of poverty, and an increased incidence of mental health problems among family carers. While many OECD countries support family and other informal carers either financially or through respite care and other non-financial benefits, it remains difficult to reconcile work and care.

Undertaking unpaid work, its timing and nature are important factors in explaining the persistent gender differences in earnings (Bonke *et al.*, 2005; Bryan and Sevilla-Sanz, 2011; Maani and Cruickshank, 2010 for a literature review). In addition to doing less unpaid work than women, men tend to engage in domestic work that is easier to fit in with working schedules – *e.g.* gardening, house maintenance, and auto repairs. By contrast, woman generally carry out daily housework, such as cooking and childcare, which cannot usually be postponed and is more difficult to fit into workplace patterns. Policies that contribute to a more equal intra-household sharing of the amount and nature of housework facilitate better female employment outcomes. Such policies should, for example, seek to intensify female labour force participation and reduce the gender wage gap (Chapter 13).

Government policies encourage female employment, but reinforce gender gaps in unpaid work

Government policies which help to reconcile work and family life (Chapter 18) often play a key role in female labour force participation. Although such policies aim to support both parents, they frequently and inadvertently reinforce the more traditional role of women as caregivers, so perpetuating gender inequality. The reason is that mothers generally make much wider use than fathers of parental leave options, part-time employment opportunities, and other flexible working time arrangements like teleworking. It is primarily mothers, for example, who avail themselves of long parental leave – and they are frequently reluctant to give up leave to their partner's benefit (OECD, 2011c). The result is a reinforcement of traditional gender roles. In fact, even when policies allow or encourage women to change the nature of their participation in employment or their hours of work, inequalities at home and in contributions to home life have a tendency to remain. A vicious circle is thus established: as long as mothers reduce employment participation when they have (young) children in the household, employers have an incentive to invest less in their female than in their male workers.

Policies that reduce differences between mothers' and fathers' labour market behaviour also have considerable potential for narrowing gender gaps in unpaid work. Dex (2010) suggests that such policies are likely to be most effective if they intervene at those critical times when men are more open to changing their behaviour – when they become fathers, for example. Men are more likely to bond with their children if they spend time caring for them from an early age. Fathers' greater involvement in childcare has beneficial effects on their children's cognitive and behavioural development (Baxter and Smart, 2011; Huerta *et al.*, 2011) and can reduce the time mothers devote to childcare.

Furthermore, while a country's average degree of happiness increases with greater gender equality (Veenhoven, 2011 and 2012), shouldering a greater burden of the housework than their male partners can negatively affect women's happiness. Mencarini and Sironi (2012) found that European women who engaged in housework for more than the median length of time in their country reported a reduced degree of happiness.

Public policy is but one determinant in the division of paid and unpaid work between men and women. This division has many of its roots in the values, attitudes and preferences of individuals and couples and is frequently built upon many generations of gender role models. The context in which people grow up and live their lives matters when they are deciding about how to use their time. Moreover, policies do not produce the most radical shifts in the division of unpaid work, but the other way round. The considerable changes that have taken place in women's and mother's employment behaviour in recent decades have led and not followed changes in policy and public opinion (Dex, 2010).

Key policy messages

- Promote a more equal use among parents of policies that enable temporarily reduced workplace participation to accomodate family and care commitments. For example, promote more balanced sharing of parental leave entitlements through the use of non-transferable leave entitlement for exclusive use by fathers; or award "bonus periods" to fathers who use parental leave.

- Promote policies that reduce gender gaps in labour market outcomes (*e.g.* narrow the wage gap) in order to promote more gender-equal sharing of unpaid work.

PART III

Chapter 18

Supporting parents in juggling work and family life

Key findings

- Work-family balance policies have contributed to higher female employment rates but more needs to be done to reduce inequalities that reinforce the gender division of labour.

- Childcare support is particularly important for facilitating higher levels of female employment.

- Many more mothers than fathers make use of family-friendly arrangements. Hence the persistence of gender inequalities in both paid and unpaid work.

Across OECD countries, governments have implemented family-friendly policies (parental leave, childcare, flexible working arrangements, etc.) with the aim of helping parents reconcile work and family responsibilities. However, there is substantial cross-national variation in the provision and generosity of such policies. Disparities in support are due to a range of factors that span policy objectives, work and family outcomes, cultural attitudes towards work and care, and the role of governments in the family sphere (Adema, 2012; OECD, 2007b and 2011c). Countries with well-balanced work and family outcomes – high female employment rates, fertility rates close to replacement levels, and a more equitable gender distribution of unpaid working time – include the Nordic countries and France. They have work-family policies that provide parents with a continuum of support throughout the early years and until children become teenagers (Thévenon, 2011).

Work-family reconciliation policies have contributed to higher female employment rates, especially among mothers with young children. In most member countries, dual-earner families have become the norm (Figure 18.1). However, the intensity of female labour market participation differs widely. In Eastern Europe, Japan, Portugal and the United States, both parents tend to work on a full-time basis, while in Australia, Austria, Germany, the Netherlands, New Zealand, Sweden and the United Kingdom a one-and-a-half earner model is more common. In Chile, Mexico and Turkey, the male-breadwinner model continues to be the norm among couples with children.

Figure 18.1. In most OECD countries, dual-earner families are the norm

Employment patterns among couple families with children aged 0-14, 2009

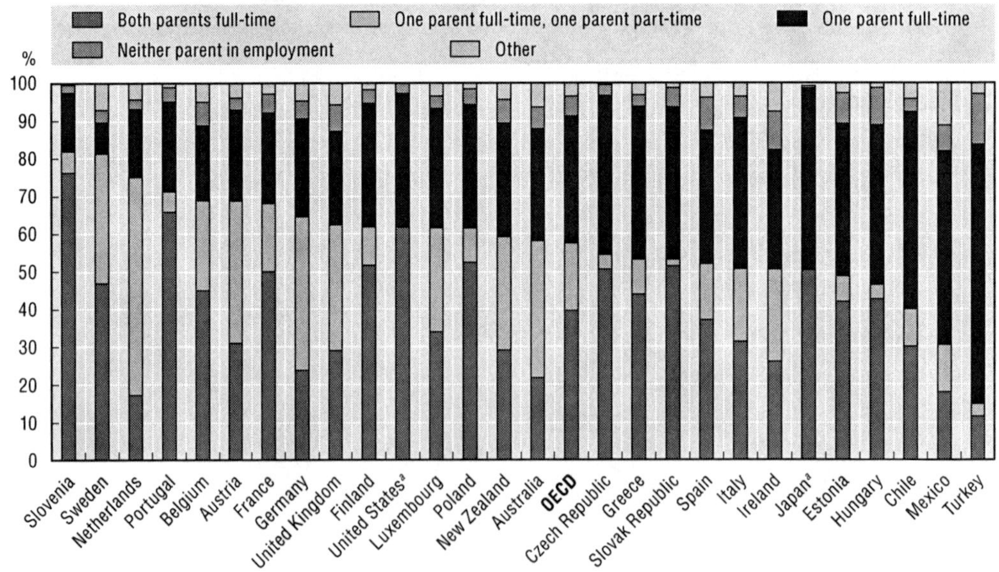

Note: Countries are arranged from left to right in descending order of the proportion of couple families where both parents are employed either full-time or part-time.

a) Not possible to distinguish between full-time and part-time work.

Source: OECD Family Database 2012.

StatLink ᴍᴤ🔗 http://dx.doi.org/10.1787/888932676412

The objectives of work-family policies are numerous and interrelated. They are designed not only to increase female employment rates, but also to reduce the opportunity costs of childbearing, help parents to have as many children as they want at the time of their choosing (Box 18.1), cut child poverty rates, and promote child development. Gender equality objectives are, however, not always pursued vigorously or prioritised. Furthermore a gender-neutral approach in family policies may reinforce the gender division of labour as women disproportionately make use of such policies (Lewis, 2009).

Box 18.1. **Female employment and fertility levels**

In 1980, most countries with high female employment rates had low fertility levels. In 2009, by contrast, those with low female employment rates also had low total fertility rates (TFRs), with the exception of Mexico. However, others combined high female employment rates with high TFRs, notably the Nordic and English-speaking countries and France. A continuum of publicly provided reconciliation support is available in the Nordic countries and France, while the Anglophones combine flexible workplace practices with income-tested childcare support and in-work benefits, as made possible, in the United States, by the low cost of domestic services (Thévenon, 2011). As a result, in these countries the choice between employment and motherhood is least stark, even if there often remains a trade-off at the individual level between having large families and working, with mothers who have three or more children far less likely to be in paid work than those with one or two (OECD, 2012a).

Motherhood and employment are less incompatible now than in 1980
Female employment and total fertility rates, 1980-2009

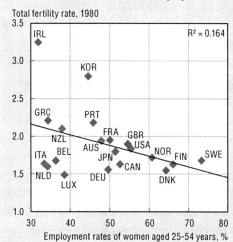

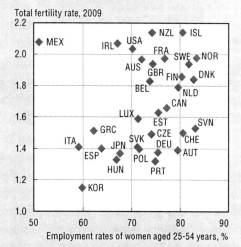

Note: The scale on the y-axis (total fertility rate) is 1.0-3.5 for 1980 and 1.0 2.2 for 2009; the x-axis (female employment rates) is 30 to 80% for 1980, and 50 to 90% for 2009.
Source: OECD Family Database 2012, *www.oecd.org/els/social/family/database*.

StatLink http://dx.doi.org/10.1787/888932676431

In other countries, where fertility rates are often much higher than in OECD countries, population issues are different. China, India and Indonesia have developed active policies to control fertility, which have contributed to a decline in TFRs from above five children per woman at the beginning of the 1960s to respectively 2.7 children per woman in India, 2.2 in Indonesia, and 1.7 in China in 2008 (see Chapter 2).

With the exception of Germany, tax and benefit systems in the OECD generally give both parents in couple families broadly similar financial incentives to work when children are of school age (Annex III.A5). However, when children are very young the financial incentives are often not strong enough for both parents to work. A wide range of factors influence parents' decisions when they consider taking up paid work: individual preferences, the duration of parental leave, the availability and cost of informal and formal childcare, earnings of the spouse, and workplace support.

To support parents in their work and family decisions, governments use different policy instruments. In the late 2000s, OECD countries spent an average of just over 2% of GDP on child and family benefits. Child-related leave policies have considerable influence on the particular time at which parents decide to (re-)enter the workforce. All OECD countries, except the United States, provide income support during maternity and/or parental leave. There are, however, wide cross-country variations in the duration and generosity of benefits (OECD, 2011c). Leave entitlements that can only be taken immediately around childbirth are likely to increase job continuity and maintain female labour force attachment. By contrast, as Box 18.2 describes, prolonged periods of leave may harm long-term earnings prospects.

Policy in many countries has been to generate change by extending parental leave entitlements to fathers. Parental leave can be granted as: i) a family entitlement – parents can share the entitlement as they choose; ii) a transferable individual entitlement – entitlements may be transferred to the other parent; and iii) a non-transferable individual entitlement – both parents are entitled to a set duration of leave.

About one-half of OECD countries grant separate paternity leave entitlements – often of short duration (OECD, 2012a). Governments of non-OECD members in Africa, Asia, and Latin America have also introduced paternity leave schemes (ILO and UNDP, 2009).

Despite efforts to encourage childcare by both parents, mothers are the predominant users of leave entitlements. When leave is granted as family or a transferable individual leave entitlement, fathers' use is low. For example, in Austria, the Czech Republic, Finland, and Poland, the proportion of fathers who take parental leave is less than 3% (Moss, 2011).

To increase take-up among fathers, in some countries they are being granted the exclusive right to parts of the parental-leave entitlement and/or associated income support. Iceland has the proportionally most gender-equal paid parental leave arrangement because one-third of the parental-leave period is reserved for men (13 weeks). The proportion is 20% in Norway (equivalent to 10 weeks) and 13% in Sweden (8.5 weeks). When Iceland introduced parental leave, it led to an increase in the proportion of parental leave days taken by fathers from 3% in 2001 to some 35% today (Eydal and Gislason, 2008). In Norway, fathers use around 13% of their leave entitlement, while the share used by their Swedish counterparts reached 22% in 2009 (Moss, 2010).

Other countries offer bonus parental-leave if fathers take up a minimum amount. In 2007, Germany reformed parental leave by granting parents two extra months if the father took at least two months of parental leave. Similarly, Portugal awards an extra month of parental leave if the father takes up a month of his entitlement. As a result, Germany saw the number of children whose father took parental leave rise from less than 9% in 2007 to 25% in the second half of 2010 (Federal Statistical Office, 2012). In Portugal, the proportion of fathers taking parental leave increased from less than 10.1% in 2009 to 22.97% in 2010.

Box 18.2. **Parental leave entitlements and female employment outcomes**

An analysis of changes in parental leave legislation over the past 40 years, conducted for this report, helps assess the effect of increased entitlements on three employment outcomes: female-to-male employment ratios, hours worked by women, and gender earnings gaps among full-time workers. A "difference-in-difference" estimator approach was used with data from 30 OECD countries between 1970 and 2010. The results suggest that extending paid leave entitlements had a small positive effect on the female-to-male employment ratio but only up to two years of leave; a longer leave has a negative effect on both the female employment rate and the female-to-male employment ratio. Results also show that extending paid parental leave had a small positive effect on weekly working hours among women but it was associated with an increase in the gender pay gap among full-time workers.

Effect of paid leave on gender differences in labour market outcomes

	Employment ratio[a]	Working hours[a]	Pay gap for full-time workers[a]
Leave duration			Number of weeks
Leave < 18 weeks	−0.099	−0.048*	−0.035
	(0.066)	(0.028)	(0.020)
Btw 19 and 52 weeks	0.014	0.018	
	(0.025)	(0.017)	
Btw 53 and 104 weeks			Squared number of weeks
	0.037*	0.034***	0.015*
	(0.020)	(0.011)	(0.008)
> 104 weeks	−0.014**	−0.019	
	(0.007)	(0.014)	
Number of observations	847	595	445
R^2	0.996	0.998	0.997

Note: The dependent variable is the female-to-male difference in the natural log of the following outcomes: employment rates (25-54 years old), average weekly working hours and weekly earnings of full-time workers. All variables include time- and country- fixed effects, and the variation in the log of GDP per capita. The effect of leave duration on employment rates and working hours is estimated with a piecewise linear regression while the effect on the pay gap is estimated using the number of weeks of paid leave and its squared value. Robust standard errors in brackets; ***, ** and *: significant at the 1%, 5% and 10%, respectively.

a) Countries: Australia, Austria, Belgium, Canada, Chile, the Czech Republic, Denmark, Estonia, Finland, France, Germany, Greece, Hungary, Iceland, Ireland, Israel, Italy, Japan, Korea, Luxembourg, Mexico, the Netherlands, New Zealand, Norway, Poland, Portugal, the Slovak Republic, Slovenia, Spain, Sweden, Switzerland, Turkey, the United Kingdom, and the United States. Data on working hours by gender for this period are not available for Canada, Japan and the United States. The analysis regarding the gender pay gap covers Australia, Germany, Finland, France, Japan, Korea, the Netherlands, Sweden, the United Kingdom and the United States.

Source: OECD Secretariat estimates based on *OECD Labour Force Statistics*, *OECD Earnings Database* and *OECD Family Database 2012*.

StatLink ᔄᓭᔕ *http://dx.doi.org/10.1787/888932677343*

Fathers' take-up remains low, however, and periods of leave are usually short. Evidence of the long-term effect on care practices and sharing of housework consequently yields mixed results. Ekberg *et al.* (2005) show that Swedish fathers' greater use of parental leave has not led to them taking more time off to look after a sick child. Haas and Hwang (2008), by contrast, argue that the more leave fathers take, the more likely they are to engage in childcare or take sole charge of the children when their spouses work. Similarly, Nepomnyaschy and Waldfogel (2007) reveal that fathers in the United States who take two or more weeks off work after the birth of their child are much more likely to be sharing childcare duties nine months later.

One of the main reasons for fathers' low take-up rates is that they often earn more than their spouses (Chapter 13), so household income loss is smaller when mothers take leave. An additional factor is attitudes: the belief that it is the mother's role to care for children may contribute to mothers rather than fathers taking leave and making greater use of family-friendly entitlements (Box 18.3).

Box 18.3. **Attitudes towards care and work**

Attitudes and behaviours towards work and care are important drivers of policy making (Kamerman and Moss, 2009; Lewis, 2009). In turn, however, policies can contribute to changing attitudes and behaviour towards family matters. Parental stances on mothers' employment vary significantly across countries (see figure in this box). In the Nordic countries, where female employment is the norm and where work-family policies have been operating for over 40 years, views of work and care are more gender-equal, even though there may be a small trend reversal among Swedish mothers. By contrast, in Germany, Hungary, Israel, Poland, Portugal, the Russian Federation and Switzerland, more than half of parents report a more traditional view of women's labour force participation and care commitments. A partial explanation of these responses may be the shortage of formal childcare for very young children – which can reinforce parents' attitudes towards employment and care (Fagnani, 2002).

Parents' attitudes towards care and work differ across countries and over time

Percentage of mothers and fathers with children aged 0 to 15 agreeing or strongly agreeing that "women should be prepared to cut down on paid work for the sake of the family", 2004 and 2010

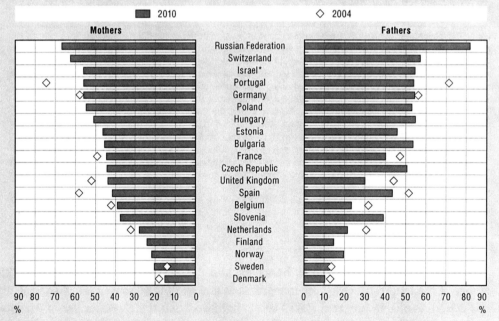

Note: Countries are arranged from top to bottom in descending order of the percentage of mothers who, in 2010, agreed that women should be prepared to cut down on paid work for the sake of the family.
* Information on data for Israel: http://dx.doi.org/10.1787/888932315602.
Source: OECD Secretariat calculations using European Social Survey 2004 and 2010.

StatLink ⬛🖳 http://dx.doi.org/10.1787/888932676450

Box 18.3. **Attitudes towards care and work** (*cont.*)

Attitudes towards work and care commitments can change over time. In most countries for which data are available, a smaller proportion of parents agreed that "mothers should cut back their number of hours of work for the sake of the family" in 2010 than in 2004. Changes over time were largest in Portugal and Spain, both countries which have seen big rises in female labour force participation since 1980 (Chapter 11), but have also experienced high unemployment since the global financial and economic crisis. This suggests that changes in views may be affected not only by historical trends but also by short-term shifts in macroeconomic factors (Chapter 19).

Return-to-work decisions by mothers depend on many factors. Tenure, qualifications, maternity leave payment rates, and family-friendly workplace support all positively affect such decisions. Mothers with low-income partners are also more likely to return to work relatively early (La Valle *et al.*, 2008). Keeping mothers informed about workplace developments while they are on leave helps nurture their sense of attachment to an employer and increases the likelihood of their returning to work (OECD, 2004b and 2007b).

However, key to the decision to return to work is the availability of affordable, flexible, good-quality childcare. Chapter 12 of this report shows that it is the main factor influencing female labour market participation and that higher public childcare expenditure is associated with higher full-time female employment. The greatest female employment and childcare enrolment rates are observed in the Nordic countries, the biggest investors in public formal childcare services (OECD, 2012a). They developed childcare services as part of a deliberate effort to increase levels of female employment (Kamerman and Moss, 2009), as the Swedish example attests: their expansion during the 1970s contributed to a rise in female employment rates from 60% to over 80% (Box 18.4).

High participation rates in formal childcare, however, do not necessarily reflect intensive use. There is considerable cross-country variation in whether childcare services are used on a part-time or a full-time basis, and/or whether they are available during holidays. For example, in Sweden very young children typically attend facilities for six hours per day, five days a week, while in the Netherlands participation in formal childcare for only one or two days a week is common. Constraints in hours of formal care pose considerable challenges to working parents: they have to find additional (usually informal) care solutions and/or reduce the number of working hours.

The affordability of good-quality care services is decisive in parental employment choices, especially for single parents and second earners in lower-income families, many of whom are mothers. Most OECD governments provide such households with financial support, but childcare costs can weaken financial incentives to work, especially for lower-income families. High childcare costs are often a barrier to paid work and contribute to the prevalence of part-time employment among women (Chapter 12). For example, in Switzerland, it does not pay for a second earner to work once childcare costs are factored into household expenditure. This is one of the factors which helps to explain why there are few Swiss couple-parent families where both parents work full-time.

Concerns over their children's development, especially when they are very young, may make mothers hesitant about working. However, recent evidence shows that other factors – such as parental education, participation in formal childcare and the quality of

Box 18.4. **Supporting all adults to pursue labour market opportunities in Sweden**

The economic boom of the post-war period created new opportunities in the labour market for Swedish women. Public policy moved towards an expansion of the public sector and social protection system, and included investment in parental leave and high-quality formal childcare (or pre-schools as they are known in Sweden). In contrast to many other welfare states developed in the 1960s and 1970s, Sweden's social model was built on the notion that all adult individuals, including parents with dependent children, should be given the opportunity to earn their own living. Some chief components of the model (Szebehely, 2001) are:

● Individual rather than household-based taxation since 1971.

● Parental leave since 1974, though maternity leave was introduced in 1938.

● Formal public childcare with major expansions in the 1970s and 1980s.

Formal childcare policy in Sweden is driven not only by concerns about gender equality or female labour supply – child well-being and development are also key. This helps to explain why childcare coverage rates have continued to increase even though female employment rates have been stable at around 80% since 1995.

Formal childcare development contributed to increasing female employment

Female employment rates (women aged 25-54) and share of children (aged 0-6)
using formal childcare, 1965-2010

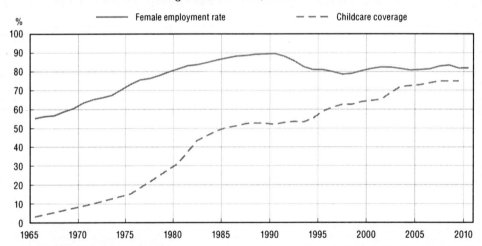

Source: Female employment rates from OECD *Labour Force Statistics*; childcare data provided by the Swedish authorities for 1965-2002, and from NOSOSCO for 2003-09.

StatLink ⫘⫘ http://dx.doi.org/10.1787/888932676469

interaction between parents and children – have greater influence on a child's early development than maternal employment *per se* (Brooks-Gunn *et al.*, 2010; Huerta *et al.*, 2011). High-quality childcare services are crucial in this respect: parents can rest assured that their children are receiving the care and attention they need while mothers pursue their labour market opportunities. This is as important in Sweden as it is in less affluent countries where childcare services are underdeveloped and female employment rates in the formal sector are low (Box 18.5 and Chapter 20).

Box 18.5. **Development of childcare services in Chile and Mexico**

Public childcare programmes in Chile and Mexico have two key objectives: to enable female participation in the workforce and promote child development (Staab and Gerhard, 2010). Programmes in both countries target poor households and require mothers to be in work, studying, or looking for a job. However, different emphasis in the underlying policy objectives yields considerable variation in programme design and policy implementation.

Mexico's federal day care programme for working mothers, "*Programa de Estancias Infantiles para Apoyar a Madres Trabajadoras*" (Child-Keeping Programme to Help Working Mothers [PEIMT]), subsidises community and home-based day care to facilitate the employment of low-income mothers. In 2011, there were 10 000 registered day centres taking care of a total of 300 000 children (SEDESOL, 2011). The programme offers both demand- and supply-side incentives: grants for individuals and civil society organisations interested in running nurseries and subsidies to low-income mothers who wish to enrol their children. The day care service comes at a low cost for users but is not entirely free. One of the greatest achievements of the programme has been the creation of female employment: by 2011, it had generated around 45 000 paid jobs for providers and their assistants, most of whom are women.

Female employment is also an objective of the Chilean scheme "*Chile Crece Contigo*" (Chile Grows With You"), although it is presented chiefly as a strategy for investing in the potential of children from low-income families. Crece Contigo provides free care for boys and girls below the age of four from the three lowest income quintiles. The services are structured by age and staffed by highly qualified professionals – pre-school or early education teachers with university or technical degrees. In 2009, a total of 4 000 nurseries were in operation. In 2011, the Chilean government introduced "*Ingreso Ético Familiar*" (Ethical Family Income), an income support scheme for very poor families. It provides a bonus payment of between USD 30 and USD 50 per month to working women; by the end of 2011 it had been paid to 36 000 women.

Promoting the value of childcare services facilitates female labour force participation and improves children's future opportunities – objectives which are important in mitigating existing gender and socio-economic inequalities.

Childcare issues, however, do not finish once children enter primary school. In most countries, a full-time working week is not compatible with regular school hours or holidays. Working parents therefore need to find alternative care solutions throughout the year. Today, many OECD countries offer out-of-school-hours (OSH) care services for school-age children, but coverage remains limited (OECD, 2011c). Some Latin American countries have also put in place public local initiatives (Piras *et al.*, forthcoming), although they need to be further developed as they provide key support to working parents and their children.

Family-friendly workplace practices also help parents combine work and care commitments more effectively. They include part-time work (Chapter 12), flexibility with regard to starting and finishing hours and working from home (teleworking).

As with leave entitlements, women are more likely to use flexible working-time arrangements than men, and are more likely to do so because of their care responsibilities (Hegewisch, 2009). One of the main reasons for the low take-up rates of such entitlements by men is workplace culture. In Japan and Korea, for example, workers show their commitment to the firm by putting in long working hours and taking less leave than they are entitled to. Such mindsets may be less pronounced in other OECD countries, but even in Sweden, working in small, male-dominated workplaces keeps fathers from using parental leave (OECD, 2011c). Fathers' underuse of parental leave is part of a vicious circle that needs to be broken. As long as women take more leave and/or are more likely to reduce their working hours, some employers will continue to perceive them as less committed to their careers than men and will be less likely to invest in their careers. The upshot from an economic perspective is that businesses do not make full, efficient use of potential labour resources (Chapter 1); from the societal perspective, the stereotypes of gender roles in paid and unpaid work are perpetuated (Chapter 17).

There has been progress in policy to assist fathers and mothers in combining work and care commitments. The more successful countries have policy packages that provide a continuum of support to parents throughout childhood, significantly facilitating male and female participation in the labour force and on an equal footing. In that sense, childcare policies are much more effective gender-equality tools than parental leave or flexible workplace arrangements, both of which actually generate different behaviour among men and women. However, childcare policies are not in themselves sufficient, as proven by Nordic countries where wide disparities in employment outcomes remain – even in Nordic countries; a more equal use of parental leave entitlements and flexible workplace arrangements is also needed to reduce prevailing gender inequalities at home and at work.

Key policy messages

- Ensure that work pays for both parents.
- Provide good-quality affordable childcare to all parents and paid maternity leave to mothers in employment.
- Promote a more gender-equitable use of flexible working time arrangements and parental leave entitlements – *e.g.* by introducing a better gender balance in the duration of parental leave entitlements that cannot be transferred to their partner.

Closing the Gender Gap
Act Now
© OECD 2012

PART III

Chapter 19

Male and female employment in the aftermath of the crisis

Key findings

- The narrowing of the gender employment gap in the immediate wake of the global financial crisis was largely due to large job losses in male-dominated sectors (notably construction and manufacturing) and an increase in the hours worked by women. Since then, however, unemployment has started to rise among women, too.

- Employment prospects for women may be affected by expected job losses in the public sector and looming government cuts in such benefits as childcare support.

Gender employment gaps have narrowed during the crisis

Although the financial and economic crisis has caused heavy job losses in most countries, it has affected men and women differently in terms of labour market outcomes. With the exception of Israel, Korea, Poland and Sweden, gender employment gaps across the OECD shrank in the three years (2007-09) following the start of the economic downturn (Figure 19.1). The countries where they narrowed the most were Turkey (by 6 percentage points), Ireland (by 8), and Spain (by 10). In the latter two, male job losses were particularly heavy, while in Turkey there was a greater rise in employment among women than among men.

Figure 19.1. **In most countries the employment gender gap narrowed during the economic crisis**

Differences between male and female employment rates in the 15-64 age range, as a percentage of male rates, third quarter of 2007 and 2011

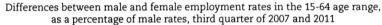

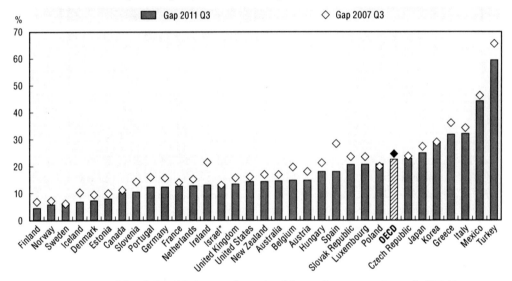

Note: Countries are arranged from left to right in ascending order of the employment gender gap in 2011. Data are not seasonally adjusted.
* Information on data for Israel: *http://dx.doi.org/10.1787/888932315602.*
Source: OECD Secretariat estimates based on national *Labour Force Surveys.*

StatLink 🔗 *http://dx.doi.org/10.1787/888932676488*

Female employment generally suffered much less than men's in the initial stage of the recent crisis – a notable deviation from historical patterns and largely due to falls in output in sectors with a predominantly male workforce (Figure 19.2). The decline in aggregate demand has been associated with a fall in trade, industry (particularly manufacturing), and construction in most countries, while employment in services – where women are predominantly employed – declined only modestly or actually rose. At the same time, women are occupying more highly skilled, better paid jobs in the European Union. The growth in female employment has been higher in the top wage quintile, mainly because of the expansion of well-paid jobs in health and education (Hurley *et al.*, 2011).

Figure 19.2. **Most employment losses are in male-dominated sectors**
Change in total employment by broad sector between 2007 and 2011,[a] whole population

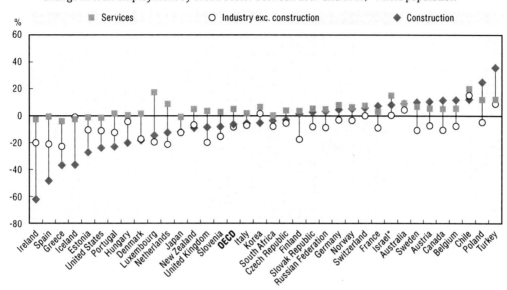

Note: Countries are arranged from left to right in ascending order of the pace of change in the construction sector.
* Information on data for Israel: *http://dx.doi.org/10.1787/888932315602.*
a) Data for 2011 corresponds to average total employment for the first three quarters of 2011 except for Australia, Canada and the United States (all-year data), Hungary, Ireland, Luxembourg, the Slovak Republic and Switzerland (first two quarters of 2011).
Source: OECD Main Economic Indicators, *www.oecd.org/std/mei.*

StatLink *http://dx.doi.org/10.1787/888932676507*

With a constant overall increase in female employment rates in recent decades, more women now have current or recent labour-market experience than in previous recessions. This development has increased their chances of successfully offsetting some of their partners' earnings losses, either by finding a job or working longer hours – often referred to as the "added-worker" effect. Households where both partners engage in active job hunting are better able to minimise income losses in the event of unemployment and to benefit quickly from improving labour market conditions. At the same time, because women often hold temporary and part-time jobs, they may be more at risk than men of losing their job if they work in the same sector.

Women have increased their hours to cushion economic shocks

Recent employment data illustrates how important female labour market experience is to reducing poverty risks. Job losses and shorter working hours among partnered men have lowered overall working hours in couple families by between 4% in the United States and just under 1% in Belgium, the Netherlands and New Zealand, while hours have remained stable in Canada, Germany and the United Kingdom (Figure 19.3, left panel). Over the same period, in some countries women's working hours have increased (Ireland, the Netherlands, New Zealand and Spain) or fallen less than men's. Figure 19.3 also shows that partnered women were significantly more likely to increase their working hours than single women. Women had higher chances to increase their working hours if they were working part-time than if they had been outside the labour market, as they often experience trouble rejoining it. Evidence from previous economic crises suggests that these difficulties can take a long time to overcome (Gong, 2011; Posadas, 2010; Stephens, 2002).

Figure 19.3. **In most countries, women increased their hours worked
to compensate for the employment loss of their partners during the crisis**

Total hours worked by men and women: changes since the onset of the crisis[a]

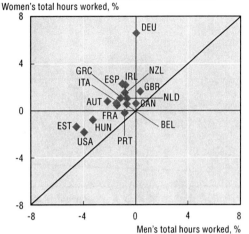

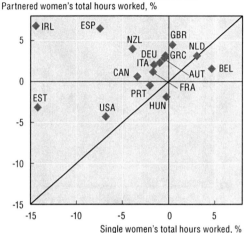

a) Changes capture differences both in employment levels and average hours worked in a job. They are measured as total hours up to 2010 for European countries and to the last quarter of 2011 for non-European countries minus total hours in the four pre-crisis quarters in each country.
b) Changes in Panel A are shown relative to family pre-crisis hours (i.e. the sum of men's and women's hours).
c) Changes in Panel B are shown relative to individual pre-crisis hours in the respective groups.
Source: OECD Secretariat estimates based on European Labour Force Surveys.

StatLink ⟶ http://dx.doi.org/10.1787/888932676526

Current policies, low wages and soaring unemployment limit labour market improvements

The degree to which partnered women are able to offset their partners' earnings losses varies between countries, with policy factors likely to play an important role. Family-related or labour market constraints can limit women's ability to help stabilise family incomes. The perceived need for them to find employment or work longer hours may not be so acute if men's earnings losses are seen as temporary (short-time working schemes, for example) or are largely compensated by government transfers. In addition, disincentives created by taxes and out-of-work benefits can affect job seeking and/or the work effort – not just for a household's principal earner, but for its second one, too. In particular, means-tested unemployment benefits, which are reduced once a partner starts to earn more, can be a sizeable obstacle to boosting female employment. Furthermore, persistent gender wage gaps mean that, even in the event of women working longer hours, family income suffers during recessions and governments need to compensate for income losses through in-work benefits for the poorest families (Mattingly and Smith, 2010).

Policies that address barriers to the participation of women in the labour market strengthen families' resilience to economic shocks, and improve their prospects of benefiting from the recovery. Labour market institutions that allow swift adjustments of work patterns, combined with support for family commitments (e.g. childcare needs), can support greater participation in the labour force. The current momentum in many OECD countries towards fairer sharing of paid work in the household suggests that the ongoing recovery presents a distinct opportunity for making progress on the gender-equality agenda.

However, in 2009 a reversal of women's initial employment gains began. At the peak of the crisis, jobless rates for women were on average just below those for men, who had borne the brunt of the initial surges in unemployment. Prior to the downturn they were 20% higher across the OECD (Figure 19.4) and up to 60% higher in Southern European countries and the Czech Republic. Between 2009 and 2011-12, however, female unemployment continued to climb while for men it declined, or rose at a slower pace, in several countries. So, although rates remain below men's or are close to parity in many countries, they exceed them in 50% of OECD countries (compared with 75% of countries before the crisis). In Chile and Turkey the gap has actually widened since 2007.

Figure 19.4. **The difference in unemployment rates between males and females is on the rise**

Difference between male and female unemployment rates in the population age range 15-64 as a % of male rates, 2007-12

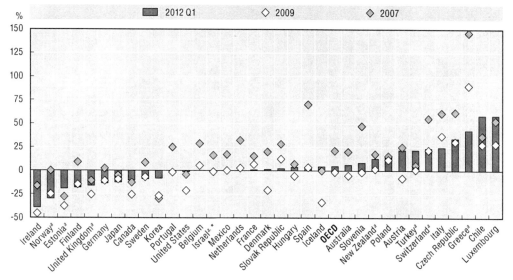

Note: Countries are arranged in ascending order of the unemployment gender gap in 2012.
* Information on data for Israel: http://dx.doi.org/10.1787/888932315602.
a) Data for Estonia, Greece, Israel, New Zealand, Norway, Switzerland, Turkey and the United Kingdom refer to the third quarter of 2011.
Source: OECD Main Economic Indicators, www.oecd.org/std/mei.

StatLink ᵃˢ http://dx.doi.org/10.1787/888932676545

Cuts in public-sector employment that have been announced or already implemented in several countries will further worsen women's position on the labour market in coming years. What's more, women might also suffer from the discouraged worker effect, particularly among the well educated, as the recession deepens and they decide to drop out of the labour force (Sabarwal et al., 2010). Evidence from previous recessions shows that, while men are more likely to lose their jobs initially, they are also more likely to find employment as the economy recovers (Maier, 2011).

Austerity measures and, in some countries, the shift in focus towards helping displaced workers back into the labour market puts the gender equality agenda at risk of becoming a low priority. Cuts in public expenditures that weaken family policies can be detrimental to women, particularly single parents. Measures that safeguard children's well-being, especially during the formative years of early childhood, should remain a high priority. In addition, work-life balance issues such as flexible working and gender parity in wages are likely to have lower priority during the current recession. Evidence from previous recessions shows that governments have used stimulus packages to cushion the impact of job losses in male-dominated sectors (*e.g.* manufacturing) – although some countries are promoting employment in the care sector. Short-time work arrangements are also more likely to benefit male workers (Leschke and Jepsen, 2011; Maier, 2011).

Key policy messages

- Ensure that the Great Recession and fiscal consolidation do not reverse progress made on gender equality in employment.
- Support increases in female working hours as a household coping strategy.

Closing the Gender Gap
Act Now
© OECD 2012

PART III

Chapter 20

The hidden workers: Women in informal employment

Key findings

- In many countries across the world, the proportion of women in informal non-agricultural employment is higher than the proportion of men. Outside agriculture, both women and men in informal employment work predominantly in non-registered enterprises, while women are more likely to work in the formal sector.

- Women in informal employment tend to be over-represented among domestic and family workers. They face high poverty risks and have limited prospects of upward mobility.

- Women in the most vulnerable informal jobs are often financially dependent on their partners and families.

Informal employment may be substantial in some OECD countries where labour taxation and benefit withdrawal may give low-wage (and part-time) earners significant incentives to work "under the radar" (Koettl and Weber, 2012). However, informal employment is considerably more widespread throughout the developing world where it concerns over half to three-quarters of non-agricultural employment. At issue is that informal employment is closely linked with low earnings, low-quality jobs and poverty (OECD, 2009b) and that women are more likely than men to work informally.

Box 20.1.   Defining employment in the informal economy

Informal employment is a job-based concept and encompasses those jobs that generally lack basic social or legal protection and employment benefits. People may be employed informally in the formal sector, informal sector, and households (ILO, 2012).

Employment in the informal sector is an enterprise-based concept which is defined as jobs in unregistered and/or small unincorporated private enterprises. Such enterprises are not constituted as separate legal entities (and are thus not officially registered) and do not maintain a complete set of accounts (ILO, 2012).

ILO (2012) shows that in 29 out of 41 countries for which data is available women outnumber men in informal non-agricultural employment. Cross-country differences can be substantial: the proportion of women in informal employment is more than 10 percentage points above that of men in El Salvador, Madagascar, Mali, Peru, Tanzania and Zambia and above 20 percentage points in Azerbaijan, Liberia and Zimbabwe. Women are more likely than men to be in informal employment in Africa and Latin America, but not in Asia and Eastern Europe (Figure 20.1). Both women and men in informal non-agricultural employment work predominantly in non-registered companies. Nevertheless, in all regions except for Central Asia and Eastern Europe, there is a higher share of women than men with informal jobs in the informal sector (Figure 20.1). Part of the reason is that more women are employed as domestic workers.

Disadvantaged groups and people with lower levels of education find it difficult to move from formal to informal work (OECD, 2009b). Female upward mobility appears to be particularly affected by limited access to finance (Chapter 24) and the need to reconcile work with family responsibilities (FAO, 2010). For example, Andersen and Muriel (2007) found that in Bolivia women have a strong preference for informal self-employment as it is more compatible with their care commitments.

Figure 20.1. **In Africa, Asia and Latin America informal employment is high and often in non-registered companies**

Informal employment (inside and outside the informal sector) as a share of non-agricultural employment by world region,[a] 2010 or latest year available

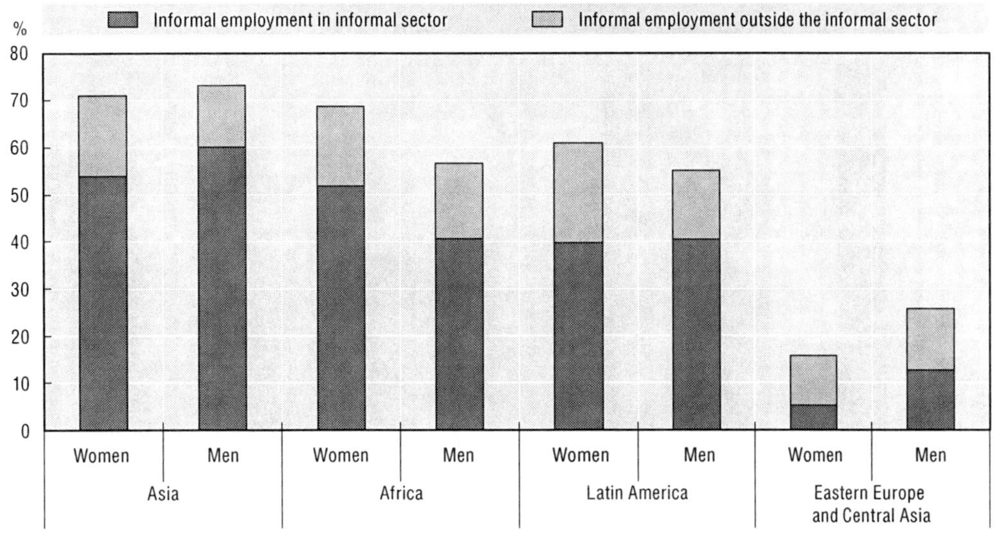

a) Regions are arranged in descending order of the percentage of women in informal employment. For the complete list of countries in each region see Annex III.A6.

Source: ILO (2012), "Women and Men in the Informal Economy – Statistical Picture", ILO, Geneva.

StatLink http://dx.doi.org/10.1787/888932676564

Women tend to be confined to the most vulnerable categories within the informal sector

Informal employment can be categorised into self-employment, family work, domestic work employed by households, and wage employment. In developing countries, a high proportion of men and women who work in informal employment tend to be self-employed. Figure 20.2 shows that this category accounts for 30% to 57% of non-agricultural informal employment, depending on the region. In more than half of the countries for which data is available, and for almost all the countries in Africa, the proportion of women in informal self-employment is larger than the proportion of men. Being self-employed in developing countries is associated with greater vulnerability and poverty, as it is closely correlated with the lack of income security and social protection (Box 20.2). Moreover, while women in self-employment tend to be concentrated among own-account workers, the proportion of men who are employers – the category with the highest earnings and the lowest poverty rates – is almost twice the proportion of women (Chen et al., 2005).

There is a hierarchy of poverty among the different categories of people in informal employment: employers and wage workers tend to be much better off, while own-account, domestic, and family workers tend to be worse off. Figure 20.2 shows that in all regions (with the exception of Eastern Europe and Central Asia) women in informal employment are more likely than men to be family and domestic workers while men work more in wage employment.

Figure 20.2. **Women in informal non-agricultural employment tend
to be concentrated among the most vulnerable work categories**[a]

Distribution of male and female informal employment by work category, 2010 or latest year available

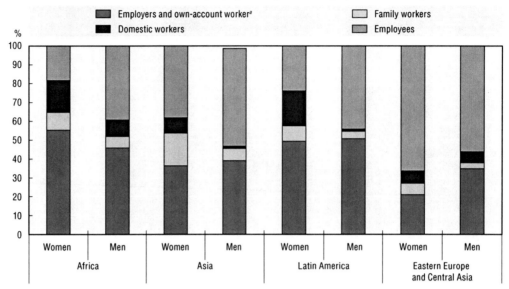

a) Including members of producers' cooperatives. For the complete list of countries in each region, see Annex III.A6.
Source: ILO (2012), "Women and Men in the Informal Economy – Statistical Picture", ILO, Geneva.

StatLink ⟨⟩ http://dx.doi.org/10.1787/888932676583

Box 20.2. **Empowering women in the informal economy: The experience of SEWA**

The Self-Employed Women's Association (SEWA) is a unique example of empowerment led by poor women working in the informal economy (OECD, 2011b). In 2005, almost 90% of women working in non-agricultural activities in India had informal jobs (ILO, 2011). Traditional trade unions had no role for these women and it was to address this failure that SEWA came into being in the early 1970s. With over 1.3 million women members, SEWA is the largest trade union of informal workers in India. More than 70% of its members are from rural areas and evenly distributed across religious groups and castes (WHO, 2008).

SEWA works to help poor women strengthen their work and income position as well as improve their social security. It is active in the areas of microfinance and insurance (mainly through the SEWA Bank), training and communication, but it is its work on labour issues – paralegal assistance, lobbying, health insurance, maternity benefits and pensions – that is at the heart of the association. Most of the women who joined SEWA experienced improvements in earnings, marketing, and working conditions. Many have been able to save on a regular basis and/or to acquire assets for the first time in their lives. But the greatest positive impact is to be seen in the increased self-esteem of its members, whose bargaining power improved within and outside the home. The main challenge for SEWA is that a large fraction of its members still do not earn enough to go beyond meeting basic daily needs or exit poverty on a long-term basis. Another key challenge is to encourage women to break the gender barrier and enter trades hitherto dominated by men (WHO, 2008).

SEWA's work has led to policy changes. Following its lobbying efforts, in 2004 the government approved a national policy for protecting street vendors and, in 2008, passed legislation on social security for informal workers. SEWA has also been able to affect policies at a global level. It was one of the main promoters of the process which led to ILO Convention 177 (1996) on the rights of home-based workers.

Box 20.3.   **Policies to tackle the vulnerability of home-based and domestic workers**

Home-based workers are people who work from their home either as own-account or subcontract workers. They are rarely visible to policy makers as they are not associated with a workplace and, in many instances, their remuneration is seen as an extension of women's unpaid house work, which further contributes to their invisibility in national surveys (Chen *et al.*, 1999). Some countries are making significant efforts to tackle the vulnerability of home-based workers. The Indian government, for example, enacted the Beedi* and Cigar Workers Act and the Beedi Workers Welfare Fund Act to protect this group of around 4 million home-based workers. The acts provide social security such as healthcare, childcare and housing for Beedi workers. The Indian government is replicating the model to protect other categories of home-based workers and sectors as it develops a national policy to that effect (*www.wigo.org*).

Domestic workers providing a range of domestic and care services in private households – women, by and large – belong to the poorest sections of society. In South Africa, domestic workers accounted for 16% of all employed women in 2009 (ILO, 2011). In 2002, the Domestic Workers Act was introduced to set a minimum wage and lay down working conditions such as hours of work, overtime pay, salary increases, and leave entitlements (South Africa Department of Labour). Domestic workers and their employers must also contribute 1% of wages to the Unemployment Insurance Fund. Hertz (2005) finds that the real wages, average monthly earnings, and total earnings of all employed domestic workers have risen since the Domestic Workers Act came into effect, while weekly hours worked and employment have fallen.

* Leaf cigarette.

Reducing women's dependency on their partners and families

Figure 20.3 shows that, in Brazil, Chile and Mexico, women earn less than the male average wage in the same informal jobs categories, even in domestic and home-based work where women are concentrated. In the other categories (employers, own-account workers, and employees), where there are fewer women than men, they also earn less. In Brazil and Chile, however, it seems that on average informal employers (both women and men) earn more than male employees in formal employment (*i.e.* the benchmark category in Figure 20.3). Yet comparisons of average earnings in informal and formal employment by job category and gender (*e.g.* between female own-account workers in the formal and informal sectors) reveal that formal employment is more lucrative than informal employment for both men and women across all categories.

In addition to lower earnings, female informal workers are less likely to be covered by social protection schemes. Although informal workers in Brazil and Chile can contribute voluntarily to social insurance, Figure 20.4 shows that contribution levels to the pension system match the job status hierarchy. Domestic, home-based and family workers, categories where women are concentrated, tend to contribute even less than the average informal worker. Social pensions that do not focus on contributory records can play a key role in reducing poverty, particularly among the elderly and women.

Figure 20.3. **Both women and men earn less in non-agricultural informal employment than in formal wage employment, but women earn even less than men**

Informal employment pay gaps[a] by gender and type of informal work, 2009

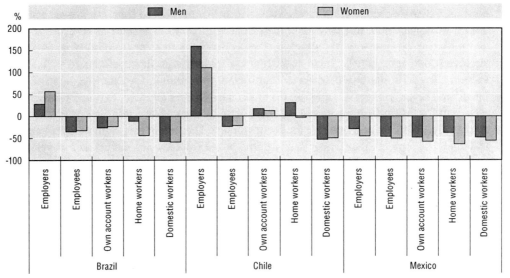

a) Pay gaps are calculated using the formal male employee's average wage as reference. Figures are calculated as the average earnings in the informal sector (by type of work and gender) minus the average wage of male formal employees, divided by the formal male employee's average wage.

Source: OECD Secretariat tabulations based on national household surveys for Brazil (PNAD, 2009), Chile (CASEN, 2009) and Mexico (ENIGH, 2010).

StatLink ⓘ *http://dx.doi.org/10.1787/888932676602*

Figure 20.4. **A significant proportion of women in non-agricultural informal employment have indirect pension coverage through their spouses**

Share of women and men contributing to the pension system or whose spouse contributes to the pension system, 2009

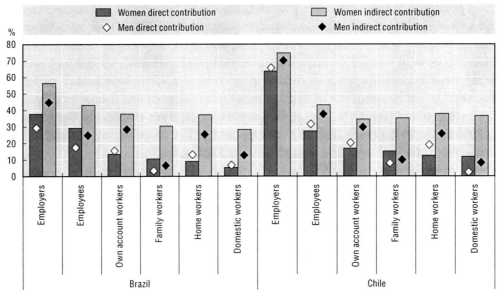

Source: OECD Secretariat tabulations based on national household surveys for Brazil (PNAD, 2009) and Chile (CASEN, 2009).

StatLink ⓘ *http://dx.doi.org/10.1787/888932676621*

A significant proportion of working women have indirect pension coverage through their spouses' contributions, which entitles them to survivor pensions should their partner die (even though women in the worst job categories in Brazil and Chile have relatively low coverage, see Figure 20.4). Nevertheless, while indirect coverage may potentially protect a significant group of women against extreme hardship in old age, it reinforces their dependency on their partner and reduces their autonomy and bargaining power within the household.

Box 20.4. **Enlarging social protection coverage to informal workers in some Latin American countries**

In the last three decades, several Latin American countries implemented social pension benefits, which are largely independent of contribution history and provide minimum income guarantees for the elderly. ILO (2002) found that social pensions in five Latin American countries sharply reduce old-age poverty among women who never had the chance to build up pension rights through (informal) employment.

In Brazil, there are two types of social pensions. One scheme targets indigent people aged 67 and over and the disabled, covering 2.1 million beneficiaries. The other is a rural scheme which covers almost 7 million beneficiaries and provides old-age, survivor and invalidity pensions, and maternity and work accident benefits for people working in the agricultural sector. In 1998, women became entitled to claim these rural pension benefits, regardless of their household status, which reduced their poverty rates from 51% in 1981 to 25% in 2001 (Camarano, 2004).

In 2002, Mexico introduced a programme called "Seguro Popular" which has considerably extended the coverage of basic health insurance and access to health services to the most vulnerable groups, that include informal workers and their families. By 2011, Seguro Popular was providing free healthcare to almost 52 million people, mostly those in the bottom two income deciles. In 2008, it introduced a women-specific provision, the "Healthy Pregnancy Strategy" (HPS), which provides affiliated women with care before, during and after childbirth. All women enjoy free access to HPS, with the exception of those in the top three income deciles who pay income-related contributions. In 2011, the HPS served almost 1.8 million pregnant women in Mexico.

Chile introduced the Basic Solidarity Pension (PBS) in 2008 (OECD, 2009c) to provide support to the over-65s who are considered poor and are not eligible for a pension on the basis of their contributory record. There is also a supplementary pension payment for those who did contribute to the pension system, but insufficiently to receive an adequate pension (Iglesias-Palau, 2009). Furthermore, Chilean pension policy grants a credit or bonus payment for each (adopted) child to low-income women (e.g. those who will receive PBS). The amount is set at childbirth – 10% of the 18 monthly minimum wage payments or CLP 327 600, around USD 670 in 2011. It is administered by a pension fund and is payable only when the mother turns 65. The number of years to retirement age and the "rate of return" set by government regulation therefore determines the total payable amount, too.

Key policy messages

- Specific interventions should target home-based and domestic workers in order to guarantee their rights and working conditions.

- If fiscal conditions allow, social pensions that are independent of contributory records and provide the elderly with minimum income guarantees should be introduced.

- Effective policies for informal workers require better gender-disaggregated statistics, particularly in those employment categories that are usually unaccounted for, such as domestic and home-based workers.

PART III

Chapter 21

Women in retirement

Key findings

- Women over 65 are about 1.5 times more likely to live in poverty than men of the same age.
- Pension payments to men are often higher than to women, but women are more likely to receive their pension payment for longer.
- Gender inequality in retirement is related more to gender differences in labour market experience and life expectancy rather than the design of pension systems.

In most OECD countries, the majority of retirees are women. Germany has the largest female share of old-age pension recipients at 68% and Greece the lowest at 45%. Women also are the bulk of poor pensioners: across the OECD the poverty rate for men aged 65 and over was 11% and 15% for women in the mid-2000s (OECD, 2008c). More recent data for 23 European OECD countries confirm this finding (Figure 21.1). Women in retirement are more likely to be poor than men for two reasons: they build up fewer pension entitlements and they often end up living alone on a relatively small income.

Figure 21.1. **Women pensioners are more likely to be poor than their male counterparts**

Poverty rates of population 65 and over at 50% of median equivalised income in European OECD countries, 2009

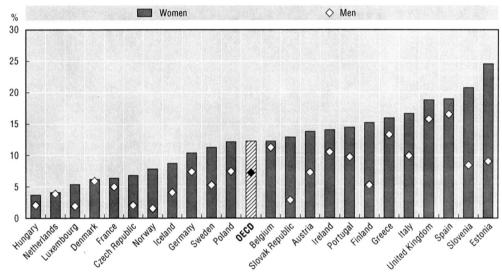

Note: Countries are arranged left to right in ascending order of women's poverty rates.
Source: OECD (2013, forthcoming), *Women and Pensions*, OECD Publishing, Paris, forthcoming.

StatLink ⬛⬛ *http://dx.doi.org/10.1787/888932676640*

Gender career differences and pension gaps

Across countries, pension entitlements are, to varying degrees, linked to a person's working career and earnings. Older generations of women generally spent less time in paid work and earned less than younger women. They also started a family earlier and had more children, often interrupting employment-participation for long periods or withdrawing from the labour force altogether (OECD, 2012a). In addition, women's pensionable age in 2010 was still below that of men in Australia, Austria, Chile, the Czech Republic, Germany, Hungary, Japan, Poland, the Russian Federation, the Slovak Republic, Slovenia, Switzerland, Turkey and the United Kingdom (OECD, 2012c). Frequent career interruptions and lower pensionable age result in shorter careers: OECD's *Women and Pensions* (OECD, 2013, forthcoming) compares 13 OECD countries and finds that women aged 65 in 2008-09 had on average been in paid work for 13 years less than men.

Women are more likely to work part-time and are over-represented in occupations and jobs that are less well paid. Since pension benefits are often earnings-related, these differences in career profiles between men and women can lead to large gender disparities in pension payments.* Furthermore, in view of their work history, older women may not meet contributory requirements and are therefore more likely to draw on non-contributory minimum (or low-level) pensions or old-age safety nets. Figure 21.2 shows that, across European OECD countries, pension payments to individuals aged 65 and over in 2009 were 34% lower, on average, for women than for men. Similarly, in the United States women's incomes from public pensions were 40% lower than that of men's in 2010 (EBRI, 2011).

Figure 21.2. **Most countries have a large pension gap**

Gender pension gap,[a] mandatory schemes,[b] selected OECD countries, 2009

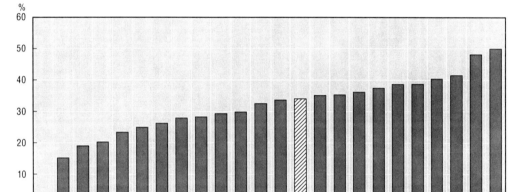

Note: Countries are arranged left to right in ascending order of gender pension gap.

a) The gender pension gap is here defined as: $\left(1 - \dfrac{\text{average gross (mandatory) pension payment to women}}{\text{average gross (mandatory) pension payment to men}}\right) * 100\%$.

b) Data for the Netherlands include pension payments derived from voluntary private pension schemes (Adema et al., 2011).

Source: OECD (2013, forthcoming), *Women and Pensions*, OECD Publishing, Paris.

StatLink ⬛📈 *http://dx.doi.org/10.1787/888932676659*

In many countries, gender pension gaps play an important role in explaining gender differences in pensioner poverty. But they do not tell the whole story, as illustrated by Estonia which has an almost negligible gender gap in pensions (Figure 21.2), but the largest one in relative income poverty (Figure 21.1). Low overall pension levels (on average about 40% of net average earnings) and a large population of elderly women who live alone and face higher poverty risks (see below) are also important factors (Sotsiaal Ministeerium, 2009).

* In defined benefit (DB) schemes, retirement income depends on earnings (either lifetime, best or final years) and the length of the career. In defined contribution (DC) schemes, retirement income is the result of the accumulation of funds in an account financed out of contributions which are a percentage of earnings (that typically increase over time). In both cases, as men are more likely to have higher tenure and earnings, their pension payments will be higher.

Women live longer on low incomes

The duration of retirement also affects gender differences in old age poverty risks. Women live longer than men: across the OECD their life expectancy at age 65 is, on average, four years higher than for men and they are likely to receive a pension for longer (Figure 21.3). They are also more likely to become widowed, live alone, and possibly rely on an often low, survivor's benefit.

Figure 21.3. **Women receive their pension for longer**
The expected retirement duration of men and women in years[a]

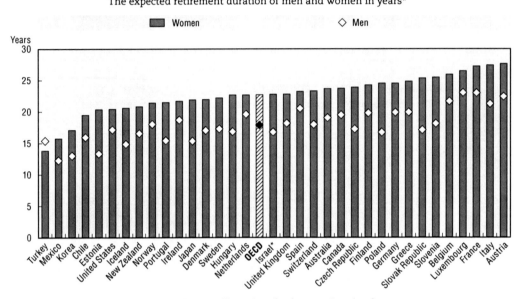

Note: Countries are arranged left to right in ascending order of retirement duration for women.

* Information on data for Israel: *http://dx.doi.org/10.1787/888932315602.*

a)   The expected duration of retirement is computed as the difference between life expectancy at the effective age of labour market exit (period 2004-09) and the pensionable age in 2010. The computations of the effective age of labour market exit concern those who were in work at age 40 and retire from the labour force at some point thereafter: calculations do not account for those who retire from the labour market before age 40, including many mothers with young children (OECD, 2006). This indicator does not, therefore, capture the labour market behaviour of all women of working age, which leads to an under-estimation of the expected duration of retirement for women. The magnitude of this effect varies across countries.

Source: OECD (2011), *Pensions at a Glance*; OECD (2013, forthcoming), *Women and Pensions*, OECD Publishing, Paris, forthcoming.

StatLink ⨳ *http://dx.doi.org/10.1787/888932676678*

Elderly persons living alone are 2.5 times more likely to be poor than elderly persons in couple households (OECD, 2012c). Moreover, older women living alone have higher poverty rates than older men living alone, except in Canada, France and Switzerland, and poverty risks are highest for women over 75 (OECD, 2012d).

Younger cohorts of women are increasingly more likely to divorce, but older woman are more frequently doing so as well. And although pension sharing in the event of divorce is allowed in some OECD countries, it is not widespread. Unless the women concerned build up their own substantial pension rights, growing divorce rates might lead to a greater reliance on old-age safety nets in the future.

Pension payments are generally lower than earnings. On average across the OECD, net replacement rates for median earners with a complete work history are about 72% (OECD, 2012c). Those who have to rely on minimum (non-contributory) safety net benefits get considerably less as such benefits are worth around 22% of economy-wide mean earnings on average across the OECD (OECD, 2011l).

The longer duration of retirement periods can also affect pension levels. For example, in defined-contribution systems, where the amount saved is converted into pension payments, women will receive a lower pension benefit than men because the same amount of "pension wealth" needs to be spread over a longer horizon. Depending on how pensions in payment are adjusted over time, a longer exposure to indexation rules may mean that the real value of women's pensions erode over time. Finally, living longer may also involve higher healthcare costs, leaving less resources for daily living expenses.

The pension policy response

Gender inequality in retirement is related more to gender differences in labour market experience and life expectancy than to the design of pension systems. Nevertheless, pension systems should be designed to avoid exacerbating retirement income gender disparities. Indeed, they should seek to mitigate them by the way in which they index pension benefits – *e.g.* through the unisex or gender-specific mortality tables used by private pension providers, or by a mix of mandatory and voluntary defined benefit and defined contribution schemes.

OECD's *Women and Pensions* (2013, forthcoming) shows that many OECD countries have specific mechanisms in place to compensate women who interrupt their careers to raise children. These mechanisms vary in terms of the pension scheme they use, their recipients, periods, and funding sources. While they help boost mothers' pension entitlements, they cannot bridge the gaps caused by career breaks. For example, the gross replacement rate of an average earner who takes a five-year childcare break is 2.5 percentage points lower than for a woman who never interrupts her career. The gap increases to 6.5 percentage points for a ten-year break. The effects vary with earnings, with the largest losses occurring at high earnings levels.

Women's pension ages are still below men's in several OECD countries, although most of these have planned or already legislated gradual increases in order to bring them into line with male pension ages. Exceptions are Chile, Israel, the Russian Federation, Slovenia and Switzerland. Having to retire earlier limits women's ability to build up pension entitlements and seems difficult to justify in view of women's longer life expectancy. Countries where pension age parity does not yet exist should move towards it.

It should be acknowledged that compelling women to work longer may have consequences for working-age families' efforts to reconcile work and family commitments, especially in countries with relatively weak formal childcare and family support policies (Chapter 18).

The majority of pension systems of OECD countries were developed with the model of a male-headed single-earner household in mind – such that the retirement income of women is "derived" primarily from husbands' pension entitlements. Even though younger generations of women will earn more own pension entitlements, there will continue to be a need for adequate survivor benefits and other design features in pensions systems which protect the elderly who live alone, from poverty in old age.

Pension policy should be seen in a wider context and use an integrated gender-focused approach with other policies and in particular family policy, tax/benefit policies and labour market policies. Pension reform in recent years has often focused on the need to ensure the financial sustainability of pension systems through, for example, less generous indexation procedures for benefit payments, a greater reliance on private and/or defined contribution schemes. The challenge for pension policy will be to find the right balance between financial sustainability, men and women's needs to save for their own retirement, and the adequacy of income support for the many men, but even more numerous women, in retirement.

Key policy messages

- Pensions systems can help to compensate women in retirement for career interruptions related to childbirth. The main barriers to equal pension entitlements, however, are related to women's work, earnings and contribution patterns.

- Until women earn full own-pension entitlements, there is a continuing need to build adequate survivor benefits and other features (*e.g.* minimum pension payments) into pension systems in order to help fight poverty in old age.

- Countries should move towards gender equality of pensionable ages.

ANNEX III.A1

Supplementary tables to Chapter 11

Table III.A1.1. **Labour force participation rates by gender, 1990, 2000 and 2010**

Proportion of people aged 15-64 in the labour force who are either in work or looking for work

Region, country or economy[c]	1990			2000			2010		
	Men	Women	All	Men	Women	All	Men	Women	All
OECD	**80.6**	**57.7**	**69.1**	**79.3**	**61.0**	**70.0**	**78.9**	**64.9**	**71.9**
Australia	85.0	61.8	73.5	82.5	65.4	74.0	82.9	70.0	76.5
Austria	80.1[a]	55.3[a]	67.7[a]	79.9	61.8	70.8	80.9	69.3	75.1
Belgium	71.3	46.1	58.7	73.8	56.6	65.2	73.4	61.8	67.7
Canada	84.9	68.4	76.6	81.9	70.4	76.2	81.5	74.2	77.8
Chile	80.9[a]	35.2[a]	57.8[a]	78.9	39.1	58.8	77.8	51.8	64.8
Czech Republic	79.6[a]	62.8[a]	71.2[a]	79.4	63.7	71.6	78.6	61.5	70.2
Denmark	87.1	77.6	82.4	84.0	75.9	80.0	82.6	76.0	79.4
Estonia	85.3	72.4	78.7	76.7	65.3	70.8	76.7	70.9	73.7
Finland	80.8	73.4	77.1	77.6	72.1	74.9	76.7	72.5	74.6
France	75.8[b]	58.5[b]	67.1[b]	75.3[b]	62.9[b]	69.0[b]	74.9	66.1	70.5
Germany	79.0	55.5	67.4	78.9	63.3	71.1	82.4	70.8	76.6
Greece	76.8	42.6	59.1	77.1	49.7	63.0	78.9	57.6	68.2
Hungary	74.4[a]	57.3[a]	65.7[a]	67.5	52.6	59.9	68.3	56.7	62.4
Iceland	87.0[a]	76.6[a]	81.9[a]	89.8	83.3	86.6	88.2	82.7	85.5
Ireland	77.5	42.6	60.1	79.8	56.4	68.1	77.9	62.6	70.2
Israel*	68.1	46.9	57.4	67.1	56.1	61.5	68.2	60.9	64.5
Italy	75.1	44.0	59.5	74.3	46.3	60.3	73.3	51.1	62.2
Japan	83.0	57.1	70.1	85.2	59.6	72.5	84.8	63.2	74.0
Korea	76.2	49.9	62.8	77.1	52.0	64.4	77.1	54.5	65.8
Luxembourg	77.4	42.4	60.1	76.4	51.7	64.2	76.0	60.3	68.2
Mexico	85.8[a]	36.0[a]	60.6[a]	84.7	41.0	61.7	83.0	46.3	63.7
Netherlands	80.0	53.1	66.7	83.2	65.2	74.3	83.8	72.6	78.2
New Zealand	83.4	63.2	73.2	83.2	67.2	75.1	83.6	71.8	77.5
Norway	83.4	70.7	77.1	84.8	76.5	80.7	80.8	75.6	78.2
Poland	77.5[a]	63.1[a]	70.2[a]	71.7	59.9	65.8	72.4	59.0	65.6
Portugal	82.8	59.6	70.9	78.9	63.8	71.2	78.2	69.9	74.0
Slovak Republic	80.7[a]	69.8[a]	75.2[a]	76.8	63.2	69.9	76.0	61.3	68.7
Slovenia	64.8[a]	56.3[a]	60.5[a]	71.8[a]	63.2[a]	67.5[a]	75.4	67.4	71.5
Spain	81.3	42.2	61.7	80.4	52.9	66.7	81.9	66.8	74.4
Sweden	86.8	82.5	84.7	81.5	76.4	79.0	82.2	76.7	79.5
Switzerland	90.8[a]	68.1[a]	79.5[a]	89.4	71.7	80.6	88.3	76.4	82.4
Turkey	83.6	36.0	59.4	76.9	28.0	52.4	75.4	30.2	52.7
United Kingdom	88.3	67.3	77.8	84.1	68.9	76.4	82.5	70.2	76.3
United States	85.6	67.8	76.5	83.9	70.7	77.2	79.6	68.4	73.9

Table III.A1.1. **Labour force participation rates by gender, 1990, 2000 and 2010** (cont.)

Proportion of people aged 15-64 in the labour force who are either in work or looking for work

Region, country or economy[c]	1990			2000			2010		
	Men	Women	All	Men	Women	All	Men	Women	All
Caribbean	**80.9**	**54.6**	**67.6**	**78.9**	**57.8**	**68.2**	**78.6**	**61.3**	**69.9**
Bahamas	81.9	68.7	75.3	78.2	71.2	74.6	83.7	75.9	79.7
Barbados	85.5	71.8	78.4	85.8	75.7	80.7	84.6	76.3	80.6
Cuba	79.0	39.6	59.5	77.8	43.3	60.7	79.4	51.0	65.4
Dominican Republic	86.0	46.5	66.3	83.1	49.7	66.4	82.9	55.1	69.0
Haiti	78.1	58.4	67.9	69.4	58.5	63.8	71.2	61.7	66.4
Jamaica	85.1	72.2	78.5	81.6	64.8	73.0	75.2	61.3	68.1
Puerto Rico	67.1	34.9	50.3	67.0	40.4	53.1	62.2	42.2	51.8
Saint Lucia	80.2	62.6	71.1	80.2	67.4	73.6	80.8	68.7	74.6
Saint Vincent and the Grenadines	85.5	48.8	67.2	84.5	55.5	70.3	83.4	60.6	72.2
Trinidad and Tobago	80.9	42.3	61.2	81.1	51.5	66.0	82.9	60.4	71.4
Central America	**85.9**	**38.6**	**62.1**	**85.7**	**44.0**	**64.6**	**84.7**	**49.7**	**66.8**
Belize	84.3	38.2	61.0	86.3	42.5	64.4	84.3	50.6	67.3
Costa Rica	87.8	35.4	62.0	85.3	40.2	63.2	83.6	50.1	67.2
El Salvador	85.1	42.5	62.7	81.7	47.6	63.5	81.8	50.5	64.9
Guatemala	89.1	41.7	65.4	87.5	43.3	64.6	90.0	50.7	69.4
Honduras	87.7	34.5	61.0	89.7	46.2	67.7	84.5	43.8	64.0
Nicaragua	84.7	36.5	60.3	84.2	39.9	61.7	82.1	48.6	65.0
Panama	82.6	41.7	62.3	85.5	48.6	67.2	86.6	53.3	70.1
South America	**84.1**	**45.5**	**64.7**	**83.5**	**52.8**	**68.1**	**83.3**	**58.2**	**70.7**
Argentina	84.1	46.5	65.1	80.7	49.0	64.7	81.5	54.4	67.8
Bolivia (Plurinational State of)	83.5	51.2	67.1	82.7	60.9	71.7	82.3	65.6	73.9
Brazil	88.6	47.6	67.9	85.4	58.6	71.8	85.4	64.6	74.8
Colombia	79.3	33.4	55.9	84.1	51.5	67.5	82.1	58.8	70.2
Ecuador	85.9	41.1	63.6	85.7	52.1	68.9	85.2	56.7	70.9
Guyana	86.1	38.4	61.8	84.9	41.2	63.1	82.6	43.6	63.1
Paraguay	93.1	55.2	74.4	88.7	53.3	71.3	88.9	60.1	74.6
Peru	79.6	48.0	63.9	84.8	60.2	72.5	86.6	70.1	78.4
Suriname	76.1	47.0	61.8	70.7	39.8	55.5	73.4	44.3	59.0
Uruguay	86.6	53.3	69.5	85.6	63.2	74.2	85.3	66.6	75.8
Venezuela (Bolivarian Republic of)	82.6	39.3	61.1	84.7	51.2	68.0	83.3	54.9	69.2
East Asia and the Pacific	**82.6**	**60.2**	**71.6**	**81.9**	**62.1**	**72.1**	**81.1**	**62.5**	**71.8**
Brunei Darussalam	84.3	45.9	66.5	82.2	57.8	70.1	80.0	58.3	69.2
Cambodia	86.2	81.0	83.3	84.1	80.2	82.1	87.5	81.8	84.5
China	88.8	79.0	84.1	87.4	78.2	83.0	85.3	75.2	80.4
China, Hong Kong Special Administrative Region	85.4	53.3	69.9	82.4	56.7	69.1	78.1	59.3	68.1
China, Macao Special Administrative Region	75.7	49.2	62.0	81.2	61.8	71.0	82.3	71.6	76.6
Fiji	85.0	29.9	57.8	79.8	40.1	60.2	81.4	40.6	61.4
Indonesia	82.6	51.9	67.2	86.7	52.2	69.4	86.3	53.2	69.7
Korea, Democratic People's Republic of	89.6	80.7	85.1	89.7	79.7	84.7	86.6	78.4	82.5
Lao People's Democratic Republic	85.2	84.7	84.9	83.6	83.3	83.4	81.5	80.4	80.9
Malaysia	82.5	45.3	64.1	83.4	46.8	65.4	78.9	46.3	62.8
Mongolia	65.6	55.8	60.6	68.2	58.8	63.5	67.3	56.9	62.1
Myanmar	81.5	75.9	78.7	83.7	78.0	80.8	84.7	78.9	81.8
Papua New Guinea	74.4	72.0	73.3	74.0	71.9	73.0	74.6	71.8	73.3
Philippines	83.9	49.3	66.8	82.9	49.9	66.5	80.9	50.9	65.9
Samoa	79.6	42.7	62.2	83.1	46.3	65.6	81.8	47.2	65.2
Singapore	83.2	54.6	69.0	84.0	58.1	71.0	82.5	62.9	72.8
Solomon Islands	79.2	54.5	67.2	80.5	54.9	68.1	81.9	55.1	68.9
Thailand	90.2	79.8	84.9	84.7	70.4	77.4	84.7	69.8	77.1

Table III.A1.1. **Labour force participation rates by gender, 1990, 2000 and 2010** (cont.)

Proportion of people aged 15-64 in the labour force who are either in work or looking for work

Region, country or economy[c]	1990			2000			2010		
	Men	Women	All	Men	Women	All	Men	Women	All
Timor-Leste	79.4	41.4	60.9	75.7	39.2	58.0	75.4	39.7	57.9
Tonga	76.8	37.7	57.3	74.5	51.7	63.3	76.9	56.4	66.6
Vanuatu	89.2	79.5	84.4	84.6	70.7	77.7	80.3	62.0	71.3
Viet Nam	88.7	81.3	84.8	86.5	79.8	83.0	84.5	78.1	81.2
Southern Asia	**84.6**	**36.9**	**61.3**	**82.4**	**39.4**	**61.3**	**82.1**	**43.6**	**63.2**
Afghanistan	83.0	15.9	50.9	82.3	13.8	49.5	81.9	15.9	50.2
Bangladesh	89.9	62.6	76.7	87.9	56.7	72.7	86.8	59.8	73.4
Bhutan	79.3	51.1	65.7	79.3	53.7	66.7	77.9	68.2	73.4
India	87.1	36.5	62.9	85.2	35.9	61.5	83.1	30.3	57.7
Iran (Islamic Republic of)	81.6	10.1	45.6	75.1	14.6	44.8	74.8	17.0	46.2
Maldives	79.0	20.6	50.7	73.0	38.1	55.6	78.4	57.2	67.8
Nepal	91.9	82.7	87.3	91.4	84.8	88.0	88.8	83.1	85.9
Pakistan	87.1	13.9	51.7	86.1	16.4	52.1	85.9	23.0	54.9
Sri Lanka	82.1	38.9	60.6	81.2	40.3	60.6	81.1	38.0	59.3
Eastern Europe and Central Asia	**77.1**	**60.6**	**68.8**	**74.6**	**59.2**	**66.7**	**73.8**	**59.0**	**66.2**
Albania	78.1	57.1	67.9	78.1	56.2	67.1	77.2	55.9	66.5
Armenia	80.6	65.3	72.7	79.1	64.9	71.5	74.3	54.8	63.7
Azerbaijan	73.4	58.0	65.5	75.5	61.9	68.4	72.0	66.4	69.2
Belarus	81.7	72.4	76.9	73.2	65.8	69.4	69.2	62.0	65.5
Bosnia and Herzegovina	60.2	38.9	49.5	64.8	38.7	51.3	67.5	42.3	54.5
Bulgaria	72.6	66.5	69.5	68.5	60.7	64.6	71.5	62.6	67.0
Croatia	75.0	55.0	65.0	72.3	56.4	64.3	70.0	59.0	64.5
Cyprus[d, e]	81.6	53.4	67.8	79.1	57.4	68.5	78.6	66.6	72.8
Former Yugoslav Republic of Macedonia (FYROM)	72.9	47.2	60.1	73.1	47.2	60.3	77.9	50.5	64.4
Georgia	77.0	59.7	68.0	76.1	57.4	66.3	77.2	59.1	67.7
Kazakhstan	81.9	69.8	75.7	80.6	71.9	76.1	81.0	74.0	77.4
Kyrgyzstan	78.0	64.7	71.3	77.7	61.4	69.5	81.4	58.9	69.9
Latvia	83.3	74.8	78.8	73.2	61.8	67.2	76.3	71.2	73.7
Lithuania	81.5	70.3	75.7	74.9	67.6	71.1	72.6	68.9	70.7
Moldova, Republic of	80.6	70.0	75.1	68.3	62.8	65.4	48.6	44.3	46.4
Romania	75.2	59.8	67.5	76.0	63.8	69.9	71.7	56.0	63.8
Russian Federation	82.1[a]	72.1[a]	76.9[a]	75.4	65.7	70.4	77.9	68.2	72.9
Serbia and Montenegro	71.5	48.5	60.0	72.8	52.9	62.9	71.7	55.2	63.5
Tajikistan	78.8	62.6	70.6	78.5	62.0	70.2	77.6	60.4	68.7
Turkmenistan	77.4	49.7	63.4	77.0	51.3	64.0	78.5	49.2	63.6
Ukraine	77.4	68.6	72.8	71.4	62.6	66.8	72.6	62.1	67.2
Uzbekistan	75.9	49.7	62.7	75.3	50.9	63.0	77.4	50.5	63.9
Middle East and North Africa	**79.7**	**21.2**	**53.3**	**79.1**	**24.6**	**54.4**	**78.7**	**27.5**	**55.9**
Algeria	77.5	10.5	44.1	79.4	12.8	46.4	75.4	15.7	45.9
Bahrain	89.4	29.0	65.8	88.1	36.3	67.4	88.5	40.6	72.0
Egypt	76.2	27.9	52.1	76.2	21.3	48.9	78.1	25.3	51.8
Iraq	74.3	11.5	41.8	72.2	13.4	42.4	71.7	15.2	43.3
Jordan	68.3	9.5	40.8	71.1	13.3	43.6	68.9	16.3	43.4
Kuwait	79.7	35.5	59.7	85.1	45.8	69.9	84.5	44.7	69.6
Lebanon	72.5	18.1	43.9	74.8	21.1	46.8	75.3	24.8	49.2
Libya	75.0	18.9	49.1	75.2	28.6	52.6	79.9	32.0	56.2
Morocco	83.1	27.1	54.6	82.0	30.5	55.6	78.3	26.4	51.6
Oman	82.3	18.4	56.7	79.4	23.8	56.7	81.6	29.2	61.8
Palestinian Authority	70.0	10.1	40.4	68.9	10.8	40.2	68.6	15.4	42.3
Qatar	94.5	44.4	81.2	92.7	40.1	76.8	95.6	53.0	87.0

Table III.A1.1. **Labour force participation rates by gender, 1990, 2000 and 2010** (cont.)

Proportion of people aged 15-64 in the labour force who are either in work or looking for work

Region, country or economy[c]	1990			2000			2010		
	Men	Women	All	Men	Women	All	Men	Women	All
Saudi Arabia	82.3	15.3	55.7	75.8	17.0	49.7	76.1	18.3	51.6
Syrian Arab Republic	82.8	19.0	50.7	81.9	21.1	51.6	74.7	13.7	44.4
Tunisia	79.1	22.1	50.5	75.7	25.6	50.6	74.0	27.5	50.7
United Arab Emirates	91.9	25.6	73.5	92.5	34.5	77.0	92.4	44.0	79.4
Yemen	75.4	16.9	45.5	73.2	23.0	48.0	73.6	25.8	49.7
Western Africa	**81.1**	**54.6**	**67.6**	**78.9**	**58.4**	**68.5**	**78.9**	**60.2**	**69.5**
Benin	89.7	58.4	73.0	81.5	65.2	73.0	78.6	68.5	73.4
Burkina Faso	92.1	79.3	85.4	91.2	79.5	85.1	91.1	79.8	85.3
Cape Verde	87.7	44.8	64.5	86.4	49.8	67.2	86.1	54.8	70.5
Côte d'Ivoire	88.3	44.3	67.9	82.2	49.5	66.6	81.9	52.4	67.5
Gambia	85.0	70.1	77.5	83.2	71.5	77.2	83.0	72.8	77.8
Ghana	73.1	71.0	72.1	77.2	73.9	75.5	72.3	68.4	70.4
Guinea	79.7	65.8	72.8	79.5	64.9	72.3	79.5	66.8	73.2
Guinea-Bissau	79.7	61.9	70.7	79.7	64.6	72.0	79.4	69.4	74.4
Liberia	64.2	56.7	60.4	61.8	59.1	60.5	64.2	58.9	61.5
Mali	67.1	39.6	52.8	67.7	38.5	52.7	70.9	37.9	54.2
Mauritania	78.6	18.9	48.2	79.0	23.6	51.1	79.9	29.0	54.6
Niger	93.1	24.8	57.3	89.0	38.4	63.2	91.1	40.2	65.4
Nigeria	75.8	39.3	57.6	67.0	44.9	56.0	62.9	48.0	55.5
Senegal	90.7	63.1	76.8	89.8	65.0	77.2	89.7	66.9	78.0
Sierra Leone	68.3	66.5	67.4	63.9	68.7	66.4	69.6	67.8	68.7
Togo	85.2	68.3	76.6	82.9	77.8	80.3	82.3	82.2	82.2
Eastern and Middle Africa	**82.7**	**65.1**	**73.8**	**81.4**	**66.1**	**73.7**	**81.4**	**67.9**	**74.6**
Angola	77.2	67.2	72.1	76.3	68.8	72.5	77.9	64.0	70.8
Burundi	90.8	91.8	91.3	85.0	86.8	86.0	82.6	84.9	83.8
Cameroon	79.7	56.7	68.1	76.8	63.2	70.0	77.4	65.6	71.5
Central African Republic	87.6	69.7	78.4	86.4	71.1	78.6	85.5	72.8	79.1
Chad	80.9	64.9	72.8	80.1	65.2	72.6	80.2	65.2	72.6
Comoros	80.3	27.6	54.0	78.7	30.8	54.8	80.8	35.4	58.2
Congo	74.1	60.5	67.2	72.5	66.1	69.3	73.8	69.7	71.8
Congo, Democratic Republic of	74.9	68.6	71.7	73.0	71.3	72.1	72.6	70.9	71.7
Djibouti	68.4	28.6	48.4	68.4	32.9	50.6	69.3	37.4	53.4
Equatorial Guinea	94.1	82.6	88.6	95.3	82.6	89.2	94.0	82.0	88.3
Eritrea	91.6	76.8	84.0	91.0	77.0	83.8	90.8	82.0	86.3
Ethiopia	91.8	74.8	83.2	92.2	75.5	83.7	90.7	80.9	85.8
Gabon	72.8	56.1	64.4	68.7	55.2	61.9	66.4	57.1	61.7
Kenya	80.1	70.1	75.1	73.3	63.3	68.3	71.9	61.8	66.8
Madagascar	89.6	85.3	87.4	90.5	85.9	88.1	89.5	85.4	87.5
Malawi	79.1	75.9	77.4	80.6	77.0	78.8	80.3	84.9	82.6
Mauritius	85.4	40.3	63.0	85.2	44.8	64.9	80.5	48.3	64.3
Mozambique	80.4	85.9	83.4	82.5	88.3	85.6	82.7	86.8	84.9
Rwanda	89.5	89.8	89.7	86.4	88.3	87.4	86.2	88.2	87.2
Sao Tome and Principe	81.1	39.9	60.1	76.6	40.8	58.4	78.9	45.8	62.1
Somalia	80.0	36.5	57.9	79.7	37.9	58.5	78.9	39.0	58.7
Sudan	79.0	27.7	53.4	75.9	30.2	53.1	76.8	32.2	54.6
Tanzania, United Republic of	92.0	88.9	90.4	91.4	89.1	90.2	91.2	90.0	90.6
Uganda	82.4	83.7	83.0	83.1	82.3	82.7	79.9	77.0	78.5
Zambia	86.4	73.9	80.1	85.7	75.2	80.4	86.1	73.5	79.8
Zimbabwe	79.8	67.9	73.8	81.8	69.2	75.5	90.4	84.3	87.3

Table III.A1.1. **Labour force participation rates by gender, 1990, 2000 and 2010** *(cont.)*

Proportion of people aged 15-64 in the labour force who are either in work or looking for work

Region, country or economy[c]	1990			2000			2010		
	Men	Women	All	Men	Women	All	Men	Women	All
Southern Africa	**74.6**	**53.0**	**63.2**	**72.8**	**56.3**	**64.3**	**72.8**	**57.5**	**65.0**
Botswana	81.4	68.9	75.1	81.3	72.1	76.7	82.8	74.8	78.9
Lesotho	84.0	68.4	75.5	81.0	69.0	74.7	74.5	60.0	67.1
Namibia	66.2	49.3	57.5	65.8	50.2	57.8	71.6	60.5	66.0
South Africa	66.4	35.3	50.7	63.2	46.5	54.7	63.2	47.2	55.2
Swaziland	74.8	43.0	57.1	72.8	43.9	57.5	71.8	44.9	58.0

* Information on data for Israel: *http://dx.doi.org/10.1787/888932315602.*

a) ILO (2012), "Key Indicators of the Labour Market (KILM)", 7th Edition, *ILO Department of Economic and Labour Market Analysis*, Geneva, available at *www.kilm.ilo.org.*

b) INSEE data, *www.insee.fr/fr/themes/tableau.asp?reg_id=0&ref_id=NATCCF03170.*

c) Country classification into world regions is based on UN and World Bank classifications.

d) *Footnote by Turkey:* The information in this document with reference to "Cyprus" relates to the southern part of the Island. There is no single authority representing both Turkish and Greek Cypriot people on the Island. Turkey recognises the Turkish Republic of Northern Cyprus (TRNC). Until a lasting and equitable solution is found within the context of United Nations, Turkey shall preserve its position concerning the "Cyprus issue".

e) *Footnote by all the European Union member states of the OECD and the European Commission:* The Republic of Cyprus is recognised by all members of the United Nations with the exception of Turkey. The information in this document relates to the area under the effective control of the Government of the Republic of Cyprus.

Source: OECD Employment Database 2012, for OECD countries and the Russian Federation, unless otherwise specified under note *a)*; ILO (2012), "Key Indicators of the Labour Market (KILM)", 7th Edition, *ILO Department of Economic and Labour Market Analysis*, Geneva, available at *www.kilm.ilo.org,* for non-OECD countries (accessed February 2012).

StatLink 🔗 *http://dx.doi.org/10.1787/888932677552*

Table III.A1.2. **Employment by broad economic activity and gender, 2010**

Percentages

Region, country or economy[k]	All				Men				Women			
	Agriculture	Industry	Services	All activities[a]	Agriculture	Industry	Services	All activities[a]	Agriculture	Industry	Services	All activities[a]
OECD	**5.5**	**24.2**	**69.9**	**100**	**6.4**	**33.7**	**59.6**	**100**	**4.5**	**12.1**	**83.0**	**100**
Australia[h]	3.3	20.9	75.7	100	4.1	30.9	65.0	100	2.3	8.9	88.7	100
Austria[h]	5.5	24.8	69.7	100	5.7	36.3	58.0	100	5.2	11.5	83.3	100
Belgium[i]	1.4	23.4	75.3	100	1.7	34.3	63.9	100	0.9	10.1	89.0	100
Canada[h]	2.2	20.2	77.6	100	3.0	30.4	66.5	100	1.2	9.0	89.8	100
Chile[h]	10.6	23.0	66.4	100	14.1	31.0	54.9	100	5.1	10.2	84.6	100
Czech Republic[i]	3.1	38.1	58.8	100	4.0	49.3	46.7	100	1.9	23.2	74.9	100
Denmark[i]	2.4	20.0	77.7	100	3.8	29.8	66.4	100	0.9	9.3	89.8	100
Estonia[i]	4.2	30.7	65.1	100	5.8	44.2	50.0	100	2.8	18.3	78.9	100
Finland[i]	4.4	23.3	72.3	100	6.0	36.1	57.9	100	2.7	9.8	87.5	100
France[i]	2.9	21.1	75.5	100	3.9	31.5	64.2	100	1.8	9.6	88.1	100
Germany[i]	1.6	28.5	69.8	100	2.0	40.7	57.3	100	1.2	14.4	84.4	100
Greece[i]	12.5	20.0	67.5	100	12.3	28.1	59.5	100	12.6	8.0	79.4	100
Hungary[i]	4.6	30.9	64.5	100	6.5	40.6	52.9	100	2.3	19.8	77.8	100
Iceland[i]	5.6	18.3	76.1	100	8.7	28.0	63.3	100	2.3	7.7	90.0	100
Ireland[h]	4.9	20.2	74.3	100	8.1	30.1	61.2	100	1.2	9.0	89.4	100
Israel*, [c]	1.7	21.7	76.5	100	2.7	31.2	66.1	100	0.7	10.7	88.6	100
Italy[i]	3.8	29.1	67.1	100	4.6	39.4	56.0	100	2.8	14.1	83.1	100
Japan[b]	4.1	26.5	69.4	100	4.3	34.2	60.7	100	4.1	15.5	79.4	100
Korea[i]	6.6	24.9	68.5	100	6.4	32.5	61.2	100	6.9	14.4	78.7	100
Luxembourg[i]	1.0	12.0	81.1	100	1.3	17.7	73.8	100	0.7	4.5	89.5	100
Mexico[i]	13.1	24.0	62.9	100	18.7	29.0	52.2	100	3.7	15.8	80.5	100
Netherlands[c]	3.3	26.7	63.6	100	3.3	25.1	71.6	100	1.7	7.7	85.7	100
New Zealand[h]	7.0	20.7	72.0	100	9.1	30.3	60.4	100	4.6	9.7	85.5	100
Norway[i]	2.5	19.7	77.7	100	4.0	31.2	64.9	100	1.0	7.0	92.0	100
Poland[i]	12.8	30.1	57.0	100	13.1	41.8	45.1	100	12.5	16.1	71.4	100
Portugal[i]	10.9	27.8	61.2	100	11.2	38.1	50.7	100	10.7	16.3	73.1	100
Slovak Republic[i]	3.2	37.1	59.6	100	4.4	50.0	45.6	100	1.8	21.1	77.2	100
Slovenia[i]	8.8	32.5	58.8	100	9.0	42.6	48.4	100	8.5	20.5	71.0	100
Spain[i]	4.3	23.2	72.5	100	5.8	34.2	60.1	100	2.5	9.5	88.0	100
Sweden[i]	2.1	20.0	77.9	100	3.2	30.9	66.0	100	0.9	7.6	91.4	100
Switzerland[b]	3.7	23.0	73.3	100	4.6	32.5	62.9	100	2.6	11.6	85.8	100
Turkey[b]	24.7	25.3	50.0	100	18.2	29.1	52.7	100	41.7	15.3	43.0	100
United Kingdom[i]	1.2	19.2	79.6	100	1.7	29.6	68.7	100	0.6	7.4	92.0	100
United States[h]	1.6	16.7	81.2	100	2.3	25.1	71.7	100	0.8	7.2	91.9	100
Caribbean	**7.4**	**19.8**	**72.2**	**100**	**10.5**	**28.9**	**59.7**	**100**	**2.8**	**8.6**	**88.3**	**100**
Antigua and Barbuda[c]	2.8	15.6	81.6	100	4.4	26.1	69.5	100	1.2	5.0	93.8	100
Aruba[d]	0.7	20.3	78.9	100	0.9	32.9	65.9	100	0.4	6.2	93.3	100
Bahamas[b]	2.9	16.0	80.8	100	5.1	27.9	66.5	100	0.5	3.7	95.5	100
Cayman Islands[c]	1.9	19.1	78.1	100	3.0	32.8	63.0	100	0.6	4.4	94.2	100
Cuba[c, g]	18.6	18.1	63.3	100	24.7	21.9	53.4	100	8.5	11.8	79.6	100
Dominican Republic[b, g]	14.5	21.9	59.8	100	21.0	26.2	47.5	100	2.1	13.7	83.4	100
Jamaica[b]	20.2	16.6	63.2	100	28.3	23.8	48.0	100	9.6	7.3	83.1	100
Puerto Rico[c, g]	1.5	18.1	80.4	100	2.3	25.0	72.8	100	0.5	9.8	89.6	100
Trinidad and Tobago[c, g]	3.8	32.2	63.8	100	5.2	43.8	50.8	100	1.8	15.3	82.0	100

Table III.A1.2. **Employment by broad economic activity and gender, 2010** (cont.)

Percentages

Region, country or economy[k]	All				Men				Women			
	Agriculture	Industry	Services	All activities[a]	Agriculture	Industry	Services	All activities[a]	Agriculture	Industry	Services	All activities[a]
Central America	**24.0**	**20.6**	**54.6**	**100**	**33.7**	**23.2**	**42.2**	**100**	**7.7**	**16.3**	**75.6**	**100**
Belize[f]	19.5	17.9	61.9	100	28.0	21.8	49.7	100	3.3	10.3	85.5	100
Costa Rica[b, g]	12.3	21.6	62.2	100	17.2	26.6	50.6	100	4.2	13.0	81.8	100
El Salvador[b]	20.9	20.7	58.4	100	32.8	22.4	44.8	100	4.8	18.3	76.8	100
Guatemala[e]	33.2	22.8	44.0	100	43.8	24.1	32.1	100	16.0	20.6	63.3	100
Honduras[d, g]	34.6	22.2	43.2	100	47.7	22.4	29.8	100	10.0	21.9	68.1	100
Nicaragua[d, g]	29.5	20.2	49.8	100	41.9	20.8	37.0	100	8.4	19.3	71.7	100
Panama[b, g]	17.9	19.1	63.0	100	24.2	24.2	51.6	100	7.3	10.4	82.3	100
South America	**16.4**	**21.3**	**62.2**	**100**	**19.5**	**28.1**	**52.3**	**100**	**11.6**	**11.8**	**76.5**	**100**
Argentina[b]	1.2	23.1	75.2	100	1.8	32.8	64.8	100	0.4	9.8	89.4	100
Bolivia (Plurinational State of)[d]	36.1	19.7	44.2	100	34.3	28.1	37.5	100	38.3	9.2	52.5	100
Brazil[b]	16.6	22.3	61.1	100	20.0	29.2	50.4	100	12.0	13.2	74.8	100
Colombia[g]	17.9	20.0	62.0	100	26.1	22.7	51.0	100	5.0	15.8	79.1	100
Ecuador[b, g]	28.7	18.8	52.5	100	33.0	23.6	43.4	100	22.1	11.4	66.5	100
Paraguay[c, g]	26.5	18.9	54.5	100	31.1	24.7	44.1	100	19.2	9.6	71.1	100
Peru[b, g]	0.8	24.4	74.8	100	1.0	32.4	66.6	100	0.5	13.7	85.8	100
Uruguay[d]	11.0	21.7	67.2	100	15.6	28.5	56.0	100	4.8	12.6	82.5	100
Venezuela (Bolivarian Republic of)[c, g]	8.5	23.0	68.3	100	12.7	30.6	56.6	100	1.9	11.1	86.8	100
East Asia and the Pacific	**32.4**	**16.9**	**50.6**	**100**	**33.2**	**20.4**	**46.3**	**100**	**31.1**	**12.4**	**56.4**	**100**
Cambodia[b, i]	72.2	8.6	19.2	100	69.3	8.1	22.6	100	75.0	9.0	15.9	100
China, Hong Kong Special Administrative Region[b, i]	0.2	12.4	87.4	100	1.0	18.9	80.1	100	0.2	4.3	95.5	100
China, Macao Special Administrative Region[c]	0.2	19.8	80.1	100	0.2	26.6	73.1	100	0.2	11.9	87.8	100
Indonesia[b, g]	39.7	18.8	41.5	100	40.2	21.2	38.6	100	38.8	14.9	46.3	100
Malaysia[c]	14.0	28.7	57.4	100	16.7	32.0	51.3	100	9.0	22.7	68.3	100
Mongolia[b, i]	40.0	14.9	45.0	100	41.2	18.6	40.2	100	38.7	10.9	50.4	100
Philippines[b]	35.2	14.6	50.3	100	42.3	17.5	40.4	100	24.0	9.9	66.0	100
Singapore[b, i]	1.1	21.8	77.1	100	1.5	25.7	72.8	100	0.6	16.6	82.8	100
Thailand[b]	41.5	19.5	38.9	100	43.7	21.2	35.1	100	39.0	17.6	43.3	100
Vanuatu[b, i]	60.5	7.0	31.1	100	59.2	10.5	29.4	100	62.3	2.5	33.3	100
Viet Nam[e, g]	51.7	20.2	28.2	100	49.6	24.4	26.0	100	53.8	15.9	30.3	100
Southern Asia	**39.2**	**20.7**	**39.1**	**100**	**35.4**	**20.5**	**41.1**	**100**	**50.7**	**19.4**	**27.6**	**100**
Bangladesh[f]	48.1	14.5	37.4	100	41.8	15.1	43.0	100	68.1	12.5	19.4	100
Bhutan[b]	65.4	6.4	28.2	100	59.1	4.0	36.9	100	72.1	9.1	18.8	100
India[h]	51.1	22.4	26.5	100	46.2	24.0	29.8	100	65.3	17.7	17.0	100
Iran (Islamic Republic of)[c]	21.2	32.2	46.5	100	19.3	33.2	47.4	100	30.6	27.3	41.9	100
Maldives[e]	11.5	24.3	60.0	100	14.0	19.9	62.2	100	7.1	31.8	56.1	100
Pakistan[c, g]	44.7	20.1	35.2	100	36.9	22.1	40.9	100	75.0	12.2	12.9	100
Sri Lanka[b]	32.6	25.1	39.6	100	30.4	25.0	27.2	100	36.6	25.3	27.1	100

Table III.A1.2. **Employment by broad economic activity and gender, 2010** (cont.)

Percentages

Region, country or economy[k]	All				Men				Women			
	Agriculture	Industry	Services	All activities[a]	Agriculture	Industry	Services	All activities[a]	Agriculture	Industry	Services	All activities[a]
Eastern Europe and Central Asia	**23.0**	**22.6**	**54.4**	**100**	**23.2**	**30.0**	**46.6**	**100**	**22.8**	**14.1**	**63.0**	**100**
Armenia[c]	44.2	16.8	39.0	100	39.4	25.4	35.2	100	49.1	7.9	43.1	100
Azerbaijan[b, i]	38.6	12.9	48.5	100	37.1	18.8	44.0	100	40.2	6.6	53.2	100
Bulgaria[i]	6.8	33.3	59.9	100	8.2	40.9	50.9	100	5.2	24.8	69.9	100
Croatia[i]	14.9	27.3	57.6	100	13.7	38.2	47.5	100	16.3	14.5	68.6	100
Cyprus[l, m, i]	3.8	20.8	75.3	100	4.8	30.3	65.1	100	2.6	9.4	87.9	100
Former Yugoslav Rep. of Macedonia (FYROM)[c]	19.7	31.3	49.1	100	19.6	33.4	47.0	100	19.8	27.9	52.3	100
Georgia[d]	53.4	10.4	36.2	100	50.5	16.5	33.0	100	56.6	3.7	39.6	100
Kazakhstan[c]	30.2	18.9	50.9	100	31.1	26.0	42.9	100	29.2	11.6	59.3	100
Kyrgyzstan[e]	36.3	19.4	44.3	100	36.9	25.7	37.4	100	35.4	10.7	53.9	100
Latvia[i]	8.8	24.0	66.9	100	12.0	33.8	53.1	100	5.8	13.9	79.8	100
Lithuania[i]	9.0	24.4	66.2	100	11.5	33.2	54.9	100	6.8	16.4	76.5	100
Moldova, Republic of[c]	31.1	19.7	49.3	100	33.7	25.7	40.6	100	28.4	13.6	58.1	100
Montenegro[f]	8.6	19.2	72.1	100	8.5	26.1	65.3	100	8.9	9.2	82.0	100
Romania[i]	30.1	28.7	41.2	100	29.1	35.5	35.4	100	31.4	20.2	48.5	100
Russian Federation[c]	8.6	28.9	62.4	100	10.5	38.4	51.1	100	6.7	19.1	74.2	100
Serbia[b]	24.0	25.1	50.9	100	24.9	32.3	42.8	100	22.9	15.7	61.4	100
Middle East and North Africa	**14.0**	**25.7**	**60.2**	**100**	**12.2**	**29.5**	**58.2**	**100**	**20.8**	**7.0**	**72.0**	**100**
Egypt[c]	31.6	23.0	45.3	100	28.2	27.3	44.4	100	45.6	5.6	48.8	100
Iraq[c]	23.4	18.2	58.3	100	17.1	21.6	61.3	100	50.7	3.7	45.6	100
Jordan[i]	2.0	18.7	79.2	100	2.2	20.5	77.2	100	1.0	9.3	89.7	100
Kuwait[f]	2.7	20.6	76.0	100	3.6	26.7	69.0	100	0.0	2.2	96.9	100
Morocco[c]	40.9	21.7	37.2	100	34.2	24.0	41.6	100	59.2	15.4	25.2	100
Palestinian Authority[c]	13.4	25.7	60.9	100	10.1	29.0	60.9	100	27.5	11.3	61.2	100
Qatar[d]	2.3	51.8	45.7	100	2.7	58.3	38.9	100	0.0	4.8	94.9	100
Saudi Arabia[b]	4.1	20.4	75.5	100	4.7	23.3	72.0	100	0.2	1.5	98.4	100
Syrian Arab Republic[g]	14.9	32.2	52.8	100	13.6	35.8	50.7	100	23.8	9.3	66.9	100
United Arab Emirates[c]	4.2	24.3	71.2	100	5.2	28.3	66.3	100	0.2	7.1	92.5	100
Western Africa	**57.4**	**9.2**	**30.9**	**100**	**60.0**	**11.0**	**26.8**	**100**	**53.1**	**7.3**	**36.3**	**100**
Burkina Faso[f]	84.8	3.1	12.2	100	82.3	3.9	13.7	100	87.2	2.1	10.2	100
Ghana[e]	57.2	13.6	29.1	100	61.4	13.4	25.1	100	53.2	13.8	33.0	100
Liberia[i]	48.9	9.2	41.9	100	49.5	13.5	37.0	100	48.3	4.8	46.8	100
Mali[e]	66.0	5.6	28.3	100	67.8	8.0	24.1	100	63.9	2.7	33.3	100
Niger[f, g]	56.9	11.1	31.1	100	64.1	8.3	26.5	100	37.8	18.4	43.0	100
Senegal[e]	33.7	14.8	36.1	100	34.1	20.2	32.7	100	33.0	4.9	42.3	100
Togo[e, g]	54.1	6.8	37.5	100	60.5	9.5	28.6	100	48.2	4.4	45.7	100
Eastern and Middle Africa	**54.7**	**11.1**	**33.8**	**100**	**51.8**	**13.7**	**34.0**	**100**	**58.0**	**7.9**	**33.9**	**100**
Congo[f, g]	35.4	20.6	42.2	100	31.3	20.0	45.9	100	39.3	21.2	38.7	100
Ethiopia[f]	79.3	6.6	13.0	100	83.2	5.1	10.4	100	74.8	8.3	16.0	100
Gabon[f, g]	24.2	11.8	64.0	100	17.3	18.6	64.1	100	33.7	2.5	63.8	100
Kenya[f, g]	61.1	6.7	32.2	100	54.5	10.8	34.6	100	68.0	2.3	29.7	100
Madagascar[f, g]	80.4	3.7	15.8	100	79.8	5.6	14.6	100	81.1	1.8	17.1	100
Mauritius[h]	8.7	28.2	63.1	100	9.5	32.1	58.3	100	7.8	22.0	70.4	100
Tanzania, United Republic of[e, g]	76.5	4.3	19.2	100	72.7	6.6	20.7	100	80.0	2.1	17.9	100
Zambia[f, g]	72.2	7.1	20.6	100	65.9	10.9	23.7	100	78.9	3.1	17.3	100

Table III.A1.2. **Employment by broad economic activity and gender, 2010** (cont.)

Percentages

Region, country or economy[k]	All				Men				Women			
	Agriculture	Industry	Services	All activities[a]	Agriculture	Industry	Services	All activities[a]	Agriculture	Industry	Services	All activities[a]
Southern Africa	**17.1**	**19.3**	**63.5**	**100**	**21.4**	**26.0**	**52.6**	**100**	**12.1**	**11.1**	**76.8**	**100**
Botswana[e]	29.9	15.2	54.9	100	35.1	19.2	45.7	100	24.3	10.8	64.9	100
Namibia[c]	16.3	17.7	65.9	100	22.7	24.4	52.8	100	8.2	9.1	82.6	100
South Africa[b, g]	5.1	25.0	69.8	100	6.3	34.5	59.2	100	3.7	13.3	82.9	100

* Information on data for Israel: http://dx.doi.org/10.1787/888932315602.

a) Data for all activities may include also "activity not adequately defined", here not reported. Sum of agriculture, industry and services may therefore not correspond exactly to 100.

b) Data refer to 2009.

c) Data refer to 2008.

d) Data refer to 2007.

e) Data refer to 2006.

f) Data refer to 2005.

g) Data refer to ISIC 2.

h) Data refer to ISIC 3.

i) Data refer to ISIC 4.

j) Information on industrial classification not available.

k) Country classification into world regions is based on UN and World Bank classifications.

l) *Footnote by Turkey:* The information in this document with reference to "Cyprus" relates to the southern part of the Island. There is no single authority representing both Turkish and Greek Cypriot people on the Island. Turkey recognises the Turkish Republic of Northern Cyprus (TRNC). Until a lasting and equitable solution is found within the context of United Nations, Turkey shall preserve its position concerning the "Cyprus issue".

m) *Footnote by all the European Union member states of the OECD and the European Commission:* The Republic of Cyprus is recognised by all members of the United Nations with the exception of Turkey. The information in this document relates to the area under the effective control of the Government of the Republic of Cyprus.

Source: OECD Employment Database 2012 for OECD countries (excluding France, Luxembourg, the United States and Brazil); ILO (2012), "Key Indicators of the Labour Market (KILM)", 7th Edition, *ILO Department of Economic and Labour Market Analysis*, Geneva, for non-OECD countries (excluding Brazil) and Luxembourg and the United States; INSEE for France.

StatLink ᴍᴤᴩ *http://dx.doi.org/10.1787/888932677571*

Table III.A1.3. **Female employment as a proportion of total employment in each industry sector according to ISIC Revision 3 and ISIC Revision 4 classifications,**[a] **2010**

Percentages

	ISIC 3, 2010								
	Agriculture and fishing	Mining, manufacturing, utilites and construction	Wholesale and retail trade, hotels and restaurant	Transport, storage and communication	Finance and real estate	Public administration and defense	Education	Health and social work	Other community activities and private households
	(A-B)	(C-F)	(G-H)	(I)	(JK)	(L)	(M)	(N)	(OP)
OECD	**29.4**	**22.5**	**49.9**	**24.5**	**45.1**	**46.0**	**69.5**	**78.2**	**58.3**
Australia	31.9	19.4	48.4	25.8	46.0	47.1	70.1	79.0	55.7
Austria	44.2	21.6	55.7	26.5	48.6	46.6	69.6	77.7	59.1
Belgium[b]	26.6	18.9	47.6	22.3	45.4	47.4	69.1	77.2	63.3
Canada[b]	27.0	22.3	49.5	29.1	49.0	49.8	66.9	82.8	61.6
Chile	18.7	17.3	47.5	15.9	41.7	38.9	68.8	70.4	69.0
Czech Republic[b]	29.8	26.9	53.0	28.0	47.4	50.3	77.4	80.5	53.3
Denmark[c]	19.7	25.1	44.8	27.7	41.4	55.7	57.8	82.9	53.3
Estonia	33.6	31.4	64.4	29.5	51.5	64.2	83.8	86.9	69.6
Finland[c]	28.9	20.7	53.8	28.2	46.0	60.2	67.3	89.3	59.9
Germany[b]	32.2	24.1	54.1	27.7	47.6	49.6	67.8	76.8	60.8
Greece[d]	42.2	17.0	43.0	19.5	46.1	36.3	62.5	64.1	61.9
Hungary[c]	24.1	29.9	52.9	27.0	50.6	55.2	78.1	77.6	55.2
Iceland	19.3	20.8	47.6	32.6	46.3	51.5	76.3	79.6	47.2
Ireland	11.5	20.7	51.2	23.3	46.4	51.8	74.1	81.5	57.7
Israel*, [c]	18.0	23.0	42.0	30.1	45.4	45.6	76.8	77.2	58.3
Italy	28.7	20.3	42.8	23.0	45.6	41.2	76.5	68.3	64.2
Japan[b]	40.8	24.7	51.6	20.6	41.1	23.4	55.0	75.7	50.3
Korea[c]	46.2	25.0	53.9	11.5	39.7	31.2	67.5	75.1	48.5
Mexico	10.7	24.9	52.7	12.4	39.2	35.6	62.4	67.0	53.9
Netherlands[c]	29.8	19.4	48.4	26.9	40.2	40.1	60.9	81.7	57.3
New Zealand	30.7	22.0	49.2	29.6	47.3	51.4	72.0	81.9	56.3
Norway[c]	22.9	18.5	50.5	25.0	37.4	52.7	65.0	82.9	52.3
Poland[d]	43.2	26.1	55.9	21.9	51.1	50.1	77.3	80.7	54.6
Portugal[c]	48.4	26.8	48.9	23.5	49.2	35.4	76.7	83.5	78.4
Slovak Republic[c]	24.0	26.8	58.7	26.8	52.6	50.9	78.6	81.7	54.4
Slovenia[c]	31.1	30.5	62.8	31.8	51.4	55.5	79.9	90.8	72.7
Spain[c]	26.0	17.1	51.1	23.3	49.7	43.4	64.3	76.9	72.1
Sweden[c]	19.8	19.3	46.0	27.3	39.9	55.0	74.6	83.4	52.6
Switzerland[c]	31.8	22.9	52.2	31.2	41.8	44.2	60.3	77.0	62.9
Turkey[b]	46.6	16.8	17.0	8.2	28.6	14.6	46.6	54.9	35.8
United Kingdom	22.9	17.9	48.9	23.4	45.0	50.7	72.2	78.9	54.3
Brazil[b]	31.1	25.3	42.7	13.8	38.6	41.7	76.2	76.1	81.3

Table III.A1.3. **Female employment as a proportion of total employment in each industry sector according to ISIC Revision 3 and ISIC Revision 4 classifications,[a] 2010** (cont.)

Percentages

	ISIC 4, 2010								
	Agriculture, hunting and forestry	Mining, manufacturing, utilites and construction	Wholesale and retail trade, accomodation and food services	Transport, storage, information and communication	Financial, real estate, professional and administrative activities	Public administration and defense	Education	Human health and social work	Other service activities, arts and entertainment, private households
	(C-A)	(B-F)	(G and I)	(H and J)	(K-N)	(O)	(P)	(Q)	(R-T)
OECD	**30.6**	**22.3**	**49.9**	**23.9**	**47.1**	**46.0**	**69.1**	**78.1**	**61.5**
Belgium	29.9	19.6	46.1	24.0	47.5	47.8	69.3	78.4	63.8
Czech Republic	26.5	26.1	55.3	26.2	50.5	49.4	76.1	79.8	60.4
Denmark	17.5	22.4	46.6	25.1	45.6	59.7	59.2	81.8	56.4
Estonia	34.0	31.1	64.5	29.6	55.5	64.2	83.8	86.7	70.3
Finland	29.6	20.6	54.9	25.5	50.0	60.7	66.7	88.4	59.4
France	29.3	21.6	47.1	29.6	47.8	52.6	67.7	78.4	70.3
Germany	33.6	23.3	54.1	28.8	49.6	49.5	68.9	76.6	66.3
Greece	40.8	16.1	43.4	20.0	47.9	37.5	65.0	68.3	67.8
Hungary	23.9	30.0	54.5	26.7	53.8	54.8	76.6	79.0	62.2
Iceland	19.3	20.3	47.6	29.8	50.4	51.5	76.3	79.3	56.8
Italy	29.3	19.8	43.0	24.0	47.4	41.3	76.0	68.6	68.6
Japan[e]	40.5	24.2	52.1	21.7	43.8	24.1	54.9	75.8	57.0
Korea	43.6	24.0	52.7	14.8	39.6	36.4	67.2	80.1	49.9
Mexico	10.7	24.8	52.7	12.4	40.0	35.6	62.4	67.0	53.9
Netherlands[b]	29.2	18.1	48.7	24.9	45.0	40.2	61.3	81.6	59.6
Norway	19.0	16.9	49.3	24.7	42.4	49.7	63.5	81.9	58.8
Poland	43.9	24.1	56.5	24.5	52.0	50.1	77.9	81.8	61.7
Portugal	45.9	27.5	48.7	23.6	50.3	38.6	77.0	83.1	81.6
Slovak Republic	24.4	25.3	59.0	25.8	53.1	48.6	80.8	84.3	64.8
Slovenia	44.3	27.8	54.6	24.5	54.4	48.7	77.7	80.1	60.6
Spain	25.8	18.2	51.0	23.1	51.0	44.4	65.7	77.2	74.5
Sweden	20.8	18.1	45.3	25.8	43.7	56.4	73.4	82.0	55.1
Switzerland[b]	33.1	22.5	52.6	28.6	43.4	43.3	60.7	76.7	68.2
Turkey[e]	47.9	17.2	18.0	9.1	28.8	14.9	46.9	56.1	35.5
United Kingdom	22.9	17.9	48.9	23.5	45.0	50.7	72.2	78.9	54.3

* Information on data for Israel: http://dx.doi.org/10.1787/888932315602.
a) ISIC 4 data were not available for Australia, Austria, Canada, Chile, Ireland, Israel, Luxembourg, New Zealand and the United States at the time of data extraction.
b) Data refer to 2009.
c) Data refer to 2008.
d) Data refer to 2007.
e) Data for water supply, sewerage and waste (E) and employment of households (T) not included.
Source: OECD Employment Database 2012; INE-Statistics Portugal for Portugal (ISIC 3 data); INSEE for France.

StatLink ᴴᵀᵗᴾ http://dx.doi.org/10.1787/888932677590

ANNEX III.A2

The determinants of female labour force participation and part-time work

The determinants of female labour market participation and part-time work can be ascertained through econometric analysis of prime-age women (25-54 years old) in 18 countries from 1980 to 2007. Two separate types of labour force determinants are considered:

● The variations in jobs and labour market characteristics.

● Policies which aim to help parents balance work and family commitments.

Jobs and labour market characteristics include the share of employment in the services sector, the proportion of part-time jobs and employment in the public sector, the OECD indicator on the strictness of employment protection legislation, and total unemployment rates.

The policy context is captured by variables measuring the incidence of paid leave, childcare services for children under the age of 3, and tax incentives for couple families to have two earners instead of one. The sensitivity of female labour market behaviour to government spending is also assessed with information on per child expenditures on leave and/or birth grants paid at childbirth, those made on other family benefits, and the expenditures for the provision of childcare services. Time-varying information on the number of years spent by women in education and birth rates are also included to account for changes in the composition of the female workforce.

Two different model specifications are considered. In the first model, the dependent variable is the total female participation rate, while the explanatory determinants include labour market characteristics and the policy variables. The drawback of this model specification is, however, that despite the use of instrumental variables, interpretation of the results is affected by the endogeneity of part-time work. Therefore, a second model is estimated which distinguishes between full-time and part-time participation as dependent variables. Two equations relating to part-time and full-time participation are thus estimated separately in a second step. Part-time work no longer appears as an explanatory factor, but is related to different factors such as the financial incentives in the tax and benefit system.

The equations are estimated by two-stage least squares with heteroskedasticity-consistent errors. All the estimated models include country-fixed effects so as to focus on the within-country and over-time variations between female labour force participation and its above-mentioned determinants. In addition, because the decision regarding care is to some extent simultaneous with the choice between work and inactivity, the use of childcare enrolment rates as a regressor introduces a risk of bias in the estimated coefficients. To reduce this risk, the enrolment rates are instrumented by their lagged values. Unemployment rates are also potentially endogenous and, for this reason, they are also instrumented by their lagged values. To minimise the risk of endogeneity, they are defined with respect to a large age group, 15-64, instead of the 25-54 age band considered for female employment.

The main results presented in Table III.A2.1 lead to the following conclusions:

Table III.A2.1. **Econometric estimates of the determinants of female labour force participation, women aged 25-54, OECD, 1980-2007**

	Labour force participation	Full-time employment	Part-time employment
Share of services in employment	0.0047*** (0.000)	0.00587*** (0.00112)	0.008 (0.005)
Share of employment in the public sector	−0.462* (0.254)	−0.359 (0.249)	−3.097*** (1.00)
Incidence of part-time employment	0.473*** (0.151)	–	–
Employment protection legislation	−0.0309 (0.029)	0.0156 (0.0190)	−0.313*** (0.115)
Average number of years of education	0.309*** (0.029)	−0.346*** (0.072)	1.910*** (0.280)
Unemployment rate	−0.0449* (0.025)	−0.023** (0.011)	−0.342*** (0.101)
Policies			
Spending on leave and birth grants per childbirth	−0.010 (0.012)	0.062*** (0.0160)	−0.192*** (0.056)
Spending on family benefits per child under 20	0.074*** (0.019)	0.028 (0.028)	0.102 (0.120)
Spending on childcare services per child under 3	0.0006 (0.005)	0.016** (0.00640)	−0.0958*** (0.029)
Duration of paid leave	−0.0107** (0.005)	0.011 (0.00770)	−0.0638*** (0.024)
Enrolment of children in formal childcare	0.0377*** (0.005)	0.032*** (0.009)	0.167*** (0.041)
Tax rate of a second earner	−0.0407*** (0.012)	−0.081*** (0.019)	–
Tax incentive to work part-time	–	–	0.0190*** (0.006)
Number of observations	156	159	152
R^2	0.997	0.993	0.980

Note: Estimates by two-stage least squares with robust standard errors in brackets. ***, ** and *: Significant at the 1%, 5% and 10%, respectively. All models include country and time dummies.

Country coverage: Australia, Austria, Belgium, Canada, Denmark, Finland, France, Germany, Ireland, Italy, the Netherlands, New Zealand, Norway, Portugal, Spain, Sweden, the United Kingdom and the United States.

The tax rate of a second earner is measured by the ratio of the marginal tax rate on the second earner to the tax wedge for a single-earner couple with two children earning 100% of average earnings. The marginal tax rate on the second earner is in turn defined as the share of the second earner's earnings which goes into paying additional household taxes.

The tax incentive to work part-time is measured by the increase in household disposable income between a situation where one partner earns the entire household income (133% of average earnings), and a situation where two partners share earnings (100% and 33% of the average earnings respectively), for a couple with two children.

Source: OECD Secretariat estimates based on *OECD Labour Force Statistics*, *OECD Earnings Database* and *OECD Family Database* 2012.

StatLink http://dx.doi.org/10.1787/888932677609

Role of education and labour market characteristics

- Female educational attainment is an important driver of female labour force participation and has contributed to an increased share of part-time employment.

- All things being equal, the increase in the share of public employment has not given rise to a significant increase in female labour market participation. The correlation between the incidence of public employment and part-time work is even highly negative, which suggests that the increase in female employment has been driven by two separate drivers: the increase in part-time work in some countries and the expansion of public employment in others.

- There is a clear negative association between the increase in part-time work and the strength of employment protection legislation.

Role of policies

- Increased enrolment of children in childcare has increased female employment on a full-time and part-time basis. Increasing public spending on childcare does not necessarily lead to greater part-time employment because it may facilitate moving into full-time work or increase the quality of childcare without affecting hours per week.

- Higher public spending on paid leave increases the share of full-time employment relative to working part-time. The duration of leave decreases the probability of working part-time.

- Higher tax rates on the second earner in a family reduce the labour force participation of women, while tax incentives to work part-time also matter.

ANNEX III.A3

Data sources for the analysis in Chapter 13

The following household surveys were used for the analysis:

United States Current Population Survey

The Current Population Survey (CPS) is a statistical survey conducted by the United States Census Bureau for the Bureau of Labor Statistics to report monthly on the employment situation. It surveys 60 000 households. An annual supplement is conducted in March on income received in the previous calendar year and used to estimate the data on income and work experience.

EU Statistics on Income and Living Conditions

The EU Statistics on Income and Living Conditions (EU-SILC) instrument has been collecting annual data for 27 European Union countries – as well as Croatia, Iceland, Norway, Switzerland and Turkey – since 2004 on a cross-sectional and longitudinal basis for 130 000 households. Variables include information on income, poverty, social exclusion and other living conditions. EU-SILC does not rely on a common questionnaire or survey but on common guidelines and procedures, common concepts (household and income) and classifications aimed at maximising comparability of the information produced.

Household, Income, Labour Dynamics in Australia Survey

Household, Income, Labour Dynamics in Australia (HILDA) Survey is an ongoing household-based panel survey funded by the Department of Families, Community Services and Indigenous Affairs. The survey started in 2001 and currently comprises seven waves. Wave 1 of the panel consisted of 7 682 households and 19 914 individuals.

Japan Household Panel Survey

The Japan Household Panel Survey (JHPS) is a panel survey of around 4 000 households conducted by the Panel Data Research Center at Keio University. The first survey was conducted in 2009 and is scheduled to be carried out annually. The survey topics include household composition, income, expenditure, assets, and housing in addition to school attendance, employment, and health conditions of respondents.

Korean Labor and Income Panel Study

The Korean Labour and Income Panel Study (KLIPS) is an ongoing household survey which has been conducted annually since 1998 and consists of 5 000 households and 13 000 individuals. The survey focuses on the study of labour market characteristics, but includes a question on life satisfaction.

Canadian Survey of Labour and Income Dynamics

The Canadian Survey of Labour and Income Dynamics (SLID) was introduced in 1993 to provide information on labour market activity and income changes experienced by individuals and families over time. The SLID sample is composed of two panels, each consisting of around 17 000 households and 34 000 individuals. Each panel is surveyed for six consecutive years, with a new panel being introduced every three years. The survey is used to investigate, among other topics, employment and unemployment dynamics, life-cycle labour market transition, job quality, low income, life events and family changes, and educational advancement.

Chilean National Socioeconomic Characterisation Survey

The Chilean National Socioeconomic Characterisation Survey (CASEN) has been conducted every two or three years since 1985. The survey provides information on the socio-economic situation of different social sectors of the country and their main needs, the incidence, magnitude and characteristics of poverty, as well as the composition and distribution of household incomes. In 2009, around 70 000 households were sampled, corresponding to around 240 000 individuals.

Mexican Household Income and Expenditure Survey

The Mexican Household Income and Expenditure Survey (ENIGH) is a long running nationally representative survey on household income and expenditure. The survey runs every two years and collects data on employment, income, and socio-demographic characteristics of household members, as well as information on housing characteristics. In 2008, the ENIGH sample consisted of around 35 000 dwellings.

South African National Income Dynamics Study

The South African National Income Dynamics Study (NIDS) interviewed around 7 300 households in 2008 and is expected to re-interview the same individuals every two to three years. The survey was designed to analyse income, consumption and expenditure of households over time. It is also designed to investigate household composition and structure; fertility and mortality; migration; labour market participation; human capital formation; and health and education.

Brazilian Pesquisa Nacional por Amostra de Domicílios

The Brazilian *Pesquisa Nacional por Amostra de Domicílios* (National Household Sampling Survey [PNAD]) is a multi-purpose household survey, which annually collects information on general population characteristics, education, work, wages and housing. In 2009, PNAD surveyed 399 387 people in 153 837 households across the country.

Egypt Labour Market Panel Survey and Jordan Labour Market Panel Survey

The Egypt Labour Market Panel Survey (ELMPS) and the Jordan Labour Market Panel Survey (JLMPS) are comparable surveys which are conducted on nationally representative samples of households.

The ELMPS re-interviewed in 2006 the same households which were selected in the 1998 survey. Individuals who had left the original 1998 households in the intervening period were also tracked and interviewed, together with their entire household. In 2006, around 8 300 households were interviewed – a total of around 37 000 individuals. The JLMPS ran for the first time in 2010 and conducted interviews with around 25 000 people in 5 000 households.

Both surveys collect information on household characteristics, employment, education, income, housing, migration, fertility and women's status.

ANNEX III.A4

Supplementary table to Chapter 15

Table III.A4.1. **Quotas on boardroom representation in Europe and sanctions for non-compliance**

Provisions	Sanctions
Since 2006, the Norwegian quota law requires all public (limited) companies listed on the Norwegian Stock Exchange – as well as state-owned, municipal, inter-municipal and co operative companies – to have at least 40% of each gender in the membership of boards where there are at least nine directors.	Legal sanctions in the event of breach of the quota law range from official warnings and financial penalties to delisting the company from the Stock Exchange.
In 2007, Spain enacted a gender equality law. It recommends that large companies with more than 250 employees and listed on IBEX 35, over an eight-year period, gradually appoint women to their boards until they have an even number of male and female members – *i.e.* between 40% and 60% of each gender.	There are no sanctions for failure to comply with obligations. But non-compliance will be taken into account when companies seek, for example, the equality label, public subsidies, or state contracts.
In 2010, the Icelandic Parliament passed legislative reform to promote gender equality on the boards of publicly owned companies and public limited companies with at least 50 employees. Boards of more than three members must have a membership of at least 40% of each gender by 1st September 2013. Moreover, companies with 25 or more employees are required to disclose the number of men and women employed as well as the number of men and women in management positions.	"Should founders, directors, managers, inspectors or others neglect their duties in accordance with the legislation, the Register of Limited Companies may invite them to discharge these duties subject to a daily or weekly fine for as long as they fail to do so. Courts of law may be consulted about the legality of the decree within a month of the serving thereof."
In 2011, France adopted a quota law that requires listed companies and companies with at least 500 employees and revenues of over EUR 50 million to appoint at least 20% of women to their boards within three years and 40% within six years.	A key penalty of the law is that the appointment of a board member which fails to meet the gender criteria will be rendered invalid.
In 2011, the Netherlands passed a law setting a minimum target of 30% of both genders on the boards (executive and supervisory) of large companies (250 employees, listed and not listed) by January 2016. The law is a temporary measure that will come under review in 2016. In 2016, the relevant articles will be rendered void.	Failure to meet this legal target must be reported in the annual report. There are no further sanctions.
In 2011, Belgium passed legislation requiring that each gender should constitute at least one-third of the membership of the management boards of state and publicly listed companies. State companies are granted one year to comply, listed companies five years, and small to medium-sized (listed) firms eight years.	Sanctions: loss of benefits by board members until the quota law has been complied with.
In 2011, Italy approved gender quotas for boards of directors and statutory auditors' boards of listed companies and state-owned companies. By 2015, boards should comprise one-third of each gender (one-fifth for a transitional period of one year). The rules are applicable to board appointments from the first year after the new law comes into effect.	Sanctions are progressive: warning, fine, then forfeiture of office by all members of the board.

Source: *http://ec.europa.eu/justice/gender-equality.*

StatLink ᵐᵍ⁵ᵖ *http://dx.doi.org/10.1787/888932677628*

ANNEX III.A5

Supplementary table to Chapter 18

Table III.A5.1. **Tax and benefit systems and their "neutrality"**

Average payments to government in % of gross household earnings at different earning distributions
of couples with two children between ages 6 and 11 (inclusive), whose income is equal
to 133% and 200% of the average worker's earnings, 2010

Gross income in terms of average worker earnings	Single-earner couples		Dominant dual earner couples		Equal dual-earner couples		Difference in net transfers to government: single and equal dual-earner couples	
	133-0	200-0	100-33	150-50	67-67	100-100	133	200
	1	2	3	4	5	6	[(1 – 5)/1]*100	[(2 – 6)/2]*100
OECD	**18.9**	**25.9**	**15.4**	**22.2**	**14.7**	**21.2**	**24.5**	**17.6**
Australia	16.9	28.0	12.9	22.8	10.5	22.3	37.6	20.5
Austria	25.7	30.7	18.3	27.1	16.9	26.3	34.3	14.2
Belgium	30.4	40.2	26.4	37.0	27.2	36.5	10.5	9.2
Canada	17.4	24.9	14.7	21.6	12.6	20.9	27.4	16.3
Chile	7.0	8.2	4.8	6.1	6.5	6.7	7.2	18.6
Czech Republic	5.3	15.9	6.6	15.9	5.3	15.9	0.0	0.0
Denmark	33.3	40.9	31.9	38.0	31.8	35.0	4.6	14.3
Estonia	11.1	15.1	11.1	15.1	11.1	15.1	0.0	0.0
Finland	29.4	36.3	20.7	28.2	18.2	26.5	38.1	27.0
France	19.8	23.2	18.3	23.6	20.2	23.9	−1.9	−2.9
Germany	25.2	28.9	26.0	32.2	26.0	33.5	−3.1	−16.2
Greece	25.6	32.2	19.9	24.6	16.3	22.4	36.4	30.5
Hungary	27.5	36.4	18.3	28.6	18.2	25.0	33.6	31.1
Iceland	20.2	29.2	19.9	27.5	19.6	27.5	3.1	5.9
Ireland	6.2	20.4	1.5	11.7	−0.6	12.3	109.3	39.7
Israel*	17.8	25.9	9.9	16.2	4.6	11.1	74.2	57.0
Italy	27.0	35.8	20.2	29.1	19.9	27.0	26.1	24.6
Japan	14.6	19.3	13.5	17.3	13.2	16.5	9.1	14.3
Korea	12.2	14.5	9.7	12.1	8.8	11.2	27.4	22.9
Luxembourg	9.0	20.1	6.3	17.3	6.3	17.3	30.2	13.5
Mexico	11.2	15.0	1.6	8.2	0.1	5.6	98.9	62.5
Netherlands	28.8	35.7	22.6	29.0	20.9	27.5	27.3	22.9
New Zealand	12.2	25.3	7.5	20.1	7.5	17.0	38.9	32.9
Norway	27.5	33.9	22.7	28.8	21.8	26.7	20.7	21.2
Poland	19.2	21.7	18.7	21.4	18.7	21.4	2.6	1.5
Portugal	16.3	23.1	12.0	20.3	12.0	20.3	26.2	12.3
Slovak Republic	9.4	16.1	8.2	16.2	9.4	16.2	0.0	−0.7
Slovenia	20.7	30.6	19.2	26.9	18.7	27.8	9.5	9.3
Spain	18.7	23.8	16.5	19.7	14.7	19.9	21.7	16.5

Table III.A5.1. **Tax and benefit systems and their "neutrality"** *(cont.)*

Average payments to government in % of gross household earnings at different earning distributions
of couples with two children between ages 6 and 11 (inclusive), whose income is equal
to 133% and 200% of the average worker's earnings, 2010

	Single-earner couples		Dominant dual earner couples		Equal dual-earner couples		Difference in net transfers to government: single and equal dual-earner couples	
Gross income in terms of average worker earnings	133-0	200-0	100-33	150-50	67-67	100-100	133	200
	1	2	3	4	5	6	[(1 – 5)/1]*100	[(2 – 6)/2]*100
Sweden	25.3	35.4	16.9	26.2	16.5	21.1	34.8	40.3
Switzerland	7.1	12.7	5.6	11.5	5.6	11.6	20.1	8.4
Turkey	28.3	31.8	27.1	29.6	26.7	28.7	6.0	9.8
United Kingdom	22.2	29.2	17.5	23.9	17.5	22.8	20.8	21.9
United States	15.1	19.9	15.1	19.9	15.1	19.9	0.0	0.0

Note: The Tax-Benefit Model assumes that no housing benefits or payments relating to a transition into work are received.

* Information on data for Israel: *http://dx.doi.org/10.1787/888932315602.*

Source: OECD Tax-Benefit Model.

StatLink ⟡ *http://dx.doi.org/10.1787/888932677647*

ANNEX III.A6

Supplementary tables to Chapter 20

Table III.A6.1. **Informal employment in non-agricultural activities by gender**
Informal employment (inside and outside the informal sector) as share of non-agricultural employment, 2010 or latest year available

Region, country or economy	Informal work in informal sector (A)			Informal employment outside the informal sector (B)			Informal employment (A + B)		
	All	Men	Women	All	Men	Women	All	Men	Women
Latin America	**39.7**	**40.4**	**38.5**	**17.5**	**14.6**	**21.2**	**57.2**	**55.1**	**59.8**
Argentina[k]	31.8	36.7	25.3	17.9	13.2	24.3	49.7	49.8	49.6
Bolivia (Plurinational State of)[d]	51.6	50.2	53.4	23.5	22.1	25.2	75.1	72.4	78.5
Brazil[j]	24.2	27.6	20.1	18.0	11.6	25.8	42.2	39.2	45.9
Colombia[l]	50.4	51.0	49.6	9.3	6.0	13.0	59.6	57.0	62.7
Costa Rica[g]	32.6	34.0	30.4	11.2	8.2	15.5	43.8	42.2	46.0
Dominican Republic[j]	29.1	32.8	23.4	19.4	13.9	28.0	48.5	46.7	51.4
Ecuador[i]	36.9	37.9	35.5	24.0	20.9	28.2	60.9	58.8	63.7
El Salvador[j]	51.6	46.6	56.4	14.8	13.5	16.0	66.4	60.1	72.5
Honduras[i]	56.9	55.4	58.5	17.0	17.6	16.3	73.9	73.0	74.8
Nicaragua[j]	50.7	51.9	49.5	15.0	13.0	17.2	65.7	64.9	66.6
Panama[h]	27.5	28.7	26.0	16.3	13.2	20.6	43.8	41.8	46.5
Paraguay[j]	37.9	38.8	36.7	32.8	29.1	37.7	70.7	67.9	74.4
Peru[j]	48.2	43.8	53.5	21.7	21.3	22.2	70.6	65.5	76.2
Uruguay[j]	30.0	34.1	25.3	9.8	5.3	15.0	39.8	39.4	40.3
Venezuela (Bolivarian Republic of)[f]	35.7	37.1	33.7	11.8	10.4	13.7	47.5	47.5	47.4
Eastern Europe and Central Asia	**9.9**	**12.7**	**5.2**	**12.5**	**13.0**	**10.5**	**22.3**	**25.7**	**15.7**
Armenia[j]	10.2	13.7	5.2	9.6	11.1	7.5	19.8	24.8	12.7
Former Yugoslav Republic of Macedonia (FYROM)[m]	7.4	10.3	2.5	5.2	5.0	5.6	12.6	15.4	8.1
Moldova, Republic of[j]	7.3	12.4	2.6	8.6	8.4	8.8	15.9	20.8	11.4
Palestinian Authority[m]	21.3	22.7	14.0	35.8	37.2	28.0	57.2	59.9	42.0
Serbia[m]	3.1	4.1	1.6	3.0	3.3	2.6	6.1	7.5	4.3
Asia	**58.2**	**60.1**	**53.9**	**14.3**	**13.0**	**17.1**	**72.5**	**73.1**	**71.0**
India[k]	66.8	68.6	58.5	16.8	14.7	26.2	83.5	83.3	84.7
Indonesia[j]	60.3	61.2	58.8	12.2	11.1	14.0	72.5	72.3	72.9
Pakistan[k]	70.1	70.3	67.7	8.3	8.3	8.0	78.4	78.7	75.7
Philippines[e]	58.5	62.8	53.3	11.5	7.1	16.9	70.1	69.9	70.2
Sri Lanka[j]	50.5	54.7	41.8	11.6	10.6	13.9	62.1	65.2	55.7
Viet Nam[j]	43.2	43.0	43.3	25.0	26.4	23.4	68.2	69.4	66.8

Table III.A6.1. **Informal employment in non-agricultural activities by gender** (cont.)

Informal employment (inside and outside the informal sector) as share of non-agricultural employment, 2010 or latest year available

Region, country or economy	Informal work in informal sector (A)			Informal employment outside the informal sector (B)			Informal employment (A + B)		
	All	Men	Women	All	Men	Women	All	Men	Women
Africa	**45.9**	**40.6**	**51.8**	**16.4**	**16.1**	**16.9**	**62.1**	**56.7**	**68.7**
Lesotho[e]	13.4	14.1	12.4	21.6	20.0	23.7	34.9	34.1	36.1
Liberia[m]	49.1	32.8	65.4	10.8	14.6	6.6	60.0	47.4	72.0
Madagascar[b]	51.7	40.6	63.8	21.9	26.2	17.2	73.6	66.8	81.0
Mali[a]	70.5	61.7	79.1	11.3	12.6	10.1	81.8	74.2	89.2
South Africa[m]	17.8	18.6	16.8	14.9	10.9	20.0	32.7	29.5	36.8
Tanzania, United Republic of[c]	51.2	52.6	49.5	25.0	18.4	33.3	76.2	70.9	82.8
Uganda[m]	55.7	52.6	59.7	13.7	14.9	12.2	68.5	67.5	71.9
Zambia[e]	57.8	51.6	67.7	11.7	11.3	12.4	69.5	62.9	80.1

a) Data refer to 2004.
b) Data refers to 2005.
c) Data refer to 2005-06.
d) Data refer to 2006.
e) Data refer to 2008.
f) Data refer to 2009 1st quarter.
g) Data refer to July 2009.
h) Data refer to August 2009.
i) Data refer to 2009 4th quarter.
j) Data refer to 2009.
k) Data refer to 2009-10.
l) Data refer to 2010 2nd quarter.
m) Data refer to 2010.
n) Data refer to 2010 4th quarter.

Source: ILO (2002), "Women and Men in the Informal Economy: A Statistical Picture", International Labour Organisation, Geneva.

StatLink ⟲ http://dx.doi.org/10.1787/888932677666

Table III.A6.2. **Distribution of male and female informal employment by work category**

Percentages, 2010 or latest year available

Region, country or economy	Employers, own-account workers and MPCs[n]		Contributing family workers		Wage employees		Domestic workers employed by households	
	Women	Men	Women	Men	Women	Men	Women	Men
Latin America	**49.4**	**50.7**	**8.1**	**3.9**	**23.9**	**44.2**	**18.6**	**1.3**
Argentina[j]	35.5	50.4	2.4	1.0	33.6	47.8	28.5	0.7
Bolivia (Plurinational State of)[c]	48.4	38.5	13.7	7.6	27.3	53.4	10.6	0.4
Brazil[j]	32.7	49.7	6.5	3.5	29.7	45.1	31.1	1.7
Colombia[k]	58.2	68.6	8.9	4.3	20.5	26.6	12.4	0.4
Costa Rica[f]	48.6	56.6	4.6	1.8	24.2	40.3	22.5	1.3
Dominican Republic[i]	39.5	64.7	5.6	2.2	25.9	31.0	29.0	2.1
Ecuador[h]	40.5	34.5	16.1	5.6	29.5	59.1	13.9	0.8
El Salvador[j]	57.9	40.9	8.7	5.3	19.0	52.2	14.5	1.6
Honduras[i]	57.2	41.9	14.9	6.5	19.4	50.6	8.6	1.0
Nicaragua[i]	55.7	45.5	10.6	5.2	15.9	45.9	17.8	3.3
Panama[g]	53.6	60.3	4.7	1.6	19.2	36.3	22.5	1.9
Paraguay[i]	37.2	30.8	7.8	5.4	28.2	61.4	26.8	2.4
Peru[i]	53.7	45.8	10.8	6.0	24.8	47.7	10.7	0.5
Uruguay[i]	55.8	68.6	4.7	1.9	14.9	28.8	24.6	0.7
Venezuela (Bolivarian Republic of)[e]	65.9	63.2	2.2	0.7	26.6	36.1	5.3	0.0
Eastern Europe and Central Asia	**21.2**	**34.8**	**5.8**	**3.1**	**66.3**	**56.2**	**6.7**	**5.8**
Armenia[i]	24.4	32.0	4.7	2.6	63.4	61.2	7.6	4.2
Moldova, Republic of[i]	20.1	54.5	3.2	2.0	68.9	42.6	7.7	0.9
Palestinian Authority[l]	19.0	18.0	9.5	4.8	66.7	64.9	4.8	12.3
Asia	**36.4**	**39.1**	**17.3**	**6.4**	**40.8**	**52.0**	**8.2**	**1.1**
India[j]	28.9	40.0	18.9	7.1	45.8	51.8	6.5	1.1
Indonesia[i]	40.2	38.9	19.0	4.3	33.5	56.2	7.3	0.7
Philippines[j]	45.2	34.4	11.3	5.2	24.5	57.6	19.1	2.8
Pakistan[d]	31.2	43.0	19.9	9.2	48.8	47.7	0.1	0.1
Africa	**55.3**	**45.8**	**9.5**	**6.1**	**18.3**	**39.3**	**16.9**	**8.8**
Lesotho[d]	8.6	6.8	2.7	2.4	38.1	51.8	50.7	39.0
Liberia[l]	80.6	56.6	11.7	11.8	6.3	28.7	1.5	2.9
Mali[a]	79.6	61.5	5.9	7.5	7.3	29.7	7.3	1.4
South Africa[m]	30.1	36.2	2.7	2.0	25.1	49.7	42.1	12.1
Tanzania, United Republic of[b]	79.2	62.0	3.6	2.3	11.0	34.3	6.1	1.4
Uganda[l]	58.8	48.5	16.3	8.6	20.2	41.7	4.7	1.2
Zambia[d]	50.4	49.3	23.6	8.0	19.9	39.4	6.1	3.3

a) Data refer to 2004.
b) Data refer to 2005-06.
c) Data refer to 2006.
d) Data refer to 2008.
e) Data refer to 2009 1st quarter.
f) Data refer to July 2009.
g) Data refer to August 2009.
h) Data refer to 2009 4th quarter.
i) Data refer to 2009.
j) Data refer to 2009-10.
k) Data refer to 2010 2nd quarter.
l) Data refer to 2010.
m) Data refer to 2010 4th quarter.
n) Members of producers' co-operatives.
Source: ILO (2002), "Women and Men in the Informal Economy: A Statistical Picture", International Labour Organisation, Geneva.

StatLink ᵃᵃˢᵖ http://dx.doi.org/10.1787/888932677685

ANNEX III.A7

General background data on employment

Table III.A7.1. Labour force participation, employment, part-time and temporary work, gender wage gaps, boardroom membership and unpaid work

	Labour force participation rate (15-64 years old) 2011		Employment/ population ratio (15-64 years old) 2011		Part-time employment[a] as a proportion of total employment 2011		Employment/population ratio full-time equivalent[b] (15-64 years old) 2011		Temporary employment as a proportion of dependent employment[c] (25-54 years old) 2011		Gender wage gap[d] 2010 or latest year	Proportion of women on boards of listed companies 2009	Average minutes of unpaid work per day[e] 1999-2010[f]		Average weekly hours dedicated to care activities 2007	
	Men	Women	Men	Women	Men	Women	Men	Women	Men	Women			Men	Women	Men	Women
OECD	**78.9**	**65.2**	**72.3**	**59.7**	**8.4**	**25.2**	**74.4**	**50.7**	**9.9**	**11.7**	**15.8**	**10.4**	**140.0**	**277.1**	**26.6**	**39.3**
Australia	82.9	70.5	78.7	66.7	13.2	38.5	79.7	51.4	4.3	6.6[k]	14.0	7.6	171.6	311.0		37.0
Austria	81.1	69.5	77.8	66.5	7.0	32.8	81.9	54.5	4.6	5.5	19.4[m]	6.0	135.3	268.9	16.0	29.0
Belgium	72.3	61.1	67.1	56.7	7.0	32.4	67.9	46.3	5.8	8.1	8.9[j]	10.8	150.8	245.0	20.0	29.0
Canada	81.5	74.2	75.0	68.9	12.9	27.2	74.6	58.5	9.7	10.7	18.8	6.3	159.6	253.6		
Chile	78.6	53.9	73.6	49.1	11.8	25.5	76.0	44.1	28.7	27.8		5.4				
Czech Republic	78.7	62.2	74.0	57.2	1.9	6.6	78.9	55.8	5.6	7.8	18.1[m]		186.1	242.8	27.0	44.0
Denmark	82.3	76.1	75.9	70.4	13.8	25.2	68.1	54.9	5.8	8.1	12.1[m]	10.2	169.0	287.8	29.0	28.0
Estonia	78.1	71.4	67.8	62.7	5.1	12.4	67.9	58.6	4.2	2.4			159.0	232.0	32.0	53.0
Finland	77.5	72.7	70.9	67.5	9.6	16.0	69.5	59.3	9.6	16.8	19.7[m]	14.9	135.9	257.6	19.0	22.0
France	74.7	66.1	68.1	59.7	5.9	22.1	69.8	51.8	10.4	12.4	13.1[j]	18.1	163.8	268.8	23.0	36.0
Germany	82.6	71.8	77.4	67.7	8.5	38.0	77.2	51.5	9.5	10.6	21.6[m]	3.5			26.0	50.0
Greece	77.7	57.5	65.9	45.1	5.6	14.0	72.5	44.4	10.3	12.0	9.6[j]	9.7	127.1	268.1	22.0	43.0
Hungary	68.8	56.8	61.2	50.6	3.4	6.4	61.5	48.9	8.8	7.8	6.4				21.0	30.0
Iceland	87.8[g]	82.4[g]	80.8	77.3	10.4	24.1	88.7	67.4	7.1	10.0	13.5[j]		129.2	296.1		
Ireland	77.2	62.6	63.3	56.0	12.6	39.3	61.9	42.7	7.2	7.9	10.4[m]	6.9			48.0	48.0
Israel*	68.2	60.9	64.3	57.5	7.1	21.1	72.1	52.3			20.3	7.0	102.9	325.8		
Italy	73.1	51.5	67.5	46.5	6.6	31.3	68.4	38.5	10.4	13.5	11.8[j]	3.9	58.6	268.7	22.0	29.0
Japan	84.4	63.0	80.2	60.3	10.3	34.8			4.5	18.7	28.7		45.0	227.3		
Korea	77.4	54.9	74.5	53.1	10.0	18.5	87.0	55.4	16.4	23.5	38.9[m]					42.0
Luxembourg	75.0	60.7	72.1	56.9	5.0	30.2	72.3	47.0	4.8	6.9		10.0	112.6	373.3	29.0	
Mexico	82.3	45.9	77.8	43.4	12.5	27.7	90.0	41.5	22.2	10.3[j]		7.4	163.0	272.8		
Netherlands	83.6	73.1	79.8	69.9	17.1	60.5	71.2	42.9	12.5	14.1	16.7[j]	4.8	141.0	264.0	31.0	53.0
New Zealand	83.6	72.2	78.2	67.2	11.2	34.3	81.9	54.3			6.8	7.8	152.2	225.3		
Norway	80.1	75.8	77.2	73.4	11.0	30.0	70.6	56.6	4.5	8.0	8.1	38.0	157.1	295.8	28.0	45.0
Poland	73.0	59.4	66.3	53.1	4.9	12.4	70.3	50.8	24.4	23.2	10.0[m]	7.4	96.3	328.2	32.0	49.0
Portugal	78.5	69.8	68.1	60.4	8.8	14.4	69.5	56.3	20.1	20.5	15.6[m]	9.7			30.0	34.0
Slovak Republic	76.7	61.0	66.3	52.7	2.7	5.7	69.0	51.8	5.0	6.1		17.8	166.5	286.2	23.0	34.0
Slovenia	73.9	66.5	67.7	60.9	6.7	10.9	68.5	58.3	11.6	15.1	11.8[m]		153.9	258.1	31.0	37.0
Spain	81.5[g]	67.9[g]	64.1	52.8	5.5	21.9	65.9	46.4	23.6	25.7		10.6	177.0	249.2	25.0	45.0
Sweden	82.7[g]	77.7[g]	76.3	71.9	9.8	18.4	73.3	61.6	9.8	13.0	14.9[m]	19.3			31.0	38.0

Table III.A7.1. Labour force participation, employment, part-time and temporary work, gender wage gaps, boardroom membership and unpaid work (cont.)

	Labour force participation rate (15-64 years old) 2011		Employment/ population ratio (15-64 years old) 2011		Part-time employment as a proportion of total employment[a] 2011		Employment/population ratio full-time equivalent[b] (15-64 years old) 2011		Temporary employment as a proportion of dependent employment[c] (25-54 years old) 2011		Gender wage gap[d] 2010 or latest year	Proportion of women on boards of listed companies 2009	Average minutes of unpaid work per day[e] 1999-2010[f]		Average weekly hours dedicated to care activities 2007	
	Men	Women	Men	Women	Men	Women	Men	Women	Men	Women			Men	Women	Men	Women
Switzerland	88.7	76.7	85.3	73.2	9.4	45.5	86.1	53.3	5.8	6.9	19.5[m]	9.5	..	..	..	..
Turkey	76.4	31.5	69.3	27.8	6.6	24.3	89.8	28.8	10.6	10.2	..	7.4	116.4	376.7	19.0	28.0
United Kingdom	82.7[g]	70.4[g]	75.5	65.3	11.7	39.3	77.4	50.9	4.3	5.2	18.4	8.1	149.9	273.4	27.0	49.0
United States	78.9[g]	67.8[g]	71.4	62.0	8.4	17.1	..	..	3.5	3.4[j]	18.8	12.0	161.1	248.2	..	..
Brazil	85.1[m]	63.5[m]	79.7[m]	56.4[m]	10.1[m]	28.1[m]	85.2[m]	50.0[m]	..	..	..	8.5	..	..	..	..
China	85.3	75.1	76.2[h]	65.3[h]	..	..	..	..	..	..	..	..	91.0	234.0	..	..
India	83.1	30.3	78.1[h]	27.7[h]	..	..	..	..	..	..	..	6.9	51.8	351.9	..	..
Indonesia	86.3	53.3	79.0[h]	46.8[h]	..	..	..	..	..	..	..	17.5	..	..	..	..
Russian Federation	77.8	68.0	72.2	63.8	2.8	5.4	..	..	9.6	5.7	..	12.1	..	..	..	..
South Africa	61.2	47.9	47.4	34.6	5.0	11.2	54.6	36.5	..	..	..	13.1	91.6	257.0	..	..

* Information on data for Israel: http://dx.doi.org/10.1787/88893215602.

a) Part-time employment refers to workers who usually work less than 30 hours per week in their main job.

b) The full-time equivalent rate is calculated as the employment/population ratio, multiplied by the average usual hours worked per week per person in employment, and divided by 40.

c) Temporary employees are wage and salary workers whose job has a pre-determined termination date as opposed to permanent employees whose job is of unlimited duration.

d) The gender wage gap is unadjusted and calculated as the difference between median earnings of men and women relative to median earnings of men.

e) Surveys for Canada, China, Denmark, France, Ireland, Japan, Korea, Mexico and South Africa do not cover a complete calendar year and thus, to varying degrees, under-represent holidays. As people do more unpaid work on weekends, excluding holidays overestimates paid work and underestimates unpaid work and leisure.

f) The years covered are: Australia: 2006; Austria: 2008-09; Belgium: 2005; Canada: 2010; China: 2008; Denmark: 2001; Estonia: 1999-2000; Finland: 2009-10; France: 1998-99; Germany: 2001-02; Hungary: 1999-2000; India: 1999; Italy: 2002-03; Ireland: 2005; Japan: 2006; Korea: 2009; Mexico: 2009; the Netherlands: 2006; New Zealand: 2009-10; Norway: 2000-01; Poland: 2003-04; Portugal: 1999; Slovenia: 2000-01; South Africa: 2000; Spain: 2002-03; Sweden: 2000-01; Turkey: 2006; the United Kingdom: 2000-01; and the United States: 2010.

g) Data refer to those aged 16-64 for Iceland, Spain, Sweden, the United Kingdom and the United States.

h) Data refer to those aged 15+ for China, India and Indonesia.

i) Data refer to 2004.

j) Data refer to 2005.

k) Data refer to 2006.

l) Data refer to 2008.

m) Data refer to 2009.

Source: OECD Employment Database 2012; ILO (2002), "Women and Men in the Informal Economy: A Statistical Picture", International Labour Organisation, Geneva; KILM for Brazil, China, India, Indonesia and South Africa (accessed February 2012). Miranda, V. (2011), "Cooking, Caring and Volunteering: Unpaid Work Around the World"; OECD (2010), "Tackling Inequalities in Brazil, China, India and South Africa – The Role of Labour Market and Social Policies"; European Quality of Life Survey, 2007; OECD-ORBIS Database.

StatLink http://dx.doi.org/10.1787/888932677704

References

Adams, R.B. and D. Ferreira (2004), "Gender Diversity in the Boardroom", *ECGI Working Paper Series*, European Corporate Governance Institute, Brussels.

Adams, R.B. and D. Ferreira (2009), "Women in the Boardroom and their Impact on Governance and Performance", *Journal of Financial Economics*, Vol. 94, No. 2, pp. 291-309.

Adams, R.B. and P. Funk (2009), "Beyond the Glass Ceiling: Does Gender Matter?", *UPF Working Paper Series*, *ECGI – Finance Working Paper*, No. 273/2010, European Corporate Governance Institute, Brussels, available at SSRN: *http://ssrn.com/abstract=1475152* or *http://dx.doi.org/10.2139/ssrn.1475152*.

Adams, R.B. and T. Kirchmaier (2012), "From Female Labor Force Participation to Boardroom Gender Diversity", Document presented at AEA meeting. San Diego, United States.

Adema, W. (2012), "Setting the Scene: The Mix of Family Policy Objectives and Packages Across the OECD", *Children and Youth Services Review*, Vol. 34, Elsevier, pp. 487-498.

Adema, W., P. Fron and M. Ladaique (2011), "Is the European Welfare State Really More Expensive", *OECD Social, Employment and Migration Working Papers*, No. 124, OECD Publishing, Paris, DOI: *http://dx.doi.org/10.1787/5kg2d2d4pbf0-en*.

Ahern, K. and A. Dittmar (2010), "The Changing of the Boards: The Impact of Firm Valuation of Mandated Female Board Representation", *Working Paper*, University of Michigan, Ann Arbor.

Ahmed, W.M. (2012), "Gender Pay Gap in Egypt", *Working Paper*, No. 14, Economic Commission for Europe, Conference on European Statisticians.

AIM (2012), *Gender Diversity in Management: Targeting Untapped Talent: First Steps*, Australian Institute of Management, 21 February.

Albrecht, J., A. Bjorklund and S. Vroman (2003), "Is There a Glass Ceiling in Sweden?", *Journal of Labor Economics*, Vol. 21, No. 1, pp. 145-177.

Andersen, L. and B. Muriel (2007), "Informality and Productivity in Bolivia: A Gender Differentiated Empirical Analysis", *Development Research Working Paper Series*, No. 07/2007, Institute for Advanced Development Studies, La Paz.

Anghel, B., S. de la Rica and J.J. Dolado (2011), "The Effects of Public Sector Employment on Women's Labour Market Outcomes", *IZA Discussion Paper*, No. 5825, Bonn.

Arulampalam, W., A.L. Booth and M.L. Bryan (2007), "Is There a Glass Ceiling over Europe? Exploring the Gender Pay Gap across the Wage Distribution", *Industrial and Labor Relations Review*, Vol. 60, No. 2, Cornell University, United Kingdom, pp. 163-186.

Baxter, J. and D. Smart (2011), "Fathering in Australia Among Couple Families with Young Children", *Occasional Paper*, No. 37, Department of Families, Housing, Community Services, and Indigenous Affairs, Australian Government.

Beauregard, T.A. and L.C. Henry (2009), "Making the Link Between Work-Life Balance Practices and Organizational Performance", *Human Resource Management Review*, Vol. 19, pp. 9-22.

Beblo, M. (2011), "An Assessment of Logib-D: Discussion Paper on Germany", *Exchange of Good Practices on Gender Equality: Reducing the Gender Pay Gap*, 5-6 December 2011, Berlin.

Beer, P. de and R. Luttikhuizen (1998), "Le 'modèle polder' néerlandais : miracle ou mirage ? Réflexions sur le marché du travail et la politique de l'emploi aux Pays-Bas", in J.C. Barbier and J. Gautié (eds.), *Les politiques de l'emploi en Europe et aux États-Unis*, Presses Universitaires de France, Paris, pp. 113-134.

Bettio, F. and A. Verashchagina (2009), "Gender Segregation in the Labour Market. Root Causes, Implications and Policy Responses in the EU", European Commission.

Bhatty, K. (2006), "Employment Guarantee and Child Rights", *Economic and Political Weekly*, 20 May, pp. 1965-1967.

BIAC/OECD/AmCham (2012), "Findings from the Conference on Business Case for the Economic Empowerment of Women", 2 February 2012, Paris.

Bianco, M., A. Ciavarella and R. Signoretti (2011), "Women on Boards in Italy", *CONSOB Working Paper*, No. 70.

BIS (2011), *Women on Boards*, Department for Business Innovation and Skills (BIS), United Kingdom, February.

BIS (2012), *Women on Boards*, Department for Business Innovation and Skills (BIS), United Kingdom, March.

Blau, F. and L. Kahn (1997), "Swimming Upstream: Trends in the Gender Wage Differential in 1980s", *Journal of Labour Economics*, Vol. 15, No. 1, pp. 1-42.

Blau, F. and L. Kahn (2006), "The US Gender Pay Gap in the 1990s: Slowing Convergence", *Industrial and Labour Relations Review*, Vol. 60, No. 1, Cornell University, United Kingdom, pp. 45-66.

Bloom, N., T. Kretschmer and J. van Reenen (2009), "Work-Life Balance, Management Practices and Productivity", in R. Freeman and K. Shaw (eds.), *International Differences in the Business Practice and Productivity of Firms*, University of Chicago Press, Chicago, United States.

Bloom, N., T. Kretschmer and J. van Reenen (2010), "Are Family-Friendly Workplace Practices a Valuable Firm Resource?", *Strategic Management Journal*, Vol. 32, No. 4, pp. 343-367.

Bloom, N., C. Genakos, R. Sadun and J. van Reenen (2011), "Management Practices Across Firms and Countries", *Working Paper*, No. 12-052, Harvard Business School, United States, 15 November.

Böhren, O. and R. Ström (2005), "The Value-creating Board: Theory and Evidence", *Research Report*, No. 8/2005, Norwegian School of Management, Department of Financial Economics, Oslo, Norway.

Bonke, J., D. Gupta and N. Smith (2005), "The Timing and Flexibility of Housework and Men's and Women's Wages", in D. Hamermesh and G. Pfann (eds.), *The Economics of Time Use*, Elsevier, Amsterdam.

Brooks-Gunn, J., W. Han and J. Waldfogel (2010), "First-year Maternal Employment and Child Development in the First 7 Years", *Monographs of the Society for Research in Child Development*, Vol. 75, No. 2, pp. 144-145.

Brown, A.H., D.L. Brown and V. Anatasopoulos (2002), *Women on Boards. Not Just the Right Thing... But the Bright Thing*, Conference Board of Canada Report, May.

Bryan, M. and A. Sevilla-Sanz (2011), "Does Housework Lower Wages? Evidence for Britain", *Oxford Economic Papers*, Vol. 63, pp. 187-210.

Buddelmeyer, H., G. Mourre and M. Ward (2005), "Part-Time Work in EU Countries: Labour Market Mobility, Entry and Exit", *IZA Discussion Paper*, No. 1550, Bonn.

Camarano, A. (2004), "Os Novos Idosos Brasileiros: Muito Além dos 60", Instituto de Pesquisa Econômica Aplicada (IPEA), Rio de Janeiro.

Campbell, K. and A. Minguez-Vera (2009), "Female Board Appointments and Firm Valuation: Short and Long-term Effects", *Journal of Management and Governance*, Vol. 14, No. 1, pp. 37-59.

Carter, D., B. Simkins and G. Simpson (2003), "Corporate Governance, Board Diversity and Firm Value", *Financial Review*, Vol. 38, No. 1, pp. 33-53.

Catalyst (2008), *Advancing Women Leaders: The Connection Between Women Board Directors and Women Corporate Officers*, United States, available at *www.catalyst.org/file/229/wco_wbd_web.pdf*.

Catalyst (2010), *Catalyst Census: Fortune 500 Women Board Directors 2010*, United States, available at *www.catalyst.org/file/413/2010_us_census_women_board_directors_final.pdf*.

Catalyst (2011), *Women on Boards*, United States, available at *www.catalyst.org/publication/433/women-on-boards*.

Chen, M., J. Sebstad and L. O'Connell (1999), "Counting the Invisible Workforce: The Case of Homebased Workers", *World Development*, Vol. 27, No. 3, pp. 603-610.

Chen, M., J. Vanek, F. Lund, J. Heintz with R. Jhabvala and C. Booner (2005), "The Progress of the World's Women 2005: Women, Work and Poverty", United Nations Development Fund for Women (UNIFEM), New York.

Childs, S. and M.L. Krook (2008), "Critical Mass Theory and Women's Political Representation", *Political Studies*, Vol. 56, No. 3, pp. 725-736.

Christofides, L.N., A. Polycarpou and K. Vrachimis (2010), "The Gender Wage Gaps, 'Sticky Floors' and 'Glass Ceilings' of the European Union", *IZA Discussion Paper*, No. 5044, Bonn.

Coles, J., N. Daniel and L. Naveen (2008), "Boards: Does One Size Fit All?", *Journal of Financial Economics*, Vol. 87, No. 2, pp. 329-356.

Conference Board of Canada (2003), "Balance at the Top: Encouraging Work-Life Effectiveness for Executives", Ottawa, available online at *www.wallnetwork.ca/inequity/2mclean.pdf*.

Connolly, S. and A. Holdcroft (2009), "The Pay Gap for Women in Medicine and Academic Medicine", British Medical Association, available at *www.medicalwomensfederation.org.uk/files/pay%20gap%20report.pdf*.

Corporate Governance Code Monitoring Committee (2010), *Second Report on Compliance with the Dutch Corporate Governance Code*, The Hague, Netherlands.

Cranfield University (2010), *The Female FTSE Board Report 2010: Opening Up the Appointment Process*, Cranfield International Centre for Women Leaders, Cranfield School of Management, Cranfield, United Kingdom.

Cranfield University (2012), *The Female FTSE Board Report 2012*, Cranfield International Centre for Women Leaders, Cranfield School of Management, Cranfield, United Kingdom.

Dahlerup, D. (1988), "From a Small to a Large Minority: Women in Scandinavian Politics", *Scandinavian Political Studies*, Vol. 11, No. 4, pp. 275-297.

De la Rica, S., J. Dolado and V. Llorens (2008), "Ceilings or Floors? Gender Wage Gaps by Education in Spain", *Journal of Population Economics*, Vol. 21, No. 3, pp. 751-776.

Del Boca, D., S. Pasqua and C. Pronzato (2009), "Motherhood and Market Work Decisions in Institutional Context: a European Perspective", *Oxford Economic Papers*, No. 61, pp. i147-i171.

Dezso, C.L. and D.G. Ross (2011), "Does Female Representation in Top Management Improve Firm Performance? A Panel Data Investigation", *Robert H. Smith School Research Paper*, No. RHS 06-104, available at *http://ssrn.com/abstract=1088182*.

Dex, S. (2010), "Can State Policies Produce Equality in Housework?", in J. Treas and S. Drobnic (eds.), *Dividing the Domestic: Men, Women, and Household Work in Cross-national Perspective*, Studies In Social Inequality, Stanford University Press, Stanford, United States, pp. 79-104.

Dijkgraaf, M. and W. Portegijs (2008), "Arbeidsdeelname en wekelijkse arbeidsduur van vrouwen", in W. Portegijs and S. Keuzenkamp (eds.), *Nederland deeltijdland, Vrouwen en deeltijdwerk*, Sociaal Cultureel Planbureau, Gravenhage.

Ding, D. and C. Charoenwong (2004), "Women on Board: Is It Boon or Bane?", Conference Paper presented at the 2004 FMA European Conference, Zürich, June.

EBRI (2011), "EBRI Databook on Employee Benefits", Employee Benefit Research Institute, Washington, DC, available at *www.ebri.org/publications/books/?fa=databook*.

Ekberg, J., R. Eriksson and G. Friebel (2005), "Parental Leave – A Policy Evaluation of the Swedish 'Daddy-Month' Reform", *IZA Discussion Paper*, No. 1617, Bonn.

European Commission (2010), *Report on Progress on Equality between Women and Men in 2010: The Gender Balance in Business Leadership*, European Union, Brussels.

European Commission (2011), *Gender Balance in Decision-making Positions Database: Judiciary*, available at *http://ec.europa.eu/justice/gender-equality/gender-decision-making/database/judiciary/index_en.htm*, accessed April 2012.

European Commission (2012a), *Women in Economic Decision-making in the EU: Progress Report*, European Union, Brussels.

European Commission (2012b), "Data on National Administrations", available at *http://ec.europa.eu/justice/gender-equality/gender-decision-making/database/public-administration/national-administrations/index_en.htm*.

Eydal, G. and I. Gislason (2008), "Equal Rights to Earn and Care – Paid Parental Leave in Iceland", Felags og Tryggingamala Raduneytid.

Fagnani, J. (2002), "Why Do French Women Have More Children than German Women? Family Policies and Attitudes Towards Child Care Outside the Home", *Community, Work and Family*, Vol. 5, No. 1, pp. 103-119.

FAO (2010), "Gender Dimensions of Agricultural and Rural Employment: Differentiated Pathways Out of Poverty – Status, Trends and Gaps", *FAO-IFAD-ILO Report*, Food and Agriculture Organisation, Rome.

Farrell, K.A. and P.L. Hersch (2005), "Additions to Corporate Boards: the Effect of Gender", *Journal of Corporate Finance*, Vol. 11, No. 1-2, pp. 85-106.

Federal Statistical Office (2012), "Geburten und Sterbefaelle", online database available at *www.destatis.de*, accessed 3 February 2012.

Felfe, C. (2012), "The Motherhood Wage Gap: What About Job Amenities?", *Labour Economics*, Vol. 19, No. 1, pp. 59-67.

Finland Central Chamber of Commerce (2010), "Female Leadership and Firm Profitability: Evaluation and Experience in Finland", Council of Europe, PACE hearing, Paris, 10 September.

Flabbi, L. and M. Tejada (2012), "Fields of Study Choices, Occupational Choices and Gender Differentials", Background paper for the *OECD Gender Initiative*.

GMI (2011), *2011 Women on Boards Report*, GovernanceMetrics International, New York, available at *www.gmiratings.com*.

Gómez Ansón, S. (2012), "Women on Boards in Europe: Past, Present and Future", *Women on Corporate Boards and in Top Management: European Trends and Policy*, Work and Welfare in Europe, Palgrave Macmillan, United Kingdom.

Gong, X. (2011), "The Added Worker Effect for Married Women in Australia", *Economic Record*, Vol. 87, No. 278, pp. 414-426.

Government of Austria (2011), "The Austrian Federal Civil Service 2011 – Fact and Figures", Bundeskanzleramt Österreich, available at *www.bka.gv.at/DocView.axd?CobId=44697*.

Government of Germany (2010), *Gleichstellung in der Bundesverwaltung – Erfahrungs- und Gremienbericht 2010*, Bundesministerium für Familie, Senioren, Frauen und Jugend Deutschland, available at *www.bmfsfj.de/ RedaktionBMFSFJ/Broschuerenstelle/Pdf-Anlagen/erfahrungs-und-gremienbericht,property= pdf,bereich=bmfsfj,sprache=de,rwb=true.pdf*.

Government of New Zealand (2010), *Human Resource Capability Survey of Public Service Departments as at 30 June 2010*, State Services Commission, available at *www.ssc.govt.nz/sites/all/files/hrc-survey-2010.pdf*.

Government of Switzerland (2009), *Promotion de l'égalité des chances entre femmes et hommes dans l'administration fédérale de 2004 à 2007 – Rapport d'évaluation au Conseil Fédéral*, Office Fédéral du Personnel de la Suisse, available at *www.efd.admin.ch/dokumentation/zahlen/00578/01476/index.html?lang=fr*.

Grosvold, J. and S.J. Brammer (2011), "National Institutional Systems as Antecedents of Female Board Representation: An Empirical Study", *Corporate Governance: An International Review*, Vol. 19, No. 2, pp. 116-135.

Guégot, F. (2011), *Rapport au Président de la République, L'égalité professionnelle hommes-femmes dans la fonction publique*, La Documentation Française, Paris, available at *www.ladocumentationfrancaise.fr/ rapports-publics/114000123/index.shtml*.

Haas, L. and P.C. Hwang (2008), "The Impact of Taking Parental Leave on Fathers' Participation in Childcare and Relationships with Children: Lessons from Sweden", *Community, Work and Family*, Vol. 11, No. 11, pp. 85-104.

Hegewisch, A. (2009), "Flexible Working Policies: A Comparative Review", *Equality and Human Rights Commission Research Report Series*, No. 16, Manchester, United Kingdom.

Hegewisch, A., H. Liepmann, J. Hayes and H. Hartmann (2010), "Separate and Not Equal? Gender Segregation in the Labor Market and the Gender Wage Gap", Institute for Women's Policy Research, *Briefing Paper*, No. 377, Washington, DC.

Hendy, R. (2012), "Female Labour Force Participation in the Middle East and North Africa: Evidence from Egypt and Jordan", Background paper for the *OECD Gender Initiative*.

Hertz, T. (2005), "The Effect of Minimum Wages on the Employment and Earnings of South Africa's Domestic Service Workers", *Department of Economics Working Paper*, American University, Washington, DC.

Holmes, R. and N. Jones (2011), "Public Works Programmes in Developing Countries: Reducing Gendered Disparities in Economic Opportunities?", Overseas Development Institution, Paper prepared for the International Conference on Social Cohesion and Development, Paris, 20-21 January.

Hsieh, C.T., E. Hurst, C.I. Jones and P.J. Klenow (2012), "The Allocation of Talent and US Economic Growth", unpublished manuscript.

Huerta, M.C., W. Adema, J. Baxter, M. Corak, M. Deding, W.J. Han and J. Waldfogel (2011), "Early Maternal Employment and Child Development in Five OECD Countries", *OECD Social, Employment and Migration Working Papers*, No. 118, OECD Publishing, Paris, DOI: *http://dx.doi.org/10.1787/5kg5dlmtxhvh-en*.

Hurley, J., D, Storrie and J.M. Jungblut (2011), "Shifts in the Job Structure in Europe During the Great Recession", European Foundation for the Improvement of Living and Working Conditions, Dublin.

Iglesias-Palau, A. (2009), "Pension Reform in Chile Revisited. What Has Been Learned?", *OECD Social, Employment and Migration Working Papers*, No. 86, OECD Publishing, Paris, DOI: *http://dx.doi.org/10.1787/224473276417*.

ILO (2002), "Pensiones No Contributivas y Asistenciales: Argentina, Brasil, Chile, Costa Rica y Uruguay", International Labour Organization, Santiago.

ILO (2011), "Statistical Update on Employment in the Informal Economy", ILO Department of Statistics, ILO, Geneva, June, available at *www.ilo.org/global/statistics-and-databases/WCMS_157467/lang-en/index.htm*.

ILO (2012), "Women and Men in the Informal Economy – Statistical Picture", ILO, Geneva, available at *http://laborsta.ilo.org/informal_economy_E.html*.

ILO and UNDP (2009), "Work and Family: Towards New Forms of Reconciliation with Social Co-responsibility", International Labour Organization and United Nations Development Programme, Santiago, Chile.

IPU (2008), *Equality in Politics: A Survey of Women and Men in Parliaments*, Inter-Parliamentary Union, available at *www.ipu.org/pdf/publications/equality08-e.pdf*.

IPU Database (2011), "Women in National Parliaments", Inter-Parliamentary Union, available at *www.ipu.org/wmn-e/classif.htm*.

Jütting, J.P. and C. Morrisson (2009), "Women, Bad Jobs, Rural Areas: What Can 'SIGI' Tell Us?", OECD Development Centre, Paris, presented at the FAO-IFAD-ILO Workshop on Gaps, Trends and Current Research in Gender Dimensions of Agricultural and Rural Employment: Differentiated Pathways out of Poverty, Rome, Italy, 31 March-2 April 2009.

Jütting, J.P., A. Luci and C. Morrisson (2012), "Why Do So Many Women End Up in Bad Jobs?: A Cross-Country Assessment for Developing Countries", *European Journal for Development Research*, Vol. 24, No. 4, pp. 530-549.

Kamerman, S.B. and P. Moss (eds.) (2009), "The Politics of Parental Leave Policy: Children, Parenting, Gender and the Labour Market", The Policy Press, University of Bristol, United Kingdom.

Koettl, J. and M. Weber (2012), "Does Formal Work Pay? The Role of Labor Taxation and Social Benefit Design in the New EU Member States", *IZA Discussion Paper*, No. 6313, Bonn, January.

Lalanne, M. and P. Seabright (2011), "The Old Boy Network: Gender Differences in the Impact of Social Networks on Remuneration in Top Executive Jobs", *CEPR Discussion Paper*, No. 8623, United Kingdom.

La Valle, I., E. Clery and M.C. Huerta (2008), "Maternity Rights and Mother's Employment Decisions", *Department for Work and Pensions, Research Report*, No. 496, United Kingdom.

Lee, P.M. and E.H. James (2007), "She-e-os: Gender Effects and Investor Reactions to the Announcements of Top Executive Appointments", *Strategic Management Journal*, Vol. 28, No. 3, pp. 227-241

Leschke, J. and M. Jepsen (2011), "The Economic Crisis – Challenge or Opportunity for Gender Equality in Social Policy Outcomes?", *ETUI Working Paper*, No. 2011.04, European Trade Union Institute, Brussels.

Lewis, J. (2009), *Work-Family Balance, Gender and Policy*, Edward Elgar, Cheltenham, United Kingdom.

Lewis, J., M. Campbell and M.C. Huerta (2008), "Patterns of Paid and Unpaid Work in Western Europe: Gender, Commodification, Preferences and the Implications for Policy", *Journal of European Social Policy*, Vol. 18, No. 21, pp. 21-37.

Li, S. and J. Song (2011), "Changes in the Gender Wage Gap in Urban China, 1995-2007", *CIBC Working Paper Series*, No. 2011-20, Centre for Human Capital and Productivity, Canada.

Linck, J., J. Netter and T. Yang (2008), "The Determinants of Board Structure", *Journal of Financial Economics*, Vol. 87, No. 2, pp. 308-328.

Liu, Y. and K. Deininger (2010), "Poverty Impacts of India's National Rural Employment Guarantee Scheme: Evidence from Andhra Pradesh", *Paper*, No. 11171 prepared for a presentation at the Agricultural and Applied Economics Association Annual Meeting, Denver, Colorado, 25-27 July.

Lo Sasso, A., M. Richards, C. Chou and S. Gerber (2011), "The $16,819 Pay Gap for Newly Trained Physicians: The Unexplained Trend of Men Earning More Than Women", *Health Affairs*, February.

Lord Davies of Abersoch (2012), "Women on Boards", London.

Lückerath-Rovers, M. (2011), "Women on the Boards and Firm Performance", *Journal of Management and Governance*, pp. 1-19.

Maani, S. and A. Cruickshank (2010), "What Is the Effect of Housework on the Market Wage, and Can it Explain the Gender Wage Gap?", *Journal of Economic Surveys*, Vol. 24, No. 3, pp. 402-427.

Macunovich, D. (2010), "Reversals in the Patterns of Women's Labor Supply in the US, 1976-2009", *Monthly Labor Review*, Vol. 133, No. 11, pp. 16-36.

Maier, F. (2011), "Will the Crisis Change Gender Relations in Labour markets and Society?", *Journal of Contemporary European Studies*, Vol. 19, No. 01, pp. 83-95.

Marinova, J., J. Plantenga and C. Remery (2010), "Gender Diversity and Firm Performance: Evidence and Dutch and Danish Boardrooms", *Discussion Paper Series*, No. 10-03, Utrecht School of Economics, University of Utrecht, Netherlands.

Marques Garcia, L., H. Ñopo and P. Salardi (2009), "Gender and Racial Wage Gaps in Brazil 1996-2006: Evidence Using a Matching Comparisons Approach", *Working Paper*, No. 681, Research Department, Inter-American Development Bank (BID), Washington, DC.

Matsumoto, M. (2011), "Wage Inequality in Indonesia: 1996-2009", unpublished manuscript, Hitotsubashi University, Japan.

Mattingly, M.J. and K.E. Smith (2010), "Changes in Wives' Employment when Husbands Stop Working: A Recession-Prosperity Comparison", *Family Relations*, Vol. 59, No. 4, pp. 343-357.

McKinsey and Company (2007), *Women Matter: Gender Diversity. A Corporate Performance Driver*.

McKinsey and Company (2008), "A Business Case for Women", *McKinsey Quarterly*, September.

McKinsey and Company (2010), *Women at the Top of Corporations: Making It Happen*.

McKinsey and Company (2011), "Changing Companies' Minds about Women", *McKinsey Quarterly*, September.

McKinsey and Company (2012), "Women Matter 2012: Making the Breakthrough", McKinsey and Company Europe, March.

Mencarini, L. and M. Sironi (2012), "Happiness, Housework and Gender Inequality in Europe", *European Sociological Review*, Vol. 28, No. 2, pp. 203-219.

Miranda, V. (2011), "Cooking, Caring and Volunteering: Unpaid Work Around the World", *OECD Social, Employment and Migration Working Papers*, No. 116, OECD Publishing, Paris, DOI: *http://dx.doi.org/10.1787/5kghrjm8s142-en*.

MMSP (2011), "Étude Conciliation travail et famille – résultats préliminaires", ministère de la Modernisation des Secteurs Publics, Rabat, Maroc.

Moss, P. (2010), "International Review of Leave Policies and Related Research 2010", *Employment Relations Research Series*, No. 115, Department for Business, Innovation and Skills, London.

Moss, P. (2011), "International Review of Leave Policies and Related Research 2011", International Network on Leave Polices and Research, London.

Muller, C. (2009), "Trends in the Gender Wage Gap and Gender Discrimination Among Part-time and Full-time Workers in Post-apartheid South Africa", *Economic Research Southern Africa Working Paper*, No. 124, South Africa.

Nepomnyaschy, L. and J. Waldfogel (2007), "Paternity Leave and Fathers' Involvement with their Young Children: Evidence from the American ECLS-B", *Community, Work and Family*, Vol. 10, No. 4, pp. 427-453.

Niehaus, P. and S. Sukhtankar (2009), "Corruption Dynamics: The Golden Goose Effect", unpublished manuscript, University of California, San Diego.

Nielsen, S. and M. Huse (2010), "The Contribution of Women on Boards of Directors: Going beyond the Surface", *Corporate Governance: An International Review*, Vol. 18, No. 2, pp. 136-148.

OECD (1994), *Women and Structural Change. New Perspectives*, OECD Publishing, Paris.

OECD (2004a), *Principles of Corporate Governance*, OECD Publishing, Paris, DOI: *http://dx.doi.org/10.1787/9789264015999-en*.

OECD (2004b), *Babies and Bosses, Reconciling Work and Family Life*, Vol. 3, *New Zealand, Portugal and Switzerland*, OECD Publishing, Paris, DOI: *http://dx.doi.org/10.1787/9789264108356-en*.

OECD (2007a), *OECD Reviews of Human Resource Management in Government: Belgium*, OECD Publishing, Paris, DOI: *http://dx.doi.org/10.1787/9789264038202-en*.

OECD (2007b), *Babies and Bosses, Reconciling Work and Family Life. A Synthesis of Findings for OECD Countries*, OECD Publishing, Paris, DOI: *http://dx.doi.org/10.1787/9789264032477-en*.

OECD (2008a), *OECD Employment Outlook*, OECD Publishing, Paris, DOI: *http://dx.doi.org/10.1787/empl_outlook-2008-en*.

OECD (2008b), *The State of the Public Service*, OECD Publishing, Paris, DOI: *http://dx.doi.org/10.1787/9789264047990-en*.

OECD (2008c), *Growing Unequal? Income Distribution and Poverty in OECD Countries*, OECD Publishing, Paris, DOI: *http://dx.doi.org/10.1787/9789264044197-en*.

OECD (2009a), *Government at a Glance*, OECD Publishing, Paris, DOI: *http://dx.doi.org/10.1787/9789264075061-en*.

OECD (2009b), "Is Informal Normal? Towards More and Better Jobs in Developing Countries", *Development Centre Studies*, OECD Publishing, Paris, DOI: *http://dx.doi.org/10.1787/9789264059245-en*.

OECD (2009c), *OECD Reviews of Labour Market and Social Policy: Chile*, OECD Publishing, Paris, DOI: *http://dx.doi.org/10.1787/9789264060616-en*.

OECD (2010a), *Progress in Public Management in the Middle East and North Africa. Case Studies on Policy Reform*, OECD Publishing, Paris, DOI: *http://dx.doi.org/10.1787/9789264082076-en*.

OECD (2010b), *OECD Employment Outlook*, OECD Publishing, Paris, DOI: *http://dx.doi.org/10.1787/empl_outlook-2010-en*.

OECD (2010c), *OECD Reviews of Human Resource Management in Government: Brazil 2010*, OECD Publishing, Paris, DOI: *http://dx.doi.org/10.1787/9789264082229-en*.

OECD (2011a), "Survey on National Gender Frameworks, Gender Public Policies and Leadership", Developed by the MENA-OECD Governance Programme, OECD Publishing, Paris.

OECD (2011b), "Women's Economic Empowerment", *Issue Paper*, DAC Network on Gender Equality (GENDERNET), OECD Publishing, Paris, April.

OECD (2011c), *Doing Better for Families*, OECD Publishing, Paris, DOI: *http://dx.doi.org/10.1787/9789264098732-en*.

OECD (2011d), *Report on the Gender Initiative: Gender Equality in Education, Employment and Entrepreneurship 2011*, Report prepared for the Meeting of the OECD Council at Ministerial Level, Paris, 25-26 May 2011, OECD Publishing, Paris.

OECD (2011e), "Exploratory Paper on Women's Entrepreneurship: Issues and Possible Research Agenda", Background paper for the OECD *Gender Initiative*.

OECD (2011f), *Society at a Glance 2011*, OECD Publishing, Paris, DOI: *http://dx.doi.org/10.1787/soc_glance-2011-en*.

OECD (2011g), *Public Servants as Partners for Growth: Toward a Stronger, Leaner and More Equitable Workforce*, OECD Publishing, Paris, DOI: *http://dx.doi.org/10.1787/9789264166707-en*.

OECD (2011h), "Survey on Gender in Public Employment", Developed by the MENA-OECD Governance Programme, OECD Publishing, Paris.

OECD (2011i), *Statistical Database*, OECD Publishing, Paris, available at *http://stats.oecd.org/index.aspx*.

OECD (2011j), *OECD Reviews of Labour Market and Social Policy: The Russian Federation*, OECD Publishing, Paris, DOI: *http://dx.doi.org/10.1787/9789264118720-en*.

OECD (2011k), *Help Wanted: Providing and Paying for Long-Term Care*, OECD Publishing, Paris, DOI: *http://dx.doi.org/10.1787/9789264097759-en*.

OECD (2011l), *Pensions at a Glance*, OECD Publishing, Paris, DOI: *http://dx.doi.org/10.1787/pension_glance-2011-en*.

OECD (2012a), *OECD Family Database*, OECD Publishing, Paris, available at *www.oecd.org/els/social/family/database*.

OECD (2012b), *Public Sector Compensation in Times of Austerity*, OECD Publishing, Paris, forthcoming.

OECD (2012c), *OECD Pensions Outlook 2012*, OECD Publishing, Paris, DOI: *http://dx.doi.org/10.1787/9789264169401-en*.

OECD (2013, forthcoming), *Women and Pensions*, OECD Publishing, Paris, forthcoming.

Olivetti, C. and B. Petrongolo (2008), "Unequal Pay or Unequal Employment? A Cross-Country Analysis of Gender Gaps", *Journal of Labor Economics*, Vol. 26, No. 4, pp. 621-654.

Piras, C., M. Saracostti and M. Sepúlveda (forthcoming), "Los servicios de cuidado infantil para niños y niñas en edad escolar primaria: La experiencia de América Latina", *Inter-American Development Bank Technical Note*.

Posadas, J. (2010), "Persistence of the Added Worker Effect: Evidence Using Panel Data from Indonesia", unpublished manuscript, World Bank, Washington, DC.

Randøy, T., S. Thomsen and L. Oxelheim (2006). "A Nordic Perspective on Corporate Board Diversity", *Nordic Innovation Centre Project*, No. 05030, Oslo, Worway.

Rhode, L.D. and K.A. Packel (2010). "Diversity on Corporate Boards: How Much Difference Does Difference Make?", *Working Paper*, No. 89, Rock Center for Corporate Governance at Stanford University, United States.

Ribberink, A. (1998), *Leidsvrouwen en zaakwaarneemsters, een geschiedenis van de aktiegroep Man Vrouw Maatschappij, 1968-1973*, Verloren b.v.

Rose, C. (2007), "Does Female Board Representation Influence Firm Performance? The Danish Evidence", *Corporate Governance: An International Review*, Vol. 15, No. 2, pp. 404-413.

Ross, S. (2003), "The Feminization of Medicine", update No. 20 of September 2003 of the Medical Women's International Association.

Sabarwal, S., N. Sinha, and M. Buvinic (2010), "How do Women Weather Economic Shocks? A Review of the Evidence", *World Bank Policy Research Working Paper*, No. 5496, World Bank.

SEDESOL (2011), "Primer informe trimestral 2011. Programas de subsidio del ramo administrativo 20, Desarrollo Social", Social Development Secretariat (SEDESOL), Mexico.

Smith, N., V. Smith and M. Verner (2006), "Do Women in Top Management Affect Firm Performance? A Panel Study of 2500 Danish Firms", *International Journal of Productivity and Performance Management*, Vol. 55, No. 7, pp. 569-593.

Sotsiaal Ministeerium (2009), *Health, Labour and Social Life in Estonia 2000-2008*, Tallinn, Estonia.

Stephens, M. (2002), "Worker Displacement and the Added Worker Effect", *Journal of Labor Economics*, Vol. 20, No. 3, pp. 504-537.

Staab, S. and R. Gerhard (2010), "Early Childhood Education and Care Policies in Latin America: For women or children or both?", *Gender and Development Programme Paper*, No. 10, United Nations Research Institute for Social Development (UNRISD), Geneva.

Sweidan, M. (2012), "Male-Female Pay Differences, Jordanian Case", *UNECE Working Paper*, No. 23, Conference on European Statisticians, Economic Commission for Europe, Geneva, 12-14 March.

Szebehely, M. (ed.) (2001), *Välfärdstjänster i omvandling* (Welfare Services in Transition), Swedish Government Official Reports (SOU), Vol. 2001:52, Fritzes, Stockholm.

Terjesen, S., R. Sealy and V. Singh (2009), "Women Directors on Corporate Boards: A Review and Research Agenda", *Corporate Governance: An International Review*, Vol. 17, No. 3, pp. 320-337.

The Economist (2011), *Closing the Gap – Special Report on Women and Work*, 26 November.

Thévenon, O. (2009), "Increased Women's Labour Force Participation in Europe: Progress in the Work-Life Balance or Polarization of Behaviours?", *Population* (English Edition), Vol. 64, No. 2, pp. 235-272.

Thévenon, O. (2011), "Family Policies in OECD Countries: A Comparative Analysis", *Population and Development Review*, Vol. 37, No. 1, pp. 57-87.

UN Statistics (2012), "Statistics and Indicators on Women and Men", available at *http://unstats.un.org/unsd/demographic/products/indwm/tab6a.htm*.

UN Women (2011), *Progress of the World Women 2011-12, In Pursuit of Justice*, UN Women, available at *http://progress.unwomen.org/pdfs/EN-Report-Progress.pdf*.

US Equal Employment Opportunity Commission (2009), *Annual Report on the Federal Work Force*, United States Equal Employment Opportunity Commission, Office of Federal Operations.

UNODC (2010), "Crime and Criminal Justice Statistics", provided by UNODC to the OECD, Vienna, Austria, available at *www.unodc.org/unodc/en/data-and-analysis/statistics/crime.html*.

Veenhoven, R. (2011), "Social Development and Happiness in Nations 1990-2010", Presentation at Conference Taking Stock: Measuring Social Development, International Institute of Social Studies, 14-15 December.

Veenhoven, R. (2012), *World Database of Happiness*, Erasmus Universiteit Rotterdam, Netherlands.

Visser, J. and A. Hemerijck (1998), *A Dutch Miracle: Job Growth, Welfare Reform and Corporatism in the Netherlands*, Amsterdam University Press.

Visser, J., T. Wilthagen, R. Beltzer and E. Koot-van der Putte (2004), "The Netherlands: from Atypicality to a Typicality", in S. Sciarra, P. Davies and M. Freedland (eds.), *Employment Policy and the Regulation of Part-time Work in the European Union, A Comparative Analysis*, Cambridge University Press, Cambridge, pp. 190-223.

WEF (2011), *The Corporate Gender Gap Report 2011*, World Economic Forum, Geneva.

White House Council (2012), "Keeping America's Women moving forward: The Key to an Economy Built to Last", White House Council on Women and Girls, Washington, DC, April.

WHO (2008), "Tackling Social and Economic Determinants of Health through Women's Empowerment, the SEWA Case Study", World Health Organization, Geneva.

PART IV

Gender equality in entrepreneurship

There are fewer women entrepreneurs then men in OECD countries and women-owned enterprises have on average lower profits. This section looks at why there are fewer women entrepreneurs than men, the different reasons they have for starting a business, and the different skills they bring to the job. It also looks at the reasons why women-owned businesses have lower profits, and why self-employed women work less, and earn less, than self-employed men. It asks whether women find it harder to finance their business than men and have less innovative enterprises. Finally, it examines policies that support female entrepreneurs in micro- and small businesses – particularly in developing countries – by encouraging entrepreneurs to exit informality and by addressing their specific needs.

Closing the Gender Gap
Act Now
© OECD 2012

PART IV

Chapter 22

Trends in women entrepreneurship

Key findings

- Across countries, there are more male than female entrepreneurs and the share of women who choose to run a business has not increased substantially in most countries.

- The number of newly created female-owned enterprises fell during the crisis, though not as much as for men.

The paucity of reliable, up-to-date information makes monitoring trends in female entrepreneurship a daunting task. It is one of the main obstacles to better understanding female entrepreneurs' challenges and effect on economic growth (OECD, 2012a).

Self-employment statistics are commonly used to measure changes in entrepreneurial activity. They reveal considerable gender differences among the self-employed, particularly those who are also employers. Figure 22.1 shows that across the 27 EU countries only 25% of business owners with employees are women (for definitions, see Annex IV.A1). The low share of women has only marginally grown over the last decade in the EU27, Canada and United States. And although the increase has been more marked in Chile, Korea and Mexico, the already low share of female employers in Japan has further diminished over the past decade.

Figure 22.1. **The proportion of female entrepreneurs has not significantly increased in most countries over the past decade**

Share of employers (self-employed with employees) who are women, 2000-10

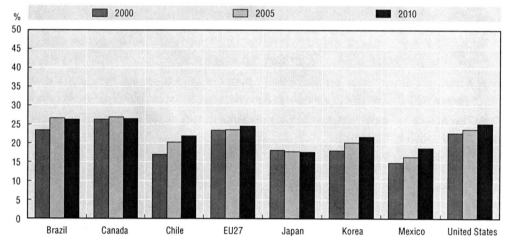

Source: OECD Secretariat estimates based on *Labour Force* and *Household Surveys*.

StatLink  http://dx.doi.org/10.1787/888932676697

Men more than women prefer to be self-employed. The 2009 Eurobarometer survey showed that 51% of European men, but only 39% of women, would rather be self-employed than employees if they had the choice (European Commission, 2009). Across 27 European countries in 2010, an average of 6.6% of unemployed men were actively seeking to become self-employed, while only 4% of women were (see Annex IV.A1 for country-level results). Eurobarometer also showed that women may have lower preferences for self-employment because they still perceive it as too risky: 7% of European women (and 5.4% of men) declared they preferred working as employees because they were afraid of the legal and social consequences if they failed as entrepreneurs.

Data on the number, characteristics and growth dynamics of female-owned enterprises exist for only a few countries. Moreover, the different definitions and methodologies they use restrict their cross-national comparability (Box 22.1). Nevertheless, they do show that female-owned enterprises contribute substantially to job creation. In the United States, women owned 7.8 million firms in 2007 and employed 7.6 million workers (US Department of Commerce, 2010). In Italy in 2010, they fully owned or majority-controlled about a quarter of all companies – almost 1.3 million (Italian Chamber of Commerce, 2010). In Canada, 16% of all small and medium enterprises (SMEs) were majority-owned by women and almost half had at least one female owner in 2007 (Jung, 2010).

Box 22.1. **Producing international statistics on "women and men-owned enterprises"**

Comparable international data on the number of businesses owned and controlled by women across countries, as well as their size, industrial specialisation and basic measures of performance are still lacking. This is due mainly to difficulties in retrieving information about the owners from standard business demography statistics, and because of the absence of international definitions of male- and female-owned enterprises. The OECD-Eurostat Entrepreneurship Indicators Programme (EIP) is addressing this gap by developing definitions and methodologies for data harmonisation and development (OECD, 2012a).

The OECD indicators on male and female-owned enterprises are being developed along three complementary axes: 1) indicators for male- and female-owned enterprises; 2) characteristics of women and men entrepreneurs; and 3) social and policy determinants of women entrepreneurship. A first data collection managed by the EIP is assessing the feasibility of building comparable business demography indicators for individual (sole-proprietor) enterprises, using data from business registers and economic censuses. Sole-proprietor statistics are being collected by gender for the following indicators: 1) number; 2) number of persons employed; 3) turnover; 4) birth rates; 5) death rates; 6) three-year survival rates; and 7) employment growth in surviving enterprises. The programme is also developing indicators on characteristics of entrepreneurs based on labour force survey data.

The OECD-Eurostat Entrepreneurship Indicators Programme (EIP) has started to collect internationally comparable data on female entrepreneurship (Box 22.1). Figure 22.2 illustrates the wide international differences in proportions of individual enterprises with female proprietors. The EIP defines an enterprise as female-owned if women are majority owners and so take the decisions as to how the business functions and develops. For the moment, data are available only for sole-proprietor enterprises, but the EIP plans to address other legal forms.

Figure 22.3 shows that the birth rate of female-owned enterprises is higher than that of male-owned ones. "Birth rate" is taken as newly created enterprises with employees as a ratio of existing enterprises, which means that, driven by newly started businesses, the number of female-owned enterprises is growing at a faster pace than male-owned ones. There is, however, no clear evidence that female-owned enterprises fail at a faster rate than male-owned ones.

Figure 22.2. **The proportion of individually-owned enterprises with a female owner varies between 20 and 40% across OECD countries**

Share of sole-proprietor enterprises owned by women, 2009

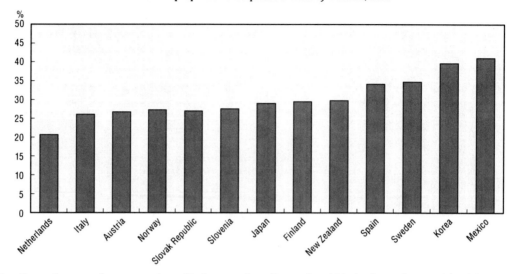

Note: Data refer to employer enterprises with the exception of Japan, for which the data refer to male and female proprietors with and without employees. Data for Norway are for 2010. Data for the Netherlands do not include service activities classified as NACE Rev. 2, Sections P, Q, R and S (Education; Human Health and Social Work Activities; Arts, Entertainment and Recreation; and Other Service Activities). Given that female owners tend to be more prevalent in these service industries, this data coverage can explain the relatively low share observed in the Netherlands. Countries are arranged from left to right in ascending order of the proportion of female-owned enterprises.

Source: OECD Secretariat estimates based on statistics produced by National Statistical Institutes.

StatLink ⬛ⱥ▸ *http://dx.doi.org/10.1787/888932676716*

Figure 22.3. **The birth rate of female-owned enterprises is higher than that of male-owned enterprises**

Birth and death rates[a] of women and men sole-proprietor enterprises, 2009

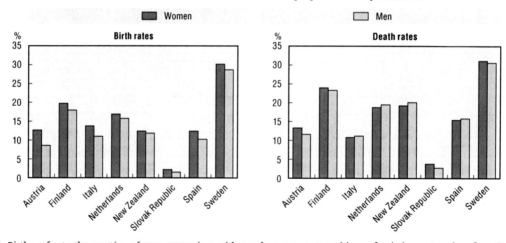

a) Births refer to the creation of new enterprises with employees or to transitions of existing enterprises from 0 to 1+ employee(s). Deaths refer to the dissolution of enterprises or to transitions to no employees.

Source: OECD Secretariat estimates based on statistics produced by National Statistical Institutes. Death rates for Italy, the Netherlands, Sweden and the Slovak Republic refer to 2008.

StatLink ⬛ⱥ▸ *http://dx.doi.org/10.1787/888932676735*

Births of female-owned enterprises dropped in 2009, but relatively less than those of male-owned ones (Figure 22.4). Part of the explanation might be women's lower propensity to enter sectors like manufacturing that have been more heavily affected by the crisis (Chapter 19).

Figure 22.4. **Births of female-owned enterprises declined less than male-owned ones during the crisis**

Percentage change in births of male- and female-owned enterprises, 2009-07 differences

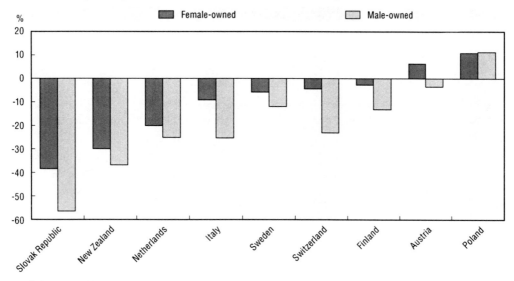

Note: All data (with the exception of data for Poland) refer to enterprises with employees. Data for the Netherlands refer to 2009-08 differences. For Switzerland, statistics are tabulated by gender of the enterprise's (sole) founder rather than by gender of the sole proprietor. Countries are arranged from left to right in ascending order of change in births of female-owned enterprises.

Source: OECD Secretariat estimates based on statistics produced by National Statistical Institutes.

StatLink ⌐ *http://dx.doi.org/10.1787/888932676754*

Policies for more female-owned enterprises

Women are a major untapped entrepreneurship resource. Policies to stimulate entrepreneurship among women should be based on thorough analysis of the factors that prevent or discourage them from going into business. Such analysis demands reliable, timely information from both quantitative and qualitative data sources and some countries have already invested in producing such information. The *Survey of Business Owners*, for example, is a rich source of information on the state of female-owned businesses in the United States. Canada's Survey on Financing and Growth of SMEs collects information on owners' genders and other characteristics, on the nature of businesses, and on access to financing. INSEE in France has developed a continuous monitoring system of new enterprises and their owners. Northern European countries have advanced systems of linked business and population data. However, the low comparability of existing data makes it complicated to produce the international benchmarks which are essential to identifying achievable targets and understanding the effects of policy reforms. More investment is needed in harmonising data on enterprise owners and their businesses, using as much existing data as possible to minimise the burden on statistical offices and curtail associated costs.

There is a clear need for policy to raise awareness of entrepreneurship as a career option for women. Programmes are also needed to boost self-esteem and growth expectations among potential and established women entrepreneurs. Men have greater faith in their entrepreneurial skills (Brush *et al.*, 2011) and are also more optimistic about the profitability of their enterprise (Eurostat, 2008). Female entrepreneur networks, which are major sources of knowledge about opportunities for successful entrepreneurship, can bolster the self-confidence of women entrepreneurs. The European Commission has set up an "Ambassadors Network" of 270 successful entrepreneurs campaigning to inspire women of all ages to set up their own businesses. A similar ambassador programme has been successfully operating in Sweden since 2008.

Key policy messages

- Develop entrepreneurial awareness campaigns in schools and for the general public. Support ambassador programmes to spread knowledge about entrepreneurial opportunities for women.
- Contribute to the work started by the Entrepreneurship Indicators Programme (EIP) to produce timely, internationally comparable information on male- and female-owned enterprises.

PART IV

Chapter 23

Motivations and skills of women entrepreneurs

Key findings

- Women often have different reasons from men for starting a business. More women than men become business owners out of necessity. Women tend also to accord more importance to the working time flexibility afforded by self-employment.

- On average, women business owners have higher levels of educational attainment than men, but less experience managing a business.

The motivations of women and men entrepreneurs

Women entrepreneurs are a highly heterogeneous group. Their motives for starting a business are a mixed bag of "push" and "pull" factors that are quite different from those that drive men. For example, Figure 23.1 shows that "realising an idea for a new product or service" is a more important motive for men than for women in Europe. Moreover, women entrepreneurs tend to attribute more importance to the time flexibility that comes with being their own boss. Evidence from the United States suggests that "achieving better work-life balance" was an important reason for starting a business for 40% of the female entrepreneurs in the smallest revenue class, but for only 12% of those in the largest revenue class (RSM McGladrey, 2008).

Figure 23.1.   **Work-life balance is a motive for starting their business for more women than men**

Key motives[a] for starting an enterprise by gender of founder and type of motivation, 2005

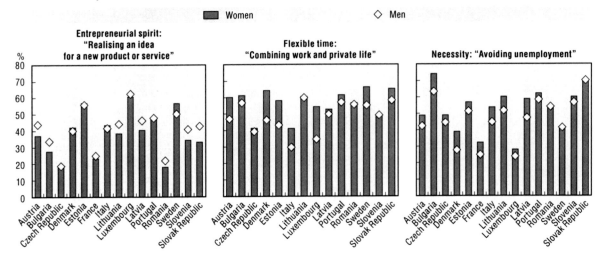

a) Respondents were allowed to select several motives.
Source: Eurostat, *Factors of Business Success Survey.*

StatLink ☞ http://dx.doi.org/10.1787/888932676773

Proportionally, more women than men start a business out of "necessity", becoming entrepreneurs because they do not see other options for entering the labour market. The relatively high rates of women entrepreneurship in emerging and developing countries are primarily due to high levels of "necessity entrepreneurship". Figure 23.2 shows that more women than men start their business in the informal sector out of economic necessity, especially in Egypt and Mexico.

Figure 23.2. **More women than men start a business out of necessity,
particularly in Egypt and Mexico**

Percentage of enterprises whose owners became entrepreneurs out of necessity,
by gender of the owner and registration status

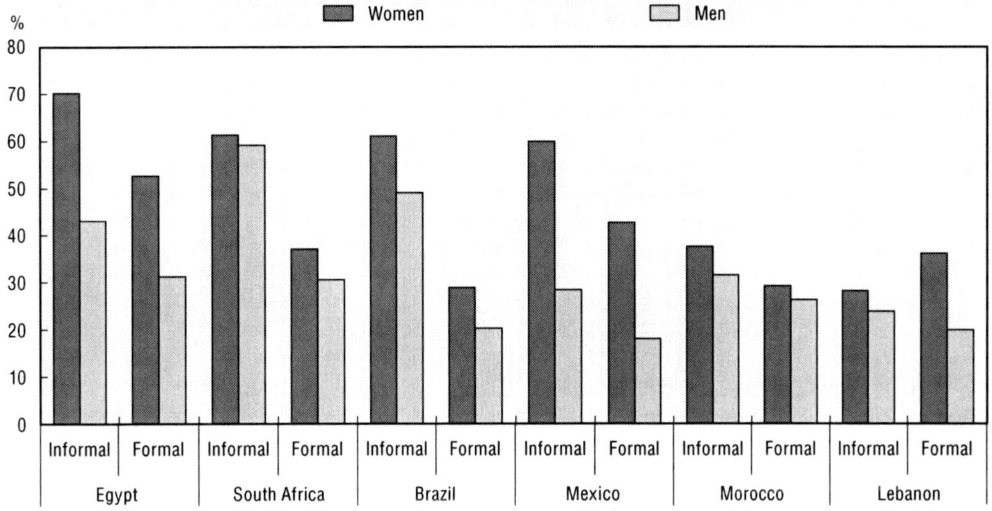

Note: Countries are arranged from left to right in descending order of the proportion of women who started an informal business out of necessity, *i.e.* he/she had no other options for earning an income.

Source: OECD Secretariat estimates based on ENAMIN 2008 (Mexico), *Economia Informal Urbana 2003* (Brazil), *Finscope 2010* (South Africa), and *ERF Micro and Small Enterprises Dataset for MENA Countries 2003* (Egypt, Morocco and Lebanon).

StatLink ᴍ⁹ *http://dx.doi.org/10.1787/888932676792*

Education and experience of female and male business owners

Figure 23.3 shows that the percentage of the self-employed with tertiary education attainment is significantly higher among women in OECD countries. However, no significant correlation exists across countries between women's educational attainment and their entrepreneurial activity, as measured by the proportion of women among the self-employed. This suggests that it is not the level but rather the type of education that matters in female entrepreneurship. Women are significantly under-represented in engineering and computing (Chapter 8), two fields of study that build the knowledge useful for starting a technology-oriented business. They are also in the minority in business degrees courses, even though their numbers have been growing. For example, in the Harvard Business School's MBA programme (*www.hbs.edu/about/statistics/mba.html*), the proportion of female students which stood at 11% in 1975 had increased to 36% by 2012. Shinnar *et al.* (2009) find that business graduates rate themselves as more entrepreneurial than those who obtained degrees in "non-business" studies and are more likely to have seriously considered starting their own business. Entrepreneurship education in primary and secondary schools is increasingly recognised as key to shaping the entrepreneurial attitudes of young women and men in OECD countries (European Commission, 2012).

Women entrepreneurs tend to have less experience than men as business owners. On average across 15 European countries, only 11.2% of women who started a new enterprise in 2002 had run another business before the start-up, compared with 18.4% of men (Eurostat, 2008). In the United States in 2007, 42% of male business owners and only 28% of female entrepreneurs had previous self-employed experience (US Census, 2009). In 2007,

Figure 23.3. **Female business owners have higher educational attainment than men**

Percentage of self-employed women and men who completed tertiary education (ISCED 5 or higher), 2010

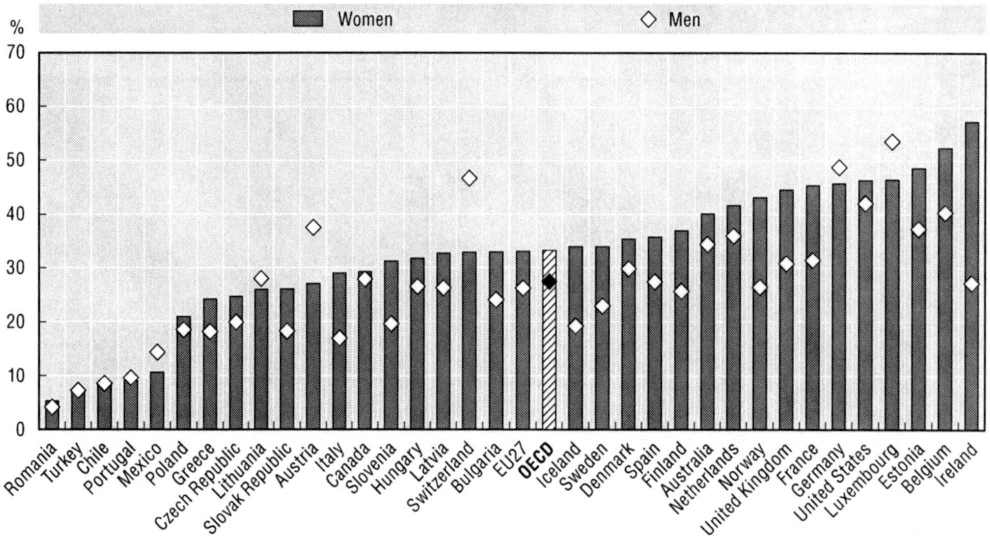

Note: Countries are arranged from left to right in ascending order of the percentage of self-employed women who completed tertiary education.

Source: Eurostat Labour Force Surveys; Estimates from *Survey of Income and Program Participation 2008* for United States; OECD Secretariat estimates from *Labour Force and Household Surveys* for 2010 in other countries.

StatLink ᵃᵐˢᵖ http://dx.doi.org/10.1787/888932676811

51% of female owners of small and medium-sized enterprises in Canada had more than ten years of management or ownership experience compared with 74% of their male counterparts (Jung, 2010).

Experience is critical for business success. For example, data on new enterprises for France show that 73% of the businesses founded by women in 2006 with three or more years of previous experience were still running three years later. The figure is 64% when there is less than three years of experience before start-up. Cohoon *et al.* (2010) show that in the United States women are more likely than men to declare that prior experience has been crucial to the success of their start-up.

Successful entrepreneurship requires talent, motivation and entrepreneurial skills – and because women often lack entrepreneurial experience they have less opportunity to build their entrepreneurial skills. Media campaigns and entrepreneurial education at schools can reduce the stigma associated with business failures, as can showcasing stories of women entrepreneurs who made it to the top through learning from trial and error. Policy makers could also design more innovative training programmes by promoting greater interaction between successful and nascent women entrepreneurs through associations and networks. Klein and Wayman (2008) and Bauer (2011) found that training programmes improve both the economic and non-economic lives of women who own small and micro businesses. International networks, such as the World Association of Women Entrepreneurs (FCEM), have the potential for transferring knowledge and experience between North and South, and East and West. Finally, many top performing women entrepreneurs in growth-oriented firms have senior management experience in corporations, where they gained experience in leadership and acquired access to valuable networks. An improved gender balance in senior management (Chapter 14) can thus have important "spillover" effects on female entrepreneurship.

Box 23.1. **Women entrepreneurs in the MENA region**

Female self-employment rates range from over 30% of working age women in Algeria to less than 2% in the Gulf countries, and only a very small proportion of businesses owned by self-employed women have more than ten employees (Stevenson, 2010 and 2011). Women's low labour force participation rates arguably limit opportunities to acquire the job skills or management experience necessary for starting a business, and only about 9% of adult women engage in early-stage entrepreneurial activity – less than half the rate of men (19%). Women entrepreneurs are a heterogeneous group, whose firm characteristics and needs vary according to location (urban *versus* rural) and education level. Against that background, a variety of policy mechanisms are necessary for accelerating women's entrepreneurship development in the region.

Governments in almost all MENA countries have adopted national development plans or gender strategies which commit to supporting women's economic integration. However, ministries responsible for implementing gender strategies seldom have strong links with ministries in charge of enterprise support. In countries where formal SME policies exist, women are rarely a target group. Businesswomen's associations exist in almost all MENA countries and provide some form of business support (mentoring, trade fairs, seminars) despite their limited financial, human and technical resources. They provide a wealth of information on the business constraints and support needs of their members, but their policy advocacy role is often limited because they are excluded from national policy dialogue.

The OECD is working with MENA governments and businesswomen's associations to improve support measures for women entrepreneurs in the region through the OECD-MENA Women's Business Forum (WBF) (*www.oecd.org/mena/investment/wbn*). The WBF is an inter-regional network of government, private sector and civil society representatives which works with governments to improve policies and legislation impacting women's economic integration. It also works with businesses, NGOs and academia to facilitate an exchange of experiences and good practices for providing concrete support to female entrepreneurs. *Women in Business: Policies to Support Women's Entrepreneurship in the Middle East and North Africa* (OECD, 2012b) highlights existing efforts by governments and other stakeholders to improve support for women entrepreneurs and identifies avenues for future action to accelerate the development of women's entrepreneurship.

Through conferences and policy studies, the WBF seeks to: *a)* support the advocacy efforts of the businesswomen's community to promote legislative reform; *b)* improve access to information about agencies which provide business support services, networks, and training to women entrepreneurs; *c)* promote access to finance, for example through targeted efforts to increase women's participation in the MENA 100 Business Plan Competition (*www.mena100.org*); and *d)* monitor changes in women's economic rights. Better quality data – about informal enterprises too – would support the development of more effective policies for promoting entrepreneurship in the MENA region. And better entrepreneurship policies would have long-term positive effects on employment opportunities for the entire population, so helping to offer a response to citizens' calls for greater prosperity which have been at the core of the recent political and social movements taking place across the MENA region.

Key policy messages

- Address women's shortage of entrepreneurial experience through innovations in the design and delivery of training programmes.
- Promote learning through role models and support networks of women entrepreneurs at multiple levels (from community groups to international networks).

PART IV

Chapter 24

Is there a gender gap in enterprise performance?

Key findings

- In most countries, there is little difference in the survival rates and employment growth patterns of enterprises with a sole proprietor, be it a man or a woman.
- Female-owned enterprises register, on average, lower profits and labour productivity than male-owned ones. The disparities can mostly be explained by differences in size and capital intensity.

Policy makers wishing to strengthen the economic impact of women entrepreneurship need a better understanding of the factors contributing to the growth and success of female-owned firms. Several studies have shown that traditional performance measures, such as growth and profits, are not always the top priority for women entrepreneurs (*e.g.* Coleman and Robb, 2012). More than men, women value balance between business activity and family and the contribution their work can make to their communities (UNCTAD, 2011). However, both male and female entrepreneurs aim to establish businesses that are profitable and sustainable, although many do not survive the first few years of activity. Figure 24.1 shows that women and men-owned sole-proprietor enterprises have similar survival rates three years after start-up.

Figure 24.1. There are wide international differences in the survival rates of women-owned enterprises

Three-year survival rates of female- and male-owned enterprises, 2009

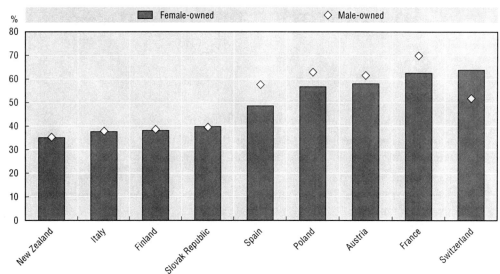

Note: Countries are arranged from left to right in ascending order of the survival rates of female-owned enterprises.
Source: OECD Secretariat estimates based on statistics produced by National Statistical Institutes. The statistics refer to employer enterprises only, with the exception of France and Poland where data cover both enterprises with and without employees. Data for Switzerland refer to two-year survival rates and are for 2008.

StatLink ᵐˢᵖ *http://dx.doi.org/10.1787/888932676830*

Female- and male-owned enterprises also perform similarly when it comes to job creation in the first few years of business (Figure 24.2). There is once again, however, considerable cross-country variation, with new female-owned enterprises performing better in France, Italy, New Zealand and Poland, while lagging behind in Finland, the Netherlands, the Slovak Republic and Switzerland.

Figure 24.2. **Female and male-owned enterprises perform similarly in terms of job creation**

Three-year employment growth rates of sole-proprietor employer enterprises by gender of the owner, 2009

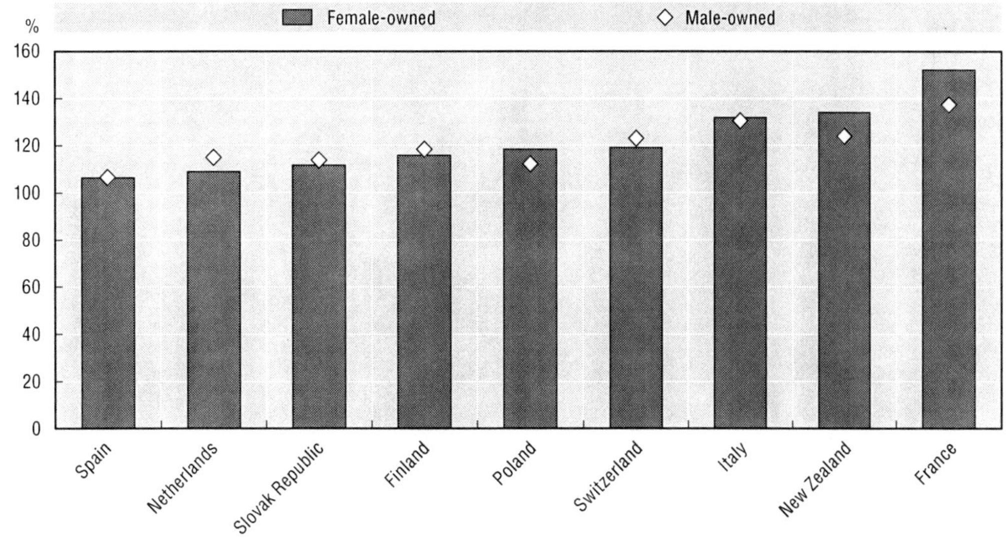

Note: Countries are arranged from left to right in ascending order of employment growth rate in female-owned enterprises.

Source: OECD Secretariat estimates based on statistics produced by National Statistical Institutes. The employment growth rate is given by the ratio of employment in year *t* and employment in year *t* – 3, multiplied by 100 (*e.g.* a value of 110 suggests employment growth of 10%). The statistics refer to employer enterprises only, with the exception of France and Poland where data cover both enterprises with and without employees. Data for Switzerland refer to two-year survival rates and are for 2008.

StatLink ⟐⟐⟐⟐ *http://dx.doi.org/10.1787/888932676849*

The most remarkable differences between female- and male-owned enterprises relate to the size of their business operations, as measured by sales or value-added. In 2009, the average turnover of individual enterprises (sole-proprietorships) owned by women was only 18% of those owned by men in the Netherlands, 26% in Italy, 38% in Mexico, and 44% in Finland. These differences are even starker when incorporated enterprises (*i.e.* enterprises with a legal form other than sole-proprietorship) are also taken into account. For example, in 2007, businesses that were majority-owned by women accounted for only 11% of sales among privately held companies in the United States (US Department of Commerce, 2010).

A key issue for policy is whether the relatively low levels of turnover among female-owned businesses are due only to women's preferences for particular sectors (and, possibly, for small-sized businesses), or are a consequence of the constraints women specifically face when starting and growing their companies. There is no definite answer to this question in the literature. While most studies find that female-controlled enterprises fare worse in terms of profits and other performance measures (Robb and Watson, 2010), several analysts argue that these differences vanish once sectors of activities and key characteristics of the business owners other than gender are controlled for (Fairlie and Robb, 2009; Gatewood *et al.*, 2009; Gottschalk and Niefert, 2011).

Figure 24.3 shows that, according to the *ORBIS Database* (see note to Figure 24.3 and Annex IV.A1), female-owned enterprises across 13 OECD countries account for a very low share of the top 10% enterprises as measured by employment, asset value, or shareholder capital. They are particularly under-represented among companies with the largest numbers of employees. The results confirm that the policy debate should focus not only on

Figure 24.3. **The share of female-owned enterprises falls among largest firms**

Share of majority female-owned companies in the top decile of employment, asset values,
and shareholder capital in the *ORBIS Database*, 2009

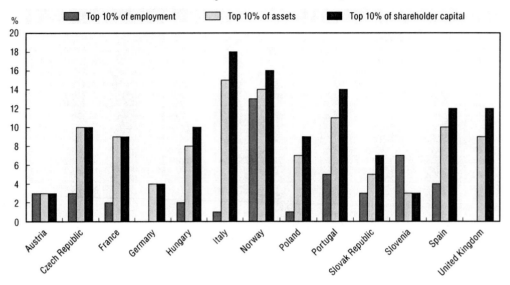

Note: The figures indicate the shares of female-owned firms out of the total of female and male-owned companies in the top decile of the employment (number of employees), value of assets and shareholder capital distributions. Firms with mixed ownership are excluded from the total. The sample is restricted to enterprises where individuals hold at least 50% of the company's shares. Only countries with over 1 000 complete observations are included in the chart. The *OECD-ORBIS Database* is the output of treatment of raw data provided to the OECD under copyright by Bureau van Dijk Electronic Publishing. It contains structural and financial information for millions of companies worldwide. The companies included in the *OECD-ORBIS Database* were classified as men or women-owned enterprises using information on the gender of the shareholders. See the Annex IV.A1. for further detail on data and definitions.
Source: OECD Secretariat estimates on basis of the *OECD-ORBIS Database*.

StatLink ⟶ http://dx.doi.org/10.1787/888932676868

how to increase the number of female-owned enterprises, but also on how to tackle the possible market or institutional failures inhibiting those already in the market from growing their firms into medium and large enterprises.

Estimates based on the ORBIS data show that average productivity (value added per employee) and profits are lower in female-owned enterprises than in those owned by men (see Annex IV.A1). However, the relatively low measured differences in productivity (4.8% for all countries' enterprises taken together, once sector, size and age of the firm are controlled for) suggest that policies should not generically give preferential treatment to women entrepreneurs.

A decomposition analysis shows that the lower capital intensity of female-owned enterprises is the most decisive factor in their lower productivity and explains 37% of the gap. The industries they operate in also account for a substantial share of the productivity disparity (22%). In sum, the gap is a result of gender differences in key strategic choices: women's choice of industry, their preferred size of business, the level of risk they are willing to accept, and the hours they can devote to their business. Further analysis of the reasons behind these different approaches can help policies to target specific market failures and the stereotypes that affect women more than men.

Policies for better performing female-owned enterprises

Policies that foster female entrepreneurship often come under the general umbrella of programmes for small enterprises. SME policies are likely to have a relatively large effect on women entrepreneurs, since most run small businesses. A mix of general policies for SMEs and instruments explicitly targeting women can be effective in prompting interest and entry into entrepreneurship. The Small Business Administration (SBA) in the United States has explicitly explored a mix of general gender-mainstreamed programmes and women-specific policies and has continuously experimented with new ones. In 2009, the SBA backed nearly 10 000 loans worth about USD 2 billion to women entrepreneurs. The SBA partners nationwide with non-profit organisations (such as the association of volunteer business counsellors "SCORE") to support the delivery of programmes tailored to the needs of small businesses owned by women and ethnic and linguistic minorities in underserved markets.

Women's entrepreneurship policies should not, however, be conceived simply as a subset of policies for start-ups and very small firms. The assumption that female business owners want to stay small is misleading for policy. There is a substantial pool of women who are eagerly pursuing growth strategies for their companies (Gatewood *et al.*, 2009). A stronger focus should be placed on instruments that can help female businesses realise their aspirations for growth. Examples of growth-focused initiatives for female-owned enterprises of all sizes would be: favourable lending ceilings and public credit guarantees; rules ensuring that small, female-owned firms have access to public procurement; and, tax credit schemes for capital investments in SMEs.

In 2003, Canada's Business Development Bank (BDC) established a fund targeted to fast-growing female-owned firms. BDC's total lending to women has increased in recent years and today represents over USD 1.8 billion. In the United States in 2010, the Women-Owned Small Business (WOSB) Federal Contract Programme authorised contracting officers to set aside certain federal contracts for eligible women-owned enterprises (White House Council, 2012). The bulk of funds in the Swedish National Programme to promote women's entrepreneurship go to business and innovation development for women, with 50% of the target group being existing female-owned businesses.

To qualify for support from such programmes and prevent abuse, companies must first meet criteria that clearly define them as "female-owned enterprises". Certification of women-owned businesses is a consolidated practice in the United States, but much less widespread in other countries.

Key policy messages

- Develop an integrated national strategy for gender mainstreaming of entrepreneurship policies. Provide specific training to staff in charge of entrepreneurship support design and delivery.
- Respond to the financial and technical support needs of women entrepreneurs wishing to increase the scale of their businesses.
- Policies for female-owned enterprises should not exclusively target start-ups and small enterprises, but include instruments to stimulate high-growth firms as well as growth and development of medium-sized and larger businesses.

Closing the Gender Gap
Act Now
© OECD 2012

PART IV

Chapter 25

Does entrepreneurship pay for women?

Key findings

- The gender gap in earnings is higher in self-employment than for wage employment.
- A major factor in the earnings gap between male and female entrepreneurs is that women devote significantly less time to their businesses than men.

A simple explanation of why fewer women than men own a business might be that entrepreneurship does not pay for women, *i.e.* earnings from business ownership are too low and/or too uncertain to attract them to entrepreneurship. Figure 25.1 shows that self-employed women earn significantly less than men across countries. The gaps in earnings from self-employment are substantial everywhere and wider than those observed in wage employment. The gap narrows, however, when calculated on the basis of earnings per hour worked, as women tend to work significantly less time on their businesses. There is also less disparity when only the self-employed with employees are considered.

Figure 25.1. **Female business owners earn significantly less than men**

Gap*a* in median earnings of self-employed women and men, 2008

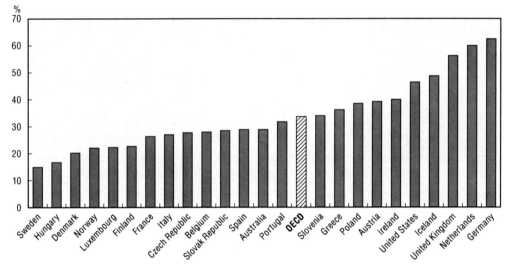

Note: The international comparability of statistics on earnings from self-employment is still limited due to differences in questions on self-employment income and in the methods used to derive the figures. Countries are arranged from left to right in ascending order of the widening gender gap.

a) Defined as the difference between male and female median earnings divided by male median earnings.

Source: OECD Secretariat estimates from *European Union Statistics on Income and Living Conditions* (EU-SILC), 2008 wave; *Survey of Income and Program Participation* 2008 for United States, *Household, Income and Labour Dynamics in Australia* (HILDA), 2008 wave.

StatLink ⟶ *http://dx.doi.org/10.1787/888932676887*

One reason for female business owners earning less than their male counterparts might be that they are less willing to take risks. Higher risk aversion naturally leads to a lower polarisation of earnings, *i.e.* less probability of incurring losses and fewer chances to reap high returns. Figure 25.2 shows that a significant number of women and men running businesses do experience net losses. The distribution of men's earnings is more skewed than women's, as the latter tend to realise low levels of profits (as shown by the considerable difference in the height of the two distribution curves for near-zero profit levels). The proportion of women who run their business at a loss is somewhat lower than for men in the United States (7.5% of women *versus* 8.7% for men).

Figure 25.2. **Most women tend to realise low profits, men being better represented among average and top earners**

Univariate kernel density estimates of profits or losses from business ownership by gender, 2008

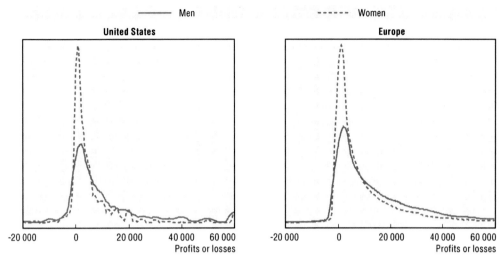

Note: The samples are restricted to business owners reporting positive or negative values of profit.
Source: EU-SILC 2008 for 24 European countries with available data on earnings from self-employment; Survey of Income and Program Participation 2008 for United States.

StatLink http://dx.doi.org/10.1787/888932676906

Women often take a different approach to business, being more cautious over the resources they commit to their ventures and preferring slow, steady expansion. The reason for their careful risk management may be greater concern about the consequences of failure (Chapter 22). Indeed, the Small Business Service (2005) in the United Kingdom found that women with family responsibilities were "particularly wary of extending commitments" and that any business venture they embarked upon would "need to be independent of family finances and self-sufficient". However, there is no conclusive evidence that women entrepreneurs are always less willing to take risks than men (Croson and Gneezy, 2009).

The differences in the average hours worked by self-employed women and men are substantial in most OECD countries, particularly in Germany, Mexico and the Netherlands (Figure 25.3). On average, 22% of self-employed women across 30 OECD countries work less than 40 hours a week against only 10% of self-employed men. Gurley-Calvez et al. (2009) show that the time-use patterns of self-employed women in the United States differ substantially from those of men: they devote less time to work-related activities and more time to their children. While it is difficult to determine an exact causal relation between hours worked and business income, findings from analyses of earnings from self-employment suggest that enabling women to work longer hours would increase the profitability of their businesses (see Annex IV.A2).

Figure 25.4 shows that self-employed women earn, on average, less than women in wage employment in European countries and the disparity is greater than for men. The earnings gaps between self-employment and wage employment are widest at the bottom and narrowest at the top end of the earning distribution. Top-earning, tertiary-educated women entrepreneurs tend to earn less than equally educated women in wage employment, while the opposite is true for men. The evidence clearly suggests that self-employment is a pathway to wealth only for a small group of well-prepared, highly motivated women. Improving the earning prospects of self-employment is critical to making it more attractive to women.

Figure 25.3. **In most OECD countries self-employed women work fewer hours than men**

Median hours worked in self-employment per week by gender, 2008

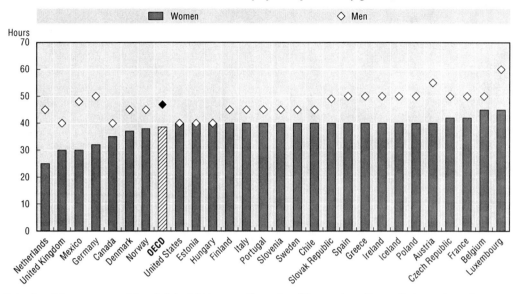

Note: Countries are arranged from left to right in ascending order of the number of hours that women work.
Source: OECD Secretariat estimates on *EU-SILC* (2008) for European countries, Survey *of Income and Program Participation 2008* for United States, *Labour Force Survey* data for the other countries.

StatLink ⏤ http://dx.doi.org/10.1787/888932676925

Figure 25.4. **Highly educated women earn more as salaried workers than as self-employed**

Earning differences[a] between self-employment and wage employment by gender and earning percentiles (pc), 2008

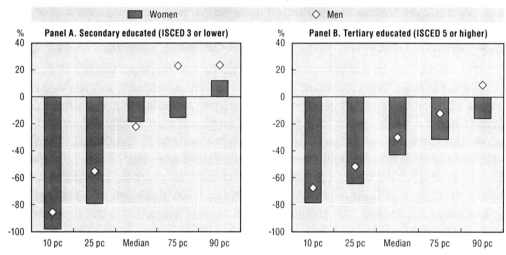

a) Earning differences are defined as the difference between self-employment and wage employment earnings divided by self-employment earnings.
Source: OECD Secretariat estimates based on *EU-SILC* (2008).

StatLink ⏤ http://dx.doi.org/10.1787/888932676944

In many countries, women entrepreneurs still gravitate towards "traditional" service and retail sectors. National and local governments can encourage more women to enter industries that provide significant opportunities for growth and wealth by developing or sponsoring web-based knowledge platforms on emerging business opportunities, mentorships for aspiring entrepreneurs, and pre-incubator workshops that help women transform their ideas into viable businesses. Successful initiatives at the local level, such as the business incubator in Styria (Austria), often rely on effective partnerships between government, educational institutions, and business associations.

An important issue is the access of the self-employed to social security and insurance. Both in the Netherlands and Norway, self-employed women are now eligible for maternity leave benefits. Cohoon et al. (2010) show that female entrepreneurs in the United States are more concerned than men about the risk of losing health insurance coverage when starting their enterprise.

The evidence makes clear that the time constraints self-employed women face can significantly affect both the type of entrepreneurial activity they engage in and the profitability of their business. Better access to high-quality, affordable childcare and eldercare may help to reduce the profitability gap between male- and female-owned enterprises. Support programmes can also be adapted to the time constraints of women. For example, distance learning may afford women greater access to training since courses can be taken at times suited to their schedules. Policy initiatives in the areas of information campaigns, training, and reducing the care burden offer a potential double dividend – greater women's empowerment and more productive businesses.

Key policy messages

- Information campaigns, targeted training programmes, and measures to reduce the burden of household duties are three complementary policy levers for increasing women's entrepreneurship and earnings.

- When evaluating the cost-benefit of affordable care services, it should be considered that they contribute to making self-employment a more attractive prospect to women. They also free up time that female entrepreneurs can devote to making their businesses more profitable.

Closing the Gender Gap
Act Now
© OECD 2012

PART IV

Chapter 26

Women's access to credit

Key findings

- Women entrepreneurs rely substantially less than men on external loans, both for start-up and for financing their activities. More analysis is needed to better understand why women are less inclined to use external finance and whether they are discouraged by discriminatory treatment in the capital markets.

- There is evidence that conditions of access to finance significantly deteriorated for both women and men during the recent economic and financial crisis.

Sources of financing for female and male-owned enterprises

Access to credit is critical to starting a new business and to its performance (Taylor, 2001). It is often argued that women have more trouble accessing credit than men. Indeed, the evidence shows that relatively more male than female entrepreneurs make use of bank loans, with or without collateral, to start their enterprises (Figure 26.1), although there are important differences in the demand for loans across countries. In 2007, only 6.3% of female-owned businesses in the United States had requested a loan from a financial institution to start their business, while 11.1% of men-owned firms had (US Census, 2009). In Eastern Europe, where entrepreneurs overall make little use of external sources for start-up financing, women generally access credit less than men. Differences also exist in the extent to which policies support start-up financing. In Sweden 22% of women entrepreneurs (*versus* 14% of men) received public financial support, but less than 1% in Denmark against 3% for men (Eurostat, 2008).

Figure 26.1. **More men than women use credit from banks to finance their start-up**

Percentage of enterprises that used a bank loan with or without collateral for financing start-up, by gender of the sole founder and current owner, 2005

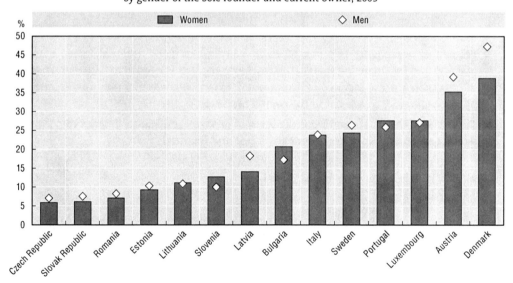

Note: Countries are arranged from left to right in ascending order of the use of start-up credit from banks among women founders.

Source: Eurostat, *Factors of Business Success Survey.*

StatLink ⟐ http://dx.doi.org/10.1787/888932676963

Smooth access to finance is crucial not only to starting a business, but to driving investment and innovation in existing enterprises. Evidence from 16 European countries in 2009 shows that female-owned enterprises are less likely than male-owned ones to rely on external financing for their investments (27% of women-owned enterprises took on no loans in the last two years versus 20% of male-owned ones). Gender differences in rejections of loan applications are less evident, even if the gap seemed to widen in late 2010 and early 2011 (Box 26.1). Evidence from other OECD countries confirms the lower reliance on debt financing from women-owned enterprises and yields mixed results as to gender differences in rejected loan applications. Data from Chile show that 55% of women-owned enterprises did not make use of debt financing in 2007 against 38% of male-owned companies (Observatorio Empresas, 2009). In the United States, women seem more likely to be discouraged from applying for loans for fear of rejection, though they are no more likely to be denied when they do apply (Cole and Mehran, 2009).

Box 26.1. **Access to credit for female-owned enterprises during the economic crisis**

There are justifiable concerns that the economic crisis has made it even harder for women to use debt financing to support the growth of their enterprises. For example, the proportion of unsuccessful loan applications rose dramatically from 1 to 27% in Ireland between 2007 and 2010 (Eurostat, 2011), increasing substantially in many other OECD countries. Problems of access faced by women in the credit market are likely to be exacerbated by the tightening of banks' credit conditions. Public interventions to strengthen banks' balance sheets and extend credit guarantees have generally lead to improvements in the financing prospects of small and medium-sized enterprises, where female ownership is more widespread. However, data monitoring the financing of enterprises in Europe show that, at the end of 2010, access to finance was the most pressing problem for more than 16% of female-owned enterprises, and rejection rates were significantly higher for women (4.3%) than for men (2.3%). Conditions for male-owned enterprises seem to have improved more and in a more sustained manner than for female-owned firms.

Conditions of access to finance have improved more for men than for women over recent months

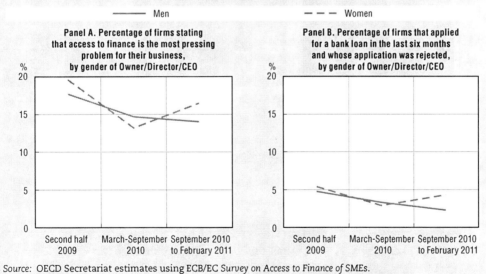

Source: OECD Secretariat estimates using ECB/EC Survey on Access to Finance of SMEs.

StatLink ᴍᴖ█ http://dx.doi.org/10.1787/888932676982

There are two very different reasons why women entrepreneurs might be treated differently in the credit markets: i) they lack significant assets (experience, capacity, cash flows, collateral) that are valued by lenders; and ii) there is cultural bias reflecting a lack of confidence in the ability of women as business owners.

Interview-based studies repeatedly report that women feel more reluctant to apply for credit and have difficulty dealing with bank officials. Female entrepreneurs in Canada had to provide lenders with more documentation – such as personal financial statements, appraisals of assets and cash flow projections – than male entrepreneurs (Jung, 2010). Muravyev *et al.* (2007), using data from 26 countries in the Eastern European and Central Asian (ECA) region, show that women are charged higher interest rates than men (0.6% more). Similarly, Alesina *et al.* (2008) reveal that women entrepreneurs in Italy pay higher interest rates and the premium they have to pay rises if they have a female guarantor.

In spite of these constraints, data on enterprises founded in 2002 in 14 countries show that there are large international differences in the share of women entrepreneurs identifying access to finance as a key difficulty for start-up (Figure 26.2). Only in half of the countries do more women than men entrepreneurs assert that financing was a primary constraint when they started their business.

Figure 26.2. **There are large international differences in the difficulties perceived by women in financing their start-up**

Percentage of women founders identifying access to finance as a key obstacle for start-up, 2005

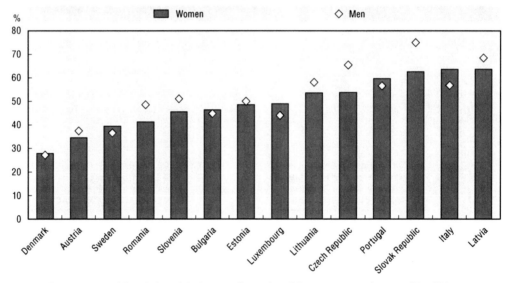

Note: Countries are arranged from left to right in ascending order of the percentage of women identifying access to finance as a key obstacle to start-up.
Source: Eurostat, *Factors of Business Success Survey.*

StatLink  *http://dx.doi.org/10.1787/888932677001*

However, many women entrepreneurs might not perceive financing as a major problem simply because they start small and have a limited demand for credit. Figure 26.3 shows that female founders in France start their enterprises with lower initial funds than men. The difference in starting capital is also wide between female and male-owned enterprises in the United States, with almost 60% of women starting their enterprise with less than USD 5 000. The relationship between size at start-up and use of finance is a

Figure 26.3. **Women create their enterprises with considerably lower amounts of initial funds**

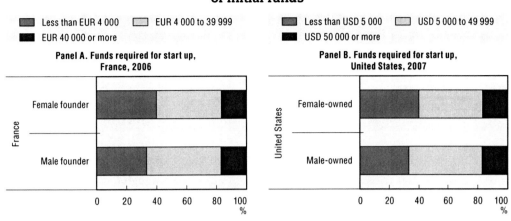

Source: OECD Secretariat estimates based on *SINE* for France and *Survey of Business Owners 2007* for United States.
StatLink ᴍᴤᴾ *http://dx.doi.org/10.1787/888932677020*

complex one. Even if many women do not seek loans because a small enterprise satisfies their ambitions, there are certainly cases when difficulties in accessing finance at competitive prices lead them to opt for a smaller business. Lower size and lower capital intensity have been shown to be key factors behind gender gaps in the profitability and productivity of enterprises (see Chapter 24, and Sabarwal and Terrell, 2008).

Better data are needed to improve understanding of the gender differences in access to finance and financing needs. The OECD has pioneered efforts in this area by developing a Scoreboard on SME and entrepreneurship finance, which comprises indicators on debt, equity, government policies, and general market conditions. However, further progress is needed to improve the comparability of gender-disaggregated data across countries.

Credit access policies for women entrepreneurs

The lower reliance of women entrepreneurs on external credit is clearly linked to demand-side differences between female and male-owned firms. However, credit providers might also discriminate against women entrepreneurs. The banks and public support policies should ensure tight supervision to prevent any discrimination. In this regard, the Consumer Financial Protection Agency (CFPA) in the United States collects data on small business credit availability by gender, race, and ethnicity and enforces lending laws to ensure that loans are granted fairly to small business owners.

National and regional business support centres should rely on best practices to bolster the self-confidence of women entrepreneurs in their dealings with credit institutions. Training programmes should be in place to help female entrepreneurs build the skills they need to better design and present their financing plans and be more successful in raising the funds they need to grow.

In the context of the continuing economic crisis, it is important to ensure that the credit squeeze does not stifle the activity of new and existing entrepreneurs. Many women and men entrepreneurs still report difficulty in accessing loans at sustainable interest rates. In response, governments in OECD countries have put in place a range of measures such as "credit mediator schemes" to ease the flow of credit to SMEs and binding codes of conduct for SME lending (OECD, 2009a). Small and credit-constrained women entrepreneurs are more likely to be the beneficiaries of such policies. In the United States, loans granted by the Small Business Administration (SBA) are three to five times more likely to go to women than conventional bank loans (White House Council, 2012). These loans have been substantially expanded through the Recovery Act and the Small Business Jobs Act. Similar credit support programmes have been operating effectively in Finland. Overall, policies seem to be particularly effective when financing instruments are supplemented with other services, such as training and consultancy, to address the additional challenges typically met by female entrepreneurs.

Key policy messages

- Address the financing gap for SMEs and micro-enterprises through measures that ease access to finance for viable businesses. Implementation mechanisms should be evaluated *ex ante* to ensure that they do not introduce a gender bias.

- Bolster the confidence of women entrepreneurs seeking funds to finance their growth by pairing financing schemes with support measures such as financial literacy, training, and consultancy services.

PART IV

Chapter 27

Financing female-owned enterprises in partner countries

Key findings

- There are large international differences in the financial inclusion of women, even across countries at similar levels of income per capita.
- Women entrepreneurs in Africa make less use of external credit than men and can rely less on credit from suppliers or advances from customers.

Financing female-owned micro-enterprises in emerging and developing economies

Women are more prone to financial exclusion than men, especially in developing countries. In other words, women are less likely to use financial institutions to borrow, save, take out insurance, and make payments. Cross-national variations in income levels account for many of the discrepancies in financial inclusion, but other cultural and institutional factors also play a role. Figure 27.1 shows that almost all adult women in high-income countries have a formal account, while there are wide disparities in the financial inclusion of women across low-income countries (Demirguc-Kunt and Klapper, 2012). For example, 1.5% of women in Niger had formal accounts with and/or obtained loans from financial institutions in 2011, while 12% of women in Mauritania had an account and 7% received a formal loan. The differences in the proportions of men and women who hold an account also tend to diminish with countries' income per capita, even if, once again, the size of the gender gap varies significantly across poor countries. Gender gaps in financial inclusion are largest in South Asia and in the Middle East and North Africa region (Klapper, 2012).

Figure 27.1. The financial inclusion of women does not depend only on income

Percentage of women with a formal account and gross national income per capita, 2011

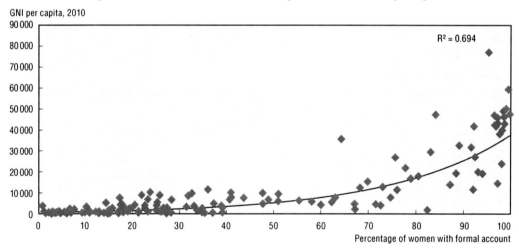

Source: Global Financial Index Database and World Development Indicators, Demirguc-Kunt, A. and L. Klapper (2012), "Measuring Financial Inclusion: The Global Findex Database", World Bank Policy Research Paper, No. 6025, Washington DC.
StatLink ᵐᵌ▇ http://dx.doi.org/10.1787/888932677039

There is a strong link between women's financial inclusion and their performance as entrepreneurs in developing countries. Enabling women to build up savings in accounts registered in their name attracts more entrepreneurs; conversely, access constraints curtail the business growth of female-owned micro-enterprises. Dupas and Robinson (2009) show that female market vendors in rural Kenya increased their daily investments by between 38 and 56% when they were provided with interest-free bank accounts.

Figure 27.2 shows that most registered female and male-owned firms in Sub-Saharan Africa have business accounts with financial institutions. However, there are marked differences between African men and women in the "demand for credit". While 29% of the firms majority-owned by men report that they asked for a loan from a financial institution in the last year, only 23% of those owned by women applied for one. There are several explanations for this gender difference. One is affordability, as women owners operate on a smaller scale and report being more discouraged than men by requests for collateral and high interest rates (Figure 27.2). An alternative reason is that African women entrepreneurs generally rely on smaller business networks and might have greater difficulty in dealing with bank officials. One indication of the networking disadvantage women face as entrepreneurs is the fact that only 2.5% of African female-owned firms have suppliers who offer them credit or customers who pay advances (versus 5.2% of men-owned firms).

Figure 27.2. **Women entrepreneurs in Africa are less likely to ask for loans than men**

Selected indicators of access and use of credit, by gender of the majority of firms' owners, 2010

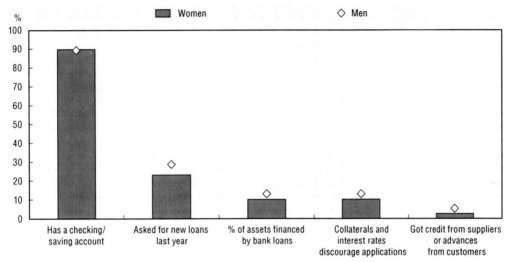

Source: World Bank Enterprise Surveys and World Bank Indicator Surveys, pooled data for registered firms in 19 African countries.

StatLink ᛘᑌ᠍ᓬᔙᔜ http://dx.doi.org/10.1787/888932677058

Access to credit for both men and women entrepreneurs is particularly hard in the start-up phase. Data on micro-enterprises (less than 15 employees) in Brazil, Mexico and South Africa show that the great majority of business owners did not use loans to start up, but relied entirely on their own funds and on support from family and friends (Figure 27.3, Panel A). When their enterprise is already up and running, women and men tend to turn to banks and other credit institutions for their financing needs (Panel B). A comparison of the two graphs suggests that financial institutions are much more likely to open a credit line to someone who has already proved his/her capacity as an entrepreneur or who can use business assets as collaterals. By operating in this way, credit markets create poverty traps with serious implications for gender equality. Poor women and men who do not have sufficient funds to finance their start-up stay out of the entrepreneurial markets and in poverty. Gender-specific effects are more pronounced in those countries where women have limited access to property rights or control over household assets (Chapter 2).

Figure 27.3. **Neither male nor female micro-enterprise owners tend to use external loans to start up**[a]

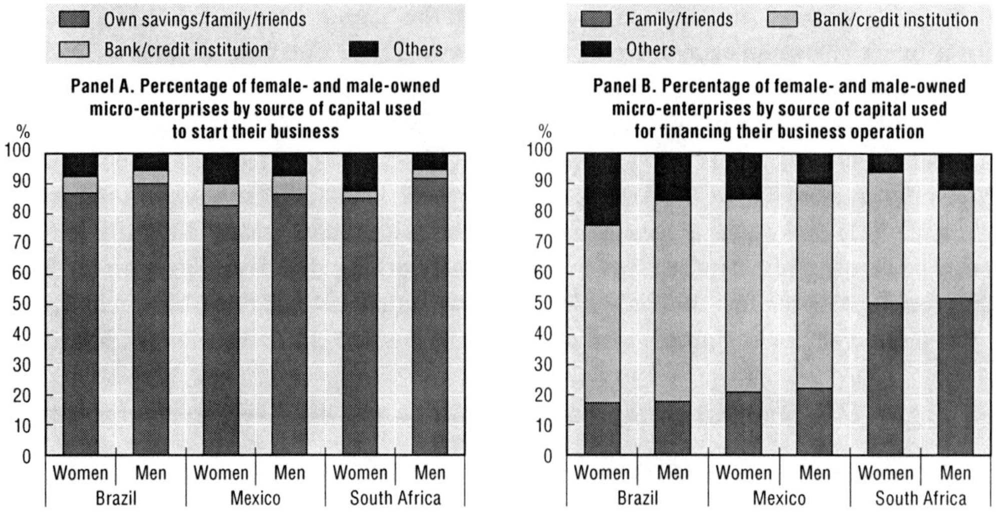

Panel A. Percentage of female- and male-owned micro-enterprises by source of capital used to start their business

Panel B. Percentage of female- and male-owned micro-enterprises by source of capital used for financing their business operation

a) Micro-enterprises are defined as enterprises that employ less than 15 employees.
Source: OECD Secretariat estimates based on ENAMIN 2008 (Mexico), Economia Informal Urbana 2003 (Brazil), and Finscope 2010 (South Africa).

StatLink ⟨⟨⟩⟩ http://dx.doi.org/10.1787/888932677077

There is ample evidence of high returns on capital in micro-businesses, generally much higher than market interest rates (Banerjee and Duflo, 2004; McKenzie and Woodruff, 2006). However, recent research proves clearly that capital injections might not be enough to enable growth, especially in female-owned micro-enterprises. Experimental evidence in Sri Lanka shows that women who have less autonomy in household and business decisions invest a smaller portion of their grant in assets that are easy to capture (De Mel et al., 2009a). For Ghana, Fafchamps et al. (2011) find that in-kind grants are more effective than cash grants in fostering business profits among Ghanaian women, suggesting that female business owners are more likely to use cash earnings for household consumption. Capital injections significantly raised profits only for a subset of high-ability women.

Policies for financially constrained entrepreneurs in developing countries

Non-governmental organisations (NGOs) and non-bank financial institutions (NBFIs) continue to play a very significant role in supporting the credit needs of self-employed women, particularly in the informal sector. Few commercial banks are, in fact, equipped to deal efficiently with very small firms, given their high mortality rates, low availability of collaterals, and demand for micro-loans. Data from the Mix Market Database show that the percentage of female borrowers from NGOs and NBFIs is much higher than from commercial banks providing micro-loans, especially in East Asia and the Pacific (where women account for 89% of the micro-borrowers from NGOs and only 35% of the borrowers from commercial and rural banks). Therefore, even if the private sector has proven to be an innovative and fast growing provider of micro-loans, subsidised credit and other public interventions still play an important role in increasing access to credit for women of all socio-economic backgrounds, thereby contributing to financial inclusion and the fight against poverty through entrepreneurship (Karlan and Morduch, 2009). In Mexico, a large micro-credit programme, the Programa Nacional de Financiamiento al Microempresario (National Programme of Microenterprise Funding), known as Pronafim, has running since 2000 and has overwhelmingly benefitted women (87% of recipients in 2011).

There is scope for commercial banks to move "downmarket" and increase their capacity to reach women micro-entrepreneurs (de Ferranti and Ody, 2007). Technological innovations like mobile banking are promising tools for extending financial services to self-employed women, particularly in rural areas. The discriminatory practices of financial institutions, such as the requirement that men should sign women's documents, must be eliminated. But formal financial institutions need to do more than merely lower the entry barriers to female micro-owners. They must improve their performance in funding the growth of female-owned businesses. Several banks in developing countries have realised that many women entrepreneurs have the potential to move up the value chain. Accordingly, they have developed specific approaches to support them. The Exim bank in Tanzania, for example, allows women running medium-sized firms to use contracts with reputable companies as collateral for their loans (IFC, 2011). Similarly, governments and donors can partner with banks to reduce the financial constraints on female-owned firms. India, for example, implements the Credit Link Capital Subsidy for financing technology upgrades in female-owned firms.

There is also scope for OECD countries to increase the gender-equality focus of their development assistance to enterprise development and financial inclusion. OECD data shows that overall aid to the economic and productive sectors focuses less on gender equality than aid to any other sector (OECD, 2011a). Greater efforts are needed to ensure such aid supports initiatives that target gender equality and women's empowerment, particularly in the areas of business and banking. Development assistance should also incorporate provisions for extending access to financial services to the poorest, most excluded women. Some innovative approaches from donors include DFID's support for EFInA (Enhancing Financial Innovation and Access), a financial sector development organisation that promotes financial inclusion in Nigeria and develops commercially viable savings products tailored to the needs of underserved women. USAID's Development Credit Authority provides loan guarantees in Kenya, which have encouraged its banking sector to greatly expand financial services to underserved segments of the population – with an emphasis on female-owned businesses.

Policy reforms can support women entrepreneurs' access to and use of finance in two main domains:

- The enforcement of legal rights and equal access to the ownership of assets that can be used as collateral.
- The strengthening of credit bureaus and other institutions that collect information on lenders and borrowers.

Aid can be scaled up to support and test innovative methods for screening the profitability of men's and women's investment activities. For example, the Entrepreneurial Finance Lab (EFL) in Harvard is pioneering the use of psychometric screening tools that assess entrepreneurial ability and honesty in order to unlock large-scale bank finance for SMEs. Such a tool could help credit institutions perform more effectively, as they would evaluate both women and men on the grounds of their entrepreneurial talent.

Programmes that give women entrepreneurs easier access to capital should be combined with training to help women keep control of their finances and obtain the highest returns for the money. Financial literacy programmes are particularly relevant since women often have lower levels of financial knowledge than men (Chapter 10). One example of these integrated financing schemes is the Inter-American Development Bank project "Strengthening Women Entrepreneurship in Peru". It currently funds 100 000 female entrepreneurs who have completed a training programme specifically designed for women.

Key policy messages

- In emerging and developing economies, private credit institutions should develop and diversify their loan terms and offerings. They should be accompanied by sustained support for not-for-profit lending institutions from governments and donors.

- Loans to women entrepreneurs should be supported by training in planning, management, and financial literacy.

- The enforcement of equal rights to property is fundamental to fostering gender equality in access to credit. Institutions and mechanisms, such as credit registers, which ease access to lender and borrower information, should be strengthened.

Closing the Gender Gap
Act Now
© OECD 2012

PART IV

Chapter 28

Do women innovate differently?

Key findings

- Enterprises founded by women produce different innovation outcomes from those founded by men. Lower levels of product and process innovation in enterprises founded by women can be explained by enterprises' characteristics (sector, start-up capital, and size) and by women's entrepreneurial experience prior to start-up.

- The venture and angel capital industries, which are instrumental in financing certain types of innovative enterprises, are still male-dominated. This, in turn, can have a negative effect on the ability of high growth women entrepreneurs in securing equity capital.

Innovation in female and male-owned enterprises

Innovation is widely acknowledged as a driving force behind the competitiveness of enterprises and the creation of jobs (Acs and Audretch, 1990). It also takes many forms (OECD, 2010). Analysis of gender differences in innovation should consider a broad notion of innovation, accounting for all changes in methods of work, in the use of factors of production, and in the types of output that improve productivity and commercial performance (OECD, 2005). In Europe, the gender gap in innovation activity is particularly pronounced for process innovation, defined as the introduction of a significant change in production and delivery methods (Figure 28.1). Differences among enterprises founded by

Figure 28.1. Female founders perceive their activity as less innovative, particularly in terms of process innovation

Percentage of male and female founders who consider their enterprise innovative, by type of innovation, 2005

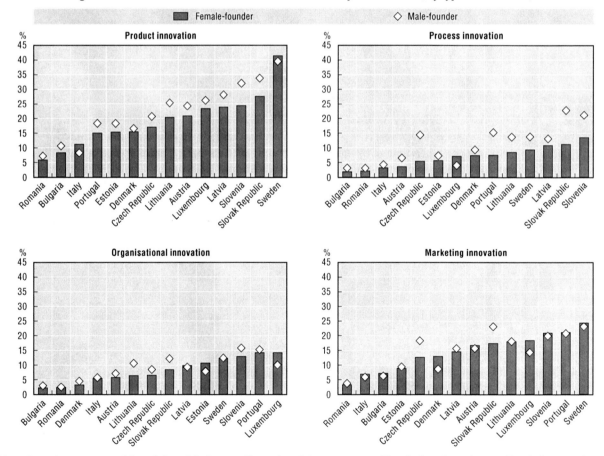

Note: Countries are arranged from left to right in ascending order of the percentage of female founders who consider their enterprise innovative by type of innovation.

Source: Eurostat, *Factors of Business Success Survey*.

StatLink 🔗 http://dx.doi.org/10.1787/888932677096

men and by women are less marked when looking at innovation in organisational methods and marketing practices, two forms of innovation that are less capital intensive. In Chile, for example, 28.5% of women-owned firms introduced a marketing innovation in 2007, while only 21.5% of male-owned firms did so (Observatorio Empresas, 2009).

There is increasing evidence that the firms' ability to innovate is closely related to characteristics of their owners (De Mel *et al.*, 2009b). Female entrepreneurs tend to lag behind men in experience in certain industries, as well as in access to the finance or networks needed to grow their businesses. These barriers affect women's propensity to invest in product or process innovation. Other less tangible differences between women and men – such as attitudes towards risk, motivation for venture start-ups, and aspirations regarding business size – have a gender dimension and can affect innovation.

Data from two surveys of young firms and their owners (the Kauffman Firm Survey for the United States and the KfW-ZEW Start-up Panel for Germany) show that entrepreneurial experience prior to start-up is one key determinant of gender differences in innovation outcomes. According to these data:

● Only 35% of the firms founded exclusively by women in the United States had at least one founder with previous experience as a business owner, compared to 49% of those founded by men. The German survey's corresponding figures are, respectively, 22% and 34%.

● In both countries, firms founded by women with previous entrepreneurial experience outperform those founded by women with none in terms of innovation outcome and investment.

● Together with the experience of the founder, differences in the types of enterprises founded by women (size at start-up, sector, and capital intensity) fully explain the observed gender gap in innovation outcomes in the United States (Annex IV.A5).

Innovation by women entrepreneurs in high-tech sectors

Innovation usually requires financial investment. External equity capital (Box 28.1) can be instrumental in financing certain types of innovation, but women entrepreneurs' lower access to these sources can affect their innovation capacity. A growing body of research demonstrates the critical role that social networks play in the funding and success of high-growth ventures (Stuart and Sorenson, 2010). Accordingly, when female entrepreneurs seek capital from other women they are more likely to be successful (Becker-Blease and Sohl, 2007), while the venture and angel capital industries are still male-dominated (Box 28.1). Figure 28.2 illustrates the overwhelmingly male composition of top management in companies that provide venture capital financing – at least 70%. In Asia the percentage is even higher (Gaule and Piacentini, 2012). The male predominance on the supply side may contribute to the low share of women's start-ups backed by venture capital: out of the founders or top managers of the 7 700 ventures that received funds in 2011 only some 10% were women.

In addition to funding, angel investors and venture capitalist make non-financial contributions to firms by helping entrepreneurs cope with uncertainty and providing oversight and strategic insights (Gompers and Lerner, 2003). The problems women have in accessing these sources of finance might explain why they appear so under-represented in emerging high-technology sectors, where returns are potentially very high but uncertainty is also greater.

Box 28.1. **Angel financing and women's entrepreneurship**

Venture capital and angel financing are important sources of funding for young, technology-based firms. Venture capital takes the form of a fund run by general partners that is used to invest in the early to expansion stages of high-growth firms. A business angel is a high net worth individual who invests his/her own funds in promising entrepreneurial businesses in return for stock in the companies.

OECD (2011b), *Financing High Growth Firms: The Role of Angel Investors* shows that women are greatly under-represented in the angel investment community. Only 5% of angel investors in Europe are women and only 13% in the US. In the venture capital industry, females comprise only 17% of professional staff and the figure is estimated to be less than 10% in Europe.

In the United States and Europe, some female angel groups have been created to encourage more women to invest. These groups introduce women to angel investing and provide training and mentoring to build their interest and confidence in investing in start-ups. In addition, there are some growing efforts to mainstream women into existing angel groups. Both approaches are important for building a greater pipeline of female investors.

Despite widespread awareness of the gender gap in angel investing and venture capital, little research has been conducted to date into understanding the barriers preventing women from participating more actively. In their 2010 white paper, "Women and European Early Stage Investing", the European Trade Association for Business Angels, Seed Funds, and other Early Stage Market Players (EBAN) proposed a number of ways to address the gap. They include conducting further research, developing best practices, raising awareness, promoting professional standards and codes of conduct that encourage greater diversity, and building networks in the female investment community.

Having more women in the angel investment and venture capital community would pay off – not only because they would widen the range of skills and expertise in the investment community, but because more doors would open for women entrepreneurs, particularly those in high-growth firms.

Gender differences in education and career choices also help explain why there are so few women among the founders of high-technology enterprises. Their under-representation in science is particularly high in tenure track positions, partly as a result of enduring gender gaps in salaries and promotion. Recent data on 12 000 inventors from 23 OECD countries show that female inventors earn lower wages than their male counterparts: 59% earn less than EUR 50 000 per year, while the figure for men is 35% (Gambardella, 2012). This gap is due not to weaker performance, but to the fact that women may put less effort into negotiating their salaries.

Male faculty members in the United States patent at more than 2.5 times the rate of their female counterparts (Ding *et al.*, 2006). Part of the reason lies in women's explicit exclusion from commercial science in its early days, which left them with few successful role models (Murray and Graham, 2007). However, Frietsch *et al.* (2009) show that the gender gap in patent applications has narrowed over time in most countries and significantly so in the United States. Women inventors commercialised 79% of their inventions, compared to 80% for all US inventors (USPTO, 2009). Interestingly, Cook and Kongcharoen (2010) find that mixed-gender patent teams commercialise their patents more than all-male and all-female patent teams.

Figure 28.2. **Venture-capital investors are predominantly male,
particularly in Asia**

Percentage of men among top managers of venture capital investment firms
by country of establishment, 2011

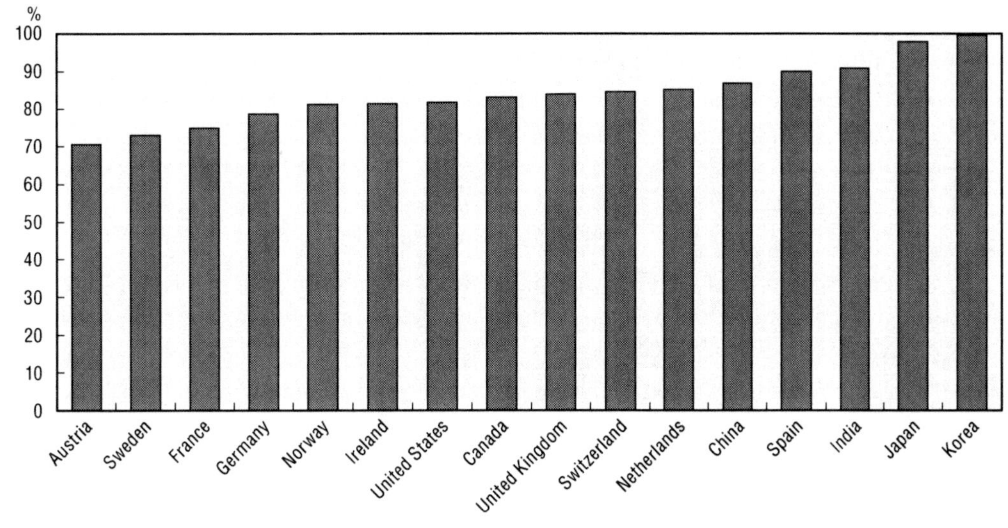

Note: Only countries with data available for at least 100 companies are shown. Countries are arranged from left to right in ascending order of the percentage of men among the top managers of venture-capital investment companies.
Source: Gaule, P. and M. Piacentini (2012), "Gender, Social Networks and Access to Venture Capital", unpublished manuscript.

StatLink ⬛⬛ *http://dx.doi.org/10.1787/888932677115*

Innovation policies for female-owned enterprises

Policies aimed at boosting innovation activity in female-owned enterprises should address three main gaps:

1. The education and career experience gap in certain innovation-intensive or high-tech fields.

2. An equity financing gap, which hinders the capacity of women to fund innovative ventures.

3. A networking gap, generated by the low numbers of women entrepreneurs in innovation-intensive industries and by the low visibility of successful innovative women.

The three gaps are interrelated and difficult to overcome given the reinforcing interactions between factors on the supply side (lower access to resources) and demand side (lower demand and expectations). Several countries are taking concrete steps to promote women innovators and high-growth entrepreneurs (European Commission, 2008), recognising that economic growth relies on the continuous marketing and application of new ideas – many of which women generate. It is increasingly clear that more diverse teams are more productive (Page, 2008) and that innovation may be hampered by male dominance in certain technological and scientific fields, equity investment networks, and top management.

Gender stereotypes in male-dominated areas of business may impair women's self-confidence, making it less likely that female entrepreneurs launch innovative firms. Public policies can tackle stereotypes by showcasing women who have succeeded in male-dominated industries with high individual and social returns (Chapter 22). The entrepreneurial mindset among women in science and technology can be fostered by integrating entrepreneurship modules into technology-oriented programmes of study, and by engaging more women in campus-based incubators, science parks and technology centres (Novakova, 2006).

Women's access to equity financing can be substantially improved by government policies that encourage private investment and address gaps in the private funding process as a whole. Gender inclusion targets can be included both in direct public funding and in public co-investment contributions to private funding. In addition to such support, public policies can facilitate women's access to risk capital through networking and information programmes. Finance South East in the United Kingdom has created a programme to facilitate women's access to risk capital. Similar networking programmes are running in Germany (National Agency for Women Start-ups) and in Poland (Gdansk Entrepreneurship Foundation).

Key policy messages

- Awareness programmes showcasing successful women in science and technology and in high-growth firms can provide useful role models for young women who may not otherwise consider such fields.

- Support programmes targeting female-owned enterprises should include modules on scaling companies and encouraging women to set higher-growth ambitions for their innovations and firms.

- Enable equal access of women innovators to equity financing. Provide financial training for women to encourage more of them to join business angel networks or venture capital firms.

PART IV

Chapter 29

Formalising female-owned businesses

Key findings

- In emerging and developing economies, the share of women among owners of small and micro-enterprises is much higher in the informal sector than in the formal one.

- Several countries are implementing measures to simplify and reduce the costs of formalisation. These policies have increased the number of women registering their businesses.

In most developing and emerging economies, small and micro-businesses play a pivotal role in the livelihoods of millions of workers and their families. Many operate in the informal economy (La Porta and Shleifer, 2008). Across countries at different level of development and with different social institutions, women represent an important share of the owners of such enterprises (Figure 29.1). In Mexico and South Africa, for example, women tend to be more prevalent in the informal sector and account for the majority of informal business owners without employees. Ownership of a micro-business in the informal sector is often the most practical source of employment for low-skilled and poor women. Most of these businesses are operated from home, which makes it easier to reconcile business and family commitments.

Figure 29.1. **Women frequently own small and micro-enterprises,
though less so in MENA countries**

Percentage of small and micro-enterprises owned by women

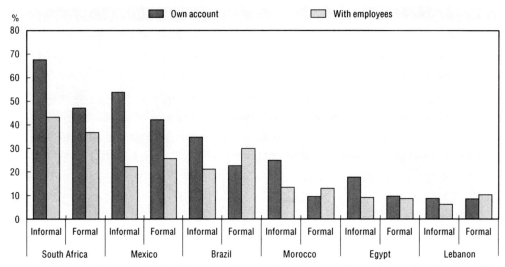

Note: Data refer to businesses with less than 15 employees (less than 5 employees in Brazil and the Mexican non-manufacturing sector). Countries are arranged from left to right in order of the decreasing percentage of female-owned enterprises in the informal sector.
Source: OECD Secretariat estimates based on ENAMIN 2008 (Mexico), Economia Informal Urbana 2003 (Brazil), Finscope 2010 (South Africa), and ERF Micro and Small Enterprises Dataset for MENA Countries 2003 (Egypt, Lebanon and Morocco).
StatLink ⌐⌐⌐ http://dx.doi.org/10.1787/888932677134

Informal enterprises are often associated with employment that is insecure and of low quality for both owners and employees (United Nations, 2008). Moreover, some analysts have stressed that informal firms generate efficiency losses because, by avoiding taxes, they rob more productive formal competitors of market shares (Farrell, 2004). Formalisation tends to increase with economic development, but there is scant evidence as to differences in the propensity of women and men business owners to move out of the informal sector when economic conditions improve. Data on micro-firms in Mexico from 1992 to 2008 show that the percentage of female owners increased more in the informal sector than in the formal one (Figure 29.2).

Figure 29.2. **The percentage of female-owned micro and small businesses has increased in Mexico both in the formal and informal sectors**

Share of micro and small enterprises owned by women in Mexico, by registration status, 1992-2008

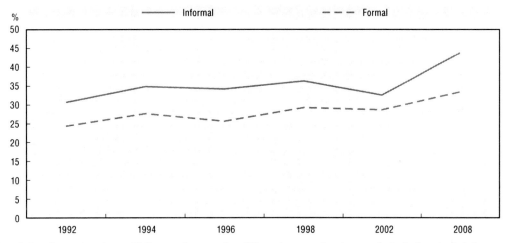

Note: Only micro-enterprises with five employees or less (15 employees or less in manufacturing) are included.
Source: OECD Secretariat estimates based on six waves of INEGI *Encuesta Nacional de Micronegocios* (ENAMIN). The data are representative of Mexican urban areas. ENAMIN 2008 data were adjusted according to estimates from the population census.

StatLink ＊ http://dx.doi.org/10.1787/888932677153

Women business owners in the informal sector are much less productive (in terms of sales per employee) than in the formal one – by 70% in Brazil, 52% in Mexico, and 34% in South Africa (see Annex IV.A4). The substantial productivity gap between registered and unregistered firms may be explained by the profiles of formal and informal entrepreneurs (De Mel *et al.*, 2009b). Interview evidence from Africa shows that women who enter and develop formal-sector companies are educated and have previous formal-sector work experience (Spring, 2009). These formal entrepreneurs target different clients and use different business networks from their informal counterparts. They perceive themselves as fundamentally different from the "survival entrepreneurs" in the informal economy and so harbour different expectations from public policies.

Perceived registration issues are a deterrent to the formalisation of small enterprises in many countries. Analysis of informal enterprises in Sub-Saharan Africa shows that, for around a quarter of female and male informal entrepreneurs, the most significant barrier to registration is the lack of information about procedures and requirements (see Annex IV.A4). Gender differences exist in the benefits expected from registration in Sub-Saharan countries. While 60% of informal women entrepreneurs expect their access to finance to improve on registration, only 53% of men do. McKenzie *et al.* (2012) also show that owners of unregistered firms in Sri Lanka are either ignorant about registration, or vastly overestimate its costs.

> ### Box 29.1. **Policy lessons: Promoting women entrepreneurship in China, India, and Indonesia**
>
> A workshop jointly organised by the Asian Development Bank (ADB) and the OECD brought together academic and policy makers from China, India, and Indonesia to discuss causes of and solutions to gender differences in education, employment and entrepreneurship (Manila, 28-29 February 2012, *http://beta.adb.org/news/events/adb-oecd-joint-workshop-gender-and-3es*).
>
> The proceedings highlighted the differences in entrepreneurial participation and the policy landscape for women entrepreneurs in the three countries. In India, the number of micro, small and medium enterprises (MSMEs) has been continuously rising – up to almost 30 million in 2010. The percentage of women-owned MSMEs is around 13%. Women in India have, over time, secured greater recognition of their capacities as entrepreneurs, but social conditioning still weighs heavily on their initiative and self-confidence. Lack of time and capital limit their potential for starting risky ventures. In Indonesia, labour force surveys show that the share of women whose status in employment is "business owner with paid workers" (employer) increased substantially between 1990 and 2011 (moving up to 1.7%). In 2006, women accounted for 29% of MSME owners in manufacturing. As in India, traditions and customs weigh on Indonesian female entrepreneurs, particularly in rural areas and among some ethnic groups. The situation of women entrepreneurs seem to have progressed at a faster pace in China, where female entrepreneurship boomed after the establishment of the new economic model in 1995. Data from the China Association of Women Entrepreneurs show that women entrepreneurs account for around 25% of all entrepreneurs, are more educated than men, optimistic about their future, and increasingly likely to seek business information from the internet and reach international markets.
>
> India is the country with the largest number of policy initiatives specifically targeting women entrepreneurs. A particular focus has been put on programmes to improve the financial inclusion of women entrepreneurs. They include preferential interest rates and credit guarantee schemes.

Policies to formalise female-owned small and micro enterprises

The design of effective policies to support female entrepreneurship in developing countries requires a deeper understanding of the heterogeneous landscapes where women operate as entrepreneurs. The distinction between formal and informal enterprises is meaningful for policy design because the profiles, needs and growth potentials are different. Female owners in the informal sector of developing countries have much less education, start out of necessity, and often earn very little from their business.

Several countries have tried to entice firms into the formal sector, primarily by reducing registration costs. Programmes to ease registration can impact extensively on women, given that the burden of complying with government regulations weighs more heavily on the low-scale businesses where female owners are prevalent (Ellis *et al.*, 2007). The SIMPLES programme in Brazil introduced simplified regulations for micro and small firms with the objective of boosting registration rates. It led to a significant increase in registration, which has in turn generated much higher revenues, employment and profits for newly registered firms (Maloney *et al.*, 2011). Brazil recently introduced a scheme, the Individual Microentrepreneur Programme (MEI), to further facilitate business registrations (Box 29.2). Mexico, too, has introduced a programme called "Sistema de Apertura Rápida de Empresas" (Quick Start System for Enterprises, SARE). It introduced a single-window point of access for services to reduce the number of procedures needed to register a business (OECD, 2009b).

> ## Box 29.2. **Encouraging micro-entrepreneurs to exit informality:**
> ### **The MEI programme in Brazil**
>
> The programme "Microempreendedor Individual", or Individual Microentrepreneur Programme (MEI), is a registration initiative designed to reduce informality among low-income entrepreneurs that was introduced in July 2009. Registration is free and can be done through an online portal (*www.portaldoempreendedor.gov.br*). Micro-entrepreneurs who register in the National Register of Legal Entities are entitled to a number of benefits:
>
> - They become eligible for social security (disability benefits, maternity pay and public pensions, subject to the payment of contributions).
>
> - They can invoice as a company.
>
> - They are granted access to low-interest credit lines in public banks such as Banco do Brasil, Caixa Econômica Federal e Banco do Nordeste.
>
> - They gain access to public procurement and business support services.
>
> In 2012, the cost of registration is the monthly state and social tax payment of BRL 6 plus BRL 31 in social contributions (in all, around USD 20). Eligibility to register is conditional on annual income from the business being less than BRL 60 000 (around USD 33 000), but above a monthly minimum wage of BRL 622 (USD 340).
>
> MEI has attracted large numbers of micro-entrepreneurs. In 2011, one full year after it was introduced, a total of 1.9 million micro-entrepreneurs formalised via MEI's online portal. Around 46% of newly formalised entrepreneurs are women. To encourage people to register, SEBRAE (the Brazilian support service for micro and small enterprises) campaigns and delivers capacity-building programmes, often targeting women. Women entrepreneurs who registered through the programme report improvements in their business operations, costs of credit, and work security. One risk of the programme is that it might create incentives to under-report real revenues (in order to benefit from the special MEI status) and reduce the attractiveness of other legal forms of business (limited-liability companies and corporations) that are generally more conducive to enterprise growth.

However, reducing the costs of registration without significantly improving the business environment is unlikely to turn millions of informal micro-businesses into competitive small and medium enterprises in the formal sector. Complementary measures are needed to enable higher growth in female-owned enterprises. Higher revenue growth would, in turn, drive faster formalisation. There is also a need to make the competitive advantages of registration more visible, particularly by improving the capacity of the private financial sector and of public business support schemes to reach very small businesses, where informality is higher.

While increasing incentives for registration, policy makers should also support women who do not consider exiting informality because they do not want to change the way they operate their business. These women can benefit from coming together in member-based associations and from being represented in economic and political organisations (Chapter 20). International research-policy networks, such as Women in Informal Employment: Globalizing and Organizing (WIEGO), can drive policy changes by documenting the role of informal women entrepreneurs as agents of poverty reduction.

In order to unlock the potential of female entrepreneurship, comprehensive policy packages need to address simultaneously the human capital deficits that most micro-business owners must contend with (education, management skills, and formal-sector business experience), together with the external constraints (high cost of capital, volatility of input prices, lack of business networks) that limit investment and diversification out of traditional small-scale, low-profit activities. Improving the skills and financial inclusion of informal, female micro-entrepreneurs is likely to have a considerable impact on poverty. However, the highest growth potential lies in those women who become entrepreneurs not to survive, but to pursue their aspirations. Support to organisations and institutions established by and for women entrepreneurs, such as the South African Women Entrepreneurs Network (SAWEN), can enable women to broaden their business and find the advice they need to compete outside their local area and in male-dominated industries.

Key policy messages

- Diversified programmes need to be put in place to meet the needs of different types of women entrepreneurs, *e.g.* informal micro-entrepreneurs and formal-sector small industries.

- Reduce the administrative burdens of registration, which tend to weigh particularly heavily on women entrepreneurs who must contend with time and resource constraints. Make the benefits from registration more visible and substantial.

ANNEX IV.A1

Methodological issues and additional findings to Chapters 22 and 24

Data and comparability issues

Self-employment data (Figure 22.1)

Figure 22.1 is based on data on self-employment by gender extracted from labour force and household surveys of OECD and non-OECD countries. Original data extractions were needed since the available datasets (*e.g.* labour force statistics published by OECD and ILO) do not provide distinct information on the self-employed with and without employees. This disaggregation is highly relevant because gender differences are generally more marked for the class of business owners with paid employees (self-employed with employees or "employers"). Both unincorporated and incorporated female and male employers are included in Figure 22.1 when the information is available. The main comparability issue relates to the classification of the "incorporated self-employed". While in the official statistics of most OECD countries the self-employed who incorporate their businesses are counted as self-employed, some countries consider them employees. To improve international comparability the number of incorporated employers and own-account workers in the United States was estimated. The estimation used information on the percentage of incorporated self-employed men and women with employees that was available for 1995, 1997, 1999, 2001 and 2005 from the Contingent and Alternative Work Arrangements Surveys. For the missing years between 1996 and 2004, the percentage was derived through linear interpolation. For the years 2006 to 2011, the percentage for 2005 was used.

EIP data on sole-proprietor enterprises by gender (Figures 22.2, 22.3, 22.4, 24.1 and 24.2)

Figures 22.2, 22.3, 22.4, 24.1 and 24.2 are based on a new data collection managed by the OECD Eurostat Entrepreneurship Indicators Programme (EIP). The statistics have been developed by national statistical offices on the basis of EIP definitions, primarily by linking business registers to population registers or other administrative data. For Mexico, the data in Figure 22.2 were derived from the Economic Census 2009. For Japan, the figure refers to the number of men and women sole-proprietors with and without employees, and not to women and men-owned sole-proprietor enterprises. Japanese data are thus not fully comparable with other countries, given that a single sole proprietor can own more than one enterprise and that there might be gender differences in the propensity to own more than one enterprise. With the exception of Japan in Figure 22.2, and of Poland and France in

Figures 22.4, 24.1 and 24.2, the data refer to "employer enterprises", defined as enterprises with at least one paid employee. Data from France, Poland and Switzerland are obtained from representative surveys of new enterprises. They are tabulated by gender of the enterprise's (sole) founder rather than by the gender of the sole proprietor.

ORBIS data on companies owned by women, men and gender mixes (Figure 24.3)

Figure 24.3 is based on the OECD ORBIS dataset, which includes structural and financial information on millions of companies worldwide. The dataset is produced by the OECD on the basis of data provided by Bureau Van Dijk Publishing. For the countries included in the table, the ORBIS dataset provides information on the names of individuals or societies owning company shares. For analytical reasons, the sample is restricted to those companies where individuals own at least 50% of a company's shares. Enterprises are defined as women (men)-owned if one or more women (men) own more than 50% of the shares. They are classified as mixed-owned if the shares of women and men are the same (*e.g.* companies owned by couples), and if neither men nor women alone account for more than 50% of the shares (*e.g.* a company 30% owned by women, 40% by men, and 30% by a non-physical person). In order to assign a gender to the different owners, an algorithm was developed to identify male and female owners on the basis of their first name. The algorithm matches the first names of the owners in the *ORBIS Database* with a database of 173 000 unique male and female first names by country compiled by the OECD and which expands the one used in Frietsch *et al.* (2009). In each country, at least 96% of the owners' names are identified as masculine or feminine. The main comparability issue is represented by the fact that ORBIS's coverage of firms is still uneven across countries. Large companies are generally over-represented.

Additional findings

Gender differences in the share of employed women who are own-account workers or employers (self-employment data)

As discussed in Chapter 22, self-employed women are less likely than self-employed men to hire employees. Figure IV.A1.1 (Panels A and B) illustrates the importance of looking at the type of self-employment in which women and men are engaged. It shows that gender differences are much more marked when focusing on the self-employed with employees ("employers"). In Chile, Mexico and South Africa, the percentage of employed who are account workers is greater among women than among men. However, women are significantly less likely to work as employers in those three countries.

Gender differences in the propensity to consider self-employment (self-employment data)

Chapter 22 argues that, compared with men, unemployed women are less likely to consider self-employment. Figure IV.A1.2 shows that this is true of all European countries, except Luxembourg.

Characteristics of female and male-owned individual enterprises (EIP data)

Sole-proprietor enterprises owned by women are significantly smaller than those owned by men. Figure IV.A1.3 shows the proportion of female- and male-owned enterprises in three size classes of the number of persons employed (1-4, 5-9, 10 or more). In most countries, women-owned enterprises are over-represented in the smallest size class.

Figure IV.A1.1. **Gender differences in self-employment
are much more pronounced among the self-employed with employees**

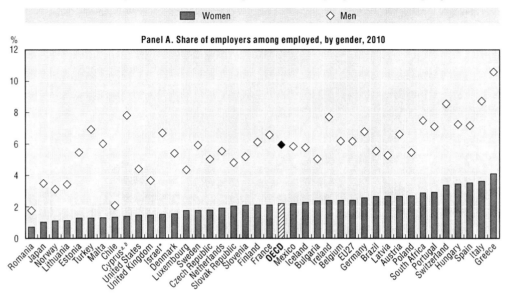

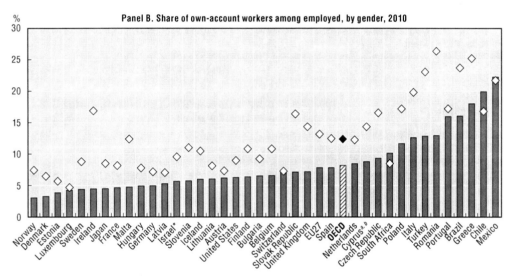

Note: In Panel A, countries are arranged from left to right in ascending order of the share of women employers; in Panel B, countries are arranged from left to right in ascending order of the share of women own-account workers.
* Information on data for Israel: *http://dx.doi.org/10.1787/888932315602.*

a) *Footnote by Turkey:* The information in this document with reference to "Cyprus" relates to the southern part of the Island. There is no single authority representing both Turkish and Greek Cypriot people on the Island. Turkey recognises the Turkish Republic of Northern Cyprus (TRNC). Until a lasting and equitable solution is found within the context of United Nations, Turkey shall preserve its position concerning the "Cyprus issue".

b) *Footnote by all the European Union Member States of the OECD and the European Commission:* The Republic of Cyprus is recognised by all members of the United Nations with the exception of Turkey. The information in this document relates to the area under the effective control of the Government of the Republic of Cyprus.

Source: OECD Secretariat estimates based on household and *Labour Force Survey* data.

StatLink http://dx.doi.org/10.1787/888932677210

Women tend to start their enterprises in different sectors from men. The proportion of female-owned enterprises is relatively higher in the wholesale and retail trade, transportation and accommodation, while it is relatively lower in manufacturing (Figure IV.A1.4).

Figure IV.A1.2. **Unemployed women are much less likely than men to consider self-employment**

Percentage of unemployed women and men who are actively searching a self-employment occupation, 2010[a]

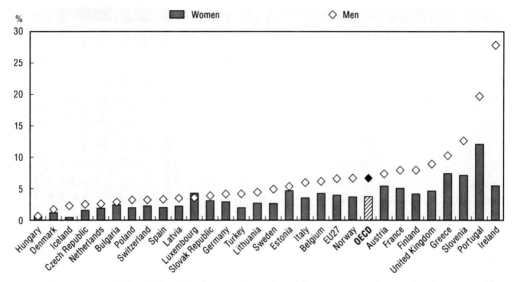

Note: Countries are arranged from left to right in ascending order of the percentage of unemployed men searching for a self-employment occupation.

a) Unemployed women and men actively searching for a job are asked if they are searching for a job as wage-employed or as self-employed.

Source: OECD Secretariat estimates based on *Eurostat European Labour Force Survey* data.

StatLink ᴴᴸᴼ *http://dx.doi.org/10.1787/888932677229*

Figure IV.A1.3. **Enterprises run by women are significantly smaller than those run by men**

Size distribution of women and men sole-proprietor enterprises, 2009

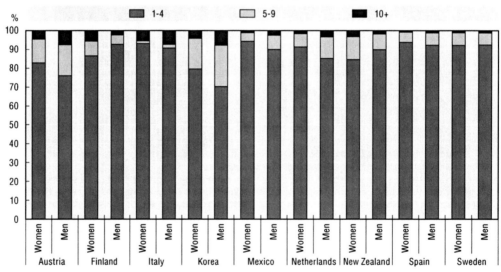

Source: OECD Secretariat estimates based on statistics produced by National Statistical Institutes. Employer enterprises only.

StatLink ᴴᴸᴼ *http://dx.doi.org/10.1787/888932677248*

Figure IV.A1.4. **Women are much less likely than men to run enterprises in manufacturing**

Distribution of women and men sole-proprietor enterprises by class of industry, 2009

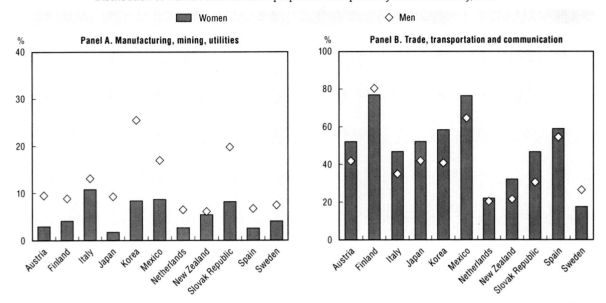

Source: OECD Secretariat estimates based on statistics produced by National Statistical Institutes. Employer enterprises only with the exception of Japan.

StatLink ⫘ *http://dx.doi.org/10.1787/888932677267*

Differences in the performances of female and male-owned enterprises (ORBIS data)

Female-owned businesses in the ORBIS dataset perform less well than male-owned ones, according to several measures of business performance. Table IV.A1.1 provides evidence on the magnitude of the performance gaps across the 21 OECD economies with available data. Column 1 presents results from a linear regression of the natural logarithm of value added per employee (a commonly used proxy measure for productivity) on a binary variable indicating female-ownership and country-fixed effects. It shows a productivity shortfall by women-owned enterprises of around 11%. In order to understand whether this productivity gap is due to the fact that women select different types of industries from men, column 2 includes these additional control variables:

- The natural logarithm of fixed asset values per employee, Ln (Capital/Employees), a measure of the business activity's capital intensity.

- The natural logarithm of the number of employees, Ln (Employees), a measure of a firm's size.

- A binary variable indicating whether an enterprise was created less than five years ago ("Recent").

- Industry-fixed effects, at 1 digit level (NACE Rev. 2 letters).

The productivity gap decreases significantly – to 4.8% – when accounting for these characteristics of a firm. The result shows that the lower productivity of female-owned enterprises is due, in large part, to the fact that they are smaller, less capital intensive, and in sectors characterised by lower average productivity. Enterprises owned by women tend to make lower profits (around 4% less), even controlling for their size, capital intensity, age, and sector of activity (column 3). The women-owned companies included in ORBIS were slightly less likely (1.2% less) to experience an increase in the number of their employees between 2005 and 2009 (column 4).

Table IV.A1.1. **Women owned-enterprises lag behind in average productivity, profits and generation of new jobs**

Estimated labour productivity (2009), profits (2009) and change in number of employees (2005-09) by gender

Variables	Ln (Value added per employee)	Ln (Value added per employee)	Ln (Profits)	Ln (Employment growth)
	OLS (1)	OLS (2)	OLS (3)	OLS (4)
Female ownership	−0.114***	−0.048***	−0.039***	−0.012***
	(0.005)	(0.004)	(0.008)	(0.003)
Ln (Capital/Employees)		0.434***	0.699***	−0.013***
		(0.002)	(0.003)	(0.001)
Ln (Employees)		0.050***	0.764***	0.127***
		(0.001)	(0.003)	(0.001)
Recent		0.042***	0.106***	0.217***
		(0.006)	(0.012)	(0.007)
Industry fixed effects	No	Yes	Yes	Yes
Country fixed effects	Yes	Yes	Yes	Yes
Constant	4.114***	1.957***	−0.283	0.333***
	(0.036)	(0.167)	(0.418)	(0.109)
Observations	231 820	247 350	224 930	152 985
R^2	0.300	0.570	0.521	0.162

Note: Robust standard errors in parentheses. ***: $p < 0.01$; **: $p < 0.05$; *: $p < 0.1$.

Source: OECD Secretariat estimates based on OECD-ORBIS Data for 21 countries. Enterprises are defined as women (men)-owned if one or more women (men) own more than 50% of the shares.

StatLink ᵐˢᵖ http://dx.doi.org/10.1787/888932677723

Table IV.A1.2 explores which firm-level characteristics matter more in explaining the mean differences in performance measures between female and male-owned enterprises. It does so through a Blinder-Oaxaca decomposition based on the regression models in columns 2 to 4 of Table IV.A1.1. The decomposition divides the performance differential between the two groups of female and male-owned enterprises into two parts: a part that group differences in firm characteristics can account for, and a residual part for which they cannot account. This "unexplained" part subsumes the effects of group differences in unobserved predictors, such as the ability or other personal characteristics of female and male business owners.

Table IV.A1.2. **Blinder-Oaxaca decompositions of the gender performance gap**

Percentages

	Ln (Value added per employee)	Ln (Profits)	Ln (Employment growth)
Contributions to the performance gap from gender differences in:			
Firm size [Ln (employees)]	9.8	52.3	87.0
Capital [Ln (Capital/Employees)]	38.3	28.1	−8.0
Sector of activity (NACE 1 digit industry fixed effects)	22.8	2.6	−32.0
Percentage of performance gap explained by firm characteristics	51.2	92.0	78.0

Source: OECD Secretariat estimates based on OECD-ORBIS Data for 21 countries. Enterprises are defined as women (men)-owned if one or more women (men) own more than 50% of the shares.

StatLink ᵐˢᵖ http://dx.doi.org/10.1787/888932677742

The values in the table show the relative contribution of firm size, capital intensity and sector of activity in explaining the gaps in productivity, profit and employment growth. As discussed in Chapter 24, the single most decisive factor in the gender productivity gap is the lower capital intensity of women-owned enterprises – it accounts for 38% of the gap. The lower average size of women-owned enterprises explains a large part of the gender differential in profits and in employment growth. If female-owned enterprises had, on average, the same characteristics (size, capital intensity, distribution by industry, age) as enterprises owned by men, then their productivity gap would be reduced by 51%, their profit gap by 92%, and their employment growth gap by 78%.

ANNEX IV.A2

Methodological issues and additional findings to Chapters 23 and 25

Data and comparability issues

Eurostat Factors of Business Success Survey data (Figure 23.1)

The Factor of Business Success Survey (FOBS) was co-ordinated by Eurostat and implemented by 15 European countries in 2005-06. FOBS collected information for the year 2005 on the enterprises that came into being in 2002 and on the characteristics of their founders. The purpose of the survey was to shed light on factors that help or hinder the success of newly created enterprises. It was conducted as a one-off survey, within the framework of data collection on business demography, using samples of enterprises in the business registers stratified by activity and employee size. The FOBS data are also used in Chapters 26 and 28.

Data on earnings of self-employed women and men (Figures 25.1, 25.2, 25.3 and 25.4)

The estimates of the earning gaps of women in self-employment are based on three different datasets:

- European Union Statistics on Income and Living Conditions (EU-SILC), 2008 wave.
- Survey of Income and Program Participation 2008 for the United States.
- Household, Income and Labour Dynamics in Australia (HILDA), 2008 wave.

The estimates are based on gross (pre-tax) cash benefits or losses from self-employment and restricted to individuals whose primary activity is self-employment. Self-employment income is one of the most problematic elements of household income to define and measure accurately. The EU-SILC programme provided detailed guidelines to statistical institutes on the criteria that should be followed for the calculation of self-employment income. However, there are still methodological hurdles that hamper the comparability of statistics across countries and periods. In fact, the self-employed often have accounting practices which make it difficult for them to provide accurate responses to survey questions. Moreover, their financial and accounting framework does not relate well to the one statisticians use in constructing national accounts or household income analysis (Eurostat, 2011).

It should be noted that comparison between self-employment and wage employment earnings (Figure 25.4) is likely to be affected by the way self-employment earnings are measured. Gaps between self-employment and wage employment earnings would be in fact lower if the measure of self-employment earnings included equity invested in the firm.

Additional findings

Table IV.A2.1 presents the results from the analysis of determinants of female and male business owners' earnings described in Chapter 25. The analysis is based on Mincer-type regressions on two separate samples of female and male self-employed.

The first column shows the results for pooled data from 24 European countries. It shows that the number of hours spent working in the business is a highly significant predictor of earnings, for both female and male business owners. Returns from potential experience, measured as *Age – Years of completed education – 5* are significant and non-linear: earnings increase with experience but at a decreasing rate, both for men and for women. The presence of children aged less than 18 in the household and home ownership are not significantly related to the earnings of self-employed women. Interestingly, tertiary-educated women in self-employment tend to earn relatively less than less well educated women in Europe. Work-limiting health conditions are significantly associated with lower earnings, both for men and for women. The most relevant difference between the results for the United States and those for Europe relate to returns from education. In the United States, better educated business owners tend to earn relatively more, an effect that is even more pronounced among women. Moreover, hours worked on the business yield relatively higher returns for women than for men in the United States (difference significant at the 10% level).

Table IV.A2.1. **Determinants of the earnings of male and female business owners**

| | Ln (Earnings) in Europe | | Ln (Earnings) in United States | |
| | (1) | | (2) | |
	Men	Women	Men	Women
Hours worked per month	0.006***	0.006***	0.003***	0.004***
	(0.000)	(0.000)	(0.000)	(0.000)
Experience	0.066***	0.051***	0.015**	0.066***
	(0.004)	(0.005)	(0.007)	(0.014)
Experience squared	−0.001***	−0.001***	−0.0001**	−0.001***
	(0.000)	(0.000)	(0.000)	(0.000)
Children less than 18	0.043***	−0.013	0.308**	0.188**
	(0.011)	(0.018)	(0.138)	(0.086)
Born in the country	−0.106**	−0.044	0.246***	−0.074
	(0.046)	(0.067)	(0.080)	(0.072)
Married	0.115***	0.049	0.077	−0.037
	(0.026)	(0.037)	(0.056)	(0.067)
Household owner	0.082***	0.058	0.112*	0.124
	(0.029)	(0.042)	(0.057)	(0.083)
Secondary educated	−0.478***	−0.230	−0.229***	0.496***
	(0.165)	(0.183)	(0.077)	(0.145)
Tertiary educated	−0.112	−0.188**	0.311***	0.990***
	(0.083)	(0.092)	(0.085)	(0.151)
Work-limiting health	−0.248***	−0.230***		
	(0.033)	(0.048)		
Constant	7.029***	7.129***	8.150***	6.363***
	(0.114)	(0.157)	(0.190)	(0.232)
Country fixed effects	Yes	Yes		
Observations	22 807	12 113	4 060	2 164
R^2	0.310	0.371	0.076	0.109

Note: Robust standard errors in parentheses ***: $p < 0.01$; **: $p < 0.05$; *: $p < 0.1$.

Source: OECD Secretariat estimates based on EU-SILC 2008 for European countries, *Survey of Income and Program Participation* 2008 for the United States.

StatLink ᴹᴱ http://dx.doi.org/10.1787/888932677761

ANNEX IV.A3

Methodological issues and additional findings to Chapter 26

Data and comparability issues

Survey on the access to finance of SMEs (Box 26.1)

Box 26.1 in Chapter 26 is based on data from the "Survey on the Access to Finance of SMEs", jointly managed by the European Central Bank and the European Commission. The objective of the survey is to provide comparable, timely, and frequent data for conditions of access to credit in the European Union. The survey provides evidence on the financing conditions faced by SMEs compared with those of large firms. The first wave of the survey was held in June-July 2009, and subsequent waves took place every six months. For the first wave (first half of 2009), it is possible to identify female and male-owned enterprises on the basis of two questions: "Has the enterprises only one owner?" and "Is the only owner male or female?" For the other waves, the enterprises can be classified as owned by women or men on the basis of the question "What is the gender of the owner/director/CEO of your firm?".

Additional findings

Table IV.A3.1 presents statistics based on the first wave of the "Survey on the Access to Finance of SMEs", discussed in Chapter 26. Enterprises owned by women are significantly less likely to ask for loans from financial institutions. In the first half of 2009, differences in means between male and female-owned enterprises were not statistically significant at the 10% confidence level for three other measures of access to credit ("Finance is the most pressing problem"; "Rejection of credit application"; and "Did not apply for fear of rejection"). Enterprises owned by one woman, however, were significantly smaller than those owned by one man in the survey. The relatively small size of women-owned enterprises may explain some of the differences in loan applications.

Table IV.A3.1. **Differences in credit use and access for enterprises owned by women and men, 2009 (16 European countries)**

	Male proprietor	Female proprietor	Difference of means
No loans in last two years	0.20	0.27	−0.06*
	(0.40)	(0.44)	
Finance is the most pressing problem	0.06	0.08	−0.01
	(0.25)	(0.27)	
Rejection of credit application	0.04	0.07	−0.03
	(0.20)	(0.25)	
Did not apply for fear of rejection	0.09	0.10	−0.02
	(0.28)	(0.30)	
Less than 10 employees	0.55	0.74	−0.19**
	(0.50)	(0.44)	

Note: Standard deviations in parentheses. **: Significant at the 5% level; *: Significant at the 1% level.

Source: OECD Secretariat estimates based on data from ECB-EU Survey on the Access to Finance of SMEs, first wave.

StatLink 🔗 http://dx.doi.org/10.1787/888932677780

ANNEX IV.A4

Methodological issues and additional findings to Chapters 27 and 29

Data and comparability issues

Global Financial Inclusion Database *(Figure 27.1)*

Data on the percentage of women and men with an account in a formal financial institution (Figure 27.1) are obtained from the *Global Financial Inclusion (Global Findex) Database*. The *Global Findex Database* is a project managed by the World Bank and funded by the Bill and Melinda Gates Foundation to measure how people in 148 countries – including both high-income economies and developing economies – save, borrow, make payments, and manage risk. The survey was carried out in 2011 by Gallup Inc. as part of its Gallup World Poll, and covered over 150 000 people. The target population was the entire civilian population aged 15 and older. Interviews were conducted face-to-face in economies where telephone coverage represented less than 80% of the population and by telephone in countries with higher coverage. For detailed information on the database, see Demirguc-Kunt and Klapper (2012).

World Bank Enterprise Surveys *(Figure 27.2 and Chapter 29)*

The selected indicators on access and use of credit indicators (Figure 27.2) are computed using recent surveys on registered enterprises in Sub-Saharan countries, collected for the World Bank's Enterprise Surveys project (*www.enterprisesurveys.org*). The selection of countries is restricted to those 18 sub-Saharan countries whose surveys include detailed information on business ownership by gender. Enterprises are defined as women (men)-owned if the majority of the owners are female (male). This classification by gender is not possible for other, non-African, countries covered by the Enterprise Surveys project, since the only information available is whether any of the owners is a woman (majority women-owned enterprises and enterprises owned by a couple cannot thus be distinguished). The countries included in Figure 27.2 are: Angola (2010), Benin (2009), Botswana (2010), Burkina Faso (2009), Cameroon (2009), the Central African Republic (2011), Chad (2009), the Democratic Republic of Congo (2010), Gabon (2009), Lesotho (2009), Liberia (2009), Madagascar (2009), Malawi (2009), Mali (2010), Mauritius (2009), Niger (2009), Sierra Leone (2009) and Togo (2009).

Chapter 29 presents data on barriers to and perceived benefits from registration of informal enterprises in 10 sub-Saharan countries. The data come from a subset of the *World Bank's Enterprise Surveys* that focus on informal enterprises in urban areas of developing countries. Again, the selection of countries was driven by availability of data allowing a clear distinction between women and men-owned enterprises. For informal surveys, women (men)-owned enterprises are defined as those enterprises whose "main owner" is a woman (man). The estimates are obtained by pooling survey data from the following ten countries: Angola (2010), Botswana (2010), Burkina Faso (2009), Cameroon (2009), Cape Verde (2009), Côte d'Ivoire (2009), Democratic Republic of Congo (2010), Madagascar (2009), Mali (2010) and Mauritius (2009).

Small and micro-enterprise surveys (Figures 23.2, 27.3, 29.1 and 29.2)

Figures 23.2, 27.3, 29.1 and 29.2 are based on the micro and small enterprise surveys described in Table IV.A4.1. For all the estimates in the chapters, the samples were restricted to enterprises with up to 15 employees. Enterprises are defined as male or female-owned on the basis of the gender of the individual responding to the survey, who is the main owner, and/or the person with the most senior responsibilities in the management of the enterprise.

Table IV.A4.1. **Description of the dataset used in Chapters 27 and 29**

	Dataset
Brazil	The *Economia Informal Urbana* (Informal Urban Economy) micro-survey was conducted in 2003 by the Instituto Brasileiro de Geografia e Estatistica (Brazilian Institute of Geography and Statistics [IBGE]). The survey was representative of Brazilian urban areas and included non-agricultural small businesses with up to five employees.
Egypt	The 2003 *Micro and Small Enterprises Dataset for MENA Countries* from the Economic Research Forum (ERF). The data was collected by a country team supervised by Dr. Alia El Mahdi (principal investigator), as part of ERF's project on "Promoting Competitiveness in Micro and Small Enterprises in the MENA region". The survey provides estimates for micro and small Enterprises with less than 50 employees on the national level and for 8 governorates in the three major administrative regions (Metropolitan area, Lower Egypt and Upper Egypt).
Lebanon	The 2003 *Micro and Small Enterprises Dataset for MENA Countries* from the Economic Research Forum (ERF). The data was collected as part of ERF's project on "Promoting Competitiveness in Micro and Small Enterprises in the MENA region". The survey was nationally representative and covered non-agricultural micro and small Enterprises with less than 50 employees.
Mexico	The *Encuesta Nacional de Micronegocios* [National Microbusiness Survey (ENAMIN)] conducted in 2008 by the Instituto Nacional de Estadística y Geografía [Institute of Geography and Statistics (INEGI)]. The survey was nationally representative and covered small businesses in urban and rural areas with up to 6 employees (including the owner) in the sectors of the extractive industry, construction, services and transport, and up to 16 employees for manufacturing.
Morocco	The 2003 *Micro and Small Enterprises Dataset for MENA Countries* from the Economic Research Forum (ERF). The data was collected by a country team supervised by Dr. Bachir Hamdouch (principal investigator), as part of ERF's project on "Promoting Competitiveness in Micro and Small Enterprises in the MENA region". The survey has a nationally representative sample and comprises urban and rural businesses with up to 50 employees.
South Africa	The *FinScope SME South Africa Survey* 2010 co-ordinated by FinMark Trust and conducted by TNS Research surveys. The survey targeted a nationally representative sample and covered urban and rural businesses with up to 200 employees.

StatLink ᵐˢᴾ *http://dx.doi.org/10.1787/888932677799*

Additional findings

In the calculation of the number of employees for Figure 29.1 of Chapter 29, only paid workers are counted as employees. For Figure 23.2, the different phrasing of the question on the prime motivation for starting a business across surveys partially limits cross-country comparability. "Necessity entrepreneurs" are, however, relatively easy to identify across the different datasets, as those who answered that they started their business because they had no other option for earning an income.

Figure IV.A4.1 shows that sales and input prices are considered by both men and women as the most important business constraint.

Figure IV.A4.1. **Business owners in Brazil and Mexico consider level of prices and sales the most important business constraint**

Percentage distribution of micro-enterprise owners according to main constraint to develop their business

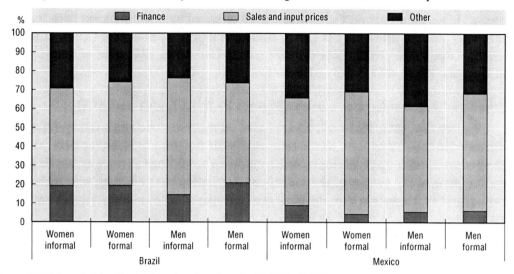

Source: OECD Secretariat estimates based on data described in Table IV.A4.1.

StatLink ⧉ http://dx.doi.org/10.1787/888932677286

Table IV.A4.2 provides descriptive statistics on the characteristics of small entrepreneurs and their businesses. As can be seen from the table, there are no wide differences in the ages of male and female owners of small enterprises. The exceptions are Lebanon and Morocco where men are older. There is no clear pattern in educational attainment, with women being on average better educated in some countries (Brazil, Lebanon, Morocco) and less educated in others (Mexico, Egypt). With the exception of Egypt, female owners spend less time running their business than men. They more often have also been running their business for a shorter length of time and they tend to employ other women.

Women have a significantly lower level of sales and sales per employee, notably in the informal sector (Table IV.A4.3). For example, female-owned enterprises in Mexico sell 63% less than male-owned ones in the informal sector, and almost 45% less in the formal sector. Evidence on the percentage differences between informal and formal sectors shows that both women and men have lower sales and productivity in the informal sector. In Brazil, Mexico, South Africa and Morocco, women tend to sell between 65% and 77% less in the informal sector than in the formal sector. Data for Lebanon are not included in the table due to sample size issues.

Table IV.A4.2. Statistics on small and micro-enterprises and their owners from surveys used in Chapter 27

	Brazil		Egypt		Lebanon		Mexico		Morocco		South Africa	
	Women	Men	Women	Men	Women	Men	Women	Men	Women	Men	Women	Men
Entrepreneur characteristics												
Age	40.59	41.13	40.40	40.35	37.66	41.88	44.48	45.02	34.60	38.61	42.39	40.93
	(12.32)	(12.60)	(15.31)	(13.18)	(12.42)	(13.03)	(13.10)	(12.73)	(9.82)	(11.81)	(13.55)	(13.55)
Number of children	0.01	0.01	1.58	2.01	1.53	2.02	–	–	1.48	1.93	–	–
	(0.15)	(0.16)	(1.56)	(1.56)	(1.40)	(1.56)			(1.16)	(1.44)		
Share of married owners	–	–	0.44	0.75	0.54	0.75	–	–	0.45	0.64	0.54	0.63
			(0.50)	(0.43)	(0.50)	(0.43)			(0.50)	(0.48)	(0.50)	(0.48)
Years in education	7.63	6.35	6.35	8.75	11.14	9.99	8.42	9.41	8.53	6.38	9.25	9.90
	(4.90)	(4.78)	(6.01)	(5.57)	(3.72)	(3.95)	(3.87)	(3.69)	(5.13)	(4.73)	(3.64)	(3.37)
Work hours per week	37.16	48.00	60.79	60.85	66.20	70.67	36.40	45.67	60.65	68.84	59.46	63.75
	(54.11)	(48.13)	(19.39)	(20.68)	(18.88)	(22.51)	(24.43)	(24.82)	(22.67)	(19.83)	(28.98)	(35.81)
Years of tenure in business	7.65	9.76	6.93	9.68	7.82	11.67	8.72	12.76	6.82	9.69	6.09	5.93
	(8.93)	(9.28)	(8.22)	(9.87)	(7.94)	(10.75)	(10.17)	(11.38)	(26.32)	(10.36)	(7.31)	(7.14)
Entreprise characteristics												
Number of employees	0.07	0.11	0.88	1.13	1.25	1.30	0.25	0.84	1.37	1.85	0.61	1.26
	(0.40)	(0.50)	(1.29)	(1.41)	(2.06)	(1.93)	(0.81)	(1.65)	(1.73)	(2.23)	(1.60)	(2.35)
Share of female employees	0.61	0.33	–	–	–	–	0.71	0.24	–	–	0.68	0.27
	(0.44)	(0.42)					(0.40)	(0.36)			(0.40)	(0.37)
Share of informal enterprises	0.94	0.90	0.32	0.22	0.44	0.51	0.71	0.62	0.52	0.43	0.84	0.74
	(0.24)	(0.30)	(0.47)	(0.42)	(0.50)	(0.50)	(0.45)	(0.49)	(0.50)	(0.50)	(0.37)	(0.44)
Sales per employee (USD 2000)	288.51	451.44	119.69	158.88	1131.49	1009.10	356.08	661.96	427.71	667.16	559.91	669.82
	(380.93)	(508.01)	(125.56)	(184.26)	(1458.77)	(1326.52)	(516.97)	(763.67)	(496.10)	(805.41)	(763.67)	(991.60)
Assets (USD 2000)	1 268.63	2 513.73	2 657.51	3 393.71	25 041.89	22 915.28	1 537.24	3 961.71	9 916.68	12 919.97	–	–
	(2 817.43)	(4 058.89)	(4 634.09)	(5 071.40)	(35 113.59)	(33 265.34)	(3 915.37)	(6 267.17)	(17 901.52)	(21 026.31)		

Note: Sample means, standard deviations in parentheses.
Source: OECD Secretariat estimates based on data described in Table IV.A4.1.

StatLink ⊟▤ᐧ *http://dx.doi.org/10.1787/888932677818*

Table IV.A4.3. **Differences in sales and sales per employee across gender and formality status**

Percentages

	Sales				Sales per employees			
	Difference by gender of the owner (female relative to male)		Difference by formality status (informal relative to formal)		Difference by gender of the owner (female relative to male)		Difference by formality status (informal relative to formal)	
	Within the informal sector	Within the formal sector	Among female owners	Among male owners	Within the informal sector	Within the formal sector	Among female owners	Among male owners
Brazil	−36.3	−11.1	−77.0	−67.8	−35.6	−17.0	−69.6	−60.8
Egypt	−40.2	−23.7	−46.9	−32.4	−24.5	−22.6	−23.1	−21.1
Morocco	−52.0	−29.4	−74.1	−61.8	−44.9	−25.5	−57.1	−42.0
Mexico	−63.0	−44.3	−65.0	−47.3	−51.6	−31.3	−52.2	−32.1
South Africa	−30.3	−16.2	−67.5	−60.9	−14.4	−4.4	−33.8	−26.0

Source: OECD Secretariat estimates based on data described in Table IV.A4.1.

StatLink ᴹᔆᴾ *http://dx.doi.org/10.1787/888932677837*

ANNEX IV.A5

Methodological issues and additional findings to Chapter 28

Data and comparability issues

Data on new firms in the United States and Germany

Chapter 28 provides evidence on gender differences in innovation investment and outcomes based on analysis of two panel datasets for the United States and Germany: the Kauffman Firm Survey (KFS) for the United States and the KfW-ZEW Start-up Panel for Germany.

The KFS is a large longitudinal study of new businesses in the United States. The panel of businesses was created using a random sample from *Dun & Bradstreet's (D & B) Database* list of new businesses started in 2004. The KFS oversampled "innovative" businesses on the basis of information on the intensity of research and development employment in the businesses' primary industries. The KFS excluded D & B records for businesses that were wholly owned subsidiaries of existing businesses, businesses inherited from someone else, and not-for-profit organisations. Data from the first wave (2004) are used to identify the owners-founders of the enterprises and to construct the variables related to their characteristics (gender, experience, etc.).

The KfW/ZEW Start-up Panel is drawn from the database of Creditreform, the largest credit rating agency in Germany. Three stratification criteria are applied in order to construct the sample of the start-up panel: year when the firm was formed, its sector of business, and whether or not it has been promoted by KfW Bankengruppe. Each year, a random sample of the firms created in the three years prior to the year of the survey is drawn. The estimates in Chapter 28 are based on data from the public use file from the first year of the survey in 2008. They result from the research project "The innovative behaviour of women-led young firms", submitted by Mario Piacentini in August 2011 and approved by the Centre for European Economic Research (ZEW) in September 2011.

Enterprises founded by men and women are defined in a comparable way across the two datasets. Women-founded businesses are those which have been founded by one woman or by an exclusively female founding team. KFS considers a founding team as the ten main owners of the business in the year it was created. Enterprises founded or owned by mixed teams are excluded. The variables relating to founder/owner characteristics are calculated as averages for the individual members of the founding team.

Additional findings

Chapter 28 discusses the importance of owners' entrepreneurial experience in explaining gender differences in innovation investment and outcomes. Table IV.A5.1 provides detailed statistics by gender for the full sample of new enterprises in the surveys conducted in the United States and Germany ("All") and for the sample of enterprises where at least one founder/owner had previous entrepreneurial experience prior to start-up ("Previously entrepreneur").

Table IV.A5.1. **Enterprises founded by women with previous entrepreneurial experience are more likely to innovate and invest in R&D**

Percentages

	United States				Germany			
	All		Previously entrepreneur		All		Previously entrepreneur	
	Women	Men	Women	Men	Women	Men	Women	Men
Product innovation	20	22	24	25	32	40	38	46
	(0.40)*	(0.42)*	(0.43)	(0.44)	(0.47)**	(0.49)**	(0.49)**	(0.50)**
Process innovation	15	18	17	21	21	28	28	36
	(0.36)*	(0.39)*	(0.38)	(0.41)	(0.41)**	(0.45)**	(0.45)**	(0.48)**
R&D	11	18	13	20	11	20	18	31
	(0.31)**	(0.38)**	(0.33)*	(0.40)*	(0.32)**	(0.40)**	(0.38)**	(0.46)**

Note: Sample means for binary (0/1) variables, standard deviation in parentheses. **: Difference in means for male-founded and female-founded statistically significant at 5%; *: Difference in means statistically significant at 10% level.

Source: OECD Secretariat estimates based on *Kauffman Firm Survey* and KfW-ZEW Start-up Panel.

StatLink ᴍᴇᴅ http://dx.doi.org/10.1787/888932677856

Table IV.A5.2 tests whether gender differences in product and process innovation and in the likelihood of expenditure on Research and Development (R&D) are statistically significant when other characteristics of both the founding team and the firms are controlled for. Additional variables are:

● Whether at least one founder/owner had previous experience as the owner of a business prior to start-up ("Previously entrepreneur").

● The founding members' average number of years of experience in the sector in which the firm operates in the year of start-up ("Experience in industry").

● The share of founders who have completed tertiary education ("Tertiary educated").

● Whether all the founders were born in the country ("Native born").

● The number of employees at the time of start-up ("Employees at start").

● Whether the enterprise operates in a high-technology industry ("High technology").

When these additional variables are controlled for, new firms in the United States no longer show significant gender differences in innovation outcomes. However, there are still gender-related differences when it comes to the probability of undertaking expenditure in R&D. Companies started up by women in Germany reveal fewer innovation outcomes and less expenditure. These gender-related disparities remain significant even when other differences between men and women-founded enterprises are controlled for.

Table IV.A5.2. **The innovation gap by gender in the United States disappears when controlling for other characteristics of firms and founders**
Marginal effects coefficients from probit models

	United States			Germany		
	Product innovation	Process innovation	R&D	Product innovation	Process innovation	R&D
	(1)	(2)	(3)	(4)	(5)	(6)
Founded by women	0.002	−0.01	−0.040**	−0.053**	−0.048**	−0.043***
	(0.022)	(0.02)	(0.019)	(0.024)	(0.022)	(0.015)
Previously entrepreneur	0.054***	0.054***	0.022	0.075***	0.092***	0.120***
	(0.017)	(0.016)	(0.015)	(0.019)	(0.017)	(0.013)
Experience in industry	−0.001	0.001	0.001	−0.037*	−0.026	−0.016
	(0.001)	(0.001)	(0.001)	(0.02)	(0.018)	(0.013)
Tertiary educated	0.042**	−0.005	0.071***	0.078***	0.044***	0.125***
	(0.018)	(0.017)	(0.016)	(0.018)	(0.016)	(0.012)
Native born	−0.050*	−0.04	−0.052**	−0.023	0.005	−0.029
	(0.027)	(0.025)	(0.025)	(0.03)	(0.027)	(0.02)
Employees at start	0.006***	0.007***	0.001	0.020***	0.017***	0.008***
	(0.002)	(0.002)	(0.002)	(0.005)	(0.004)	(0.003)
High technology	0.119***	0.068***	0.182***	0.079***	0.085***	0.123***
	(0.027)	(0.025)	(0.027)	(0.018)	(0.016)	(0.012)
Pseudo R^2	0.024	0.02	0.0591	0.03	0.02	0.1
Observations	2 381	2 376	2 336	3 426	3 449	4 819

Note: Robust standard errors in parentheses. ***: $p < 0.01$; **: $p < 0.05$; *: $p < 0.01$.
Source: OECD Secretariat estimates based on *Kauffman Firm Survey* data (United States) and KfW Start-up Panel (Germany).
StatLink ᵐˢ⅃ http://dx.doi.org/10.1787/888932677875

Table IV.A5.3 uses data from the *Kauffman Firm Survey*. It shows that in the United States (as across European countries) gender differences in innovation outcomes tend to disappear when less capital- and research-intensive forms of innovation are considered. The only significant differences between men and women-founded enterprises relate to expenditure in design, software, and databases.

Table IV.A5.3. **Differences in expenditure on different forms of innovation by new enterprises founded by women and men in the United States**

	Men founded	Women founded
Expenditure in design of new products and services	0.20	0.17
	(0.40)*	(0.37)*
Expenditure in software and databases	0.26	0.21
	(0.44)*	(0.40)*
Expenditure in brand development (advertising and marketing)	0.31	0.29
	(0.46)	(0.46)
Expenditure on organisational development	0.07	0.06
	(0.25)	(0.24)
Expenditure on training of employees	0.20	0.20
	(0.40)	(0.40)

Note: Binary (1/0) variables, equal to 1 if positive expenditure. Sample means for enterprises where all the owners were men at the start-up date (men founded) and where all the owners were women (women founded). Standard deviation in parentheses.
Source: OECD Secretariat estimates based on *Kauffman Firm Survey* 2009 data.
StatLink ᵐˢ⅃ http://dx.doi.org/10.1787/888932677894

References

Acs, Z.J. and D.B. Audretsch (1990), "The Determinants of Small-Firm Growth in US Manufacturing", *Applied Economics*, Vol. 22, No. 2, pp. 143-153.

Alesina, A.F., F. Lotti and P.E. Mistrulli (2008), "Do Women Pay More for Credit? Evidence from Italy", *NBER Working Paper*, No. 14202, National Bureau of Economic Research, Inc., Cambridge, United States.

Banerjee, A. and E. Duflo (2004), "Do Firms Want to Borrow More? Testing Credit Constraints Using a Directed Lending Program", *CEPR Discussion Paper*, No. 4681, London.

Bauer, K. (2011), "Training Women for Success: An Evaluation of Entrepreneurship Training Programs in Vermont, USA", *Journal of Entrepreneurship Education*, Vol. 14, pp. 1-24.

Becker-Blease, J.R. and J.E. Sohl (2007), "Do Women-owned Businesses Have Equal Access to Angel Capital?", *Journal of Business Venturing*, Vol. 22, pp. 503-521.

Brush, C.G., P.G. Greene, D.J. Kelley and Y. Litovsky (2011), *2010 Women's Report*, Global Entrepreneurship Monitor Executive Report, Babson College, United States.

Cohoon, J., V. Wadhwa and L. Mitchell (2010), "The Anatomy of an Entrepreneur: Are Successful Women Entrepreneurs Different from Men?", Ewing Marion Kauffman Foundation, United States.

Cole, R.A. and H. Mehran (2009), "Gender and the Availability of Credit to Privately Held Firms: Evidence from the Surveys of Small Business Finances", *Federal Reserve Bank of New York Staff Report*, No. 383, August.

Coleman S. and A.M. Robb (2012), *A Rising Tide, Financing Strategies for Women-owned Firms*, Stanford University Press, Stanford, United States.

Cook, L.D. and C. Kongcharoen (2010), "The Idea Gap in Pink and Black", *NBER Working Paper*, No. 16331, Cambridge, United States.

Croson, R. and U. Gneezy (2009), "Gender Differences in Preferences", *Journal of Economic Literature*, Vol. 47, No. 2, pp. 448-474.

De Ferranti, D. and A.J. Ody (2007), "Beyond Microfinance: Getting Capital to Small and Medium Enterprises to Fuel Faster Development", *Brookings Policy Brief Series*, No. 159, The Brookings Institution, Washington, DC.

De Mel, S., D. McKenzie and C. Woodruff (2009a), "Are Women More Credit Constrained? Experimental Evidence on Gender and Microenterprise Returns", *American Economic Journal: Applied Economics*, Vol. 1, No. 3, pp. 1-32.

De Mel, S., D. McKenzie and C. Woodruff (2009b), "Innovative Firms or Innovative Owners? Determinants of Innovation in Micro, Small, and Medium Enterprises", *IZA Discussion Paper*, No. 3962, Bonn.

Demirguc-Kunt, A. and L. Klapper (2012), "Measuring Financial Inclusion: The Global Findex Database", *World Bank Policy Research Paper*, No. 6025, Washington, DC.

Ding, W., F. Murray and T.E. Stuart (2006). "Gender Differences in Patenting in the Academic Life Sciences", *Science*, Vol. 313, No. 5787, pp. 665-667.

Dupas, P. and J. Robinson (2009), "Savings Constraints and Microenterprise Development: Evidence from a Field Experiment in Kenya", *NBER Working Paper*, No. 14693, Cambridge, United States.

Ellis, A., J. Cutura, N. Dione, I. Gillson, C. Manuel and J. Thongori (2007), *Gender and Economic Growth in Kenya: Unleashing the Power of Women*, World Bank, Washington, DC.

European Commission (2008), *Evaluation on Policy: Promotion of Women Innovators and Entrepreneurship – Final Report*, GHK-Technopolis, Brussels, available at *http://ec.europa.eu/enterprise/newsroom/cf/_getdocument.cfm?doc_id=3815/*, accessed 7 February 2012.

European Commission (2009), *Flash Eurobarometer: Entrepreneurship in the EU and beyond*, European Commission, Brussels.

European Commission (2012), "Entrepreneurship Education at School in Europe: National Strategies, Curricula and Learning Outcomes", Education, Audiovisual and Culture Executive Agency (EACEA), Eurydice and Policy Support, Brussels.

Eurostat (2008), "Statistics Explained: Factors of Business Success Survey", Luxembourg, available at *http://epp.eurostat.ec.europa.eu/statistics_explained/index.php/Factors_of_business_success*, accessed 27 January 2012.

Eurostat (2011), "Statistics Explained: Access to Finance Statistics", Luxembourg, available at *http://epp.eurostat.ec.europa.eu/statistics_explained/index.php/Access_to_finance_statistics*, accessed 27 January 2012.

Fafchamps, M., D. McKenzie, S.R. Quinn and C. Woodruff (2011), "When Is Capital Enough to Get Female Microenterprises Growing? Evidence from a Randomized Experiment in Ghana", *NBER Working Paper*, No. 17207, Cambridge, United States.

Fairlie, R.W. and A.M. Robb (2009), "Gender Differences in Business Performance: Evidence from the Characteristics of Business Owners Survey", *Small Business Economics*, Vol. 33, No. 4, pp. 375-395.

Farrell, D. (2004), "The Hidden Dangers of the Informal Economy", *McKinsey Quarterly*, No. 3, pp. 26-37.

Frietsch, R., I. Haller, M.F. Vrohlings and H. Grupp (2009), "Gender-specific Patterns in Patenting and Publishing", *Research Policy*, Vol. 38, No. 4, pp. 590-599.

Gambardella, A. (2012), *Final Report the Inventor Survey in Europe, the US, and Japan*, Report for the EU INNOS&T PROJECT, *http://bcmmnty-qp.unibocconi.it/QuickPlace/innovativest/Main.nsf/h_Toc/6F62C34308AE1B45C1257460004519ED/?OpenDocument*, accessed 7 February 2012.

Gatewood, E.J., C.G. Brush, N.M. Carter, P.G. Greene and M.M. Hart (2009), "Diana: A Symbol of Women Entrepreneurs' Hunt for Knowledge, Money, and the Rewards of Entrepreneurship", *Small Business Economics*, Vol. 32, No. 2, pp. 129-144.

Gaule, P. and M. Piacentini (2012), "Gender, Social Networks and Access to Venture Capital", unpublished manuscript.

Gompers, P. and J. Lerner (2003), "Short-Term America Revisited? Boom and Bust in the Venture Capital Industry and the Impact on Innovation", *NBER Chapters*, in A. Jaffe, J. Lerner and S. Stern (eds.), *Innovation Policy and the Economy*, Vol. 3, pp. 1-28, National Bureau of Economic Research, Inc., Cambridge, United States.

Gottschalk, S. and M. Niefert (2011), "Gender Differences in Business Success of German Start-up Firms", *ZEW Discussion Paper*, No. 11-019, Mannheim.

Gurley-Calvez, T., K. Harper and A. Biehl (2009), "Self-Employed Women and Time Use", *Small Business Administration*, Office of Advocacy, available at *http://archive.sba.gov/advo/research/rs341tot.pdf*.

IFC (2011), "Strengthening Access to Finance for Women-Owned SMEs in Developing Countries", Global Partnership for Financial Inclusion and International Finance Corporation, available at *www1.ifc.org/wps/wcm/connect/a4774a004a3f66539f0f9f8969adcc27/G20_Women_Report.pdf?MOD=AJPERES*.

Italian Chamber of Commerce – Unioncamere (2010), "Dati dell'Osservatorio sull'Imprenditoria Femminile", available at *www.unioncamere.gov.it/P43K6300/imprenditoria-femminile.htm*, accessed 24 January 2012.

Jung, O. (2010), "Women Entrepreneurs", *Small Business Financing Profiles*, Industry Canada, Small Business and Tourism Branch, Ottawa.

Karlan, D. and J. Morduch (2009), "Access to Finance", in D. Rodrik and M. Rosenzweig (eds.), *Handbook of Development Economics*, Elsevier, Amsterdam.

Klapper, L. (2012), "Two Persistent Divides in Financial Inclusion: Gender and Rural", CGAP, Consultative Group to Assist the Poor, available at *http://microfinance.cgap.org/2012/04/25/two-persistent-divides-in-financial-inclusion-gender-and-rural/*.

Klein, J. and C. Wayman (2008), "Encouraging Entrepreneurship: A Microenterprise Development Policy Agenda", Community Investments, pp. 15-30, available at *www.frbsf.org/publications/community/investments/0812/klein_wayman.pdf*, accessed 30 January 2012.

La Porta, R. and A. Shleifer (2008), "The Unofficial Economy and Economic Development", *NBER Working Paper*, No. 14520, Cambridge, United States.

Maloney, W.F., P. Fajnzylber and G. Montes-Rojas (2011), "Does Formality Improve Micro-firm Performance? Evidence from the Brazilian SIMPLES Program", *Journal of Development Economics*, Elsevier, Vol. 94, No. 2, pp. 262-276.

McKenzie, D.J. and C. Woodruff (2006), "Do Entry Costs Provide an Empirical Basis for Poverty Traps? Evidence from Mexican Microenterprises", *Economic Development and Cultural Change*, Vol. 55, No. 1, pp. 3-42.

McKenzie, D., S. De Mel and C. Woodruff (2012), "The Demand for, and Consequences of, Formalization Among Informal Firms in Sri Lanka", *Policy Research Working Paper Series*, No. 5991, World Bank, Washington, DC.

Muravyev, A., D. Schafer and O. Talavera (2007), "Entrepreneurs' Gender and Financial Constraints: Evidence from International Data", *Discussion Paper*, No. 706, German Institute of Economic Research, Berlin.

Murray, F. and L. Graham (2007), "Buying Science and Selling Science: Gender Stratification in Commercial Science", *Industrial and Corporate Change Special Issue on Technology Transfer*, Vol. 16, No. 4, pp. 657-689.

Novakova, J. (2006), *Promoting Women's Entrepreneurship in Technology Sectors: Good Practice Examples from the EU and Other Countries*, Report for the project "Reducing Causes of Professional Segregation", available at *www.athenaswan.org.uk/downloads/research/Latvia6.pdf*, accessed 9 February 2012.

Observatorio Empresas (2009), "Encuesta longitudinal de empresas: resultados seleccionados por género", available at *www.wim-network.org/2010/09/chile-encuesta-longitudinal-de-empresas-resultados-seleccionados-por-genero/*, accessed 3 February 2012.

OECD (2005), *Oslo Manual: Guidelines for Collecting and Interpreting Innovation Data*, 3rd Edition, OECD Publishing, Paris, DOI: *http://dx.doi.org/10.1787/9789264013100-en*.

OECD (2009a), "The Impact of the Global Crisis on SME and Entrepreneurship Financing and Policy Responses", OECD Publishing, Paris, available at *www.oecd.org/dataoecd/40/34/43183090.pdf*, accessed 3 February 2012.

OECD (2009b), "Is Informal Normal? Towards More and Better Jobs in Developing Countries", *Development Centre Studies*, OECD Publishing, Paris, DOI: *http://dx.doi.org/10.1787/9789264059245-en*.

OECD (2010), *The OECD Innovation Strategy: Getting a Head Start on Tomorrow*, OECD Publishing, Paris.

OECD (2011a), "Aid in Support of Women's Economic Empowerment", OECD Publishing, Paris, available at *www.oecd.org/investment/aidstatistics/46864237.pdf*.

OECD (2011b), *Financing High Growth Firms: The Role of Angel Investors*, OECD Publishing, Paris, DOI: *http://dx.doi.org/10.1787/9789264118782-en*.

OECD (2012a), *Entrepreneurship at a Glance 2012*, OECD Publishing, Paris, DOI: *http://dx.doi.org/10.1787/entrepreneur_aag-2012-en*.

OECD (2012b), *Women in Business: Policies to Support Women's Entrepreneurship in the Middle East and North Africa*, OECD Publishing, Paris, DOI: *http://dx.doi.org/10.1787/9789264179073-en*.

Page, S.E. (2008), "The Difference: How the Power of Diversity Creates Better Groups, Firms, Schools, and Societies", Princeton University Press, United States, out of print.

Robb, A. and J. Watson (2010), "Comparing the Performance of Female- and Male-Controlled SMEs: Evidence from Australia and the US", *Frontiers of Entrepreneurship Research*, Vol. 30, No. 8, pp. 1-12.

RSM McGladrey (2008), "2007 Survey of Women Business Owners", available at *http://mcgladrey.com/Knowledge-Center/Downloads/WBOSurvey2007-1/wbosurvey2007.pdf*, accessed 30 January 2012.

Sabarwal, S. and K. Terrell (2008), "Does Gender Matter for Firm Performance? Evidence from Eastern Europe and Central Asia", *IZA Discussion Paper*, No. 3758, Bonn.

Shinnar, R., M. Pruett and B. Toney (2009), "Entrepreneurship Education: Attitudes Across Campus", *Journal of Education for Business*, Vol. 84, No. 3, pp. 151-158.

Small Business Service (2005), *Myths Surrounding Starting and Running a Business*, DTI Small Business Service, London.

Spring, A. (2009), "African Women in the Entrepreneurial Landscape: Reconsidering the Formal and Informal Sectors", *Journal of African Business*, Vol. 10, No. 1, pp. 11-30.

Stevenson, L. (2010), *Private Sector and Enterprise Development: Fostering Growth in the Middle East and North Africa*, Edgar Elgar and International Development Research Centre (IDRC), Ottawa.

Stevenson, L. (2011), "The Role of Women's Entrepreneurship in the Middle East and North Africa Labour Market", High-Level Consultation of the MENA-OECD Initiative on Governance and Investment for Development, 16 May 2011, Paris.

Stuart, T.E. and O. Sorenson (2010), "Strategic Networks and Entrepreneurial Ventures", *Strategic Entrepreneurship Journal*, Vol. 1, No. 3-4, pp. 211-227.

Taylor, M.P. (2001), "Self-employment and Windfall Gains in Britain: Evidence from Panel Data", *Economica*, Vol. 68, No. 272, pp. 539-565.

UNCTAD (2011), "Women's Entrepreneurship and Innovation: A Comparative Perspective", United Nations, Geneva.

United Nations (2008), "Making the Law Work for Everyone", Vol. 1, *Report of the Commission on Legal Empowerment of the Poor*, UNDP, New York.

US Census (2009), "Results from the 2007 Survey of Business Owners", available at *www.census.gov/econ/sbo/*, accessed 30 January 2012.

US Department of Commerce (2010), "Women-owned Businesses in the 21st Century", Department of Commerce, Washington, DC.

USPTO (2009), "US Patents – Custom Data Extracts", United States Patent and Trademark Office, United States.

White House Council (2012), "Keeping America's Women Moving Forward: The Key to an Economy Built to Last", White House Council on Women and Girls, Washington, DC, April.

General note on figures and tables

OECD country ISO codes

Australia	AUS	Japan	JPN
Austria	AUT	Korea	KOR
Belgium	BEL	Luxembourg	LUX
Canada	CAN	Mexico	MEX
Chile	CHL	Netherlands	NLD
Czech Republic	CZE	New Zealand	NZL
Denmark	DNK	Norway	NOR
Estonia	EST	Poland	POL
Finland	FIN	Portugal	PRT
France	FRA	Slovak Republic	SVK
Germany	DEU	Slovenia	SVN
Greece	GRC	Spain	ESP
Hungary	HUN	Sweden	SWE
Iceland	ISL	Switzerland	CHE
Ireland	IRL	Turkey	TUR
Israel	ISR	United Kingdom	GBR
Italy	ITA	United States	USA

Unless otherwise stated, the OECD figure refers to the unweighted average for OECD countries for which data are available.

Other major economy country ISO codes

Brazil	BRA	Indonesia	IDN
China	CHN	Russian Federation	RUS
India	IND	South Africa	ZAF

Conventional signs

.. Not available.

Notes

Note on Israel

The statistical data for Israel are supplied by and under the responsibility of the relevant Israeli authorities. The use of such data by the OECD is without prejudice to the status of the Golan Heights, East Jerusalem and Israeli settlements in the West Bank under the terms of international law.

Note on Cyprus

Footnote by Turkey: The information in this document with reference to "Cyprus" relates to the southern part of the Island. There is no single authority representing both Turkish and Greek Cypriot people on the Island. Turkey recognises the Turkish Republic of Northern Cyprus (TRNC). Until a lasting and equitable solution is found within the context of United Nations, Turkey shall preserve its position concerning the "Cyprus issue".

Footnote by all the European Union Member States of the OECD and the European Commission: The Republic of Cyprus is recognised by all members of the United Nations with the exception of Turkey. The information in this document relates to the area under the effective control of the Government of the Republic of Cyprus.

References

Adams, R.B. and D. Ferreira (2007), "A Theory of Friendly Boards", *Journal of Finance*, Vol. 62, No. 1, pp. 217-250.

Auriol, L. (2010), "Careers of Doctorate Holders: Employment and Mobility Patterns", *OECD Science, Technology and Industry Working Paper*, No. 2010/04, OECD Publishing, Paris, DOI: *http://dx.doi.org/10.1787/5kmh8phxvvf5-en*.

Australian Public Service Commission (2011), *State of the Service 2010-11*, available at *www.apsc.gov.au/stateoftheservice/1011/report.pdf*.

Beck, T., A. Demirgüç-Kunt and R. Levine (2007), "Finance, Inequality and the Poor", *Journal of Economic Growth*, Vol. 12, No. 1, Springer, pp. 27-49.

Becker, G. (1985), "Human Capital, Effort and the Sexual Division of Labor", *Journal of Labor Economics*, Vol. 3, No. 1, Part 2, pp. S33-S58.

Breen, R. and L.P. Cooke (2005), "The Persistence of the Gendered Division of Domestic Labour", *European Sociological Review*, Vol. 21, No. 1, pp. 43-57.

Bremer, J. (2009), *Position Paper: Introducing Gender Analysis into Regulatory Frameworks*, Report prepared for the first meeting of the Gender Focus Group of the MENA-OECD Governance Programme on "Addressing Gender in Public Management", available at *www.oecd.org/dataoecd/54/50/43088074.pdf*.

Buddelmeyer, H., G. Mourre and M. Ward (2008), "Why Europeans Work Part-time? A Cross-country Panel Analysis", in W. Polachek and K. Tatsiramos (eds.), *Work, Earnings and Other Aspects of the Employment Relation, Research in Labor Economics*, Vol. 28, Emerald Group Publishing Limited, pp. 81-139.

Catalyst (2007), *The Bottom Line: Corporate Performance and Women's Representation on Boards*, United States, available at *www.catalyst.org/file/139/bottom%20line%202.pdf*.

Centre for State and Local Government Excellence (2011), "Comparing Compensation: State-Local versus Private Sector Workers", available at *http://slge.org/wp-content/uploads/2011/12/BC-brief_Comparing-Compensation_12-082.pdf*.

Chen, M. and G. Raveendran (2012), "Urban Employment in India: Recent Trends and Patterns", Paper for the *Workshop on Growth and Inclusion: Theoretical and Applied Perspectives*, 13 January, Delhi.

D'Souza, A. (2010), "Moving Toward Decent Work for Domestic Workers: An Overview if the ILO's Work", *Working Paper*, No. 2, Bureau for Gender Equality, ILO, Geneva.

Da Costa, R., J.R. de Laiglesia, E. Martinez and A. Melguizo (2011), "The Economy of the Possible: Pensions and Informality in Latin America", *OECD Development Centre Working Paper*, No. 295, OECD Publishing, Paris, DOI: *http://dx.doi.org/10.1787/5kgj0vdgrk8v-en*.

Dee, T.S. (2007), "Teachers and the Gender Gap in Student Achievement", *Journal of Human Resources*, Vol. XLII, No. 3, pp. 528-554.

Deloitte (2011), *The Gender Dividend: Making the Business Case for Investing in Women*, available at *www.deloitte.com/investinginwomen#*.

Département Fédéral des Finances et Office Fédéral du Personnel (2009), "LOGIB pour l'Administration Fédérale", Bureau International de l'Égalité entre Femmes et Hommes, Suisse, *www.ebg.admin.ch/dienstleistungen/00017/index.html?lang=fr*.

Département Fédéral des Finances et Office Fédéral du Personnel (2011), *Valeurs cibles et indicateurs stratégiques pour la gestion du personnel*, Stratégie concernant le personnel de l'administration fédérale pour les années 2011-15, Suisse.

Duryea, S., G. Marquez, C. Pagés, S. Scarpetta and C. Reinhart (2006), "For Better or for Worse? Job and Earnings Mobility in Nine Middle and Low-Income Countries", Brookings Trade Forum, Global Labour Markets, The Brookings Institution, Washington, DC, pp. 187-209.

Edward, M. and M. Kremer (2004), "Worms: Indentifying Impacts on Education and Health in the Presence of Treatment Externalities", *Econometrica*, Vol. 72, No. 1, pp. 159-217.

EUROFOUND (2010), *Addressing the Gender Pay Gap: Government and Social Partners Actions*, European Foundation for the Improvement of Living and Working Conditions, available at *www.eurofound.europa.eu/pubdocs/2010/18/en/2/EF1018EN.pdf*.

EZI (2010), *European Board Diversity Analysis 2010: Is It Getting Easier to Find Women on European Boards?*, Egon Zehnder International.

Finnie, R. and M. Frenette (2003), "Earning Differences by Major Field of Study: Evidence from Three Cohorts of Recent Canadian Graduates", *Economics of Education Review*, Vol. 22, No. 2, pp. 179-192.

German's Federal Act on Equal Opportunities between Women and Men in the Federal Administration and the Courts of the Federation available online at *www.gesetze-im-internet.de/bgleig/index.html*.

Government of Canada (2011), *Eighteenth Annual Report of the Prime Minister on the Public Service of Canada*, Privy Council Office Canada, available at *www.clerk.gc.ca/local_grfx/docs/18rpt-eng.pdf*.

Government of New South Wales (2008), *Making the Public Sector Work Better for Women 2008-12*, available at *www.dpc.nsw.gov.au/__data/assets/pdf_file/0005/30299/Making_the_public_sector_work_better_for_women_-_Strategy_2008-2012.pdf*.

Hemerijck, A., B. Unger and J. Visser (2000), "How Small Countries Negotiate Twenty-five Years of Policy Adjustment in Austria, the Netherlands and Belgium", in F. Scharpf and J. Visser (eds.), *Welfare and Work in the Open Economy*, Vol. II, Oxford University Press, Oxford, United States, pp. 176-263.

IIPS (2007), "National Family Health Survey 2005-06 India", Vol. I, International Institute for Population Sciences, Mumbai, India.

ILO and OECD (2011), "Questionnaire on Statistics of the Public Sector Employment. and International Labour Organization", *Labour Statistics Database*, available online at *http://laborsta.ilo.org/*.

INSEE (2005), "Secteur public, secteur privé : Quelques éléments de comparaison salariales", Institut national de la statistique et des études économiques, Paris, available at *www.insee.fr/fr/ffc/docs_ffc/salfra05b.pdf*.

INSEE (2011), "Fiches thématiques : Synthèse des actifs occupés", *Emploi et Salaires*, Edition 2011, Institut national de la statistique et des études économiques, Paris, available at *www.insee.fr/fr/ffc/docs_ffc/ref/empsal11h.pdf*.

IPU (2006), *The Role of Parliamentary Committees in Mainstreaming Gender and Promoting the Status of Women*, Inter-Parliamentary Union, Geneva, available at *www.ipu.org/pdf/publications/wmn_seminar06_en.pdf*.

Jacob, M., C. Kleinert and M. Kuehhirt (2009), "Trends in Gender Disparities at the School to Work Transition in Germany", Mannheimer Zentrum fuer Europaeische Sozialforschung (MZES), Mannheim.

Kanazawa, S. (2005), "Is Discrimination Necessary to Explain the Sex Gap in Earnings?", Journal of Economic Psychology, Vol. 26, No. 2, pp. 269-287.

Kay, R., B. Günterberg, M. Holz and H.J. Wolter (2003), "Female Entrepreneurs in Germany", Expert opinion on behalf of the Federal Ministry of Economics and Labour presented by the Institut für Mittelstandsforschung, Bonn, 31 March.

Kremer, M., M. Edward and R. Thomton (2009), "Incentive to Learn", *Review of Economics and Statistics*, Vol. 91, No. 3, pp. 437-456.

Lee, K.W. and K. Cho (2005), "Female Labour Force Participation During Economic Crisis in Argentina and the Republic of Korea", *International Labour Review*, Vol. 144, No. 4.

Mavriplis, C., R. Heller, C. Beil, K. Dam, N. Yassinskaya, M. Shaw and C. Sorensen (2010), "Mind the Gap: Women in STEM Career Breaks", *Journal of Technology Management and Innovation 2010*, Vol. 5, No. 1, pp. 140-151.

Morrison, A. and S. Sabarwal (2008), "The Economic Participation of Adolescent Girls and Young Women: Why does it Matter?", The Adolescent Girls Initiative Note, World Bank, Washington, DC.

Nordman, C.J. and L. Pasquier-Doumer (2011), "Transitions and Occupational Changes in a West African Urban Labour Market: The Role of Social Network", CSAE 25th Anniversary Conference 2011 "Economic Development in Africa", 20-22 May 2011, Oxford, United Kingdom.

Norwegian Ministry of Children and Equality (2009), *Gender Equality 2009? Objectives, Strategies and Measures for Ensuring Gender Equality*, Oslo, available at *www.regjeringen.no/upload/BLD/Rapporter/2008/BLD_likestillingsrapport_eng_.pdf*.

O'Reilly, J. and C. Fagan (1998), "Part-Time Prospects: An International Comparison of Part-Time Work in Europe, North America and the Pacific Rim", Routledge, London.

OECD (2006), *Live Longer, Work Longer*, OECD Publishing, Paris, DOI: *http://dx.doi.org/10.1787/9789264035881-en*.

OECD (2011a), *OECD Employment Outlook*, OECD Publishing, Paris.

OECD (2011b), *Divided We Stand: Why Inequality Keeps Rising*, OECD Publishing, Paris, DOI: *http://dx.doi.org/10.1787/9789264119536-en*.

Office of the Auditor General of Canada (2009), *Spring Report of the Auditor General of Canada*, Ontario, Canada, available at *www.oag-bvg.gc.ca/internet/English/parl_oag_200905_01_e_32514.html#hd5e*.

Portegijs, W. (2008), "Opvattingen over arbeidsduur van vrouwen", in W. Portegijs and S. Keuzenkamp (eds.), *Nederland deeltijdland, Vrouwen en deeltijdwerk*, Sociaal Cultureel Planbureau, Gravenhage.

Premier and Cabinet Office for Women's Policy of New South Wales, Australia (2011), "Key Facts and Trends in Part-time Work: NSW Women", New South Wales, Australia, available at *www.dpc.nsw.gov.au/__data/assets/pdf_file/0019/115255/women_parttime.pdf*.

Privy Council Office Canada (2011), *Eighteenth Annual Report of the Prime Minister on the Public Service of Canada*, Canada, available at *www.clerk.gc.ca/local_grfx/docs/18rpt%1eeng.pdf*.

Puerto, O.S. (2007), "Labor Market Impact on Youth: A Meta-analysis of the Youth Employment Inventory", Background paper for the *World Bank's 2007 Youth Employment Inventory*, conducted by the Social Protection and Labor Unit of the Human Development Network, Washington, DC.

Report of the Minister for Gender Equality in Denmark to the Parliament (2009), *2009 Perspectives and Action Plan*, Copenhagen, available at *http://miliki.dk/fileadmin/ligestilling/PDF/PHplan/PH_plan_2011_eng.pdf*.

Steger, G. (2010), "Gender Budgeting – The Austrian Experience", PowerPoint presentation delivered at the 3rd Annual Meeting of Middle East and North Africa Senior Budget Officials (MENA-SBO), Dubai, United Arab Emirates, 31st October-1st November 2010, available at *www.oecd.org/dataoecd/14/58/46384463.pdf*.

Torberg Falch, T., L.E. Borge, P. Lujala, O.H. Nyhus and B. Strøm (2010), "Completion and Dropout in Upper Secondary Education in Norway: Causes and Consequences", Centre for Economic Research at Norges Teknisk-Naturvitenskapelige Universitet, Trondheim, October.

Treasury Board of Canada Secretariat (2010), "Demographic Snapshot of the Federal Public Service", available at *www.tbs-sct.gc.ca/res/stats/demo-eng.asp*, accessed 24 February.

United Nations (2010), *The World's Women 2010: Trends and Statistics*, Department of Economics and Social Affairs, United Nations, New York.

UN Commission on the Status of Women (2010), "Interactive Expert Panel on the Evolving Status and Role of National Mechanisms for Gender Equality", United Nations, available at *www.un.org/womenwatch/daw/beijing15/hlroundtables/Issues%20paper%20national%20mechanisms_11%20Feb.pdf* and *www.un.org/womenwatch/daw/beijing15/interactive_panel_VI/Panel%20VI%20%1e%20Jahan,%20Rounaq.pdf*.

UNDP (2011), *Human Development Report 2011*, United Nations Development Programme, New York, available at *http://hdr.undp.org/en/media/HDR_2011_EN_Tables.pdf*.

US Department of Labour (2011), "Data on Wages and Salaries in the State and Local Government and the Private Industry by Occupational Group", US Department of Labour, Bureau of Labour Statistics, available at *www.bls.gov/news.release/ecec.toc.htm*.

US Merit Systems Protection Board (2009), *Fair and Equitable Treatment: Progress Made and Challenges Remaining*, Report to the President and Congress of the United States by the US Merit Systems Protection Board, Washington, DC.

Watson, N. and M. Wooden (2010), "Data Survey: The HILDA Survey: Progress and Future Developments", *Australian Economic Review*, Vol. 43, No. 3, pp. 326-336.

World Bank (2009), "Youth and Employment in Africa: The Potential, the Problem, the Promise. African Development Indicators 2008/2009", World Bank, Washington, DC.

World Bank (2010), "Active Labour Market Programs for Youth. A Framework to Guide Youth Employment Initiatives", *World Bank Employment Policy Primer*, No. 16, Washington, DC, November.

World Bank (2012), "Women, Business and the Law – Removing Barriers to Economic Inclusion", IBRD, World Bank, Washington, DC, available at *http://wbl.worldbank.org/~/media/FPDKM/WBL/Documents/Reports/2012/Women-Business-and-the-Law-2012.pdf*.

ORGANISATION FOR ECONOMIC CO-OPERATION AND DEVELOPMENT

The OECD is a unique forum where governments work together to address the economic, social and environmental challenges of globalisation. The OECD is also at the forefront of efforts to understand and to help governments respond to new developments and concerns, such as corporate governance, the information economy and the challenges of an ageing population. The Organisation provides a setting where governments can compare policy experiences, seek answers to common problems, identify good practice and work to co-ordinate domestic and international policies.

The OECD member countries are: Australia, Austria, Belgium, Canada, Chile, the Czech Republic, Denmark, Estonia, Finland, France, Germany, Greece, Hungary, Iceland, Ireland, Israel, Italy, Japan, Korea, Luxembourg, Mexico, the Netherlands, New Zealand, Norway, Poland, Portugal, the Slovak Republic, Slovenia, Spain, Sweden, Switzerland, Turkey, the United Kingdom and the United States. The European Union takes part in the work of the OECD.

OECD Publishing disseminates widely the results of the Organisation's statistics gathering and research on economic, social and environmental issues, as well as the conventions, guidelines and standards agreed by its members.

OECD PUBLISHING, 2, rue André-Pascal, 75775 PARIS CEDEX 16
(81 2012 10 1 P) ISBN 978-92-64-17936-3 – No. 60201 2012-02

Trocaire Libraries

CPSIA information can be obtained at www.ICGtesting.com
Printed in the USA
BVOW020558170513

320982BV00002B/4/P

9 789264 179363